The Making of National Economic Forecasts

Edited by

Lawrence R. Klein

Benjamin Franklin Professor of Economics Emeritus, University of Pennsylvania, USA and 1980 Nobel Laureate in Economic Sciences

Edward Elgar

Cheltenham, UK • Northampton, MA, USA

Published by
Edward Elgar Publishing Limited
The Lypiatts
15 Lansdown Road
Cheltenham
Glos GL50 2JA
UK

Edward Elgar Publishing, Inc.
William Pratt House
9 Dewey Court
Northampton
Massachusetts 01060
USA

A catalogue record for this book
is available from the British Library

Library of Congress Control Number: 2009930432

FSC
Mixed Sources
Product group from well-managed
forests and other controlled sources
www.fsc.org Cert no. SA-COC-1565
© 1996 Forest Stewardship Council

ISBN 978 1 84720 489 9

Printed and bound by MPG Books Group, UK

Contents

Contributors

Sudip Ranjan Basu, United Nations Conference on Trade and Development (UNCTAD) and University of Geneva, Geneva, Switzerland

You Chan 'Kevin' Chung, Carnegie Mellon University, Pittsburg, USA

Alfredo Coutiño, Moody's Economy.com

Vladimir Eskin, PROGNOZ, Washington, DC, USA

Mikhail Gusev, Institute of Economic Forecasting, Moscow, Russia

Giselle Guzmán, Columbia University, New York, USA

Yoshihisa Inada, Konan University, Kobe, Japan

Lawrence R. Klein, Benjamin Franklin Professor of Economics Emeritus, University of Pennsylvania, USA and 1980 Nobel Laureate in Economic Sciences

Fyodor I. Kushnirsky, Temple University, Philadelphia, USA

Wendy Mak, Temple University, Philadelphia and International Monetary Fund and PROGNOZ, Washington, DC, USA

Süleyman Özmucur, University of Pennsylvania and Decision Economics, Inc., USA

Andrei Roudoi, Global Insight, Washington, DC, USA

Preface

This volume focuses on methods and some recent estimates for predicting macroeconomic results for national economies around the world. The economies of the world, as they might be listed in major multinational economic reports from institutions, such as the International Monetary Fund, the World Bank or the United Nations, are very numerous – more than 200 – but these sources do not provide explicit national accounting details and recent performance results for all of them. They do, however, pay attention to major interesting performance results for between 150 and 200.

Naturally, the largest economies of the world are given separate treatment. These include the USA, Japan, Germany and China, the four largest in that order, although China is moving forward in 'leapfrog' style.

Another feature of the various chapters in this book is that the methods being used are generally applicable to countries in North America, Asia, Europe and Latin America. In Asia, where superior macroeconomic performance is now taking place, the apparent competition for economic stardom is between China and India. India has been one of the most-studied countries in the world, ever since achieving independence from the UK, but its hugely successful economic expansion did not get under way until a few years ago, when it appeared that India was becoming a major factor in outsourcing of valuable economic services, using information technology (IT) software in building up export activity. This recent burst of activity may not seem, by itself, to put India in a position for special consideration as regards its economic potential. India, however, was adversely burdened with meteorological uncertainty with respect to a kind of cyclical or random fluctuation of rainfall – monsoon activity, if you like. Until the emergence of offshoring activity and provision of other international services, India suffered the uncertainty of climate change for its large agricultural sector, and poor times in primary activity offset much of the growth of manufacturing, and even imputed cyclical movement to those sectors that are dependent on agriculture. For example, cotton or other raw material for inputs into textile manufacturing contributed to a spread of perverse monsoon conditions, from time to time. Now, outsourcing of IT software provides a buffer to keep the economy on a more predictable and profitable path.

India's new economy of the past ten or more years has been able to grow more consistently, and realize the gains from new technologies, steady growth of more primary sectors, improved living conditions, expanded tourism, and durable consumer goods, such as cars. India's reformed economy constitutes a second Asian growth center that is close on the heels of China's growth trajectory. Our model projections indicate an Indian growth path of 7–9 percent annually by Dr Sudip Basu (Chapter 3), close on the heels of China's 9–11% annually by Wendy Mak (Chapter 2).

It is remarkable that these two Asian giants are the most populous countries of the world, each at 1 billion persons or more. This book aims to provide a short-run basis for tracking this peaceful economic contest between two different systems.

Our forecasting experience with China has been developed on a fuller and more substantial base, while India has been closely examined on a comparative basis for less than one year, but steps are being taken to bring the Indian material, for comparative purposes, up to date as quickly as possible.

China emphasizes economic policy guidance and control under close political supervision, and ongoing measures for economic enhancement are stated to be implemented 'in the Chinese way'. By contrast, Indian economists and general policy executives claim that they are moving in expansionary directions by 'democratic principles'. It is evident that India is exploiting an important advantage that China does not have, namely, a higher educational system along British lines, based on fluency in the English language, now the main language for IT. These two giant economies are clearly different, but together they are dominant in the present Asian surge, and the authors plan to observe this contest going forward by tracking the two economies frequently, every fortnight for China and every month for India.

Another feature of this volume is to show how economic systems in transition can be studied through repeated forecasts by the methods featured in this book.

The two major economies in transition from plan to market are China and Russia. The Chinese case is presently in competition with the Indian case, as discussed above, but in 2002 several Western-oriented economists challenged China's estimates of its GDP (gross domestic product) records of strong growth rates, claiming that they were exaggerated and not believable. In order to clear the atmosphere of that period of accusation, Süleyman Özmucur and I turned to the use of the method of principal components, based on direct measurement of many straightforward estimates in quantitative physical terms or accepted indexes in much the same manner as generations of 'Kremlinologists' examined Soviet and

Chinese data on well-understood and observed statistics of tonnages, kWh, gallons, bushels, etc. to approximate, for intelligence officials, how the centrally planned economies were growing.

The students of planned economies, however, had no satisfactory guidelines on bundling these diverse physical measures of different kinds of production. Professor Özmucur and I estimated principal components of diverse time series of quantitative magnitudes and studied the multiple correlation estimates between published GDP values for China and some principal components. We found very high correlation relationships between the official GDP estimates and principal components of major quantitative magnitudes of observable economic flows.

When it became urgent to turn to modern Russian growth for a presentation in recognition of St Petersburg's Tercentenary in 2002, I, with the guidance of Dr Vladimir Eskin and Dr Andrei Rudoi, drew upon the method of principal components for estimation of Russia's GDP expansion path, and came to the conclusion that principal components of several quantitative measures of physical economic time series correlated well with the dynamics of Russia's GDP estimates. Not only did we find good agreement, much like the Chinese results, but also we found that the Russian economy exhibited dynamics much like many other large countries that were not in transition. The method of principal components turns out to be very good for estimating and forecasting macroeconomic dynamics. There are few long, historical data series on production, employment, infrastructure and price dynamics for transition countries, especially for the extremely important cases of China and Russia. China, at the present time, is building highly usable national statistics that will soon permit econometric studies on a par with those that can be made in Europe, North America, Japan, South Korea, Australia and New Zealand, but at this juncture, it is wise to turn to intensive use of principal components, as demonstrated in this volume, for economies that do not have long-standing data files in the time dimension, but do have such data files for relatively short histories across areas or sectors of important economic activity. Wendy Mak (Chapter 2) is able to make an intensive analysis of the Chinese economy, including meaningful fortnightly forecasts from detailed analysis of principal components. Correspondingly, Dr Vladimir Eskin and Mikhail Gusev (Chapter 4) produced similar results for Russia, although the Russian official agencies for data analysis of the modern economy needed to be much more fully developed in order to access the potential information flows that fully describe the workings of the economy.

Significant attention has been paid among economists and investors to the grouping of countries by The Goldman Sachs Group according to an acronym, BRIC, which stands for Brazil, Russia, India and China. The last three countries have received individual chapter treatment, and it was recognized that special treatment should be accorded to Brazil.

Andrei Roudoi, who prepared the chapter on Germany (Chapter 5), one of the major advanced countries in our presentation of forecasting systems, had special knowledge about Brazil, when studied from the viewpoint of our procedures using principal component estimation for generating high-frequency forecasts.

Accordingly, Dr Roudoi prepared a special treatment for Brazil in a forecasting mode, and it has been set apart in an Appendix. He followed the same statistical steps that have been used in this volume on forecasting techniques for other countries, and prepared such a system for Brazil, which can be used for making the same kinds of forecasts that are presented for other countries.

Mexico is an unusual case of a developing Latin American economy, in that it has a very strong and lengthy database going back to a period before the Second World War; so it can be studied, to good advantage, by our preferred methods of econometric analysis. Dr Alfredo Coutiño does this in his chapter (Chapter 6), with appropriate attention paid to the close linkage between the Mexican and US economies. Mexico does not quite match Brazil's economic status, but is well advanced among developing countries. Dr Alfredo Coutiño has crafted an excellent high-frequency model system for Mexico.

Japan and the Republic of Korea are major economies in the Asia-Pacific area. Both are modern manufacturing economies, but of course Japan is much larger. They have close economic ties with one another and trade significantly with China. Economic ties with the whole world, and the USA in particular, since the end of the Second World War are important.

Japan, South Korea and China are partners with Russia, Mongolia and North Korea in organized cooperation for the economic development of Northeast Asia at the Economic Research Institute for Northeast Asia (ERINA). Japan and South Korea have trading relationships in goods and services with the whole world, including the USA, on a large scale. The aims and objectives of this volume are enhanced by Professor Yoshihisa Inada of Konan University in Japan (Chapter 7). He makes economic forecasts every two weeks for the Japanese economy based on the high-frequency techniques that are prominent in this volume, and Kevin Chung disseminates monthly forecasts of the Republic of Korea in the same way (Chapter 8).

In addition to rounding out the BRIC composite forecasts, Dr Andrei Rudoi has also chosen the largest economy in Western Europe, namely

Germany, for presentation of high-frequency forecasts (Chapter 5). The postwar economic history of Germany needs analysis along the lines of this volume because its postwar history contains strained relationships between West and East Germany, which constituted two very different economic systems until unification after the tearing down of the Berlin Wall. The shorter sample, after unification, is well handled with the principal components approach across sectors of the economy as well as across time periods.

A major national group living in Germany is the Turkish immigrant population. Accordingly, Süleyman Özmucur has made a separate analysis for Turkey (Chapter 9). His chapter is very informative for its economic content, but he has also undertaken to explain the definitive and mathematically sound statement about the meaning, interpretation, and use of principal components analysis.

Most of the chapters in this book relate to country performance, requiring appreciation of the general economic background for each country, as a case study, followed by specific statistical techniques for making high-frequency forecasts up to two quarters (or six months) ahead. There are, however, some different but related interests.

In the case of the US current quarter model (CQM) there was an important methodological point; individual components of the GDP (or its specific sub-groupings) and individual monthly prices that can be found in advance of the target values could be used as surrogate approximations for specific GDP or price components.

Süleyman Özmucur and I conceived a representation of the US Treasury's yield curve (the curve of interest rates on specific maturities, ordered by the length of the maturity). We also had another objective in mind, namely to enquire whether it would be possible to make even higher-frequency estimations of the yield-curve concept, that is much closer to real-time computational sequencing. Our deep interest in high-frequency economic forecasting has been based for several years on quarterly and monthly economic statistics. The chapter on the treasury yield curve (Chapter 10) attempts to provide insight into this important curve at weekly, daily, or intra-daily intervals. In a sense, we explore the issue: how close to real-time economic forecasting can we get? For this approach we must use statistical data that are available at 'any time' during the market working day.

We describe a trading day as one that functions on a supply–demand market-clearing basis continuously from 9.00 am until 4.00 pm. At the beginning, end or any working time during the regular market day's trading in US government bills, notes or bonds we can forecast treasury yields. The bulk of our empirical work on the yield curve views time in this way for US government securities transactions. What do we know at 9.00

am on a regular trading day? We know how markets have functioned in the Pacific Far East, in mainland Asia, in Europe and in futures markets in the USA, Canada and Latin America. In econometric language, these readings of market performance, up to the opening of US market trading, are 'predetermined variables'.

We classify treasury securities by their maturity date spread over 11 different maturities, from one month to 30 years. From our point of view, we are not simply looking for a bivariate relationship between yield and maturity; we estimate, instead, separate multivariate equations among yield, maturity date, central bank quotations, realized inflation (marketing opening time), public debt, tax legislation and whatever is found to influence the observed yield during the trading day. In the USA we estimate a separate equation for the yield on each major maturity. At any time during the day, up to market closing time, we can use our estimated yield equations, for each maturity, to provide a yield estimate from each equation, in order. A graphic display of computed estimates of yield, ordered by maturity, traces out a curve, which is our conception of a yield curve. In our chapter, we show forecast accuracy tables for our calculations of yield (e.g. on the ten-year treasury) against simple rules for more mechanistic estimates. According to our concept of the yield curve and the several equations ordered by maturity, our approach leads to more accurate yield forecasts and more meaningful descriptions of what is meant by the 'yield curve'.

Countries that want macroeconometric forecasts and approach some of the economists involved in the development of this book usually ask, after being shown high-frequency models, 'What is your method and estimate for a longer-term horizon?' They want, in addition to short-term forecasts of two or even three quarters ahead (or six to nine months ahead), forecasts for one, two or three future years.

As long ago as the highly productive days of Jan Tinbergen at the League of Nations in Geneva, there was intense interest in using the available databases of the interwar period of the 1920s and 1930s in constructing models of a national economy, with an aim to make economic forecasts or plausible scenarios annually. In the 1930s, Tinbergen wanted to unlock the secrets of the business cycle. There were no databases or computer facilities like those of today, in either richness or depth. Professor Kushnirsky (Chapter 11) has interpreted results from an unusual database, one that permits both low- and high-frequency information to lead to very short-run forecasts, up to one year at most, and also more information to enhance the model through its application to forecasts of up to three or more years in advance. Professor Kushnirsky puts together a short-run database for estimating a model and its extrapolation of two to four quarters in the future and then considers the use of this informative step for the use of a lower-frequency model, say an annual model, or even a structural quarterly model that can be solved for one, two or three years into the future. The high-frequency model thus provides initial input information for the low-frequency system.

The high-frequency information can be used as input into the low-frequency system, and some corresponding equations can be suppressed for the latter. Kushnirsky also considers whether the high-frequency information implies higher or lower activity levels in the low-frequency system and devises rules for allowing the high-frequency system to change the solution trajectory of the low-frequency system. This obviously requires the use of two models in tandem, for medium-term forecasting, over horizons that are long enough to satisfy model users, and indicates how this could have been used in judging the macroeconomic forecasts of the Fox Administration in Mexico.

In addition to special chapters on short-term yield-curve forecasting and longer-term forecasting, Giselle Guzmán (Chapter 12) investigates forecasting broad market averages (S&P500, Russell 1000, Russell 2000) for some different investor groups, with special reference to the use of sample survey information, which is available prior to trading periods.

She deals significantly with several sample surveys that are well known, and regularly the subject of media reporting, but they are not completely unrelated to one another; therefore she turns to the method used frequently in this volume, namely, principal components analysis in order to deal with the mutual correlations of the various surveys. Much new ground for security market analysis is covered by this chapter.

1. Background to national economic forecasts and the high-frequency model of the USA

Lawrence R. Klein

GUIDING HYPOTHESES

Two main hypotheses about a national economy are in the background here, shaping the national economic forecasts described in this volume:

1. The national economy is viewed as a highly multivariate macroeconomic concept.
2. The ultimate test of the validity of economic propositions is their ability to forecast.

Economists are often ridiculed for being 'two-handed' – on the one hand a certain outcome to an economic event could result, but on the other hand a quite different outcome could also occur. The user of economic interpretation of actual events generally wants one specific interpretation and not two or more. There is an inherent reason for the ambiguity or confusion that often accompanies professional economic assessment. Economics is a social science in which controlled experimentation, in a strict sense, is not possible. This distinguishes social science from natural science. In the latter field of study or knowledge, controlled experimentation is generally possible.

There have been attempts to introduce experimental methods into economics, but they do not have the clear-cut power to prove or disprove hypotheses about economic behavior. Some social sciences have more opportunity for experimental control than do others, and some pedagogical findings can be developed for making limited decisions, but these are very special cases and not generally applicable to a wide variety of economic analyses, certainly not to the macroeconomics of large human populations, in a realistic national or international setting.

Also, there are some non-experimental natural sciences that are much more precise or accurate than are analyses of macro- or microeconomic behavior. The often-cited fields of study for considering some non-experimental analyses in natural science are astronomy, meteorology, seismology and cosmology. Those and other natural sciences are different from most social sciences in that their noise-to-signal ratios are much smaller or much better known and appreciated than are the noise-to-signal ratios of economics or other social sciences.

To study properties of a national economy, the economist must state many conditions before drawing significant conclusions. In a broad sense those conditions usually cover many circumstances, namely the conditions that constitute a level playing field on which economic behavior takes definite shape. These conditions cover such things as equal opportunity and ability to have total information about constraints to economic decision-making. All economic agents must have equal access to relevant information, and access to the appropriate use of that information. There must be equal opportunity for all agents to use external information. There must be no obstruction to market forces in determining such things as relevant prices, interest rates, wage rates and international exchange rates. There must be no restraints of trade through manipulation of availability of goods and services. Civic law and order must prevail.

If all these conditions, and more, that constitute the level playing field are in operation, then economic outcomes may be said to be optimal and leading to an economic equilibrium state that cannot be improved upon, with 'no economic entity left behind'.

Of course, the conditions mentioned above are very stringent and not entirely satisfied, but if they were, optimality conditions would prevail, especially if economic entities were given enough time to work out all the details among themselves. In general, the national economies would settle down into situations that deviate from optimal situations only by random error. The error should not only be random, but it should be small, in some sense, say according to probability limits to its statistical variance–covariance measures.

It should be evident that this optimal outcome requires that many, many economic variables, covering prices and quantities, must fall into place. Innumerable variables are involved. At any moment some significant error can occur, and the community of economists will be called upon to say how the general economy will react to the change of conditions. It hardly ever happens that only a single disturbance or change occurs, and the outcome cannot be simply analyzed by judging from a bivariate relationship. Many prices, many quantities, many rates will generally be reacting and the outcome will depend on all, at the same time. The failure to judge the movements of several economic variables, all at once, is the source of skepticism that will accompany expert economic response to the changed situation. Too many economists struggle to analyze a bivariate economic relationship for explanation of changing events when several multivariate relationships are at work. This is why economic assessments are often wrong and not found to be acceptable. In this volume, our approach will hardly ever involve quick responses to univariate change derived from a bivariate relationship.

The role of forecasting is often eschewed by philosophical economists. After all, our subject is often dated from Adam Smith, the moral philosopher. Cosmology is defined in *Webster's Student Dictionary* as 'the branch of philosophy which deals with the physical universe as an orderly system', but the debates among astronomers and other space scientists are founded on many quantitative relationships used in many aspects of outer space leading to many precise predictions, with some notable mistakes or failures. Space exploration has encountered some significant failures. The build-up of successes, however, depends on the ability to make good predictions, correcting past mistakes. Much of the excellent predictive work in the non-experimental aspects of meteorology and space science, in general, is their ability to draw upon advances in computing and information science to make better and better predictions.

A major motivation and avenue of research in this present study of national economic forecasting is to try to do just that for economics. The contemporary flow of information, new sources, faster flows, and better processing have led the authors of the present volume to try to improve economic forecasting to the point at which it becomes extremely valuable to the using community.

The ability to forecast, in a useful sense, for economics does not follow from the historical procedures of data-mining for high correlations, especially bivariate correlations alone, for the making of economic forecasts. The emphasis in this volume is on assembling the relevant data for a variety of national economies and on testing the ability to look ahead. High correlations alone are not sufficient to lead one to useful and improved economic forecasts. The main procedure is to study historical data files, in fresh intricate pathways, to see if repeated usage of multivariate economic relations can be extrapolated ahead, period after period, within improving informative error bands. High correlations among historical data are not adequate, by themselves, for making future judgments because the parameter estimates derived from past data are chosen so as to minimize past deviation between system estimates and observations. This provides only limited judgment whether these systems can look ahead. That is why the studies in this volume are based on highly repetitive forecasting attempts that compare actual and projected values, period by period into the future, where there is no attempt to choose, in advance, parameter estimates that have done little beyond making historical relationships look as accurate as possible, say by minimizing squared deviations.

Modern database systems and repetitive extrapolations are, in this advanced information era, required to pass a more severe battery of tests to see how extrapolations beyond historical statistical samples provide useful forecasts.

NATIONAL ECONOMIES FOR STUDY

Econometric model building for purposes of studying macroeconomic fluctuations, even to the point of studying the business-cycle phenomenon that started in a formal sense with the studies of Jan Tinbergen, who began first to analyze dynamic economics in his own country, moved later to build a model of the USA for the League of Nations, in order to gain understanding of the Great Depression of the 1930s, and finally to examine the economy of the UK during the period of the gold standard (Tinbergen, 1937; 1939; 1951). After the Second World War Tinbergen's work led to systematic modeling for the Central Planning Bureau of the Netherlands, which continues at the present time.

In those earlier studies, relevant data were sparse and, for macroeconomic analysis, confined to annual statistics. This is particularly the case for systems of national accounts. At the present time many countries maintain and publish, at regular intervals, complete systems of accounts. In the USA, where such accounts are meticulously maintained, these tabulations are known as national income and product accounts (NIPA). They are maintained in a double-entry accounting system so that all the major accounts for households, business firms, public bodies and the rest of the world (ROW) are balanced by use of a double-entry system based on debits and credits, or expenditures and receipts.

Shortly after the Second World War these accounts were estimated quarterly, as well as annually, and now it is commonplace for many countries to have quarterly NIPA statistics.

To move to the use of quarterly accounts in building a database for econometric estimation was a natural step, and the USA was a major leader in making NIPA statistics widely available for economic analysis. Many other countries followed suit after the Second World War, and other pioneers besides those in the USA also did this.

For the large cohort of economic analysts studying the national economy of the USA, and eventually many other countries, some NIPA statistics have been made available at monthly intervals, with successive revision of the relevant quarterly national statistics. Some countries publish selected macroeconomic statistics at monthly or even more frequent intervals, but the field of study called applied econometrics produces comprehensive estimates of projected NIPA systems on a quarterly basis. That is to say, the time unit of the macro models is quarterly, but updating and recalculation of system solutions take place more often. In the USA, some very important NIPA components, however, are made available slowly. Figures for exports, imports and company earnings lag by approximately one or two months.

A main interest of the present volume is to build statistical models that can provide estimates of economic conditions more frequently than quarterly. The accounting period for NIPA entries remains quarterly, but the frequency of access and implementation of systematic economic patterns can be daily, weekly, fortnightly or monthly. The information technology (IT) achievements that blossomed in the last quarter of the twentieth century make possible high-frequency economic analysis.

The main focus of the present volume is to show how high-frequency macroeconometric models can be built and used in the forecasting of national economic performance. Indeed, in this volume, the research avenue will be followed up to the point of daily or even intra-daily analysis. For the most part, high-frequency analysis will be presented on the basis of 'anytime' model performance in monthly terms in the framework of the quarterly NIPA systems that prevail at 'any time'. To a large extent this will be displayed in chapters devoted to individual advanced economies and to some economies that aspire to be classified as advanced, but are mainly considered to be economies in transition. Often such economies are in the stage of moving from plan to market systems for allocation of economic resources.

A principal tool of analysis will be forecasting, understood as extrapolation outside the data set for which the equation systems are estimated. The guiding principle for the concept of forecasting is that the most important and most demanding assessment of econometric systems is their ability to predict. If economic equilibrium is found to be achievable, even on a partial basis, that piece of theoretical knowledge will be used, but dynamic economies that are in motion will rarely, if ever, be in theoretical equilibrium. The premature imposition of theoretical equilibrium conditions can be far off the mark in terms of predictive performance. Systems of applied econometrics are best stated in probability terms, and the presence of error will be taken into account in the national models in this volume. Also it is recognized that significant one-time events do occur in the course of economic performance. These may be due to international conflict, disease, human fallibility, incomplete knowledge of new technologies, and other possible external shocks.

The NIPA framework is at the base of analysis in this volume, but a more complete accounting framework must recognize intermediate flows of goods and services, and that calls for attention to, and use of, input–output systems. Another accounting system is the flow-of-funds system, which is important for the introduction of financial conditions for the operation of our systems. Input–output analysis and flow-of-funds analysis are not used as extensively in the work that follows for individual country models, but the concepts and uses are applied in very specific markets. For flow-of-funds analysis, treasury yield curves for the USA are estimated on nearly a real-time basis for the study of market interest rates in Chapter 10.

For input–output analysis, we refer to interpretations of high-frequency forecasting for the USA, particularly in the period of recovery in the 1990s following the productivity slowdowns of the 1970s and 1980s.

METHODOLOGY OF HIGH-FREQUENCY FORECASTING

Other approaches to forecasting of national economies at high frequency have been used, but the general procedure used in this volume follows a specific pattern.

The generation of regular quarterly NIPA statistics for the USA and other countries studied in the succeeding chapters is based on one principle that is closely tied to the availability of informative data about entries in time periods shorter than one calendar quarter and published in real time, or at daily, weekly, or monthly intervals.

It was noted above that comprehensive international trade statistics and corporate profit statistics are noteworthy laggards for reporting purposes, but many statistics that are closely related to corresponding entries in NIPA become available early – prior to NIPA publication.[1] It is well known that the statistician–economists in the national accounting division of the US government examine the statistics of retail trade in order to estimate components of consumer expenditures in NIPA. The monthly sales of motor cars and light trucks become available within days or hours at the end of each month, and this information is directly relevant for predicting consumer outlays for such vehicles. Retail sales of major department stores and chains are available at about the same time as total retail sales. Real-estate companies publish figures for monthly building of new homes and sale turnover of existing homes. Early monthly statistics are available for industrial production, construction, stocks of key energy products, and many services. All these early indicators form the basis for the first of three regular monthly releases of quarterly NIPA (advance, preliminary and final). Statistics on employment, unemployment, wage rates and hours worked, all based on sample surveys, are made available monthly, approximately one month after the surveys take place. Other indicators are prices, government outlays, construction activity, orders for industrial goods, agricultural production, and many other economic activities. Most major entries in quarterly NIPA have access to some earlier monthly, weekly or daily statistics that bear a close relationship with a desired NIPA entry. This is the point at which the technical advances in information delivery play an important role in making possible high-frequency estimates of NIPA components.

One can try to do (approximately and in principle) what the NIPA statisticians do and rely on the flow of monthly or other high-frequency data reporting in order to assemble as soon as possible a set of indicators of pieces of the NIPA. For the USA, this is done weekly at the University of Pennsylvania (at the close of business each Friday), namely to relate each NIPA entry to available corresponding indicators. In Table 1.1, the left-hand-side entries refer to components of the NIPA structure of the

Table 1.1 NIPA entries and corresponding indicators

NIPA, demand side	Indicators available quickly and frequently
Durable goods for consumption	
Autos and parts	Unit sales of cars and light trucks
Furniture and household equipment	Retail sales of such items as furnishings, furniture, household equipment
	Sales of clothing, food, energy, gasoline
Services	Medical, entertainment, house rental or imputed homeowner equivalent for shelter
Fixed investment	Business machinery, progress on structural building, or new transport equipment (materials or people usage)
	Computers, software
	Building equipment
Inventory change	Stock building or drawdown by major businesses
Exports	Port statistics
Imports	Other shipping, insurance, water and air freight statistics
Public spending	State/local and national factor payments, including military requirements

demand side of GDP, while the right-hand side lists well-known indicators, available early at monthly frequency and closely related to corresponding NIPA entries.

Table 1.1 presents simply a stylized display. In actual forecasting activity (at high frequency) for an economy as complicated as the USA, with many areas of detail, it requires at least 50 indicators to be available weekly (none changing simultaneously each week).

For every NIPA entry, a simple linear or log-linear relationship is maintained in ready-to-use form. This allows us to estimate NIPA entries on the basis of their ongoing relationships to each subdivision needed for forecasting each element of the NIPA (both income and expenditure sides). We do this by using sample regression of NIPA entries on the indicators that are most closely tied to any NIPA variable being estimated, with appropriate time lags.

What has been discussed in some detail is a high-frequency economic table for the (final) demand side that captures the results of those equations in the model that are available for computing each week's NIPA items in a complete system of accounts, including a similar layout for the supply side. The double-entry accounting system is followed in order to make sure that all identities from the dual-entry nature of the system of accounts aggregate to the final set of forecast values. This also involves attention to the income, or supply, side, as well as to the demand side.

The relationships used to compute NIPA accounting values are called 'bridge' equations. The 'bridge' exists between the accounting entries, properly added or summed, that appear in the estimated 'bridge' relations, while the high-frequency indicators are found in each week's reported data collected day by day. The indicators provide only approximate information, i.e. retail sales indicate aspects of consumption outlays in the macro accounts, but they do so imperfectly. Also, more than one single high-frequency indicator may be needed in order to provide relevant information.

As soon as an indicator value becomes known, fully or partially, for the desired period of accounting flows, it can be used in generating forecasts. For example, unit sales of motor vehicles in a given month are important information for estimating not only vehicle purchases, but also sales of gasoline and other vehicle-use inputs. A rule of behavior for the high-frequency forecaster is that as soon as data become available, partially or fully, for a high-frequency interval, they should be used immediately in estimation of appropriate account entries. Therefore forecasters must be nimble, and make use of pieces of information as soon as they are made public. During a typical week, there are always some new pieces of information that can be acted upon in forecast mode.

The economic forecaster must, however, look beyond current values and create plausible future values for the chosen indicators. To do this, by extrapolation, outside the sample of observed indicator values, the econometrician must resort to time-series analysis to estimate some future NIPA entries. In the next step of forecasting, the econometrician must collect as much forward-looking data as possible, over a period of two to four quarters ahead. This projection is usually done by inputting the most recent and also the lagged values of the relevant indicators and extrapolating from dynamic equations, one or more quarters ahead, to generate forecasts. For a high-frequency model, forecasts one year ahead (by quarters) would seem to be valuable. Beyond that period of extrapolation, a low-frequency companion model should take over and make calculations up to the horizon limit of the lower-frequency model.[2]

Published quarterly descriptive statistics of the modern economy are far superior to those made available during the past century or earlier, but there are still mistakes, missing data and uncertain judgment that give rise to other sources of error. Among the various methods of processing accounts of an economy, there has never yet been complete absence of error; therefore data input and statistical model output for the future will always be subject to revision. On the various methods of determining the value of macroeconomic magnitudes there is never complete agreement. For example, gross domestic product (GDP) can be independently estimated from the demand side, from the supply side, and from different approaches within the demand and supply sides. This gives rise to an important but thorny estimate of the item known as 'statistical discrepancy'. In best-practice econometrics, this important item should be tested as one of the significant variables of the system. For the USA, an economic interpretation of the statistical discrepancy has been examined (Klein and Makino, 2000).

To summarize:

1. Build a database of quarterly or monthly and annual macroeconomic data covering the whole economy and some particular trading partners (in the case of the USA: Mexico, Canada, China, India, Japan, the EU).
2. Build a database of monthly, or more frequent, indicators that are tied to system performance or of economic interest in their own right.
3. Estimate bridge relations between strategic indicators at high frequency and elements of NIPA, also extended to lower frequency (annual and quarterly).
4. Each week, some indicators are published in reports, and bridge equations are re-estimated and extrapolated over the forecast horizon.

5. Standard NIPA tables are updated and examined for effects on movement of the economy.
6. Fresh NIPA tables are analyzed throughout the period of extrapolation. For the USA, the tables provide data for three estimates of GDP and two of the GDP deflator. One is a demand-side estimate; another is an income (or supply-side) estimate. A third estimate is obtained by using principal components (to be explained below) of major indicators of GDP and its deflator. The final estimate of GDP and its price deflator are formed as simple averages. The methods proposed in this chapter are similar to that developed for 'real-time' forecasts at the US Treasury by John Kitchen and Ralph Monaco.
7. Interpret results, judge their consistency and plausibility, keeping in mind that the week-to-week changes should nearly always be in historical ranges.

THE USE OF PRINCIPAL COMPONENTS AND THEIR EXTRAPOLATION FOR OTHER FORECASTS

In this volume, the chapters to follow will, to a large extent, rely on the method of principal components and some time-series methods for predicting the movement of several other national economies.

The chapters dealing with particular countries are chosen so that we can study the main features of statistical information systems and stages of economic development. To some extent, the approach will be much like that shown for the USA, but the databases and uses of model-based economic forecasts are often specific to the country being studied, and this requires explanation.

A starting point for construction of a national economic forecasting system appearing in this volume is an explanation of use of the statistical method of principal components for making high-frequency forecasts of individual economies that can be readily used in order to look ahead six months at least, and possibly up to one year. Beyond that kind of forecast horizon, the model of choice will be a structural system based on macroeconomic analysis that encompasses both the supply side and the demand side of producer and consumer behavior, with an explicit public sector.

Many of the economies examined in this volume have a limited history of quantitative economic information; therefore we use principal components, which demands detail across certain sectors of the economies that have comparatively short record-keeping. The method of principal components brings behavioral and other structural economic characteristics into play rather than relying primarily on relatively short historical records of revealing statistical information. This methodology is also useful even for major economies that do have good historical data. First, let us consider the movement of major macroeconomic target variables of special interest, such as aggregate production (GDP), inflation, international trade (exports and imports), exchange rates and employment (unemployment). This list of magnitudes to be predicted ahead can readily be extended, but the methodology can be made clear with these starting magnitudes, which are of interest to all economies.

In addition to the magnitudes, or variables, to be projected forward, or in other words extrapolated into the unobserved future, there will be indicator variables. They will be chosen from an economy's major supply-side indicators, demand-side indicators and market-clearing indicators. Since some of the most interesting cases in our portfolio of national economies to be studied are those countries in the stage of transition, i.e. from plan to market, it is of unusual importance to include market-clearing variables as indicators. These are prices, wage rates, interest rates, exchange rates, rental rates, futures rates and other market-sensitive indicators.

On the supply side, we shall make significant use of factor inputs such as physical capital, labor, advanced technological services, traditional services and infrastructure. On the demand side, major indicators are retail sales, orders, wholesale sales, residential services, inventories of goods for sale or productive use, taxes and subsidies. In addition, indicators of exports, imports, quality of life, health and other societal features will be used where applicable and when available.

The principal components are estimated as simple linear equations of these indicators. We denote as Y_{it} the ith economic variable to be explained and by X_{jt} the jth indicator that has some degree of relationship to the explanation of movement of Y_{it}. A simple model that relates the indicator variables to the major economic variable to be explained is

$$Y_{it} = \alpha_{i0} + \alpha_{i1}C_{1t} + \alpha_{i2}C_{2t} + \ldots + \alpha_{im}C_{mt} + e_{it} \tag{1.1}$$

$$C_{jt} = V_1X_{1t} + V_2X_{2t} + \ldots + V_nX_{nt} \tag{1.2}$$

In equation (1.1) the economic variable is expressed as a linear function of m principal components $C_{1t}, \ldots, C_{mt}$. The final statistical form of this equation depends on the empirical significance of the components. In equation (1.2), each component at time t is a different linear function of the n indicators, where n must be less than the number of observations of each indicator variable at time $t = 1, 2, \ldots, T$ $(n \leq T)$. To repeat, each component is a linear function of indicators, and the variable to be explained (Y_{it}) is a linear function of some components, where $m \leq T$.

For simplicity of presentation, linear relationships are shown in equations (1.1) and (1.2). It must be stressed that transformations of variables from conventional units to logarithmic or rates-of-change units of measurement are implemented where convenient or revealing. The final choice of parametric specification will generally be made on the basis of performance. For illustrative purposes, however, plain linearity is used at this point of explanation of procedures.

Before the method of principal components became popular in econometric analysis, this statistical technique was used in other social sciences, where the variable to be explained was often not directly measurable. It was then called a 'latent' variable, and was used in order to obtain a measured value for such a notion as IQ (intelligence quotient), when that variable was not directly observable or measurable. The method provides a plausible route for approximately estimating something as elusive as IQ, even though IQ is not directly measurable.

An early econometric user of principal components analysis was Richard Stone (1947). He simply computed principal components for a time series of NIPA tables with 17 income and product accounts. He then associated the first, second and third component, each being a different vector of all the individual accounts, and determined that total national income (NI) was highly correlated with the first principal component, the change in NI with the second component, and the trend in NI with the third component. In this way he gave specific and meaningful content to those components that carried the most weight in representing the entire NIPA collection that was available at that stage of economic information and analysis. In the early postwar period (1947), the macroeconomic variable of choice was NI, but now the attention is centered on GDP.

In this volume, the various authors use principal components in a different way. We use as many components as are needed from time series of indicators, to account for as much systematic variability as can be found in the original set of variables being used as indicators.

Among the first few components, usually under ten, we find that a high fraction of the overall variance of the entire set of indicators is accounted for. At this stage we have not established formal statistical interpretation of the individual components, differing from Stone's approach. Instead, we compute regression relationships between the NIPA variables being investigated, using as many of the first strategic set of components as are found to be statistically significant in a relation between each variable that is to be extrapolated, such as GDP, or GDP deflator, or trade, or whatever variable is being made ready for forecasting. Ours is not a latent variable approach. We use, instead, those explicit measured variables that make up our forecast positions. For each major variable of interest to be explained, a fresh principal-component investigation is made because different indicators are known, *a priori*, to have a closer relationship with the individual variables to be projected ahead.

The final regression equation to be tested, over and over again, for its forecasting records thus depends on its own set of principal components and relevant external variables, such as world market prices for estimating domestic inflation, or demographics when there are known economic effects of their variation. In this process of estimating forecasting equations from strategic principal components and other major known predictors, we examine the residual variation, for we are pursuing the goal of separating signal from noise, where the noise must be estimated as white noise (i.e. purely random variation). We estimate white-noise effects by including autoregressive moving-average (ARMA) terms, also as explicit regressors. The ARMA variables have feedback effects on the coefficients of the other variables in each regression.

In the high-frequency forecasting system for the USA, we make weekly estimates of principal components for GDP and for its price deflator, PGDP. The GDP- and PGDP-observed values are then regressed on their respective principal components to provide another set of forecasts in addition to the two that have already been described above, where GDP is estimated from its regression relationship to specific monthly or more frequent indicators. We now make another estimate by regressing GDP and PGDP on their respective principal components, which are brought up to date each week, or more often, if needed.

We select 14 indicators for estimating real GDP and six for the implicit price deflator (PGDP) to determine their principal components in the form of equation (1.2) above (see Box 1.1).

These components are computed as weighted combinations of the indicators, where the weights are elements of eigenvectors (or characteristic vectors) associated with the indicators X_{jt} as V_j in equation (1.2). We then regress historical quarterly values of GDP_t on those C_{jt} that are empirically established as significantly related to GDP_t over the sample period. A second regression is computed for $PGDP_t$. A typical pair of regressions for those two variables is shown in Box 1.2, with not only the relevant principal components but also some other variables that may be separately related to GDP_t and $PGDP_t$. These are the forecasting equations and are shown with specific extrapolations that make up the repeated weekly forecasts. Every week, at the close of financial and business activity at the week's end, a fresh forecast is made using the latest reports from government or businesses that can have an effect on the prediction.

It should be noted that, in building the forecast equations from regression analysis, the indicator variables that we use must be known

BOX 1.1 INDICATORS USED FOR PRINCIPAL COMPONENTS ANALYSIS IN THE US MODEL

For GDP:

1. Industrial production index
2. Manufacturers' orders, deflated by producer price index
3. Manufacturers' shipments, deflated by producer price index
4. Manufacturers' unfilled orders, deflated by producer price index
5. Yield spread between six-month commercial paper and six-month treasury bills
6. Real interest rate (six-month commercial paper yield adjusted by consumer price index)
7. Real M1, adjusted by consumer price index
8. Real retail sales, adjusted by consumer price index
9. Real personal income, adjusted by consumer price index
10. Real ten-year treasury yield
11. Yield spread between ten- and one-year treasury bills
12. Non-farm payrolls
13. Average weekly hours, production workers: total private
14. Trade-weighted value of the US dollar, nominal broad-dollar index

For PGDP:

1. Consumer price index
2. Index of prices received, all farm products
3. Producer price index finished goods
4. Producer price index intermediate materials, supplies and components
5. Import price index for all commodities
6. Average earnings per hour, production workers: total private

in advance; they are not in a simultaneous feedback relation with the variables that we are forecasting; that is, the indicators affect the NIPA variables or strategic indexes for the macroeconomy, but they are advance indicators that contribute to the determination of the variables of ultimate interest. When it is relevant, the indicators are available at higher

BOX 1.2 FORECAST EQUATIONS

$$\begin{aligned}\text{Dlog}\,(QGDP) = {} & 0684 - 0.954\ \text{Dlog}\ C_1 + 0.304\ \text{Dlog}\ C_2 \\ & - 0.0661\ \text{Dlog}\ C_6 - 0.295\ \text{Dlog}\ C_7 \\ & + 0.581\ \text{AR}(1) - 0.677\ \text{MA}(1)\end{aligned}$$

$$\begin{aligned}\text{Dlog}\,(QPGDP) = {} & 0.817 - 2.463\ \text{Dlog}\ C_1 + 0.925\ \text{Dlog}\ C_2 \\ & + 1.383\ \text{Dlog}\ C_3 - 5.113\ \text{Dlog}\ C_4 \\ & + 4.189\ \text{Dlog}\ C_5 - 2.233\ \text{Dlog}\ C_6 + 0.908\ \text{MA}(4)\end{aligned}$$

frequency, such as months, weeks, or days, in order to forecast some variables that are available only at quarterly or other frequency. In the case of some price variables that are not NIPA deflators, however, the final objective in forecasting may be monthly and based on monthly indicator variables that are observed in advance.

There are different methods for following the course of an economy and trying to track its path ahead of actual performance, so that officials can plan for the future. There will, of course, always be error. The point of this intensive method of forecasting is to try to make the errors as small as possible, by some criterion, such as minimum squared error or minimum absolute error. Modern computing and reporting technologies enable one to intervene and re-estimate as often as needed, in order to limit the size of error boundaries.

Time variation and spatial variation are two dimensions in which the investigator can adapt to the presence of a significant disturbance. Because the economic system is large and complex, and disturbances can come from many parts of the economy, spatial variation across many indicator sightings is important. Patterns of historical time variations are also used, but there is a great benefit in looking for signals in many varied spaces of the economy, especially for countries that have weak or unusable historical records in time variation. This is particularly the case now for economies in transition, but the advances in computing equipment facilities and in software enable one to follow both sources of variation.

All the bridge equations, between a NIPA or other significant economic magnitude, are used in order to establish forecast values as soon as each indicator variable is available to be placed in the relevant equation to determine values that are to be estimated ahead, in time. In the principal components analysis, all the indicator values that are not fully known for forecasting purposes are extrapolated ahead, in time, from estimated ARMA equations, that are always available, on call, in order to obtain values for the variables that are being forecasted. All the identities and

Table 1.2 Forecast update overview (3 March 2007, for business week of 5 March 2007)

Date	Economic indicator	Month	Latest	Prior month
Mar. 01	**Construction spending**	**January**	**0.5%**	**0.7%**
Feb. 02	Non-farm payroll employment	December	111,000	206,000
Mar. 01	**Auto sales**	**February**	**16.5 million**	**16.7 million**
Feb. 07	Consumer credit outstanding	December	$6.0 billion	$13.7 billion
Feb. 15	Export/import price index	January	0.3%, –1.2%	0.7%, 1.1%
Feb. 16	Producer price index, total & core	January	–0.6%, 0.2%	0.9%, 0.2%
Feb. 14	Retail sales, total & ex-auto	January	0.0%, 0.3%	0.8%, 1.5%
Feb. 15	Industrial production	January	–0.5%	0.5%
Feb. 14	Business inventories	December	0.0%	0.4%
Feb. 21	Consumer price index, total & core	January	0.2%, 0.3%	0.4%, 0.1%
Feb. 16	Housing starts	January	1.41 million	1.64 million
Feb. 13	Trade balance	December	–$61.2 billion	–$58.1 billion
Feb. 27	**Durable goods orders & shipments**	**January**	**–7.8%, 0.2%**	**2.8%, 0.5%**
Feb. 02	Manuf. shipments, inventories & orders	December	2.4%, 1.4%, 0.1%	1.2%, 0.2%, 0.2%

Notes: This forecast incorporates the following national income and product accounts:

FEB 28 GDP (based on chain 2000 weights) for 2006Q4: 2.2%.
MAR 01 Personal income and consumption for January: 1.0%, 0.5%.

The latest current quarter model (CQM) forecast incorporates new monthly economic indicators (in bold) that were not included in the previous forecast.

display rules are activated in order to establish inputs for all the tables and graphs that make up the final product.

The forecast output for the US model, at the end of every business week (or between weeks), takes the following form: on the first page, latest values for key indicator variables are listed as in Table 1.2. The newest weekly values are in bold type; others are repeated as carry-over values from previous weeks. In Table 1.3 and Figures 1.1 and 1.2, two key values, among many for the whole system, are listed by date of forecast computation. Official government estimates are in italic type and are not our forecasts. Our weekly forecasts, as they are developed week by week, are listed over a five-month span, to reveal how forecast information evolved – for real quarterly GDP (QGDP), and the quarterly price deflator for personal

Table 1.3 Recent track record: weekly forecasts of the quarterly percentage change (SAAR) of real GDP and quarterly percentage change (SAAR) of the (chain-type) price index of PCE

2006	Real GDP				PCE price index				Official release
	06Q3	06Q4	07Q1	07Q2	06Q3	06Q4	07Q1	07Q2	
Jun. 12	2.21				4.22				
Jun. 19	2.07				4.29				
Jun. 26	2.07				4.29				
Jul. 03	2.41				3.58				
Jul. 10	2.41				3.58				
Jul. 17	2.01				4.29				
Aug. 07	1.96	1.65			3.98	4.04			
Aug. 14	2.18	1.55			3.98	4.04			
Aug. 21	2.02	1.50			4.26	4.17			
Aug. 28	2.04	1.49			4.26	4.17			
Sep. 04	3.10	2.05			3.55	3.53			
Sep. 11	2.90	1.87			4.26	4.17			
Sep. 18	2.77	1.79			4.14	4.02			
Sep. 25	2.76	1.82			4.14	4.02			
Oct. 02	2.60	2.03			3.40	3.34			
Oct. 09	2.59	2.05			3.40	3.34			
Oct. 16	2.14	1.40			4.14	4.02			
Oct. 23	2.42	2.02			3.83	2.95			
Nov. 06	*1.58*	2.37	2.17		*2.48*	2.94	3.70		≤=1st 2006Q3
Nov. 13	1.45	2.87	2.62		2.46	2.12	3.05		
Nov. 20	1.43	3.07	3.11		2.46	0.85	2.48		
Dec. 04	*2.21*	3.09	3.03		*2.42*	1.99	3.25		≤=2nd 2006Q3
Dec. 11	2.22	2.93	3.38		2.42	0.70	2.00		
Dec. 18	2.21	2.96	3.68		2.42	0.73	2.02		
Dec. 25	*1.96*	2.88	3.55		*2.35*	0.73	2.30		≤=3rd 2006Q3
2007									
Jan. 01		2.88	3.55			0.73	2.30		
Jan. 08		2.98	3.57			0.73	2.30		
Jan. 15		2.87	3.78			0.73	2.30		
Jan. 22		2.67	3.31			0.94	3.03		
Jan. 29		2.68	3.31			0.94	3.03		
Feb. 05		*3.47*	3.56	2.97		*−0.79*	3.02	2.71	≤=1st 2006Q4
Feb. 12		3.12	3.41	3.01		−0.91	3.02	2.71	
Feb. 19		3.00	2.65	2.84		−0.91	3.04	2.75	
Feb. 26		3.00	2.71	2.87		−0.91	2.88	2.67	
Mar. 05		*2.22*	3.08	2.08		*−0.86*	2.88	2.67	≤=2nd 2006Q4

Notes: Official figures released by the Department of Commerce are in italic.
SAAR: seasonally adjusted at annual rate.

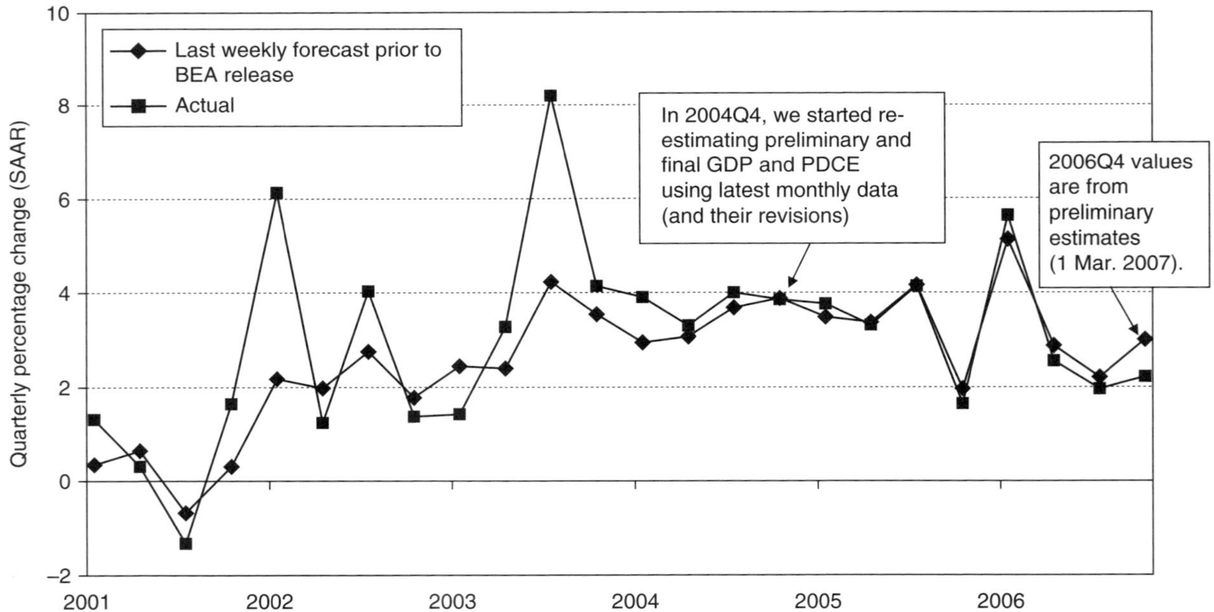

Notes:
BEA: Bureau of Economic Analysis.
PDCE: price deflator of consumer expenditure.
SAAR: seasonally adjusted at annual rate.

Figure 1.1 Real GDP (2001Q1–2006Q4)

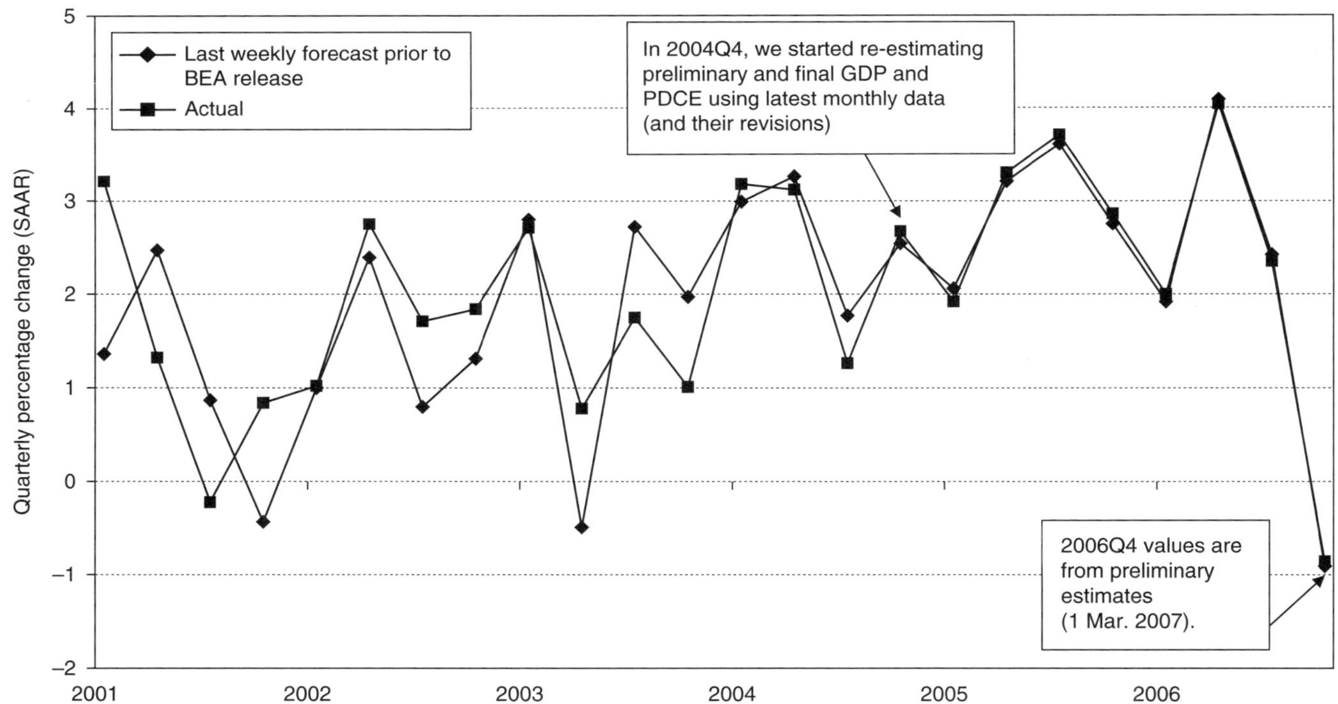

Notes: As for Figure 1.1.

Figure 1.2 PCE price deflator (2001Q1–2006Q4)

consumption expenditures (QPCE). The price deflator is listed as the main inflation forecast. This does not always provide the same insight as the GDP deflator. The economic story told by the records is discussed below for an unusual period.

Table 1.4 summarizes three forecasts: (1) real GDP; the price deflator of GDP (not the consumer deflator in Table 1.3); and nominal (current price) GDP. The principal components method, which is a third approach to GDP estimation, is listed separately in tables, with GDP estimated from the expenditure side and income side of NIPA.

The particular forecast of the US economy, discussed here and made every week, is worth close examination because it came at a time of heightened uncertainty for business-cycle developments. The Federal Reserve governors have made a policy statement that bears watching because they tried to execute monetary decisions that would bring the macroeconomy to a 'soft landing' (i.e. economic slowdown, short of recession) that would in their opinion reduce the rate of inflation to movement in a target zone between 1 and 2 percent annualized rate of change of the price level. Their policy target was formulated in terms of the 'core' rate of inflation, measured by movement in the consumer price index (the 'core' value of the price 'index' that is listed in Table 1.2) without including prices for food and energy components. This is an inadequate indicator, in our opinion, because food and fuel products are so important in nearly every citizen's lifestyle.[3]

In a turbulent period of more than one week there were unusual fluctuations in securities markets because of significant breaks in Chinese financial markets, where such fluctuations provide an unknown element to market dynamics for an economy in transition. Markets around the world felt the actions and reactions, including both economies in transition and advanced economies with well-established markets. The US economy, in particular, was affected by the Chinese shock.

The regular weekly report on high-frequency modeling of the total US economy runs to more than 20 pages. Two of those pages, shown in Table 1.3 and Figures 1.1 and 1.2, provide interesting summary results. The first analytical page, Table 1.3, gives weekly and historical forecasts of real GDP and an important consumer price index, so that the 'trail' of very short-run forecasts is in full view. This forecast was made from data reported or generated prior to 6 March 2007. Table 1.2 lists latest release numbers for 14 strategic variables as well as data for fourth-quarter GDP (2006), monthly personal income and monthly consumer spending for January 2007. The monthly data are recomputed and extrapolated forward in time on a weekly basis in Table 1.3. The first columns show the trail for predicting GDP. The second columns contain forecasts ahead, by the week, for an index of prices of personal consumption expenditures (PCE). When an official release is made, the stated number in the release is in italics.

Looking at the columns for real GDP and PCE price index 2006Q4, we cite the entries for Feb. 05. In the case of GDP, in 2006Q4 the report for the advance estimate by the Bureau of Economic Analysis is 3.47, considered to be evidence of a strong economy, operating near its full potential, while the entry for consumer price inflation is estimated to have been –0.79, a low number because oil prices in that quarter receded from high values. By the methods that have been established for high-frequency forecasting for the US economy, the weekly estimate for GDP growth, which had been apparently too low, at 2.7 percent, before Feb. 05, is, after the advance report, recalculated to be reduced by our model to 3.00 percent by Feb. 26. When the advance estimates were reconsidered by BEA for release on Mar. 05, growth had been downgraded to 2.22. Our calculations suggested that 3.47 percent was too high and 2.22 percent possibly too low. When we used our measurement approach for extrapolation to 2007Q1, the economy seemed to be growing at 3.08 percent. One interpretation might be that 3.47 was obviously too high and 2.22 percent might have been too low.[4] We do, however, accept the general viewpoint that GDP growth started to be less rapid as early as 2006Q4 and was not expected to be significantly higher by 2007Q1 or 2007Q2.

In the case of inflation forecasting, we confirm the advance estimates at negative reported values for price growth until later in 2007 when it was estimated between 2 percent and 3 percent.

In the tabular summary (Table 1.4), we conclude, by our estimates for 2006Q4 and extrapolations for 2007Q1 and 2007Q2, that GDP would be approximately 2.0 percent or 3.0 percent in 2007Q1 and 2007Q2, and that the GDP deflator, a different measure of inflation, would be between 2 percent and 3 percent in those same two quarters; also that the estimation of GDP growth in early 2007 would be lower if measured from the income side over three quarters rather than the expenditure side over the same three quarters, although the difference is small (2.76 percent versus 2.81 percent). These observations are meant to show how the high-frequency estimates could be interpreted, but they remain as estimates before being stated as numerical observations. They indicate how the high-frequency results can be interpreted in the immediate short run, especially in uncertain times of strong volatility of economic developments.

Apart from focusing attention on the particular period of market turbulence, Figures 1.1 and 1.2 show fluctuations in output and inflation since 2001. The time curves of our forecasts in relation to official preliminary estimates show that the inflation forecasts are extremely close to the official releases and, except for two or three unusual quarters (subject to official revision), the GDP forecasts are also quite close to the targets.

Table 1.4 Forecast summary, GDP, 5 March 2007 (billions of (chained 2000) dollars, SAAR)

	2006Q2	2006Q3	2006Q4	2007Q1	2007Q2
	Actual			Forecast	
Real GDP					
(i) Expenditure-side GDP	11 388.1	11 443.5	11 506.5	11 596.1	11 644.2
% previous Q, AR	2.56	1.96	2.22	3.15	1.67
% year before	3.51	2.95	3.07	2.47	2.25
(ii) Income-side GDP	11 388.1	11 443.5	11 506.5	11 585.4	11 630.9
% previous Q, AR	2.56	1.96	2.22	2.77	1.58
% year before	3.51	2.95	3.07	2.38	2.13
(iii) Principal components est. GDP	11 388.1	11 443.5	11 506.5	11 600.5	11 686.8
% previous Q, AR	2.56	1.96	2.22	3.31	3.01
% year before	3.51	2.95	3.07	2.51	2.62
Average real GDP	11 388.1	11 443.5	11 506.5	11 594.0	11 654.0
% previous Q, AR	2.56	1.96	2.22	3.08	2.08
% year before	3.51	2.95	3.07	2.45	2.33
GDP deflator (2000=100)					
(i) Expenditure-side PGDP	115.9	116.4	116.9	117.6	118.2
% previous Q, AR	3.30	1.88	1.65	2.17	2.25
% year before	3.28	2.92	2.52	2.25	1.99
(ii) Income-side PGDP: same as (i)	115.9	116.4	116.9	117.6	118.2
% previous Q, AR	3.30	1.88	1.65	2.17	2.25
% year before	3.28	2.92	2.52	2.25	1.99
(iii) Principal components est. PGDP	115.9	116.4	116.9	117.6	118.1
% previous Q, AR	3.30	1.88	1.65	2.32	1.79
% year before	3.28	2.92	2.52	2.29	1.91
Average GDP deflator	115.9	116.4	116.9	117.6	118.2
% previous Q, AR	3.30	1.88	1.65	2.22	2.10
% year before	3.28	2.92	2.52	2.26	1.96
Nominal GDP					
(i) Expenditure-side GDP$	13 197.3	13 322.6	13 449.9	13 631.8	13 764.7
% previous Q, AR	5.94	3.85	3.88	5.52	3.96
% year before	6.89	5.96	5.65	4.79	4.30
(ii) Income-side GDP$	13 197.3	13 322.6	13 449.9	13 619.2	13 748.9
% previous Q, AR	5.94	3.85	3.88	5.13	3.87
% year before	6.89	5.96	5.65	4.70	4.18

Table 1.4 (continued)

	2006Q2	2006Q3	2006Q4	2007Q1	2007Q2
	Actual			Forecast	
(iii) Principal components est. GDP$	13 197.3	13 322.6	13 449.9	13 641.9	13 804.4
% previous Q, AR	5.94	3.85	3.88	5.83	4.85
% year before	6.89	5.96	5.65	4.87	4.60
Average nominal GDP	13 197.3	13 322.6	13 449.9	13 630.9	13 772.7
% previous Q, AR	5.94	3.85	3.88	5.49	4.22
% year before	6.89	5.96	5.65	4.79	4.36

Notes:
SAAR: seasonally adjusted at annual rate.
AR: annualized rate of growth.

The use of principal components analysis for high-frequency forecasting is an important feature of the present volume, but some more tentative and preliminary steps are illustrated in a volume that deals with financial crises (Klein and Shabbir, 2006).

SIGNIFICANT ECONOMIC FORECASTING

While the emphasis in this volume is on forecasting for the modern national economy, it should be noted that all forecasts are not of equal importance for national economies. Systematic forecasting by econometric methods did not take place until after the Second World War, particularly on a macroeconomic basis. There were many specific forecasting attempts for individual processes, variables or sectors. In particular, agricultural forecasting for individual crops or products was attempted, but few, if any, macroeconomic forecasts were involved.

The first major attempts at macroeconomic forecasting were implemented in connection with the ending of the Second World War. In particular, would the USA return to the dynamics of the Great Depression, or would it avoid an immediate postwar decline?

The immediate response from the Cowles Commission at the University of Chicago in 1945, at the request of the Committee for Economic Development, was to challenge popular opinion and forecast a growing economy on the basis of extrapolation of an econometric macro model of the USA (see Bodkin et al., 1991, pp. 66 and 83, fn. 20).

The next major forecast, the first in a series of excellent predictions by the Research Seminar in Quantitative Economics of the University of Michigan, was to estimate that there would be a small recession after the end of the Korean War, and not a major collapse as warned by Colin Clark in an article in the *Manchester Guardian Weekly*.[5] Ironically, the King's College investment portfolio at Cambridge, England, known for its perceptive analysis, was shifted towards gilt securities on the basis of Colin Clark's forecast, and Professor Richard Kahn told me later that he should have been following the forecasts of the Klein–Goldberger model instead of making King's investment decisions on a more personal judgment.

Another important forecast concerned the estimate of recession in the US and the world economy as a whole, from the model at the Wharton School of the University of Pennsylvania in 1969, at the end of the Vietnam War, which predicted that the US economy would go into recession but not collapse, as a result of the failure to pay for war costs during the conflict.

A world recession, including the dynamics of the US economy, was forecasted by the world model of Project LINK, within weeks of the imposition of the first oil price shock in the early 1970s. In fact, both the US model component of LINK and the entire world system were predicted by LINK to go into recession as early as November 1973.

Most of the very important macroeconometric forecasts were tied to war-and-peace processes, but the expansion of the USA in the 1990s was appropriately captured by the intensive use of a time series of input–output tables that were made to coordinate with macro models (see Klein et al., 2004).

These are singular examples of very meaningful econometric forecasts that have provided guidance for decades and influence much of the start of research for the twenty-first century in model-building for national economic forecasting.

Intensive attention to frequent details has been possible for the USA, and high-frequency forecasting has become relevant for objective tracking of the largest economy in the world. The high-frequency approach to forecasting is being implemented in many other economies – some large and dominant on the present world economic scene, some for countries that aspire to play prominent roles in the economic development of the twenty-first century. Brazil, Russia, India and China, the so-called BRIC economies, so named by economists at Goldman Sachs Company, are large in terms of population and growing fast. Russia and China are countries in transition from plan to market. They are developing useful data files that are suitable for application of the quantitative economic methods that are being applied in this volume. They are not yet ready for conventional time-series analysis because their economic histories do not cover a sufficiently long period of time to give full interpretation of their present dynamic movement. They are, however, well situated for the quantitative study across sectors of their respective economies and of their interaction with other economies at the present time, thus suggesting principal components analysis.

India is not in a similar transition stage. It has participated for a longer period as a market economy, with reasonable historic data files, but it is distinctive for this volume of studies because of its involvement with the most modern and sophisticated economic activities, especially in IT, and with a long historical experience with personal service in trade, finance and agriculture. It also qualifies for the studies taken up in this volume for large populations.

The countries of Western Europe, Japan and North America are well endowed with quantitative data, fine universities, and historical experience with market processes. The studies in this volume are not exhaustive; for example, we do not have forecast investigations for Australia, Brazil, the UK, and Western European countries, except Germany, at the present time, but the studies of advanced countries that are included are indicative of what can be achieved in economic forecasting. The countries of Eastern Europe could also be studied by the same methods, as well as many in Asia and Latin America.

In the chapters to follow, forecasting studies for Mexico (Latin America) and the Republic of Korea represent cases that show the potential for sound quantitative forecasting for the remaining parts of the world.

Some, or nearly all the cases, for the developing world of Europe, Asia and Africa could potentially be treated in the same way as the cases presented in the following chapters of this volume.

NOTES

1. The eagerly awaited international trade statistics for May 2007 became available on 12 July 2007. The NIPA data for the second quarter (April, May, June 2007) were initially based on judgmental estimates only in August 2007. Corporate profit statistics share a similar reporting delay. In real terms (dollars of 2000), second-quarter net exports rose more than $40 billion, as reported over the holiday weekend, 1 September 2007, while annual rate corporate profits rose almost $100 billion.
2. A systematic demonstration of constructing models of mixed (high and low) frequency can be found in Klein and Kushnirsky (2005).
3. Before the end of 2007, the Federal Reserve Board based their explicit monetary policies on concepts that went beyond 'core' values of the price index.
4. The data of 13 July 2007 bear out this interpretation, with GDP estimated, officially at 2.45 percent, between 3.47 percent and 2.22 percent. Consumer price inflation went up to 3.5 percent, year over year.
5. *Manchester Guardian Weekly*, 19 and 26 November 1953 and 17 January 1954.

REFERENCES

Bodkin, Ronald G., Lawrence R. Klein and Kanta Marwah (1991), *A History of Macroeconometric Model Building*, Aldershot, UK and Brookfield, USA: Edward Elgar.

Kitchen, John and Ralph Monaco (2003), 'Real-time forecasting in practice: the US Treasury staff's real-time GDP forecasting system', *Business Economics*, **38** (4), p. 14.

Klein, Lawrence R. and Fyodor I. Kushnirsky (2005), 'Econometric modeling at mixed frequencies', *Journal of Economic and Social Measurement*, **30**, 1–27.

Klein, L.R. and J. Makino (2000), 'Economic interpretations of the statistical discrepancy', *Journal of Economic and Social Measurement*, **26**, 11–29.

Klein, Lawrence R. and Tayyeb Shabbir (2006), *Recent Financial Crises: Analysis, Challenges and Implications*, Cheltenham, UK and Northampton, MA, USA: Edward Elgar, pp. 291–5.

Klein, Lawrence R., Vijaya Duggal and Cynthia Saltzman (2004), 'Contributions of input–output analysis to the understanding of technological change in the information sector in the United States', in Erik Dietzenbacher and Michael L. Lahr (eds), *Wassily Leontief and Input–Output Economics*, Cambridge: Cambridge University Press, pp. 311–61.

Stone, J.R.N. (1947), 'On the interdependence of blocks of transactions', *Supplement to Journal of the Royal Statistical Society*, **VIII**, pt 1, 1–32.

Tinbergen, Jan (1937), *An Approach to Business Cycle Problems*, Paris: Hermann & Cie.

Tinbergen, Jan (1939), *Statistical Testing of Business Cycle Theories: Business Cycles in the United States of America, 1919–1932*, Geneva: League of Nations.

Tinbergen, Jan (1951), *Business Cycles in the United Kingdom, 1870–1914*, Amsterdam: North-Holland.

2. Forecasting the sustainability of China's economic performance: early twenty-first century and beyond

Wendy Mak

INTRODUCTION

China's economic progress in the past several decades has been exceptional. Since the end of the Cultural Revolution around the late 1970s, the Chinese economy has been strengthening year after year, with only one interruption, in 1989, during the Tiananmen Square uprising. Such a record long expansion caught many economy-watchers by surprise. Between 1980 and 2000, the Chinese economy quadrupled its GDP (see Figure 2.1). During those 20 years, China gradually evolved from a tightly planned economy to a more market-oriented structure. Throughout its economic transition, income inequality has greatly increased, but at the same time, the poverty crisis has lessened significantly. According to a World Bank report, 400 million of China's population were raised out of poverty between 1980 and 2000 (Ravallion and Chen, 2004).

In recent years, while developed countries in the Western world have struggled with lackluster economic performance, China has proven its resilience, with double-digit economic expansion. An abundant supply of

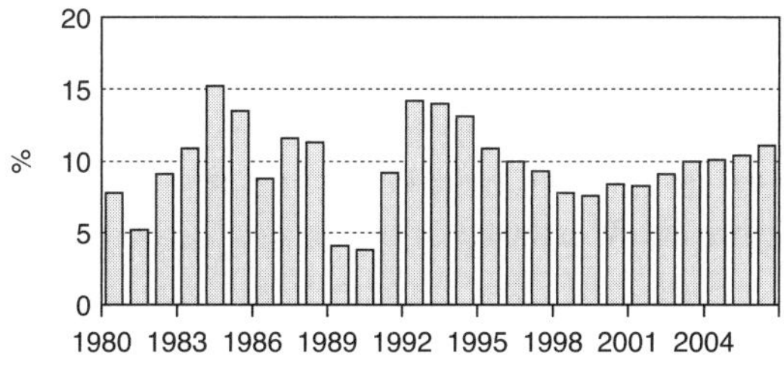

Source: The National Bureau of Statistics, China.

Figure 2.1 Annual GDP growth rates (1980–2006)

inexpensive labor, among other factors, has become China's competitive edge against its trading partners in the manufacturing sector. Trade and investment have been expanding at record paces month after month. By 2006, China had become the world's fourth largest economy, in terms of aggregate GDP, and can likely surpass Germany to become the third largest in 2007–08. The nation is also the world's largest foreign reserve holder (well above US$1 trillion) and has been a major foreign buyer of US treasuries. China has established itself as an engine of growth for the global economy. As China strengthens its position in the world economy, an important question is whether it can sustain its strong economic performance; and assuming the answer is positive, the next question is: for how long can China sustain such a strong pace of economic growth?

According to the latest IMF *World Economic Outlook*, China leads the pack of Asian countries in terms of economic growth in 2007 and 2008. Indeed, in 2007, China was the only Asian country with a real GDP growth rate forecasted above 10 percent, to be followed by India, with an estimated growth rate of 8.9 percent. With its strong economic growth momentum and increasing trade ties with neighboring economies, China could prove itself to be the growth engine in the Asian region during the next several years, based on IMF figures (see Table 2.1).

The current government administration is optimistic about economic sustainability. To quote Vice Premier Madam Wu Yi, the government's plan is to establish a strong economy by 2020, which will benefit both Chinese individuals and support economic growth in neighboring economies. Based on the government's projection, China's GDP in 2020 could quadruple that of 2000 and reach US$4 trillion. One reason that Madam Wu's thinking is plausible is China's hosting of the 2008 Beijing Olympic Games, and the Shanghai Expo in 2010. Both events will support construction activities and related investment. Another policy that will support further economic expansion is the government's sensible technique of strengthening the expansion of special economic zones (SEZs), which have become important centers for commerce and have provided job opportunities for many workers. They have also become critical gateways for foreign businesses to enter the Chinese market, which enables Chinese workers to gain business know-how and achieve technological advancement from the Western world.

CHINA'S ECONOMIC REFORM

The major events noted (Olympic Games and Expo) and the SEZs are some of the contributing factors to recent economic growth in China. To understand

Table 2.1 Asian countries: real GDP, consumer prices and current account balance

	Real GDP (annual % change)				Consumer prices (annual % change)				Current account balance (% of GDP)			
	2005	2006	2007	2008	2005	2006	2007	2008	2005	2006	2007	2008
Emerging Asia[1]	8.7	9.3	9.2	8.3	3.5	3.7	4.9	4.2	4.5	5.8	6.6	6.5
China	10.4	11.1	11.5	10.0	1.8	1.5	4.5	3.9	7.2	9.4	11.7	12.2
South Asia	8.6	9.1	8.4	8.0	5.0	6.4	6.6	6.9	−1.0	−1.4	−2.3	−2.7
India	9.0	9.7	8.9	8.4	4.2	6.1	6.2	4.4	−1.0	−1.1	−2.1	−2.6
Pakistan	7.7	6.9	6.4	6.5	9.3	7.9	7.8	7.0	−1.4	−3.9	−4.9	−4.9
Bangladesh	6.3	6.4	5.8	6.0	7.0	6.5	7.2	6.3	—	1.2	1.3	0.8
ASEAN-4	5.1	5.4	5.6	5.6	7.3	8.2	4.0	4.2	2.1	5.2	4.7	3.7
Indonesia	5.7	5.5	6.2	6.1	10.5	13.1	6.3	6.2	0.1	2.7	1.6	1.2
Thailand	4.5	5.0	4.0	4.5	4.5	4.6	2.0	2.0	−4.5	1.6	3.7	2.2
Philippines	4.9	5.4	6.3	5.8	7.6	6.2	3.0	4.0	2.0	4.3	3.8	2.6
Malaysia	5.2	5.9	5.8	5.6	3.0	3.6	2.1	2.4	15.3	17.2	14.4	13.3
Newly industrialized Asian economies	4.7	5.3	4.9	4.4	2.3	1.6	2.0	2.3	5.5	5.6	5.4	4.9
Korea	4.2	5.0	4.8	4.6	2.8	2.2	2.6	2.7	1.9	0.7	0.1	−0.4
Taiwan	4.1	4.7	4.7	3.8	2.3	0.6	1.2	1.5	4.5	6.8	6.8	7.1
Hong Kong	7.5	6.9	5.7	4.7	0.9	2.0	2.0	3.2	11.4	10.8	11.2	9.5
Singapore	6.6	7.9	7.5	5.8	0.5	1.0	1.7	1.7	24.5	27.5	27.0	25.4

Note: 1. Emerging Asia consists of developing Asia, the newly industrialized Asian economies and Mongolia.

Source: IMF, *World Economic Outlook*, October 2007, p. 84, Table 2.3.

how China is where it is now, it is pertinent to discuss some major issues that the country has faced (or is still facing) in the past several decades.

In 1978, under the leadership of Deng Xiaoping, China experienced its first phase of economic reforms, where fundamental economic changes were introduced. First, the government introduced the 'household responsibility system', which helped strengthen the agricultural sector and handled the adequacy of food problem at an early stage of development. Unlike the old way, in which farmers worked collectively, the new system assigns farmers their individual pieces of land and allows them to retain any food surplus they produce beyond the state quotas. This gives farmers incentives to work hard on the farm and to increase agricultural production. Another part of the rural reform was the introduction of enterprises owned by townships and villages (TVEs), which covers various activities such as rural development through agricultural technology, education and business. The TVEs allow farmers to take advantage of economies of scale in operations. The TVEs also conduct 'off-season' manufacturing activities, which absorb workers during the off-peak agricultural months, and provide a second source of income for rural households.

The second part of the reform involved state-owned enterprises, SOEs. During the early 1980s, the government decided to decentralize the decision-making process to state and local management in these enterprises. Managers were given more autonomy on fiscal planning and resource allocation. Bonus incentives were introduced to encourage entrepreneurship. This marked the beginning of China's transformation from traditional planned economy to market-based economy. Under the new system, production expanded rapidly, and so did employment opportunities outside the agricultural sector. China's economic activities diversified into the more stable, more predictable manufacturing sector, and reduced the country's reliance on the agricultural sector, which is affected by unpredictable weather. This is in contrast to the claim of many external 'Western' observers that inefficient SOEs retard growth.

The third part of the reform was the government's adoption of an open-door policy in 1979. The government gradually relaxed its rules on accommodating foreign investment and international trade. In Guangdong and Fujian provinces it began to practice flexible policies, and subsequently established the first four SEZs in Shenzhen, Zhuhai, Shantou and Xiamen. Following that, the government established 15 free trade zones, 32 state-level economic and technological development zones, and 53 high-tech industrial development zones, and diversified economic development from Beijing to cities along the coastal and border areas. Foreign trade increased rapidly, in both exports and imports (see Figure 2.2). From US$20 billion in 1978, China's total trade volume jumped to US$38 billion in 1980, and later to US$115 billion in 1990. By 2007, China's trade volume totaled US$2.2 trillion. Foreign capital also flowed into China. FDI was less than US$1 billion in 1983, but topped US$11 billion by 1992, and surged to US$75 billion in 2007. Trade and investment have emerged to be major economic drivers for China, and have supported urban development, new job opportunities and wealth creation.

These reform measures stimulated China's economic development. Agricultural output strengthened, and net per capita income of rural households rose from 133.6 yuan in 1978 to 2785.1 yuan in 2006, a 20-fold increase, more than enough to grow in 'real' terms, after taking price increases into account (see Table 2.2). It should be noted that these reforms were executed in a step-by-step approach as the government deemed fit at

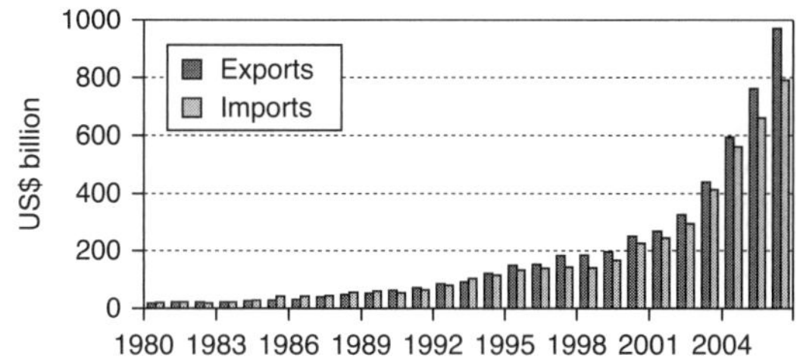

Source: The National Bureau of Statistics, China.

Figure 2.2 China's trade with the rest of the world

Table 2.2 Average annual net per capita income of rural households, 1978–2006

Year	Income/capita (yuan)
1978	133.6
1980–89	378.0
1990–99	1428.8
2000–06	2785.1

Source: National Bureau of Statistics, *China Statistical Yearbook*, 2007.

that particular time. From the government's perspective, the importance of economic and social stability should not be underestimated.

THE EMPHASIS ON ECONOMIC AND SOCIAL STABILITY

The strong need for all-round stability stemmed from the hardship that China and its people had suffered for more than 2000 years. The People's Republic of China (PRC) was established in 1949. Prior to that, China went through more than 20 dynasty changes (since 200 BC), each preceded by years of wars and famine, and constant internal and external power struggles, resulting in significant loss of lives. This was followed by the Sino-Japanese War between 1937 and 1945, and the Civil War between the Nationalist Party (Kuomintang, KMT) and the Chinese Communist Party (CCP). Millions of lives were lost, especially those of young males enlisted in the troops. The power struggle continued through the Cultural

Revolution during the late 1960s. Almost all economic activities came to an end. The government was in huge debt, the railroad system was in ruins, and the education system was failing. After the Cultural Revolution, China was left with an enormous population of under-educated citizens, making illiteracy a major problem. The economic contraction, the significant loss of lives and the social chaos were all major setbacks that confronted China after the Cultural Revolution. Therefore, as Deng Xiaoping introduced major economic reforms in 1978, the policies were executed carefully in a gradual manner. This was to give individuals and businesses time to adjust and to minimize the possibility of disruption to economic and social stability. In later reforms, the 'step-by-step' approach in the Chinese manner remains a critical priority for the Chinese government.

CHINA'S POPULATION SIZE AND POPULATION-CONTROL POLICY

China's population currently stands at about 1.32 billion people (close to 20 percent of the world population), to be followed by India (1.10 billion), the EU (493 million) and the USA (303 million) (see Figure 2.3). China represents a huge retail sales market with substantial growth potential for foreign companies. Its enormous population also gives the country a competitive edge, with an inexpensive and abundant supply of workers. However, since the government has been upholding the one-child-per-family demographic policy for about 30 years, China may soon face the problems of an aging population, and its subsequent economic impact (see Figure 2.4).

The government introduced the one-child policy in the early 1970s, and it has since become one of the most fundamental and strictly enforced policies in China. The population-control policy gradually led to a decline in China's fertility rate. From 5.8 percent before the policy was implemented, the fertility rate had fallen below the replacement rate needed for zero population growth by the 1990s. Slower population growth has allowed China to build a 'demographic dividend'. Between 1978 and 1997, the decline in the fertility rate added 1.3–2.0 percentage points to China's annual GDP growth rates, 0.8–1.5 percentage points to labor productivity and 1.7–3.0 percentage points to per capita spending.[1] Therefore, at the beginning of the restraint, the policy seemed to generate major economic success, which foreshadowed the burden to come.

The current government administration remains committed to the population-control policy, but some demographers and economy-watchers are increasingly concerned about an aging population, judging from the issues that currently confront Japan and some European countries. The

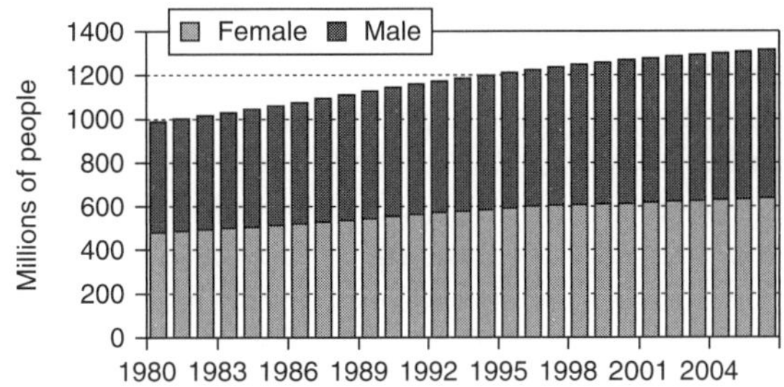

Source: The National Bureau of Statistics, China.

Figure 2.3 China's population dynamics

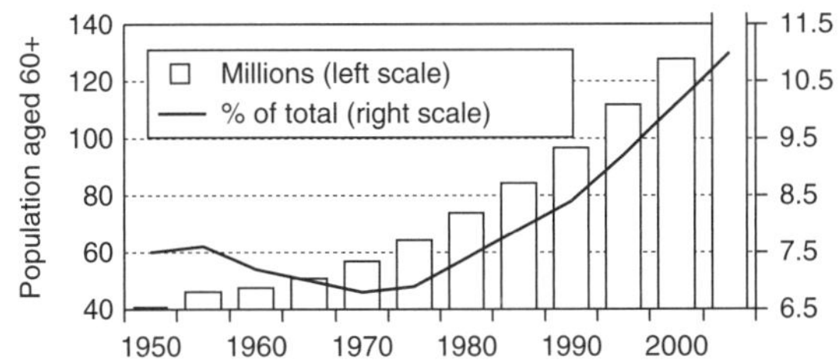

Source: The National Bureau of Statistics, China.

Figure 2.4 China's aging demographics, at five-year intervals

gender ratio is also distorted, with a ratio at about 118 boys to 100 girls in 2005.[2] The distortion problem is even more serious in rural areas, because sons are traditionally preferred to daughters for economic reasons (more suitable for labor-intensive work on the farm and for parent care in their old age). Chinese demographers also warn about the possibility of rising social tension as it becomes difficult for Chinese men to find wives.

The one-child policy continues to be a fundamental doctrine for China, but it seems that the government has softened its tone somewhat. China's population size and the government's decision on demographics will have a major impact on the country's long-term economic development.

THE CHINESE ECONOMY IN RECENT YEARS

Aside from the economic reform in the past decades, the government's step-by-step approach and the one-child policy, further progress in China's economic development and changes in the world economy have also contributed substantially to shaping the Chinese economy. In this section, we shall discuss some main features that are crucial in the Chinese economic picture.

Wage Differential

China's abundant supply of inexpensive labor has given the nation a distinct comparative advantage in relation to its trading partners. Companies worldwide often consider the option of establishing operations in China to take advantage of lower production costs. The booming manufacturing sector has transformed China from an agricultural-based economy to one that is industrially based, which helps support stable economic development. As labor demand increases, the wage differential between China and its Western trading partners has narrowed. Chinese wages in the manufacturing sector were 1/40 of those in the USA a decade ago, but have since risen to about 1/20 a few years ago, and to about 1/15 according to the latest data (see Figure 2.5).[3] At the moment, rising wages have brought a better life to Chinese workers. However, as the wage differential continues to narrow, China's comparative advantage will lessen gradually, especially as other developing Asian economies, such as Vietnam and Malaysia, seek to compete with China. That said, with its huge working-age population, China's competitive edge with respect to labor supply will likely be sustained in the short term, but, as forecasters, we must monitor closely China's labor market development for possible changes over the medium-term horizon.

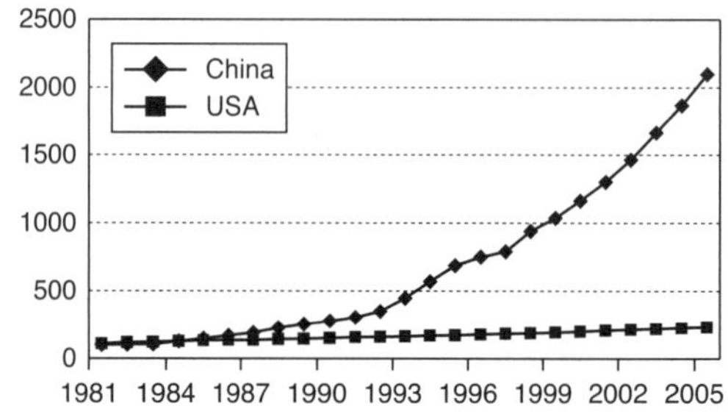

Source: The National Bureau of Statistics, China and Department of Labor, USA.

Figure 2.5 Nominal wage indexes in the manufacturing sector (1980 = 100)

World Trade Organization Accession

In December 2000, China was accepted for membership in the WTO. The Chinese government agreed to provide broader access for foreign companies. This related in particular to the Chinese service sector, which was previously closed to foreign participation. China also agreed to eliminate WTO-inconsistent tariffs, quotas and export subsidies, and to follow WTO-related regulations. From the Chinese perspective, domestic companies have experienced a surge of joint-venture opportunities with foreign firms, allowing Chinese businesses to gain know-how and technology from the Western world. Such learning processes range from the construction and use of the German magnetic levitation train in Shanghai (MAGLEV), the increased use of robotics technology, and in increasingly value-added manufacturing activities (autos, aircraft, high-tech equipment and pharmaceuticals). Urban development has also expanded substantially. The government plans to invest another $20–30 billion to improve the national railway infrastructure. The rapid establishment of skyscrapers and high-end residential construction in Beijing, Shanghai and other cities signifies the recent urban development, with some degree of foreign participation.

The previously closed service sector has grown rapidly. In the telecommunications industry, the infrastructure has become more extensive, in both cities and rural areas. The use of wireless technology has also increased at an exponential pace. Likewise, the banking sector has experienced significant improvement in operations and service to customers. Exports of Chinese goods also surged. In 2007, China provided 80 percent of toy exports around the world. Chinese exports of clothing and footwear have also skyrocketed, following the expiration of a three-decades-long global textile quota system (see Figure 2.6). Although, in the following months, both the USA and the EU introduced import quotas on Chinese clothing, China has become a major supplier of clothing and footwear in the world market.

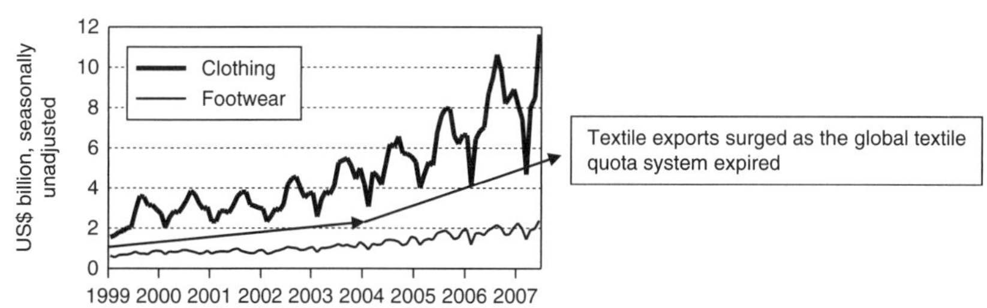

Source: The National Bureau of Statistics, China.

Figure 2.6 Chinese exports of textile products

Foreign Direct Investment

In 2007, FDI totaled US$75 billion, following years of double-digit growth (see Figure 2.7). Foreign capital has helped strengthen manufacturing activities and provide job opportunities. In the past few years, several Japanese automakers established factories in China, following developments by Volkswagen, GM and other manufacturers. Boeing also has an agreement with Chinese companies to manufacture parts and assemblies for their fleet. On the high-tech side, Microsoft is strengthening its presence in the Chinese consumer market and has recently established a research arm in Beijing. Other major high-tech players such as Google, Intel and Dell all have some operations in China. Pharmaceutical and biotech companies are also increasing production in China. The government is encouraging diversification into high-tech and even higher-value-added products. In 2007, Chinese exports rose 26 percent to US$1.3 trillion. More than half of these Chinese exports were driven by foreign-funded companies.

FDI is also crucial in educating the Chinese labor force. Chinese workers get to learn the latest technology from the Western world, while management is taught to be more efficient. The spillover effect of education and research on overall economic growth cannot be underestimated. In the post-Cultural Revolution period, under a closed economic structure, teachers lacked the expertise to teach economics and science. Foreign firms have brought their Western knowledge to train workers and university graduates, and have encouraged the build-up of scientific research and innovation. In recent years, ivy-league and public American schools have established campuses in Beijing or Shanghai. Among various studies, MBA and executive education classes are often the most popular among university students.

FDI helps push forward the development of the Chinese real-estate

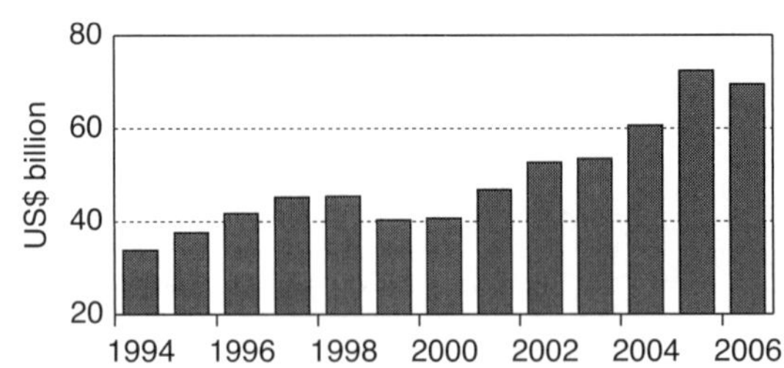

Source: The National Bureau of Statistics, China.

Figure 2.7 Foreign direct investment, utilized

market. In recent years, FDI contributes about 15–20 percent of real-estate financing.[4] In 2006, FDI in the real-estate sector totaled US$8.2 billion, up 51 percent from 2005. This did not include foreigners' purchases of existing real-estate properties, which totaled US$3.4 billion in 2005, and could be even more in 2006. Foreigners' strong appetite for Chinese real-estate properties has kept prices rising rapidly. Average prices in the residential real-estate market rose more than 40 percent in 2006, with even sharper price increases in major cities such as Beijing, Shanghai and Shenzhen.

In May 2006, the government introduced tighter regulations to limit foreigners' participation in the real-estate market and to reduce short-term speculative activities in the market. Indeed, housing prices have appreciated at such a record pace that the government is concerned about a possible housing market bubble and the subsequent impact on economic stability. The sharp appreciation of housing prices has also made it difficult for some Chinese households to become home-owners. Following the government's initiatives, the real-estate boom has eased slightly, but housing prices continued to increase in double digits in 2007. While US construction activities struggle and the Japanese real-estate market remains weak, the strong price increase in the Chinese real-estate market continues to draw foreign investment.

Foreign Reserves

In 2007, China had foreign reserves of US$1.5 trillion and was the world's largest foreign reserve holder (see Figure 2.8 for comparison with Japan). China is also the second largest buyer of US treasuries. In early 2007, the government announced that it would gradually diversify its foreign reserve holdings into assets of other currencies. China has become a major investor in the global financial market, with investors monitoring closely what the nation plans to do with its reserves. China is also diversifying its

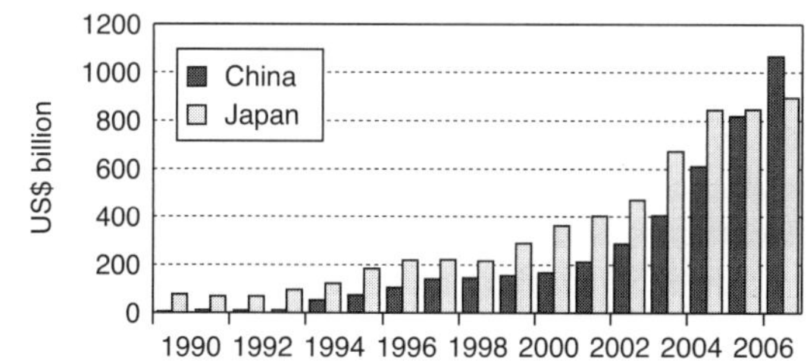

Source: The National Bureau of Statistics, China, and the Ministry of Finance, Japan.

Figure 2.8 Foreign reserves, Japan versus China

investment abroad, as evidenced by its active purchases of US and other companies. Some purchases were successful, while some failed due to political pressure. In electronics, the Lenovo Group purchased the personal-computer line from IBM in 2004. In home appliances, Haier offered to buy Maytag, but later withdrew its bid. In the energy sector, Cnooc (with 70 percent state ownership) competed with Chevron for Unocal, but the deal fell through as a result of political pressure. The Chinese purchases are often compared to the Japanese acquisitions of high-profile properties and art in the 1980s. From the Chinese perspective, their acquisitions are more strategy-oriented. In the Lenovo–IBM deal and Haier's attempt to acquire Maytag, the US companies had established sales and distribution channels and could strengthen the 'made-in-China' image for Lenovo and Haier. For Cnooc, more than half of Unocal's energy reserves are in Southeast Asia, and could have been a partial solution to China's energy shortage problem.

After several failed attempts in the US marketplace, China decided to shift some foreign investment to other countries. For example, Haier planned to establish an R&D plant in Israel in 2008. China has also invested in oil companies in Russia, Canada and some Latin American countries. China has also strengthened its ties with African countries, which are known for their raw materials, in particular timber. Most of the investment abroad is in line with the government's goal to resolve the problem of raw materials shortage. Meanwhile, China continues to expand its presence in the global economy, which is feasible, due to its strong foreign reserves.

Financial Markets

The most noticeable recent change in the Chinese financial markets is the Central Bank's decision to ease its control over the renminbi in July 2005, which was previously fixed at 8.28 yuan per dollar. Under the new regime, the renminbi was allowed to float as a managed rate against a basket of currencies. The yuan–dollar rate was given a ±0.3 percent band, which was widened to ±0.5 percent in 2007. In the past three years, the government has been diligent in following the 'step-by-step' approach, despite foreign governments' pressure on China to expedite and enlarge the currency reform process. The Chinese government has also been working actively to strengthen domestic financial market operations to support currency trading. In early 2008, the Chinese renminbi traded at about 7.20 yuan per US dollar, corresponding to a 13 percent appreciation of the renminbi since the peg was removed in 2005 (see Figure 2.9). With much outside speculation on the renminbi, the government is easing its control

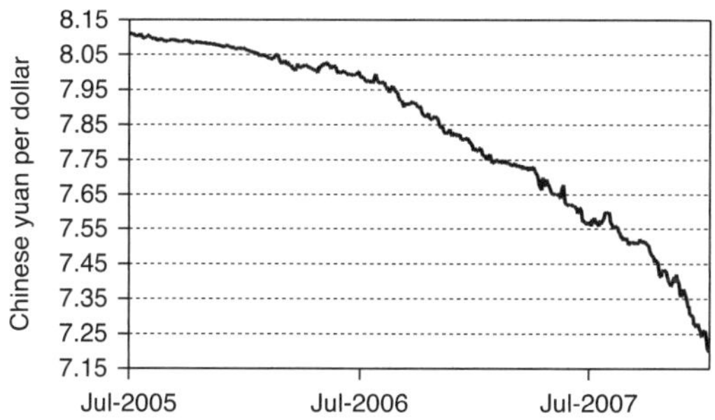

Source: The People's Bank of China.

Figure 2.9 Daily exchange rate

on the home currency gradually, to minimize possible disruption of economic activities.

In the past, the Central Bank rarely conducted its monetary policies via interest rate changes, altering interest rates only twice between mid-1999 and 2005. Instead, it relied on fiscal instruments and provided guidance or targets to SOEs. As its market structure has strengthened, and its economy has become increasingly open, the Central Bank has been conducting more of its monetary policies through interest rate changes. In the latest tightening cycle, which started in 2006Q2 and is still in place, the Central Bank raised both the reserve requirement ratio and short-term interest rates several times. The Central Bank also continues to announce its targets for annual money supply (M2) growth to the public at the beginning of each year. The Central Bank monitors closely signs of inflation in the economy. It is believed that a band of 2–3 percent annual increase in price levels (measured by total consumer price index (CPI)) is within the comfort zone of the Central Bank. However, it should be noted that the Central Bank does not specifically focus on inflation targeting. Economic stability remains critical, and the Central Bank is cautious about the impact of interest rate increases on the economy's capacity to absorb workers. The Central Bank also focuses on specific issues such as the possibility of overinvestment in specific industries (cement, textiles, autos and steel), the rapid price appreciation in the residential real-estate market, and the surge of Chinese stock prices, which are closely linked to the stability and sustainability of China's economic development.

The banking sector has also undergone reform throughout the years. Following the Cultural Revolution, the government provided low-interest-rate loans to SOEs (see Figure 2.10), and gave them flexibility in timing of principal repayments. As the years passed, the SOEs accumulated

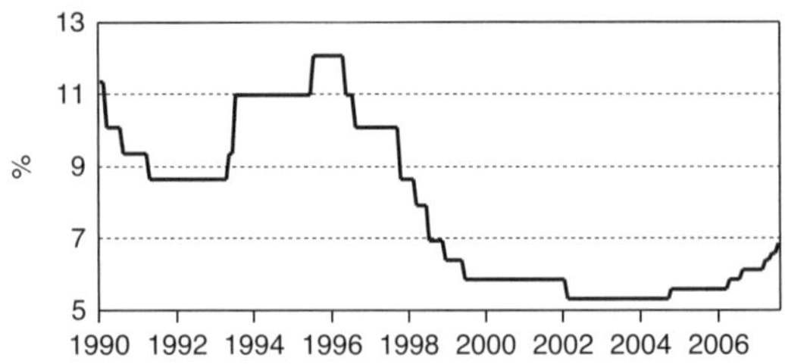

Source: The People's Bank of China.

Figure 2.10 China's one-year lending interest rate

so many loans that they could not repay at all. In the late 1990s, non-performing loans accounted for about one-quarter of total loans in the four big state banks. The financial burden has posed a huge threat to the survival of domestic banks, especially since China is committed to opening the banking industry to foreign competition upon its WTO entry. The government has been working towards commercializing the banking sector's interests, i.e. to switch the objectives from assisting SOEs and serving the government to maximizing profits. This will also allow the interest rate to reflect market-clearing conditions better. Domestic banks continue to work towards strengthening their financial position and reducing the non-performing loan burden. At the moment, banking sector reform remains in progress. Domestic banks lag foreign institutions in terms of competitiveness. For years, the state banks were protected with their monopolistic position, and as such, are poor in service quality, product variety, operation transparency and reliability. In 2000, foreign financial institutions set up about 190 offices or subsidiaries in specific cities. Following that, China is gradually allowing entry to more foreign banks and new domestic banks and easing geographical restrictions. State banks are forced to be more competitive to survive.

Another recent development in Chinese financial markets is the stock market's rapid price boom. In 2007, the Shanghai composite stock index doubled (see Figure 2.11). Despite the gains, Chinese stock prices remain volatile. In February 2007, rumors spread that the government might impose regulations to limit illegal offshore share offerings, which sent the market on a selling rampage, with the Shanghai index tumbling 9 percent. This was not surprising, considering the price swings of the index by a similar magnitude in the past. What caught market-watchers off guard is the 'domino' impact on foreign stock markets. Stock market indexes in the USA, Europe, Japan and Hong Kong all closed lower.

Source: Yahoo! Finance (http://finance.yahoo.com/q/hp?s=000001.SS).

Figure 2.11 Shanghai composite stock index, daily close

This incident is clear evidence of China's increasing presence in the global marketplace. It also shows that an increasing number of investors, both institutional and individual, have increased their exposure to the Chinese market. Indeed, with a 400 percent gain within two years and steady appreciation of the renminbi, the Chinese stock markets are attractive for investors worldwide. This includes Chinese investors, who have been riding along the bullish stride in the Chinese stock markets, and have realized favorable wealth creation led by robust capital gains, which, in turn, support stronger consumer spending, particularly on luxury goods.

From the government's perspective, the stock market boom might not be that favorable. The government's concern is that the Chinese stock market operations are far from mature, as they lag in terms of technology, transparency, liquidity and overall sophistication in operations. Many activities are either speculative or short-term trades, which add to the volatility in stock prices. The possibility of a sharp downturn in stock prices imposes significant downside risks in upsetting consumer and business spending. Therefore, in its latest tightening cycle, the Central Bank has often voiced its concerns about an irrational rise in asset prices.

Raw Materials Shortage

China's rapidly growing manufacturing sector leads to strong demand for raw materials. Power shortages have become an increasingly severe problem, especially during the summer peak usage period. Since 1992, China's annual energy consumption has surpassed domestic production

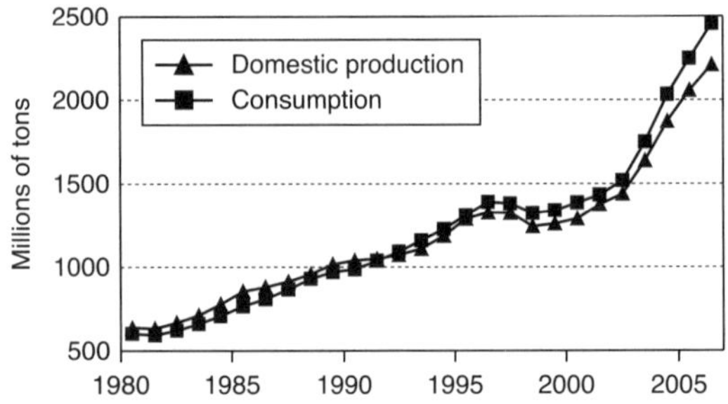

Source: The National Bureau of Statistics, China.

Figure 2.12 China's energy demand and supply

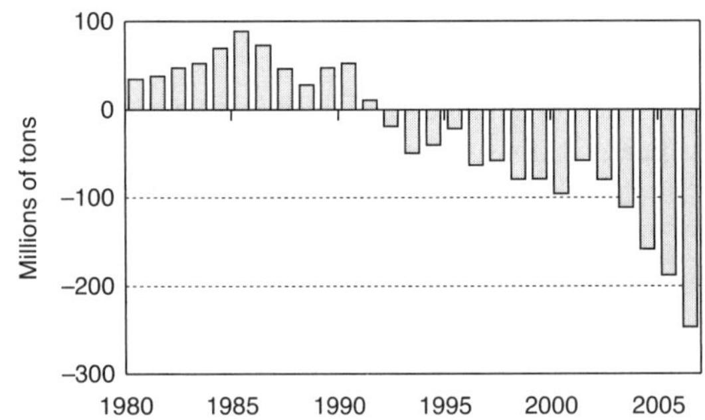

Source: The National Bureau of Statistics, China.

Figure 2.13 China's domestic energy balance

(see Figures 2.12 and 2.13). The gap continued to widen over the years. Not only do power shortages cause disruption to industrial production and other business activities, they also cause inconvenience and discomfort to Chinese households. Such intermittent power outages are unacceptable according to living standards in industrialized economies. China has been boosting energy production capacity by more than 10 percent on an annual basis, but energy consumption continues to grow faster than domestic production. China also seeks to secure energy resources abroad (as discussed earlier). Indeed, China has become the world's largest consumer of coal and the second-largest consumer of electricity and oil. Similar to other industrialized countries, China also embraces ethanol production as an alternative fuel. In the past year, China has surged to be the third-largest ethanol producer, after Brazil and the USA.

China also faces scarcity of other resources, ranging from various types of metals (iron, copper and aluminum) to cotton and timber. As the government indicates, continued raw materials shortage has caused major bottleneck problems for the economy; it has therefore been directing investment into the energy and metals sectors.

AN EMPIRICAL APPROACH

Going back to the question of sustainability of China's economic performance, we take a scientific approach by building a statistical forecasting model for the major economic indicators. In the previous sections, we identified some recent key characteristics of the Chinese economy, which will guide us in the formation of the empirical work. In recent years, Chinese data availability has improved significantly, especially in terms of higher-frequency data, such as monthly, weekly and daily data. The availability of high-frequency data suggests that we can apply principal components analysis to study the Chinese economy from 1980 to the latest date in very short-term successive steps. Principal components analysis has been used for a long time, especially in other fields of social science and psychological studies. The method takes variables (which may be interrelated) as inputs and calculates corresponding eigenvectors as outputs. These eigenvectors are mutually independent linear combinations of the input variables, and have the same overall variance as the sample set of the original variables. The method proves to be useful for studying the Chinese economy, as many economic indicators correlate strongly over time, where they have all been expanding rapidly in the post-reform years. Principal components are canonical forms, i.e. they constitute linear mathematical combinations of a group of separate but interrelated variables.

DATA SOURCES AND AVAILABILITY

As the Chinese economy moves forward, the National Bureau of Statistics (NBS), which is the government's main statistical agency, has been increasingly able to provide more data to the public (see Table 2.3 and Figure 2.14). Such data have improved in terms of both breadth of coverage and historical span. Technological improvement has also allowed the NBS to improve on the technique of data collection (accuracy and reliability) and the speed of delivery (via internet and monthly bulletins). The NBS has also broadened its data coverage from data with annual frequency to quarterly and monthly frequency. This is important for the research

Table 2.3 Estimates of GDP and sector breakdowns, before and after revisions (trillions of yuan)

Year	GDP		Primary industry		Secondary industry		Manufacturing		Construction		Tertiary industry	
	New	Old	New	Old	New	Old	New	Old	New	Old	New	Old
1993	3.5	3.5	0.7	0.7	1.6	1.6	1.4	1.4	0.2	0.2	1.2	1.1
1994	4.8	4.7	0.9	0.9	2.2	2.2	1.9	1.9	0.3	0.3	1.6	1.5
1995	6.1	5.8	1.2	1.2	2.9	2.9	2.5	2.5	0.4	0.4	2.0	1.8
1996	7.1	6.8	1.4	1.4	3.4	3.4	2.9	2.9	0.4	0.5	2.3	2.0
1997	7.9	7.4	1.4	1.4	3.8	3.7	3.3	3.2	0.5	0.5	2.7	2.3
1998	8.4	7.8	1.5	1.5	3.9	3.9	3.4	3.3	0.5	0.5	3.1	2.5
1999	9.0	8.2	1.5	1.4	4.1	4.1	3.6	3.5	0.5	0.5	3.4	2.7
2000	9.9	8.9	1.5	1.5	4.6	4.5	4.0	3.9	0.6	0.6	3.9	3.0
2001	11.0	9.7	1.6	1.5	5.0	4.9	4.4	4.2	0.6	0.6	4.5	3.3
2002	12.0	10.5	1.6	1.6	5.4	5.3	4.7	4.6	0.6	0.7	5.0	3.6
2003	13.6	11.7	1.7	1.7	6.2	6.1	5.5	5.3	0.7	0.8	5.6	3.9
2004	16.0	13.7	2.1	2.1	7.4	7.2	6.5	6.3	0.9	1.0	6.5	4.4

Source: The National Bureau of Statistics, China.

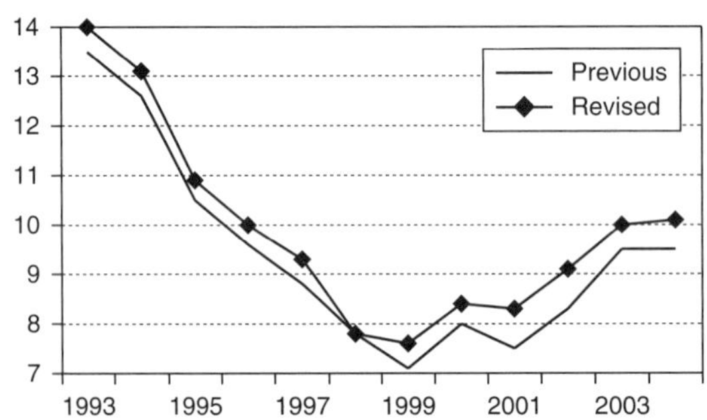

Source: The National Bureau of Statistics, China.

Figure 2.14 Gross domestic product revision (year-over-year % change)

techniques of this volume, as we can now take the latest high-frequency data from the NBS to forecast China's economic performance – first in the very short run (days, weeks, months) and eventually in the medium to long run, over several years. Furthermore, the NBS, at the beginning of the year, publishes the data release schedule on its website, so users are aware of the timing of data releases. All in all, the NBS is pushing its data-reporting standards closer to those of the Western world. One example of such improvement is its re-estimation of output growth in the secondary and tertiary industries in 2005. The NBS improved its accounting methods of the service sector, including IT, telecommunications, retail trade and real-estate activities, which allowed it to discover informative additional output on the state of the economy.

The NBS is the main data source for our econometric model. We collect data on a routine basis, from its website, monthly bulletin and yearbook. We also collect data from some other government agencies, such as the Customs Bureau, the Ministry of Commerce, the Ministry of Finance and the Ministry of Meteorology. Data on interest rates and exchange rates, by daily frequency, are collected from the website of the People's Bank of China.

One major, and very common, criticism that observers make relates to the reliability of Chinese data. In particular, some observers claim that China's economic growth in the past three decades has been overstated. Lawrence Klein and his colleagues presented two analyses that indicate otherwise. The first study, with Süleyman Özmucur, presented a principal components analysis of China's expansion to a Project LINK meeting in New York (Klein and Özmucur, 2002–03). In a subsequent study, Klein et al. (2007) argued that the economic expansion in China was underestimated, rather than exaggerated as critics had claimed. In their paper, they indicated that if China's CPI were to be measured for the same reasons, but by different techniques, as those used for the USA by the Boskin Committee, the results would show that Chinese households experienced similar quality of life improvement as US consumers did in the same general period measured by the Boskin Committee.

Aside from data from Chinese government agencies, data in the global market are also important for our analysis. China is a major importer of raw materials, and its demand for world commodities will likely continue to increase. Commodity prices in the world market are crucial for our analysis. In addition, since China is a big consumer of rice, we also incorporate the international (Thai) rice price index as an indicator in our econometric model.

CHINESE CURRENT QUARTER MODEL (CQM)

In the Chinese current quarter model, the objective is to use the latest high-frequency data available (monthly, weekly or daily) as inputs for principal components analysis and forecasts of GDP and prices (both CPI and producer price index (PPI)) for six months ahead. In this section, we present the characteristics of our model and forecast.

Gross Domestic Product

We construct GDP from three measurement approaches and three systems of principal components analysis. The first system is based on the aggregate approach, where we use a set of 30 indicators that represent broadly based economic activities in China. The second system is to construct GDP from the supply (production) side, by adding up results of primary, secondary and tertiary sectors, separately. The third system is from the demand (expenditure) side, where we add up personal consumption (using real monthly retail sales as a proxy), investment (business investment and residential investment, separately), government spending and exports, minus imports. We then average the results of these three systems to generate the final forecast for GDP every fortnight.

Selection of Economic Indicators and Correlation Analysis

The majority of economic indicators used as inputs in the principal components analysis are monthly data, with some indicators such as interest rates, exchange rates, or prices in the world market averaged from daily to monthly frequency. Some economic indicators, however, are in quarterly frequency, such as earnings and employment figures, where we interpolate from quarterly to monthly frequency. Although these indicators are at low frequency, they provide valuable inputs to our model.

The economic indicators are chosen based on their relevance to the dependent variable measured. The indicators are chosen to represent macro markets from the demand side and the supply side, with market-clearing conditions.

The selection process of the economic indicators involves testing the correlation (with principal components, where needed) of economic indicators, and the dependent variables to be forecasted. We also look for effects of time in order to improve the dynamics of our relationships of timely lags of economic indicators with the dependent variables. In some cases, certain economic indicators have a stronger influence on the dependent variables than others. For example, in building the model for the PPI, we understand that raw energy and basic metal prices in the world markets have a dominant role in driving PPI movements in China. Therefore, in our model, we separate these indicators from the principal components analysis and use them as explicit independent variables in the final regression equations that are to be extrapolated into the unknown future.

Transformation of Economic Indicators

The National Bureau of Statistics reports GDP figures on a year-to-date, year-over-year basis, with the same period of the previous year set at 100. This is a crude way for the NBS to handle seasonal factors. In addition, in our regression analyses, we use logarithms of dependent variables. To ensure that the set of economic indicators is measured in the same way as the dependent variables, we transform the economic indicators to a year-to-date, year-over-year basis, and we use logarithms of the transformed indicators as inputs in the principal components analysis. In addition, since the NBS reports GDP growth in real terms, we also take the necessary step of adjusting many nominal economic indicators for price changes. The adjustment often involves the use of an appropriate price index, which can be the corresponding CPI, PPI or export/import prices of the variable being used. In the absence of appropriate price indicators, we also consider the use of ratios in nominal form, such as the ratio of government spending to GDP, both in nominal terms.

Treatment of Special Events

We monitor the occurrence of unusual events, such as the SARS (severe acute respiratory syndrome) epidemic, incidence of avian flu, the WTO textile quota, and the latest – various recall issues for Chinese exports. We are interested in understanding how these events might affect the current forecasts. In the case of SARS, we introduced a dummy variable in our estimation in 2004 to account for the outbreak. But as our sample period lengthened in 2005, the SARS effect ceased to be statistically significant. We also account for one seasonal factor that is specific to China, namely the dating of the Chinese New Year. Since the Chinese lunar calendar is not the same as the Western calendar, the Chinese New Year will sometimes fall in January of the Western calendar, and sometimes in February. We observe that, prior to the beginning of the holiday, industrial production and retail sales will likely strengthen. Meanwhile, during the Chinese New Year, consumer prices will often spike in response to strong demand for food products. To account for such seasonal features, we introduce dummy variables into the system to correspond to the different dates of the Chinese New Year in the Western calendar.

Methodology and ARMA Adjustments

After taking into consideration the set of monthly economic indicators, the normalization process, and the treatment of possible special factors, we calculate the monthly principal components computed from the 'transformed' indicator variables. These principal components are then averaged to quarterly frequency, and are used as independent variables in the regression analysis, where the dependent variable will be GDP (or individual sector output), the price variables, or other macroeconomic variables that we try to forecast. In the first attempt at estimating regression equations, we often start with the principal components that account for at least 80 percent of overall variance of the sample set. Step by step, we eliminate insignificant principal components in the regression equation based on their computed statistical significance. In our regression analysis, we check the results of the Durbin–Watson test and introduce autoregressive and/or moving-average (ARMA) terms of residual values in the equations if necessary. The objective is to extract all information available to provide the best possible forecast, with error terms that reflect white noise.

Interpolation of Monthly Economic Indicators

After we have established the regression equation, the next step will be to use the regression for forecasting purposes. In the current quarter model, we forecast GDP for two quarters ahead and CPI or PPI for six months ahead. For the set of monthly economic indicators, we take the objective approach (with the minimum subject input) by using an ARIMA (autoregressive integrated moving-average) approach to extrapolate these series for six months ahead, which are then used as inputs for forecasting the dependent variables. The ARIMA approach can be applied either to the economic indicators themselves or to the calculated principal components. In China's case, we apply the ARIMA approach on the individual economic indicators.

Test of Goodness of Fit

In our early experimentation for establishing the models, we test the closeness of fit and dynamic validity of the model. The Durbin–Watson test mentioned earlier is one critical test for serial correlation in the error term. We also monitor the residual plots of the regression equation, to check for unusual discrepancy between the actual and fitted values of the dependent variable of the equation. To check for the validity of the model, one test involves shortening the sample size by two quarters (or six months for monthly variables), applying the same model specification, and testing how well the model stands over time, in out-of-sample extrapolation. It should be noted that the Chinese economy has been changing at a very rapid pace, and there has been much progress by the NBS in data reporting, so we are seeing new information being made available to the public. We often have to consider the availability of new data (or discontinuation of obsolete data) and also the changing economic environment in terms of changing the selection of economic indicators, or searching for appropriate economic scenarios.

Frequency of Forecast and Track Record

At the moment, we generate forecasts on a bi-weekly basis. The mid-month forecast usually incorporates the latest monthly updates from the National Bureau of Statistics, while the end-month forecast includes month-end data on interest rates, exchange rates and world prices. In each estimate, we incorporate the latest data available, and we recalculate the monthly principal components based on the updated monthly data set. Using the new principal components (which are averaged into quarterly frequency) but keeping the same model specification, we re-estimate the regressions for GDP, CPI and PPI, and other macroeconomic variables. In our forecast report, we maintain a rolling calendar that shows how the forecast figures change every two weeks, to reflect the impact of the updates in the indicator set and the direction of changes in the forecast. We also maintain track records of how our forecasts compare with the actual figures released by the NBS.

FORECASTING GDP, CPI AND PPI – PRINCIPAL COMPONENTS ANALYSIS

In the Chinese CQM, we forecast both GDP and prices. Eventually we expect to forecast additional variables. On the GDP side, we forecast GDP from three approaches: aggregate, demand side and supply side. The forecast results from these three approaches are averaged to form the final GDP forecast. On prices, we forecast both the CPI and PPI. Figure 2.15 provides an overview of the structure of the Chinese CQM, and is followed by detailed lists of monthly indicators used in forecasting each independent variable.

In selecting the monthly economic indicators for each independent variable, we choose and experiment with indicators that are crucial or complementary to each independent variable we forecast. In addition, we consider the conditions, such as interest rates, wages and foreign exchange rates, that satisfy the market-clearing conditions for the selected independent variable. We also present the OLS (ordinary least squares) equations

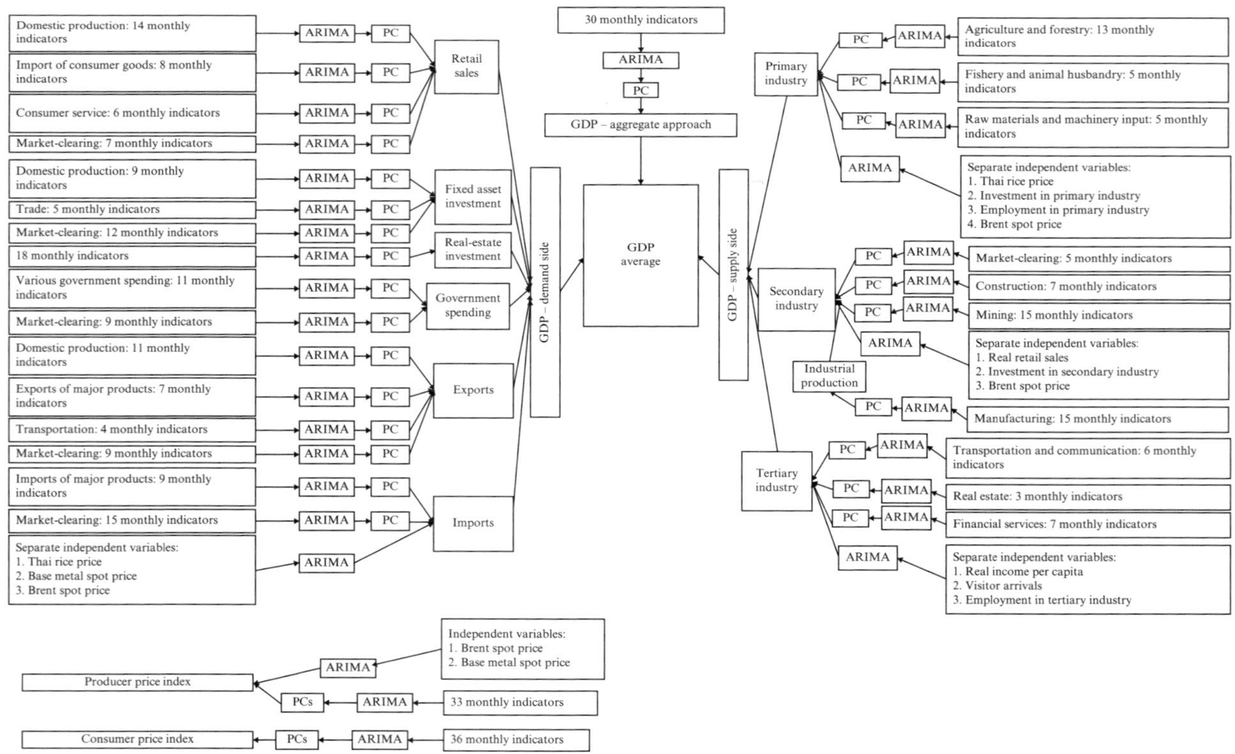

Notes:
ARIMA: autoregressive integrated moving average.
PC: principal component.

Figure 2.15 Structure of the Chinese current quarter model

for GDP (aggregate approach), CPI and PPI, and the track record of our forecasts for recent quarters (Table 2.4). Following that, we select the aggregate approach of GDP estimation as an example to elaborate on the OLS results and forecasts.

GDP – Aggregate Approach

- Imports – aluminum (tons)
- Central Bank benchmark interest rate – reserve requirements (percent per annum)
- Industrial production – cement (millions of tons)
- Commercial buildings, under construction (thousands of square meters)
- Imports – copper (tons)
- Exports – cotton yarn (tons)
- Imports – crude petroleum oil (thousands of tons)
- Industrial production – total energy production (millions of tons)
- Ratio of utilized FDI to GDP, with appropriate lags
- Industrial production – chemical fertilizer (thousands of tons)
- Industrial production – garments (millions of pieces)
- Ratio of government expenditure to GDP, with appropriate lags
- Ratio of industrial sales to GDP
- Industrial production – iron ore (thousands of tons)
- Exports – live pigs (thousands)
- Industrial production – plastic products (thousands of tons)
- Exports – plastic articles (tons)
- Exports – live poultry (thousands)
- Industrial production – power generated (billions of kWh)
- Real retail sales, consumer goods – total (billions of yuan)
- Imports – refined petroleum products (thousands of tons)
- Ratio of fixed assets investment (state-owned & other ownerships) to GDP, with appropriate lags
- Imports – steel products (thousands of tons)
- Industrial production – steel (thousands of tons)
- Exports – sugar (tons)
- Exports – tea (tons)
- Exports – vegetables (thousands of tons)
- Relative wage rate between China (numerator) and USA (percentage change from a year earlier)
- Velocity, based on M2 (percentage change from a year earlier)
- Exports – apparel and clothing accessories, deflated by clothing CPI

Table 2.4 Quarterly track record

	Official figure	CQM forecast figure	Official figure	CQM forecast figure	Official figure	CQM forecast figure	CQM forecast month
	GDP (year-to-date, year-over-year index)		CPI (year-over-year index)		PPI (year-over-year index)		
2006Q1	110.3	109.2	101.2	100.6	102.9	102.8	Oct. 05
		108.7		101.1		103.1	Nov. 05
		108.8		101.1		102.3	Dec. 05
		109.6		101.5		103.1	Jan. 06
		109.9		101.5		103.0	Feb. 06
		109.8		101.3		102.9	Mar. 06
		109.8		101.3		103.0	Apr. 06
2006Q2	110.9	109.6	101.4	101.4	102.6	102.8	Jan. 06
		109.7		101.4		102.6	Feb. 06
		109.7		101.2		102.4	Mar. 06
		110.3		101.0		102.5	Apr. 06
		110.6		101.2		101.7	May 06
		110.2		101.3		102.2	Jun. 06
		110.7		101.4		102.2	Jul. 06
2006Q3	110.7	109.9	101.3	101.0	103.5	102.1	Apr. 06
		110.0		100.9		101.6	May 06
		109.6		100.9		102.6	Jun. 06
		110.4		101.3		103.8	Jul. 06
		110.1		100.6		103.5	Aug. 06
		110.2		101.2		103.3	Sep. 06
		110.5		101.2		103.3	Oct. 06
2006Q4	110.7	110.0	102.0	101.0	102.9	103.3	Jul. 06
		110.0		100.5		103.1	Aug. 06
		110.0		101.2		103.0	Sep. 06
		110.6		101.2		103.3	Oct. 06
		110.9		101.3		102.8	Nov. 06
		110.6		101.7		102.7	Dec. 06
		110.6		101.6		102.7	Jan. 07
2007Q1	111.1	110.0	102.7	100.9	102.9	103.0	Oct. 06
		110.3		101.0		102.4	Nov. 06
		110.1		101.4		102.1	Dec. 06
		110.1		101.4		102.1	Jan. 07
		110.3		102.2		102.2	Feb. 07
		110.4		102.4		102.8	Mar. 07
		110.7		102.4		102.8	Apr. 07

Table 2.4 (continued)

	Official figure	CQM forecast figure	Official figure	CQM forecast figure	Official figure	CQM forecast figure	CQM forecast month
	GDP (year-to-date, year-over-year index)		CPI (year-over-year index)		PPI (year-over-year index)		
2007Q2	111.5	110.1	103.6	101.5	102.7	100.9	Feb. 07
		109.9		101.6		101.8	Mar. 07
		110.5		102.7		102.0	Apr. 07
		110.8		102.6		102.7	May 07
		110.9		103.2		102.8	Jun. 07
		110.6		103.2		102.7	Jul. 07
2007Q3	111.5	109.9	106.1	101.6	102.6	101.1	Apr. 07
		109.9		101.7		102.1	May 07
		109.9		102.7		102.5	Jun. 07
		110.6		103.7		102.2	Jul. 07
		111.1		105.3		102.0	Aug. 07
		111.2		106.1		102.5	Sep. 07
		111.2		106.1		102.6	Oct. 07
2007Q4	111.4	110.1	106.6	102.4	104.4	101.7	Jul. 07
		110.8		104.0		101.8	Aug. 07
		110.9		105.4		102.5	Sep. 07
		111.5		105.5		102.8	Oct. 07
		111.5		106.3		103.1	Nov. 07
		111.5		106.6		104.1	Dec. 07
		111.5		106.6		104.1	Jan. 08

GDP – Demand Side

Real retail sales

Domestic production of consumer goods

- Industrial production – cameras (thousands)
- Industrial production – television sets (thousands)
- Industrial production – VCRs (thousands)
- Industrial production – home theatre systems (thousands)
- Industrial production – washing machines (thousands)
- Industrial production – household refrigerators (thousands)
- Industrial production – air conditioners (thousands)
- Industrial production – garments (millions of pieces)

- Industrial production – cigarettes (billions)
- Industrial production – gasoline (thousands of tons)
- Industrial production – power generated (billions of kWh)
- Industrial production – medicine (thousands of tons)
- Industrial production – autos (thousands)
- Industrial production – computers (units)

Imports of consumer goods

- Imports – cereals and flour (millions of US$)
- Imports – refined petroleum products (millions of US$)
- Imports – autos (millions of US$)
- Imports – television sets (millions of US$)
- Imports – furniture (millions of US$)
- Imports – travel goods and handbags (millions of US$)
- Imports – clothing (millions of US$)
- Imports – footwear (millions of US$)

Consumer service

- Passenger traffic (billions of passenger-kilometers)
- Telephone users in cities (millions)
- Telephone users in rural areas (millions)
- Mobile phone subscribers (millions)
- Real consumer spending on recreational and educational services (yuan)
- Real consumer spending on medical services (yuan)

Market-clearing

- Real money supply, M2, deflated by CPI (year-over-year percent change)
- Household savings deposit rate, 1 year (percent)
- Chinese yuan per basket of US$, euro and yen currencies, monthly average
- Foreign direct investment, utilized (millions of US$)
- Number of employees – wholesale & retail trade (millions)
- Number of employees – accommodation and catering trade (millions)
- Brent oil spot price (US$ per barrel)

Fixed asset investment

Domestic production of major products

- Industrial production – garments (millions)
- Industrial production – television sets (thousands)
- Industrial production – refrigerators (thousands)

- Industrial production – total energy production (millions of tons)
- Industrial production – cement (millions of tons)
- Industrial production – steel (thousands of tons)
- Industrial production – autos (thousands)
- Industrial production – computers (units)
- Number of cell phone subscribers (millions)

Trade

- Imports – iron ore and concentrates (millions of US$)
- Imports – refined petroleum products (millions of US$)
- Imports – plastics in primary forms (millions of US$)
- Imports – steel products (millions of US$)
- Imports – mechanical and electrical products (millions of US$)

Market-clearing

- Real money supply, M2, deflated by CPI (billions of yuan)
- Financial institution loans, deflated by PPI (billions of yuan)
- Nominal lending interest rate – 1 year (percent)
- Real earnings of employees, deflated by CPI (billions of yuan) – from quarterly data
- Foreign direct investment, utilized, year-to-date (millions of US$)
- Number of employees, construction (millions of persons)
- Number of employees, manufacturing (millions of persons)
- Industrial production, light industry (percent change from a year earlier)
- Industrial production, heavy industry (percent change from a year earlier)
- Real wages, construction, deflated by CPI (yuan)
- Real wages, manufacturing, deflated by CPI (yuan)
- Real business profit, deflated by PPI (millions of yuan)

Real-estate investment

- Industrial production – cement (millions of tons)
- Commercial buildings under construction, year-to-date (thousands of square meters)
- Residential buildings under construction, year-to-date (thousands of square meters)
- Imports – wood in the rough (millions of US$)
- Imports – steel products (millions of US$)
- FDI in real estate, utilized, year-to-date (millions of US$) – interpolated from quarterly data

- Number of employees, construction (millions of persons)
- Number of employees, real-estate management (millions of persons)
- Real estate climate index (2000 = 100)
- Working population, age 16–64 (number of persons)
- Real income per capita, deflated by CPI (millions of yuan)
- Real business profit, deflated by PPI (millions of yuan)
- Nominal long-term interest rates, over 5 years (percent)
- Real bank loans to construction sector (millions of yuan)
- Real investment in construction (millions of yuan)
- Retail sales of household electronics and appliances
- Retail sales of furniture
- Retail sales of building materials

Government spending

Various government spending

- National defense spending, year-to-date, year-over-year percent change
- Government price subsidies, year-to-date, year-over-year percent change
- Real earnings, healthcare, social security and welfare (deflated by CPI)
- Real earnings, education services (deflated by CPI)
- Real earnings, scientific research (deflated by CPI)
- Real earnings, public administration (deflated by CPI)
- Fixed asset investment, public infrastructure (deflated by PPI)
- Fixed asset investment, education (deflated by PPI)
- Fixed asset investment, healthcare (deflated by PPI)
- Fixed asset investment, culture and sports (deflated by PPI)
- Fixed asset investment, scientific research (deflated by PPI)

Market-clearing (and other relevant indicators)

- Government tax revenue (deflated by CPI)
- Reserve requirement ratio (percent)
- Benchmark interest rate (percent)
- Real money supply, M2, deflated by CPI (billions of yuan)
- Real earnings, deflated by CPI (millions of yuan)
- Real tourism revenue, deflated by CPI (millions of yuan)
- Real business profit, deflated by PPI (millions of yuan)
- Foreign reserves (millions of US$)
- Number of employees, total (millions of persons)

Exports

Domestic production of major exports

- Industrial production (deflated by PPI), year-to-date, year-over-year percent change
- Industry sales (deflated by PPI), year-to-date, year-over-year percent change
- Industrial production – televison sets (thousands)
- Industrial production – refrigerators (thousands)
- Industrial production – air conditioners (thousands)
- Industrial production – garments (millions of pieces)
- Industrial production – cement (millions of tons)
- Industrial production – autos (thousands)
- Industrial production – computers (units)
- Industrial production – pharmaceutical products (units)

Exports of major products

- Exports – mechanical and electrical products (millions of US$)
- Exports – garments (millions of US$)
- Exports – footwear (millions of US$)
- Exports – plastic articles (millions of US$)
- Exports – toys (millions of US$)
- Exports – cement (millions of US$)
- Exports from special economic zones (millions of US$)

Transportation

- Freight traffic by water, total (100 million ton-kilometers)
- Freight traffic by air, total (100 million ton-kilometers)
- Imports – ships (thousands)
- Imports – aircraft (thousands)

Market-clearing

- Relative wage rate between China and US (percent change from a year earlier)
- Chinese yuan per basket of US$, euro and yen, monthly average
- Number of employees, manufacturing (millions of persons)
- Foreign direct investment, utilized, year-to-date (millions of US$)
- Real money supply, M2, deflated by CPI (billions of yuan)
- Nominal lending interest rate – 1 year (percent)
- Fixed asset investment, manufacturing sector (percent change from a year earlier)

- Number of visitors (millions)
- Real business profit, deflated by PPI (millions of yuan)

Imports

Imports of major products

- Imports – mechanical and electrical products (millions of US$)
- Imports – electronic parts (millions of US$)
- Imports – crude oil (millions of US$)
- Imports – plastics in primary form (millions of US$)
- Imports – steel (millions of US$)
- Imports – iron (millions of US$)
- Imports – aircraft (millions of US$)
- Imports – autos (millions of US$)
- Imports – cereal (millions of US$)

Market-clearing

- Industrial production, heavy industry (percent change from a year earlier)
- Industrial production, light industry (percent change from a year earlier)
- Government tariffs (percent change from a year earlier)
- Real earnings of employees, deflated by CPI, year-to-date (billions of yuan) – from quarterly data
- Real business profit, deflated by PPI (millions of yuan)
- Chinese yuan per basket of US$, euro and yen, monthly average
- Foreign direct investment, utilized, year-to-date (millions of US$)
- Real money supply, M2, deflated by CPI (billions of yuan)
- Nominal lending interest rate – 1 year (percent)
- Velocity measured by M2
- Foreign exchange reserves (billions of US$)
- Working population, age 16–64 (number of persons)
- Number of employees, total (millions of persons)
- Fixed asset investment, manufacturing sector (percent change from a year earlier)
- Fixed asset investment, retail sector (percent change from a year earlier)

Separate independent variables

- Thai rice price (US$ per metric ton)
- Brent oil spot price (US$ per barrel)
- Base metal price index (US$)

GDP – Supply Side

Primary industry

Agriculture and forestry

- Industrial production – yarn (thousands of tons)
- Industrial production – silk (thousands of tons)
- Industrial production – sugar (thousands of tons)
- Industrial production – salt (thousands of tons)
- Exports – edible oil seeds, soybeans (thousands of tons)
- Exports – edible oil seeds, peanuts (thousands of tons)
- Exports – tea (tons)
- Exports – vegetables (thousands of tons)
- Production – rapeseeds (thousands of tons)
- Production – flue-cured tobacco (thousands of tons)
- Production – fruit (thousands of tons)
- Industrial production and imports – chemical fertilizer (thousands of tons)
- Industrial production – chemical pesticide (millions of tons)

Fishery and animal husbandry

- Exports – aquatic products (thousands of tons)
- Industrial production – dairy products (tons)
- Exports – live pigs (thousands)
- Exports – frozen chicken (tons)
- Exports – fresh eggs (millions)

Raw materials and machinery input for primary industry

- Industrial production – processed crude oil (millions of tons)
- Industrial production – power generated (billions of kWh)
- Industrial production and imports – chemical fertilizer (thousands of tons)
- Industrial production – tractors (thousands)
- Industrial production – chemical pesticide (millions of tons)

Separate independent variables

- Thai rice price (US$ per metric ton)
- Fixed asset investment in primary industry, with appropriate lags (millions of yuan)
- Brent spot price, with appropriate lags (US$ per barrel)
- Employment, primary industry (millions of persons)

Secondary industry

Manufacturing

- Industrial production – electronics (cameras, TVs, VCRs, radios, etc.) (thousands)
- Industrial production – computers (computers and micro computers) (units)
- Industrial production – autos (thousands)
- Industrial production – appliances (washers, fridges, air conditioners, and freezers) (thousands)
- Industrial production – textile items (millions of meters)
- Industrial production – beverages (beer and white liquor) (millions of liters)
- Industrial production – canned goods (thousands of tons)
- Industrial production – pharmaceuticals and medicines (thousands of tons)
- Industrial production – plastics and plastic products (thousands of tons)
- Industrial production – business equipment (power generating units, alternating current generators, and internal combustion machines) (thousands of kilowatts)
- Industrial production – metal-cutting machines (thousands)
- Exports – apparel and clothing accessories, deflated by clothing CPI
- Employment, manufacturing (millions of persons)
- Chinese yuan per US$, monthly average
- Chinese yuan per euro, monthly average

Construction

- Industrial production – paints (thousands of tons)
- Industrial production – cement (millions of tons)
- Industrial production – plated glass (thousands of cases)
- Imports – steel and steel products (thousands of tons)
- Commercial buildings under construction (thousands of square meters)
- Residential buildings under construction (thousands of square meters)
- Employment, construction (millions of persons)

Mining and quarrying

- Industrial production – iron ore, pig iron and iron alloy (thousands of tons)

- Industrial production – steel and steel products (thousands of tons)
- Industrial production – phosphorus ore, non-ferrous metal, copper, alumina and aluminous products (millions of tons)
- Employment, mining (millions of persons)

Market-clearing

- Velocity, based on M2 (percent change from a year earlier)
- Relative wage rate between China and USA (percent change from a year earlier)
- Chinese yuan per US$, monthly average
- Chinese yuan per euro, monthly average
- Chinese yuan per 100 yen, monthly average

Separate independent variables

- Brent spot price, with appropriate lags (US$ per barrel)
- Real retail sales (yuan)
- Secondary industry fixed asset investment (percent change from a year earlier)
- Real value-added of industry (percent change from a year earlier)

Tertiary industry

Transportation and communication

- Freight traffic, total (100 million ton-kilometers)
- Passenger traffic, total (100 million person-kilometers)
- Post and telecommunication services (100 million yuan)
- Industrial production of buses and coaches (thousands)
- Brent spot price (US$ per barrel)
- Imports of aircraft (units)

Real estate

- Real-estate investment, with appropriate lags (millions of yuan)
- Commercial buildings under construction (thousands of square meters)
- Residential buildings under construction (thousands of square meters)

Financial market

- Real M1, deflated by CPI (billions of yuan)
- Nominal lending rate, 1 year (percent)
- Financial institution loans (billions of yuan)
- Signed FDI (millions of US$)

- Consumer price index (percent change from a year earlier)
- Producer price index (percent change from a year earlier)
- Commercial real-estate price index (yuan per square meter)

Separate independent variables

- Monthly income per capita in urban areas, deflated by CPI (yuan)
- Visitor arrivals (thousands)
- Employment, tertiary industry (millions of persons)

Consumer Price Index

- Import price – aluminum (US$ per metric ton)
- Export price – aquatic products (US$ per metric ton)
- Import price – motor vehicles and chassis (US$ per unit)
- Export price – coal (US$ per metric ton)
- Import price – copper (US$ per metric ton)
- Export price – cotton yarn (US$ per metric ton)
- Import price – petroleum oil (US$ per metric ton)
- Household saving deposit rate – demand (percent per annum)
- Import price – cotton woven fabrics (US$ per meter)
- Utilized FDI, year-to-date (millions of US$)
- Import price – fertilizers (US$ per metric ton)
- Import price – synthetic fibers for spinning (US$ per metric ton)
- Urban household survey, monthly income per capita – 35 cities average (yuan)
- State-owned fixed asset investment (millions of yuan)
- Import price – iron ore and concentrates (US$ per metric ton)
- Money supply M1 (billions of yuan)
- Export price – edible oil seeds, peanuts (US$ per metric ton)
- Import price – refined petroleum products (US$ per metric ton)
- Export price – live pigs (US$ per unit)
- Export price – plastic articles (US$ per metric ton)
- Export price – live poultry (US$ per unit)
- Commercial real-estate price index (yuan per square meter)
- Price index of rice
- Import price – synthetic rubber (US$ per metric ton)
- Export price – raw silk (US$ per metric ton)
- Export price – edible oil seeds, soybean (US$ per metric ton)
- Import price – steel products (US$ per metric ton)
- Export price – sugar (US$ per metric ton)
- Export price – tea (US$ per metric ton)
- Import price – TV sets, including CKD and SKD (US$ per unit)

- Import price – edible vegetable oils, including palm oil (US$ per metric ton)
- Import price – cereals and cereal flour, wheat (US$ per metric ton)
- Import price – woven fabrics of synthetic filament yarn (US$ per meter)
- Chinese yuan per US$, monthly average
- Chinese yuan per euro, monthly average
- Chinese yuan per 100 yen, monthly average

Producer Price Index

- Import price – cereals and cereal flour (US$ per ton)
- Import price – edible vegetable oils, including palm oil (US$ per ton)
- Import price – sugar (US$ per ton)
- Import price – synthetic rubber (US$ per ton)
- Import price – wood in the rough (US$ per cubic meter)
- Import price – synthetic fibers for spinning (US$ per ton)
- Import price – iron ore and concentrates (US$ per ton)
- Import price – refined petroleum products (US$ per ton)
- Import price – fertilizers (US$ per ton)
- Import price – plastics in primary forms (US$ per ton)
- Import price – cotton woven fabrics (US$ per meter)
- Import price – steel products (US$ per ton)
- Export price – live pigs (US$ per unit)
- Export price – live poultry (US$ per unit)
- Export price – tea (US$ per ton)
- Export price – coal (US$ per ton)
- Purchasing price index, building materials and non-ferrous metals (past year = 100)
- Purchasing price index, chemical materials (past year = 100)
- Purchasing price index, ferrous metal materials (steel included) (past year = 100)
- Purchasing price index, fuels and power (past year = 100)
- Purchasing price index, non-ferrous metal materials & electric wire (past year = 100)
- Purchasing price index, timber and paper pulp (past year = 100)
- Value-added of industry (billions of yuan)
- Industrial sales (billions of yuan)
- Government expenditure – capital construction (billions of yuan)
- Real-estate investment, year-to-date, office buildings (millions of yuan)

- Real-estate investment, year-to-date, commercial buildings (millions of yuan)
- Commercial buildings, sales, year-to-date, total (millions of yuan)
- State-owned fixed assets investment (millions of yuan)
- Utilized FDI, year-to-date (millions of US$)
- Chinese yuan per US$, monthly average
- Chinese yuan per euro, monthly average
- Chinese yuan per 100 yen, monthly average

Separate independent variables

- Brent oil spot price, with appropriate lags (US$ per barrel)
- Base metal price index, with appropriate lags (1985=100, includes aluminum, copper, lead, nickel, tin and zinc)

GDP – Aggregate Approach

$$\text{LOGGDP} = \underset{(1145)}{4.6915} - \underset{(-4.36)}{0.0024}\,{*}\text{A1} + \underset{(2.62)}{0.0011}\,{*}\text{A3} - \underset{(-2.48)}{0.0015}\,{*}\text{A4}$$

$$+ \underset{(1.97)}{0.0012}\,{*}\text{A9} + \underset{(2.81)}{0.0037}\,{*}\text{DUMMY} + \underset{(5.63)}{0.8284}\,{*}\text{AR(1)}$$

Sample (adjusted): 1997Q3 2007Q4
Adjusted R^2 0.8721 Durbin–Watson stat. 1.9378

Ai = ith principal component
AR = autoregressive error transformation
MA = moving-average error transformation

Consumer Price Index

$$\text{LOGCPI} = \underset{(1574)}{4.6146} - \underset{(-6.51)}{0.0040}{*}\text{A1} + \underset{(2.33)}{0.0013}{*}\text{A2} + \underset{(2.53)}{0.0013}{*}\text{A8} - \underset{(-1.94)}{0.0007}{*}\text{A12}$$

$$+ \underset{(3.68)}{0.0023}{*}\text{DUMMY} + \underset{(11.54)}{1.102}{*}\text{AR(1)} - \underset{(-2.71)}{0.2358}{*}\text{AR(2)}$$

Sample (adjusted): 1997M02 2007M12
Adjusted R^2 0.9415 Durbin–Watson stat. 1.8836

DUMMY is to account for the Chinese New Year dates

Producer Price Index

$$\underset{}{\text{LOGPPI}} = \underset{(93.91)}{4.4608} + \underset{(3.86)}{0.0034*\text{A1}} + \underset{(4.03)}{0.0021*\text{A13}}$$

$$+ \underset{(3.38)}{0.0175*\text{LOGBRENTSPOT}} + \underset{(1.74)}{0.0150*\text{LOGBASEMETAL}(-1)}$$

$$+ \underset{(30.69)}{0.9471*\text{AR}(1)} + \underset{(2.89)}{0.2676*\text{MA}(1)}$$

Sample (adjusted): 1997M02 2007M12
Adjusted R^2 0.9784 Durbin–Watson stat. 2.0000

The principal components analysis we use is quite similar across the different independent variables. In this case, we shall elaborate on a specific one, the aggregate approach for GDP, to give readers a better idea of the methodology involved (Figure 2.16). To test the fit of the equation, we examine the residual graph of the OLS equation, as shown below. We also examine the partial elasticity of GDP to the monthly indicators (Table 2.5).

Based on the regression for the aggregate approach, we expect that the Chinese economy will grow 11.3 percent and 11.4 percent, respectively, in 2008Q1 and Q2. We use similar methodologies and obtain forecasts from both the demand and supply sides of GDP forecast. Averaging the three forecasts, our final GDP forecast is for 11.2 percent and 11.0 percent, respectively, for 2008Q1 and Q2 (Table 2.6).

CONCLUDING REMARKS

We started our discussion with the following two questions in mind: whether China can sustain its strong economic performance; and, assuming the answer is positive, then for how long can China perform at such a strong pace of economic growth? By taking into account the history of Chinese economic development, and the present economy's special characteristics, we apply principal components analysis to obtain short-term forecasts of China's GDP, CPI, PPI and major economic indicators. We maintain our forecast on a routine bi-weekly basis. Based on the latest forecast, the Chinese economy is expected to lie between two plausible error boundaries, one above and one below the extrapolated values.

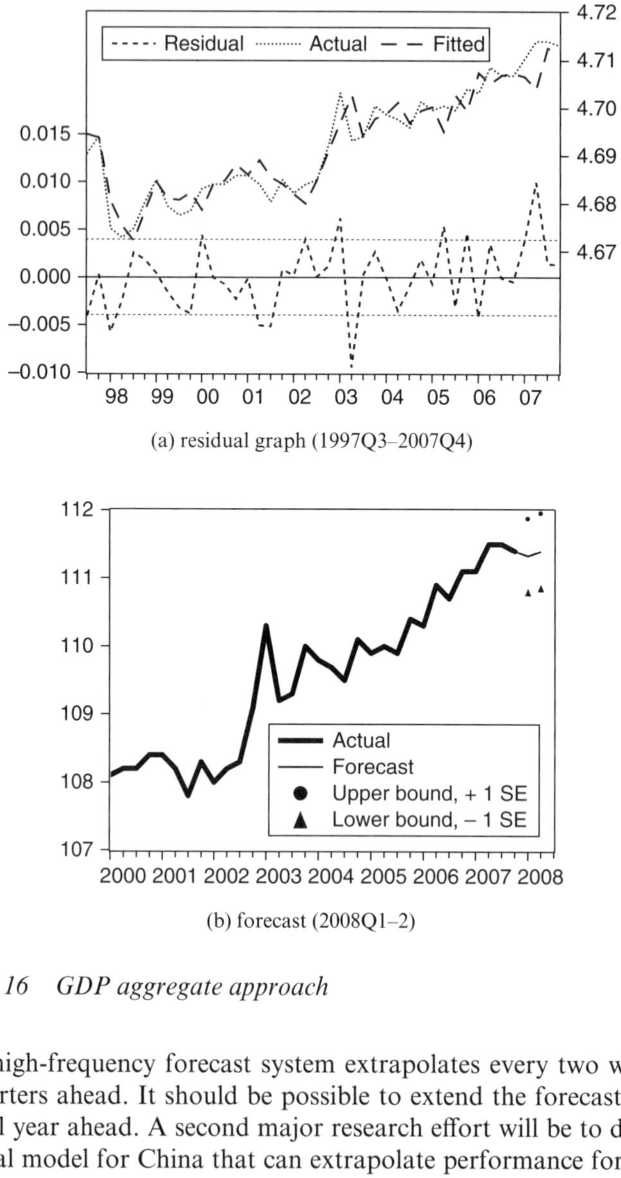

Figure 2.16 GDP aggregate approach

This high-frequency forecast system extrapolates every two weeks for two quarters ahead. It should be possible to extend the forecast horizon for a full year ahead. A second major research effort will be to develop a structural model for China that can extrapolate performance for a three- to five-year horizon and join the two systems along the lines of Professor Kushnirsky's chapter in this book (Chapter 11). That will require a major research effort; our fortnightly system is but a first step.

Table 2.5 Partial elasticity of GDP to the monthly indicators

Partial elasticity of LOGGDP w.r.t.		Rank of importance (by absolute value)
LOGALUMINUMIM	−0.000084	27
LOGBENCHMARK	0.001079	2
LOGCEMENTIP	0.000578	14
LOGCOMBUILDUNDER	0.000712	9
LOGCOPPERIM	−0.000748	7
LOGCOTTONX	−0.000118	26
LOGCRUDEIM	0.000218	22
LOGENERGYIP	0.000968	3
LOGFDIURATIO(−6)	0.000124	25
LOGFERTILIZERIP	0.000322	20
LOGGARMENTIP	0.000392	18
LOGGOVEXPRATIO(−6)	−0.000484	16
LOGINDSALESRATIO	0.000802	6
LOGIRONIP	0.000911	5
LOGPIGX	0.000237	21
LOGPLASTICPIP	0.000742	8
LOGPLASTICX	−0.000036	28
LOGPOULTRYX	−0.000664	13
LOGPOWERIP	0.000706	10
LOGREALRETAILTOTAL	−0.000475	17
LOGREFPETROIM	0.001116	1
LOGSTATEINVRATIO(−3)	−0.000175	23
LOGSTEELIM	0.000004	30
LOGSTEELIP	0.000559	15
LOGSUGARX	−0.000921	4
LOGTEAX	−0.000006	29
LOGVEGX	−0.000144	24
LOGRELWAGERMB	0.000687	11
LOGVELOCITYM2	0.000357	19
LOGGARMENTX	0.000681	12

Table 2.6 GDP forecast (year-to-date, year-over-year percent change)

	Average	Aggregate approach	Demand side	Supply side
2008Q1	11.2	111.3	110.7	111.6
2008Q2	11.0	111.4	109.8	111.7

NOTES

1. Source: National Population and Family Planning Commission of China.
2. Source: Census Bureau.
3. Chinese wage data are from the National Bureau of Statistics, while US wage data are from the Bureau of Labor Statistics.
4. Source: Ministry of Commerce.

REFERENCES

Klein, Lawrence, Huiqing Gao and Liping Tao (2007), 'Adjustment to China's CPI-based inflation rate to account for the "true" cost of living, 1993–2004', in Lawrence R. Klein and Tayyeb Shabbir (eds), *Recent Financial Crises: Analysis, Challenges and Implications*, Cheltenham, UK and Northampton, MA, USA: Edward Elgar, pp. 260–95.

Klein, Lawrence and Süleyman Özmucur (2002–03), 'The estimation of China's economic growth rate', *Journal of Economic and Social Measurement*, **28** (4), 187–202.

Ravallion, Martin and Shaohua Chen (2004), 'How have the world's poorest fared since the early 1980s?', *World Bank Research Observer*, **19**(2), 141–70.

3. The economic growth story in India: past, present and prospects for the future

Sudip Ranjan Basu*

1. INTRODUCTION

India has certainly become a country of worldwide attention over the past decade or so, mostly because of its high economic growth and outsourcing hub for major US and European corporations. From the man in the street to heads of state, India is now a significant destination not only for their travel to learn yoga and attain Nirvana, but also a key marketplace for business and investment opportunities. India's image has gone beyond that of a country full of snake-charmers and cows on the busy streets. It is now very different, with Indian Bollywood cinema catching the imagination of people from all walks of life with its beauty and colour, while Indian software companies, steelmakers and business personalities show that the sky is the limit for success. Everywhere 'Indianness' is the buzzword that has captured the spirit of democracy, hope and prosperity for the future.

India's economy has undergone many changes over the last six decades. The process of development depends on various aspects, namely socioeconomic linkages, cultural and political ideologies, class–clan structures and climatic conditions. Policies adopted by the government in New Delhi and at the sub-national level vary according to the characteristics and the nature of the political parties operating at that specific point in time, and those of the different stakeholders and interest groups. Hence the evolution of the Indian economy over the decades reflects considerable variety in economic policies and has subsequently prompted differences in the levels of growth and the development process over the years.

Thus, to analyse the growth prospects and to enhance the development dividend of the socioeconomic policies, we ought to look in detail at the variations in these policy phases and responses. This provides policy-makers with the necessary instruments to enhance the usefulness of understanding the current socioeconomic phenomenon of growth and development outcomes.

All-round development of the Indian economy requires that the different aspects of society be taken into consideration to make policies harmonious and broadly based. The central government must play a significant role in reducing regional disparities and in bringing about evenness in the development level across the states/regions. The importance of a good monsoon should not be forgotten in the Indian context and in setting the overall growth strategy for the country.

When India gained independence in 1947, the country was handicapped by mass poverty, very low literacy, a stagnating agriculture sector, and an industry with obsolete machines; it faced a very low level of productivity growth and an abysmally low per capita income. The first prime minister of India, Jawaharlal Nehru, initiated the planning model to bring the economy and society into the path of economic progress and development. The planning model emphasized the role of heavy industry for development, which was also known as the Nehru–Mahalanobis model. This strategy was aimed at accelerating economic growth to increase India's overall development potential, and thus help to reduce mass poverty.[1] To bring countries out of the low-level equilibrium trap, the leadership believed that the state should take up the 'commanding heights of the economy'. It may be noted that since independence, there have been many tangible changes in every sphere of life. The society has become a highly diversified economy with a well-developed industrial sector and immense potential for sustainable growth and development (see Agarwal and Basu, 2005 for further discussion on development strategy).

The initiation of the First Five-Year Plan in April 1951 was a move to accelerate a process of development aimed to 'raise the standards and open out new opportunities to the people for a richer and more varied life'.[2] It was sought to achieve this by a set of planning strategies for development, self-reliance, social justice and equality among the people in every sphere of life.

In 1991, Indian economic reform policies were initiated under a severe balance-of-payments problem.[3] This crisis has finally helped India to change her economic system (from an inward-looking to an outward-looking policy), which India has pursued over the last four decades.[4] In the wake of such an event, the Rao–Singh government took the initiative of reforming the Indian economy, with support from international organizations, such as the IMF–WB, to open the economy to the world. After the new economic reform strategies of 1991, Indian economic growth picked up significantly and stood at a rate near 9 per cent in 2007.

The present chapter provides an overview of the Indian economic growth story from 1950 to 2007, and then makes an economic growth forecast for 2007–08. Section 2 describes the evolution of economic policies in India since the initiation of the planning process. The trends and patterns of India's economic growth are discussed in Section 3. The current quarter model (CQM) is employed to prepare high-frequency quarterly GDP forecasts for the Indian economy in Section 4. The final section describes the challenges for sustainability of the GDP growth rate of the Indian economy.

2. EVOLUTION OF INDIAN ECONOMIC POLICIES SINCE INDEPENDENCE

India started with a Soviet Russian style planning model to eradicate mass poverty and inequality, rural–urban gaps and male–female inequality by giving the state a predominant role in accelerating and continuing the process of economic growth.

Since the initiation of the Indian planning process in 1950, there has been tremendous optimism among its instigators. The economy was depressed, with high rates of poverty, inequality, disease and death. A strong economic upturn was absolutely necessary to overcome these difficulties. The Planning Commission had to devise development strategies to accelerate the growth rate. The planning framework then rested on three legs: (1) generating the additional savings to finance the investments; (2) seeking to make escalated growth credible to private investors so that they could invest in a self-fulfilling prophecy; and (3) expanding social opportunity through land reforms and social programmes and expenditures on health and education, in particular.[5]

Against such a background, the Constitution of India in 1950 had adopted in its *Directive Principles for State Policy* the objectives of planning for national development. It stated: 'The State shall strive to promote the welfare of the people by securing and protecting as effectively as it may a social order in which justice, social, economic and political, shall inform all the institutions of the natural life.'

The First Five-Year Plan (1951–56) had initiated the policies to bring in modern technology for raising capital accumulation as one of the key factors in promoting development. The aim to step up the role of capital formation and thereby increase productivity would allow expanding levels of income and employment. The First Five-Year Plan set the overall interventionist framework of Indian economic policy-making, while the Second Five-Year Plan, whose theoretical basis was provided by P.C. Mahalanobis, contained the analytical foundation for a development strategy that was pursued in its fundamentals until 1991. The Mahalanobis model emphasized the need to achieve self-sufficiency through an increase in the allocation of productive and investible resources to capital goods industries for a subsequent acceleration in the growth of the output of consumer goods and thereby overall economic growth.

At the beginning, the growth-accelerating strategy was placed at the forefront to attack poverty, and to increase the investment rates further in India. India chose a more 'inward-looking' economic strategy, the so-called 'import substitution industrialization' (ISI) strategy, to protect the domestic industries for development, and adopted anti-export-biased policies. In the agricultural sector, the policies emphasized mechanization and R&D. This is often known as the 'Green Revolution' in Indian agriculture, and in 1970 the Nobel Peace Prize was awarded to Norman Ernest Borlaug for his intellectual achievements in world agriculture.[6]

After almost four decades of closed economic policies and planning models, major economic reforms were initiated in 1991 to bring the Indian economy out of a so-called 'Hindu rate of growth' of a modest 3–3.5 per cent. The change of economic policies in 1991 is often seen as a significant turning point for the Indian economy. This policy was a direct response to the foreign exchange crisis due to the Gulf War in June 1990, which subsequently worsened the balance-of-payments position through rising oil prices and reduced worker remittances. The then Indian prime minister, Narashima Rao, introduced a whole package of economic reforms, which in effect abolished all sorts of 'licence raj' or red tapism. The new package was known as 'a programme of macroeconomic stabilization and structural adjustment' under the guidance of the IMF and the World Bank. The adoption of economic reforms was believed necessary to achieve the purpose of accelerating the economic growth and development process of national trade and development strategies. Since the early 1990s, the main aim of this reform has been to increase efficient resource allocation, including material distribution, foreign exchange and financial markets, with well-specified attention to reforming the banking sector.

The key element of India's reform strategy initially included 'structural measures', consisting of industrial policy reform, trade and exchange rate reform (i.e. external sector), and reform in the financial sector, public sector reform and measures to streamline tax reforms, among many other series of reform measures.[7] Deregulating private sector investment, trade liberalization and opening the door to foreign direct investment and foreign institutional investment (FDI and FII), and *vis-à-vis* the financial sectors, are also some of the policy measures. Moreover, some of the important public sector industries were opened up (e.g. iron and steel, heavy plant machinery, telecommunications, air transport services etc.)

to the private sector.[8] Series of measures were directed to deregulation of imports and general opening up of the trade and investment regime to outside competition, which also constitutes a step towards India's attempt to integrate with the world economy, easing the quantitative restrictions (QRs) that were used as an instrument to restrict the imports of not only finished consumer goods, but also input of raw material components, and capital goods. In the first phase of the reform, import licensing was dismantled with respect to industrial raw materials, intermediate components and capital goods. However, in keeping with the WTO commitment, the Indian government promised that QRs on all imports would be phased out within a period of six years starting from 1998.[9]

In line with international standards (WTO regulations), India had to reduce the average rate of tariff, as India's import duties were extremely high, at more than 200 per cent on certain items. Exchange rate management is another area where the reform has been implemented with care. There was a strong desire among the reformers to tap foreign investment (both short-term and long-term) in the economy, as public sector investment was no longer feasible and sustainable, given the huge losses and inefficiency in resource mobilization. The law allowed FDI of up to 51 per cent foreign equity in a defined list of 48 industries and up to 74 per cent for nine high-priority industries.[10] The deregulation of the price regime was also a crucial component of the overall structural adjustment policy, along with the setting up of the Disinvestment Commission in 1996, to privatize the chronic loss-making public sector units, and to sell their shares in the market.[11]

Another key issue was that of opening up the market for foreign investors (including short-term investment), by lowering import tariff rates to promote a level playing field for both domestic and foreign entrepreneurs. The channel of foreign investment should attract more FDI and other long-term investment which is regarded as the crucial route to trade openness and integration. To achieve this objective India set up export processing zones (EPZs) and special economic zones (SEZs), as these policies were used to a great extent in the Chinese reform process.[12] The main objective of this sectoral reform was to encourage exports in order to create a substantial foreign exchange reserve, and to support the import of advanced technology and equipment. The non-resident Indians (NRIs) have recently been provided with many incentives for investing heavily in India.

To sum up, India's initiative in agriculture was not encouraging. However, India initiated land tenure and land reform way back in the 1950s, but failed (except in Communist Party ruling states of West Bengal and Kerala) in its land redistribution efforts. The industrial sector was the heart of India's reform process. The economic policies sought to achieve a proper balance of heavy and big industries *vis-à-vis* small-scale industries, which was crucial for successful reform. In India, the government had failed to keep the balance between small and large-scale industries, because of several political and bureaucratic vested interests as well as lack of governance structure. This has led to disparities in socioeconomic well-being (see Basu, 2002 and 2003). Moreover, on labour market policies, the Indian approach has been very weak. The Indian labour laws and unions/lobbies are too strong to allow government to pass a full-fledged bill on this policy. Thus India has yet to rationalize 'flexibility' in labour markets.

3. TRENDS AND PATTERNS OF ECONOMIC GROWTH IN INDIA

With the onset of the twenty-first century, the 'India rising' slogan has picked up steadily. Private sector participation in business activities is overwhelming, and multinational corporations have moved in huge numbers to gain from the consumer power of the middle class and the financial market upswing. So, more than 60 years of the development planning process has yielded tremendous opportunities for economic prosperity and welfare for people from all walks of life. Millions of people have been lifted out of poverty since independence. Overall economic well-being has improved significantly, leading to a lowering of social inequality across different income-class and economically backward groups of society. In this section, we briefly describe some of the major achievements.

A snapshot of the overall development performance of the Indian economy since 1950 shows that the population was about 361.10 million in 1950–51 and has skyrocketed to 1.03 billion in 2006; that amounts to an average population growth rate of 2.3 per cent per annum over the last 60 years. There has also been a steady increase in population density from 117 per sq. km in 1950–51 to 368 per sq. km in 2005. Employment in the organized sector has increased from 12.1 million in 1960 to 26.5 million in 2004, while employment in the public sector has also gone up from 10.7 million in 1970 to 18.2 million in 2004. The above results are a strong indication of the substantial improvement in every sphere of India's society and economy since the time of independence over the last five decades.

India has now become a classic case for academicians to show that economic opening up has actually benefited the economy by increasing per capita income level and growth, thereby helping to reduce poverty. The current global decline in the poverty rate has been possible mostly due to the decline in the poverty rates of India and China. The proportion of people living below the national poverty line declined in India from 42 per cent in 1993/94 to about 22 per cent according to the latest Planning Commission statistics.[13]

Table 3.1 presents some key indicators before and after the adoption of economic reform policies in 1991. The simple statistics show that the GDP growth rate was 3.9 per cent in 1960–61, and declined to 0.9 per cent in the year of economic crisis, 1990–91. However, the situation has changed dramatically, and the GDP growth rate reached 9 per cent in 2006–07. Similarly, real per capita GDP has also gone up significantly, from $176 in 1960 to $588 in 2005.

We also observe that there has been a constant improvement in educational levels and provisioning of health services. The adult literacy rate increased from as low as 18.33 per cent in 1951 to 65.38 per cent in 2001. More importantly, the percentage of girls enrolled in primary school has increased from 28.11 to 43.17 during the same period. We observe that the number of upper primary educational institutions has also increased 13 times, and there is an improvement in the teacher–pupil ratio as well, indicating a considerable development in primary and upper primary educational quality over the last 50 years. Also the number of medical practitioners and beds (all types) has registered an increase during the period. The information in Table 3.1 shows that the mortality rates for infants have been steadily declining, and the life expectancy rates have been steadily increasing, indicating that more resources have been channelled to education and health services.[14] Per capita expenditure on education and health has increased considerably during the period. Now, we look at the most talked-about phenomenon of the Indian economy: the prevalence of poverty. Poverty alleviation programmes have been on the national economic policy agenda since independence, although the proper importance and need to design policies to alleviate poverty made a significant presence only with the Fourth Five-Year Plan.[15] Strategies were designed to attack poverty directly through several rural development and employment-generating programmes. As a consequence of all these strategies, the percentage of the population below the poverty line has declined significantly, from 54.88 in the first half of the 1970s to 35.97 in 1993–94, according to a Planning Commission expert group. The Gini coefficient of inequality of consumption, however, has increased for urban India, and has been more or less stable for the rural population.

In terms of progress in social outcome indicators such as literacy, infant mortality and life expectancy, the information clearly indicates that there has been an immense improvement. The rise in educational achievement is noticeable, with a literacy rate of 24 per cent in 1960 that went up to about

Table 3.1 A profile of India's economic growth and development

	1960	1980	1991	2005
Growth indicators				
GDP growth (annual %)	3.9	6.7	0.9	9.2
GDP per capita (constant 2000 US$)	176.3	223.2	313.7	588.4
Social indicators				
Literacy rate, adult total (% of people aged 15 and above)	24.02	43.67	52.21	64.84
Mortality rate, infant (per 1000 live births)	146	113	80	56
Life expectancy at birth, total (years)	44.3	54.2	59.1	63.5
Human Development Index				
Trade and Development Index				
Economic indicators				
(a) Savings–investment				
Gross fixed capital formation (% of GDP)	15.3	18.7	21.9	33.4
Gross domestic savings (% of GDP)	12.6	15.5	21.9	29.7
(b) Sectors				
Agriculture, value-added (% of GDP)	46.5	38.9	31.5	18.3
Industry, value-added (% of GDP)	19.4	24.5	26.4	27.3
Manufacturing, value-added (% of GDP)	13.7	16.3	16.1	15.7
Services, etc., value-added (% of GDP)	34.2	36.6	42.1	54.4
(c) External sector				
Exports of goods and services (% of GDP)	4.6	6.3	8.6	20.5
Imports of goods and services (% of GDP)	7.3	9.5	8.6	24.2
Manufactures exports (% of merchandise exports)	43.3	58.6	72	70.3
Foreign direct investment, net inflows (% of GDP)	0.1* (1970)	0	0	0.8
Trade (% of GDP)	11.9	15.7	17.2	44.7
(d) Urbanization				
Urban population (% of total)	17.9	23.1	25.7	28.7

65 per cent in 2005. This improvement in education has been quite instrumental in many areas of economic advancement, including the rising skill content of the labour force (see Basu et al., 2006 for discussion of factors related to welfare improvement in India).

Other economic indicators, such as the savings rate, have increased since the 1960s, together with domestic investment, leading to a higher growth rate in the post-reform period. In terms of sectoral distribution, it is quite obvious that over the years there has been a significant structural transformation of the Indian economy. India had started with a favourable contribution from the agricultural sector, but from the beginning of the new millennium, the contribution to GDP from the service sector has increased rapidly. This implies that industrial development was not that favourable for economic growth in India, and there was stagnation for a long period in the 1980s and early 1990s. In terms of external sector performance, the Indian record has been rising with the opening of its economy. Exports of goods and services, as well as imports, have increased significantly over the years. Interestingly, manufacturing exports in total merchandise are increasing with India's integration in the world economy. Urbanization is another key indicator to show the movement of people from rural areas to cities and other metropolitan areas in search of jobs and a better lifestyle.

India has many natural resources, and at the beginning of the planning process the bulk of the population was based in agriculture. So, when the development model was initiated, it was thought wise to set up a modern domestic industrial sector to produce industrial goods, and intermediate capital goods, so as to protect their infant industries from competition by foreign industries. Then the state initially imposed a high level of tariffs and non-tariff barriers under an anti-export-bias economic strategy. The import-substituting industrialization or closed-door economic policy was encouraged to raise the role of capital-intensive production, with less emphasis on labour-intensive industries. This had actually hurt the growth process, and failed to reduce poverty incidence in the pre-reform era.

The basic argument for reform was then to open the economy to the rest of the world and reap the benefit of trade and exchange of information technology. The policies were redirected to boost industry and attract foreign investment. With trade liberalization, India reduced high tariff levels on imported goods and eliminated quota restrictions. This immediately helped to attract significant foreign resources and investment in the domestic economy. The policies were designed to boost exports and build efficiency of resource allocation in line with comparative advantage, as advocated by neoclassical trade theory.

Trade expansion and industrial development have been strong, attracting FDI inflow with export growth. Recent economic information clearly shows that with trade expansion, service sector development has gone up, but industrial development has not been that impressive. The other crucial effect of economic reform can be seen in the manufacturing sector, in industrial development and increased FDI. The manufacturing sector now needs a contribution to overall economic growth that generates employment in labour surplus countries such as India. Industrial expansion helps export diversification, leading to a rise in manufacturing output, and, in turn, increases employment. Another significant aspect of the economic reform is enhancement of technical change in the economy, leading to a rise in the productivity rate, which, in turn, increases real wage rates in the manufacturing sector. The higher wages help the economy to reduce the poverty rate, and induce a higher rate of growth. Experience shows that Indian labour productivity, measured by GDP per person employed, has been increasing over time, in step with the wage rate. This has helped India to reduce the poverty rate significantly during the reform period.

One of the reasons is that supply-side factors such as public spending on human capital, through provision of basic health and education, are key to sustaining a higher level of growth and poverty reduction (see Basu and Krishnakumar, 2005 for detailed results of the status of poverty and inequality across socioeconomic groups in India). The figure (average of 1990s) from the World Bank shows that total public spending as a percentage of GDP is 15.88. The health and education expenditures are 5.01 per cent and 3.26 per cent. Also per capita primary student expenditure as a percentage of per capita GDP is 8.44 per cent. However, such investments can work only if the infrastructure development takes place and institutional arrangements are effective so as to translate social programmes (such as poverty alleviation, employment guarantee and a mid-day meal for school children) into successful implementation (see Nagar and Basu, 2002 for the relationship between infrastructure development and economic growth, and Basu, 2002 for the interlinkages between governance arrangements and economic well-being).

Latest Developments in the Indian Economy, 2007

In the year 2007, India witnessed record-breaking economic performances. This section presents some recent trends of the Indian economy. India's GDP exceeded US$1 trillion for the first time in history. India is now the twelfth country in the list of those that have passed this mark. This elite group consists of the following countries: the USA, Japan, Germany, China, the UK, France, Italy, Spain, Canada, Brazil and Russia. This has led to an increase in real per capita income from Rs 20 734 (about US$500 at the current exchange rate) for the year 2005–06 to Rs 22 483 (about US$550) for the year 2006–07 at 1999–2000 prices.

The Indian economy has continued to grow at an impressive rate. Indian GDP grew by 9.4 per cent in the financial year 2006–07 as compared to the year 2005–06 at constant 1999–2000 prices. According to the latest estimates released by the Central Statistical Organization (CSO) of the Government of India and other institutions, real GDP at factor cost is about 8.5 per cent to 9.0 per cent year on year. The current *Asian Development Outlook 2007* update report of the Asian Development Bank projects India's real GDP to grow by 8.5 per cent year on year in 2007 and 2008. The report also noted that India's GDP grew by 9.4 per cent in the fiscal year 2006–07, the fastest expansion in the last 18 years. The Reserve Bank of India (RBI) projected the Indian economy to grow at 8.5 per cent in 2007–08 against an expected 9.2 per cent for 2006–07. GDP growth continues to be robust due to a good monsoon season, rising investment (both domestic and foreign), and an expansion in service sector activities.

Furthermore, the continuing real GDP growth is possible as a result of the growth of the overall industrial and service sectors. This industrial production was mainly driven by good performance of the manufacturing subsectors as well as the growth of six core infrastructure industries. The construction, housing and infrastructure industries all over India are experiencing a boom. The majority of core manufacturing sectors have recorded higher growth rates compared to a year earlier.

The index of industrial production (IIP) expanded by 11.8 per cent year on year in October 2007–08. The IIP for the manufacturing sectors for October grew 13.3 per cent from a year earlier. Output of consumer goods grew 12.5 per cent. Output of capital goods and intermediate goods grew 20.5 per cent and 14.2 per cent, respectively. This trend is expected to continue in the near future. The index for the mining, manufacturing and electricity sectors grew by 8.1 per cent, 8.3 per cent and 7.1 per cent, respectively, in 2007–08Q2 as compared to the growth rates of 2.6 per cent, 13.0 per cent, and 8.0 per cent, respectively, in 2006–07Q2. The boom in real-estate activity has led to growth in production of cement and finished steel of 9.9 per cent and 9.6 per cent, respectively, in 2007–08Q2. The rising purchasing power of 500 million Indian middle-class people enables them to demand more and more consumption and capital goods.

Another key sector in India's manufacturing growth figures is the automotive industry, which constitutes about 5 per cent of total GDP in dollar terms, and the Government of India expects the industry to contribute about 10 per cent by 2016. Passenger car sales stand at 842 000 for the period January–July 2007.

The service sector continued to grow rapidly in this period. The subsector 'trade, hotels, transport, and communication', with a growth rate of 11.4 per cent for 2007Q2 to 2008Q2 over 2006Q2 to 2007Q2, was strengthened by 'finance, insurance, real estate and business services' at 10.6 per cent, and 'community, social and personal services' at 7.8 per cent.

In recent years, the telecommunications industry has shown robust growth. The total telephone subscription numbers have exceeded 200 million, while the total number of mobile phone subscriptions rose to 162.5 million in February 2007. Also the total stock of telephone connections (including WLL – wireless in local loop – and cellular) grew by 46.3 per cent in 2007Q2 to 2008Q2 over 2006Q2 to 2007Q2.

The growing number of worldwide mergers and acquisitions (M&A) activities has attracted a rise of Indian companies' acquisitions of foreign companies. A recent study shows that during the first nine months of 2006, Indian companies announced 115 foreign acquisitions worth $7.4 billion, a seven-fold increase since 2000. The Government of India estimates indicate that India could capture around 15 per cent of the knowledge process outsourcing (KPO) industry worldwide by 2010.

Apart from outsourcing boom, the IT sector has given India an impressive edge in the service sector as compared to other developing countries. The recent boom in the IT market is likely to continue in the next few years. Some estimates predict that the service sector will grow to $10.73 billion by 2011. Rising domestic demand and increasing reliance on foreign firms have been instrumental in expanding market opportunities. In recent years the earnings from IT services can be seen as a real economic 'stabilizer' to help India overcome any short-run global and/or national economic crisis.

A recent report shows that India is the fastest-growing healthcare IT market in Asia and is expected to grow at an average of 22 per cent year on year, followed by China and Vietnam. The total market value for IT in the healthcare industry in Asia was $2.95 billion in 2006, and is expected to reach $4.83 billion by 2010. The healthcare industry has opened up new business opportunities for Indian companies and professionals, and attracts foreign visitors with favourable pricing of personal services.

The agriculture, forestry and fishing sector registered a modest increase. The growth rate here registered a 3.6 per cent increase in 2007Q2 to 2008Q2. There is some indication that inflation is coming under control, as the Reserve Bank of India has tightened fiscal and monetary policies, and prices of food items have stabilized over the past few months. The RBI set the tolerance threshold of the inflation rate, based on the wholesale price index (WPI) of all commodities, at 4.0–4.5 per cent. Indian annual average inflation based on the WPI was 3.50 per cent in the week ended 22 December 2007, while the annual rate of inflation stood at 5.78 per cent in 2006–07. So, over the past several months, the inflationary pressure on the Indian economy has continued to show a downward trend.

The latest A.T. Kearney's annual Global Retail Development Index (GRDI), a measure of retail investment attractiveness among 30 emerging markets, ranked India as the most attractive market for retail investment, followed by Russia and China. India continues to be one of the most attractive destinations for foreign investors. The share of FDI in India's GDP has gone up and accounts for 2.31 per cent in the latest available statistics.

The Indian economy continues to attract a large amount of foreign investments. For the first time the net investments by foreign institutional investors (FIIs) crossed the $10 billion mark during the months of January to July 2007, which is significantly higher than $7.99 billion for the 2006 calendar year. Furthermore, with a reduction of the US Federal Reserve interest rate, there has been an impressive rise of foreign institutional investment (FII) in India, reaching $1.5 billion. Similarly, total foreign investment flows now stand at US$5.0 billion, while foreign direct investment rose to US$2.7 billion from 1.0 billion a year ago.

India is also pushing for a growth model based on attracting foreign investments through operating SEZs. The latest statistics show that there are 133 approved SEZs, which have attracted investment worth about $10 billion. The SEZs have absorbed directly more than 35 000 people and provided double the number indirectly through different chain operations. The government estimates that the employment opportunity will reach 100 000 people and investment will increase to about $23 billion by the end of 2007. It is envisaged that SEZs will create about 3–5 million jobs by 2009.

India has gradually emerged as a global power in international trade. According to the United Nations, India's total merchandise trade stood at $295 billion, while services trade reached $140 billion in 2006. Hence India's overall trade in merchandise and services has risen from $126 billion in 2000 to $435 billion in 2006. Moreover, India's share in world merchandise and services trade stood at 1.5 per cent in 2006.

4. HIGH-FREQUENCY CURRENT QUARTER MODEL FOR FORECASTING QUARTERLY GDP FOR THE INDIAN ECONOMY

4.1 The Prelude to the Forecasting Model

The major change in the Indian economy over the past decade has prompted policy-makers and market experts to look carefully at the evolution of economic prospects. The statistical modelling technique of principal components (see Stone, 1947; Nagar and Basu, 2002) has been used to explore prospects for the Indian economy. Furthermore, the Indian high-frequency forecasting methodology is based on the CQM for the US economy developed at the University of Pennsylvania (see Klein and Young, 1980; Klein and Park, 1993; and Klein and Özmucur, 2002–03). Although a structural model could have been an appropriate option for building a full model of economic growth, instead we make use of a CQM to prepare short-run forecasts.

The availability of consistent high-frequency information on economic activities has provided opportunities to prepare short-term forecasts. It is now believed that a high-frequency model can be used to set up correctly preliminary groundwork for the structural equation model over a longer horizon, without any subjectivity. Many of the indicators of economic activity are now available on an hourly, daily, weekly or monthly basis.

Monthly economic indicators are used in this chapter to forecast the quarterly GDP of the Indian economy from a principal components analysis. This forecast can be made similarly from the production side and the expenditure side. The principal components methodology primarily uses a set of strategic monthly indicators that are closely linked to GDP to estimate the main independent sources of variation. The forecast values of the set of monthly indicators are obtained with use of ARIMA (autoregressive integrated moving-average) equations over the future horizon.

The expenditure-side model is based on the aggregation of final purchases for a country detailed in the national income accounts. The demand-side components are the following: consumption (private and public), investment (private and public), and the difference between exports and imports. The estimation of all demand components will provide the final estimate of the GDP. The production-side model is based on the summation of value-added across three sectors of production: primary, secondary and tertiary. The aggregated estimation of three sectors will provide the final estimates of GDP.

The principal components methodology avoids the problem of multicollinearity among the strategically selected monthly indicators. The principal components are a set of mutually uncorrelated variables that explain variation of the strategic monthly indicators. GDP is then regressed on the principal components to obtain the forecast equations for extrapolations.

4.2 Forecasting Quarterly GDP by Principal Components Methodology

The principal components technique is used here to make forecasts of India's real GDP on the basis of a set of strategic monthly indicators. The principal components are normalized linear functions of the monthly indicators that represent the economy as a whole, and they are mutually orthogonal. These components can be considered as a canonical form. These mutually uncorrelated principal components provide the main sources of the joint variation, but some particular external variables, such as major primary prices like the world crude oil price, are used as regressors in addition to principal components values.

The first step is to select a set of strategic monthly indicators such as industrial production, interest rate, investment, trade, remittances and software earnings. We replace the set of monthly indicators by an equal or smaller number of their principal components. The monthly principal components are converted to three-month averages to yield quarterly series. Quarterly GDP is then regressed on some or all principal components. The quarterly regression equation is then used to extrapolate GDP and related macroeconomic variables.

The main purpose of this approach is to select a set of strategic monthly indicators from the set of economic indicators that are highly correlated with real GDP. These indicators are obtained from industrial production, interest rates, trade and other indicators. These indicators are critical for representing the short-term variation of real GDP, which is forecasted on a quarterly basis. However, most of the strategic indicators are reported on a monthly frequency from respective official sources.

The selections of strategic monthly indicators are carried out by taking into account the supply side and demand side of the economy. We have also included a set of market-clearing indicators. Moreover, some of the indicators are chosen to identify the future potential of the economy. On the other hand, some indicators are chosen by investigating their historical importance and established trends.

Indian monthly data for a large number of indicators are available only from 1997. The CQM is based on monthly strategic indicators starting in 1997–98. So, this time span allows us to extrapolate estimates for as long as two quarters in advance. The forecast of GDP is a function of 29 monthly indicators (see Table 3.2 for the list of monthly indicators).

For the purpose of estimating and forecasting real GDP, we have added three independent indicators. We have included only those indicators that have a common starting point. So, we specify a semi-reduced-form model for the Indian economy by using the principal components (PC) methodology. The PCs are estimated from quarterly data for 26 indicators and three independent variables to account for estimation of GDP. The first ten components account for 79.3 per cent of the overall variation of the whole set. Moreover, the first component accounts for 27.1 per cent, and has a large coefficient for the export of manufactured goods in the corresponding eigenvector. We have finally selected 15 PCs for the estimation of GDP that account for 91.1 per cent of the total variation of the sample. We exclude the rest because they represent a small proportion of total variance of the original set of 26 strategic indicators.

The regression estimate of the logarithm of quarterly $(GDP)_t/(GDP)_{t-4}$ shows the following result in equation (3.1). All the monthly indicators are converted to a logarithm of quarterly average *PC*s, PC_t/PC_{t-4}. The coefficients

Table 3.2 List of 29 monthly indicators used in forecasting GDP

Indicators	Unit	Indicators	Unit
1 Money supply (M2)	Rs.crore	18 Leather & leather manufactures export	US$ million
2 Bank credit to commercial sector	Rs.crore	19 Chemicals & related products export	US$ million
3 Bank rate	Per cent		
4 Sugar production	'000 tonnes	20 Textiles (excluding ready-made garments) export	US$ million
5 Rubber production	Tonnes		
6 Jute goods production	'000 tonnes	21 Ready-made garments export	US$ million
7 Fertilizer production	'000 tonnes	22 Other manufactured goods export	US$ million
8 Aluminium production	Tonnes	23 Market rate of rupee *vis-à-vis* US$	Rs/US$
9 Passenger car sales	Numbers	24 Foreign direct investments (including acquisition of share)	US$ million
10 Railway earnings from goods traffic	Rs.crore		
11 Food & related items imports	US$ million	25 Software services earnings, gross	US$ million
12 Chemicals and related products imports	US$ million	26 Private transfers (remittances), gross	US$ million
		27 Actual rainfall in India	Millimetres
13 Capital goods imports	US$ million		
		28 Crude oil (petroleum); dated Brent	US$ per barrel
14 Other commodities imports	US$ million		
		29 Rice, 5 per cent broken milled white rice, Thailand nominal price quote	US$ per tonne
15 Tea export	US$ million		
16 Iron ore export	US$ million		
17 Manufactured goods export	US$ million		

obtained from the regression estimates indicate the elasticity, meaning that if there is a 1 per cent increase in quarterly PCs or three independent variables (price of Thai rice, price of Brent oil and rainfall), the quarterly GDP will increase by an estimated coefficient in percentage points.

The regression results strongly reflect the general situation of the Indian economy. The principal components generally represent the movement of 26 broad-based economic indicators. The regression estimate is based on 36 observations from 1998Q2 to 2007Q3. We initially include the first 15 indicators as possible regressors. We dropped the PCs that are insignificant, and kept the significant PCs to estimate real GDP. The final regression is obtained by including nine PCs and three independent indicators, as well as a moving-average process of residuals.

So, the equation for year-over-year growth in quarterly GDP and the regression period covers 1998Q2 to 2007Q2 (i.e. 1998:2–2007:2). The regression is estimated by using ordinary least squares (OLS) and is given as:

$$
\begin{aligned}
D\log\frac{GDP_t}{GDP_{t-4}} = {} & 4.8847 + 0.006D\log\frac{PC1_t}{PC1_{t-4}} - 0.003D\log\frac{PC2_t}{PC2_{t-4}} \\
& + 0.002D\log\frac{PC4_t}{PC4_{t-4}} + 0.007D\log\frac{PC5_t}{PC5_{t-4}} \\
& + 0.007D\log\frac{PC6_t}{PC6_{t-4}} + 0.009D\log\frac{PC9_t}{PC9_{t-4}} \\
& - 0.0137D\log\frac{PC12_t}{PC12_{t-4}} + 0.004D\log\frac{PC14_t}{PC14_{t-4}} \\
& + 0.015D\log\frac{PC15_t}{PC15_{t-4}} + 0.015D\log\frac{RAIN_t}{RAIN_{t-4}} \\
& - 0.032D\log\frac{RICETHAI_t}{RICETHAI_{t-4}} - 0.03D\log\frac{OILBRENT_t}{OILBRENT_{t-4}} \\
& - 0.997MA(1) \qquad (3.1)
\end{aligned}
$$

Adjusted $R^2 = 0.932$, DW = 2.554, F = 38.012, LM (2) = 0.000, ARCH (0.435), n = 36.

The adjusted R^2 indicates that these nine PCs and three independent variables account for 93.2 per cent of the variation of real GDP. We find that all the regression coefficients are significant at least at the 5 per cent level. Interestingly, the results clearly indicate the importance of three independent indicators that we have included in the estimation of quarterly GDP. The positive and significant coefficient for *RAIN* indicates the importance of the monsoon in India, while increases in the price of rice and oil have a negative impact on GDP. This implies that the Indian economy is now closely related to international prices of commodities, and the higher price of these commodities can restrain the growth rate of the economy.

The equation has serially uncorrelated errors (according to Durbin–Watson and Breusch–Godfrey LM tests). Furthermore, there is no autoregressive conditional heteroscedasticity (ARCH) of residuals. This regression has therefore been able to reproduce the historically quarterly real GDP

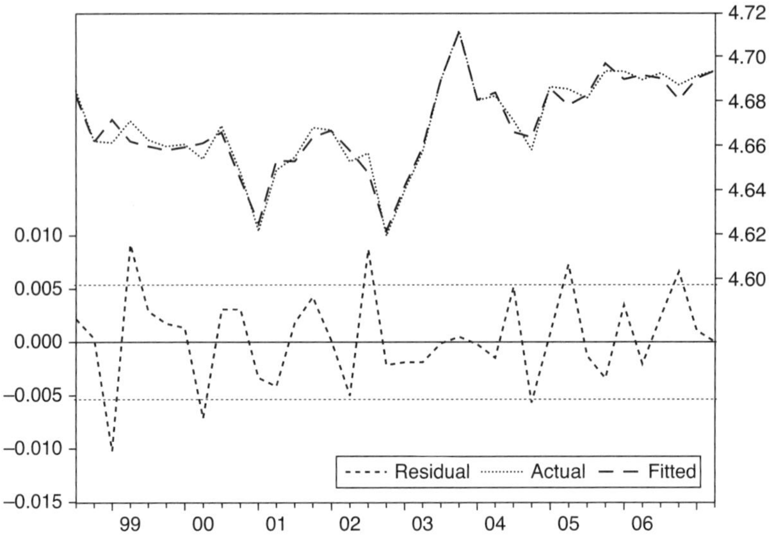

Figure 3.1 GDP equation plot (1997–98Q3 to 2007–08Q4)

growth rates with a significant degree of precision. Figure 3.1 presents clearly the observed and fitted real quarterly GDP growth rates. The use of these principal components and three extra variables is consistent with the movements of the government's official estimates of the real GDP growth rate.

The CQM for quarterly real GDP is estimated in order to make forecasts and validate the official releases. The model allows us to make two-quarter-ahead estimates. Table 3.3 shows the forecast results of real GDP. The first column is the year and quarter for which the forecast is made, the second column is the logGDP and the third column is the real GDP year-over-year percentage change. The last two rows of the second and third columns are the forecasts for the third and fourth quarters of 2007. The fourth column indicates if the number represents official release or the CQM high-frequency forecast (see also Figure 3.2 for the two forecasted quarters of 2007–08).

We expect that the Indian economy will continue to experience strong growth momentum in the first half of 2008. For the third quarter, CQM forecasts 9.03 per cent real GDP growth, which should be followed by a slightly slower rate of increase (7.92 per cent) in the fourth quarter (on the basis of year-over-year percentage change).

The coefficients of the regressions and of the corresponding eigenvectors together produce the partial elasticities of the strategic indicators that are included in the estimation to make forecasts of real quarterly GDP (see Table 3.4). The manufacturing sectors of the economy are positively related

Table 3.3 Real quarterly GDP forecast for 2007Q3–08Q3 to 2007Q4–08Q4 (forecast by out-of-sample extrapolation)

Year/quarter	LOGGDP	Real GDP (%)	Type (actual/ forecast)
2006–07 Q1 (April–June)	4.694	9.30	Actual
2006–07 Q2 (July–September)	4.690	8.89	Actual
2006–07 Q3 (October–December)	4.693	9.22	Actual
2006–07 Q4 (January–March)	4.688	8.64	Actual
2007–08 Q1 (April–June)	4.692	9.08	Actual
2007–08 Q2 (July–September)	4.694	9.34	Actual
2007–08 Q3 (October–December)	**4.692**	**9.03**	**Forecast**
2007–08 Q4 (January–March)	**4.681**	**7.92**	**Forecast**

Notes:
The LOGGDP variable stands for the logarithms of the ratio of GDP to its value one year ago. (*D* log GDP at constant 1999–2000 prices.)

to GDP growth rate at the margin, while some indicators such as software earnings, FDI and fertilizer production have a small impact on GDP growth rates. These indicators have been growing in recent years; therefore we need a few more years to realize their impact on overall economic activities.

5. SUSTAINABILITY OF INDIA'S ECONOMIC GROWTH

This sustainability of high economic growth of the Indian economy has become a subject of intense debate among policy-makers. To keep the economy moving requires balanced policies on many fronts of the planning process, given the fast-changing economic developments in India. India recorded an average growth rate of around 9 per cent in 2007. But at the same time, there have been some factors that have posed risks of reducing overall GDP growth, such as rising international crude oil prices, increasing domestic fiscal deficits and emerging environmental challenges,

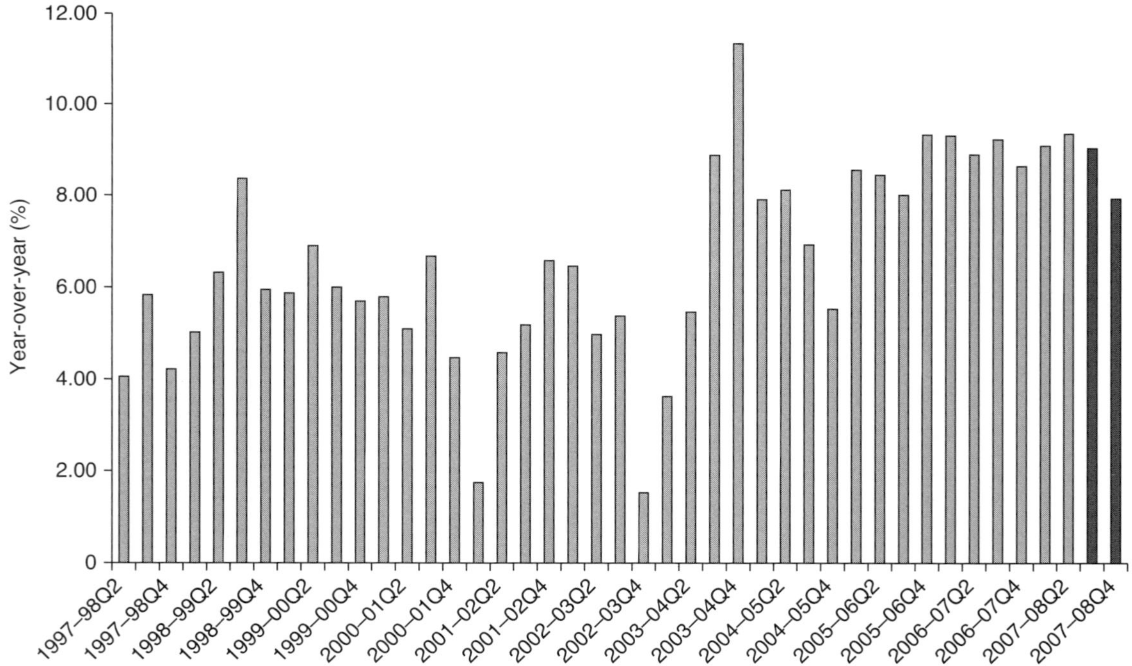

Sources: Central Statistical Office, Centre for Monitoring the Indian Economy and author's estimates.

Figure 3.2 *Quarterly forecasts of real GDP (year-over-year percentage change with the same quarter of prior year, at constant 1999–2000 prices)*

Table 3.4 Partial elasticity of real quarterly GDP with respect to monthly indicators

	Partial elasticities	Rank (by absolute value of partial elasticity)
Manufactured goods export	3.067	1
Leather & leather manufactures export	2.580	2
Other manufactured goods export	2.202	3
Capital goods imports	2.159	4
Ready-made garments export	2.105	5
Aluminium production	1.970	6
Bank credit to commercial sector	1.944	7
Money supply (M2)	1.939	8
Chemicals & related products export	1.909	9
Textiles (excluding ready-made garments) export	1.802	10
Iron ore export	1.746	11
Market rate of rupee *vis-à-vis* US$	−1.678	12
Tea export	1.412	13
Chemicals & related products imports	1.408	14
Sugar production	1.304	15
Jute goods production	−1.178	16
Rubber production	1.154	17
Bank rate	0.999	18
Private transfers (remittances), gross	−0.794	19
Railway earnings from goods traffic	0.618	20
Passenger car sales	0.572	21
Other commodities imports	−0.518	22
Food & related items imports	−0.518	23
Fertilizer production	−0.314	24
Foreign direct investments (including acquisition of share)	−0.063	25
Software services earnings, gross	−0.004	26

including uncertainty about monsoon rainfall. Furthermore, some possibilities of an upward trend in inflation could be fuelled by three major components, such as increases in commodity prices (oil and metal prices in international markets), money supply and public expenditure.

Yet there are growing business and investor expectations and confidence in strong industrial and service sector activities. IT-enabled service sector growth, from both export earnings and growing employment opportunities, and optimism centred around the concept of 'India rising' are likely to continue to make their positive impact on GDP growth rate and overall development.

Of course, Indian policy-makers need to focus on some key factors to bring about equitable growth phenomena in their national development framework. The planning process should aim at challenges that could derail India's march towards becoming an economic superpower:

- a growing rich–poor divide creates the notion of socioeconomic inequality;
- regional polarization, with some regions outperforming others and thereby increasing regional socioeconomic differences;
- rural–urban migration, bringing a rising level of economic prosperity in cities setting up new industrial and service sector activities. People are now leaving their low-wage work in primary sectors;
- an increasing role of regional political parties that may retard the economic process. The regional political leaders are becoming more interested in preparing their local industrial and service sector hubs by wooing investors from abroad with attractive incentives;
- environmental degradation, causing pollution, and other industrial activities that also contribute negatively to the environment and other human activities;
- politicization of caste and religion creates social tensions among some economically backward groups and raises major challenges in different government institutions and regions.

Against this background, the high-frequency CQM of national income and product accounts provides key indicators to the direction of movement of the Indian economy. Future studies will be carried out to prepare regular forecasts for the consumer price index, the producer price index, and the trade balance of the Indian economy.

NOTES

* I would like to express my sincere thanks to Lawrence R. Klein for his insightful comments and suggestions at all stages of preparation of this chapter. I am thankful to Süleyman Özmucur, Wendy Mak, Vladimir Eskin and A.L. Nagar for useful comments on the technical part. Thanks are also due to Gayatrika Gupta for giving me useful research suggestions. The views expressed in this chapter are those of the author and do not necessarily reflect the views of the United Nations Secretariat or its members. Any errors in this chapter are the responsibility of the author.

1. According to Bhagwati (1998, p. 25), this growth rate was an 'instrumental variable, a policy outcome that would in turn reduce poverty'.
2. First Five-Year Plan, Planning Commission, 1951–56.
3. The annual inflation rate reached nearly 14 per cent, gross fiscal deficit of the central government reached 8 per cent (of GDP), central government debt reached 51 per cent (of GDP), the current account deficit peaked at nearly 3 per cent (of GDP), and external

debt went up to more than 26 per cent (of GDP) in 1990. *World Development Indicators 2001*, World Bank. See Agarwal (1997) for further discussion.

4. There was tremendous pressure on India's foreign exchange reserve, as it stood at US$3.105 billion in 1989, and went to US$1.205 billion in 1990 according to the International Monetary Fund, and could sustain only two weeks of import coverage.
5. See Bhagwati (1998) for a detailed discussion of the Indian planning process.
6. The Green Revolution started in India in 1966, mostly in the states of Punjab, Haryana and West Bengal, and consisted of three basic elements: continued expansion of farming areas; double-cropping existing farmland; and using seeds with improved genetics – high-yielding varieties (HYV), of which the K68 variety for wheat is most important.
7. The Committee on Tax Reform was set up in 1992; it proposed that the share of customs duties in total taxes should be reduced and the share of direct taxes should be raised. More revenue needed to be mobilized via excise duties by transforming them into value-added taxes. Maximum rates of personal and corporate income taxes were reduced.
8. The production of certain items in the small-scale sector has been maintained to keep the interest of the small-scale units.
9. The central government in New Delhi under the 'United Front' coalition government introduced this phasing out of QRs in 1998. After that the BJP government took over power and endorsed phasing out of QRs. As a first step it removed QRs from 350 items in April 1998, which still leaves 2200 items subject to QRs (Ahluwalia, 1999).
10. In 1993, foreign institutional investors (FIIs) were, for the first time, allowed to invest in Indian equity once they fulfilled certain minimum standards, and further policies were simplified to enable them to trade in debt instruments through secondary market purchases in the stock market. Another channel for portfolio investment was provided by allowing Indian companies to issue fresh equity abroad through the new mechanism called global depository receipts (GDRs).
11. The Commission was set up by the United Front government to restructure public sector undertakings (PSUs), either by privatizing them or offloading shares in favour of workers. The objective of the plan is to divert the revenues generated from such disinvestment to be utilized for allocations for education and health, and to create a fund to strengthen public sector enterprises in the future.
12. For further discussion on SEZs policies, visit http://sezindia.nic.in/HTMLS/about.htm and http://sezindia.nic.in/HTMLS/SEZs_notified_under_SEZ_Act_2005.pdf. See also Sachs et al. (2002) for discussion on such new trade promotion policies in India.
13. The UNDP *Human Development Report*'s (2003) finding is that the first of these global targets (Millennium Development Goal 8), reducing by half the proportion of people living on less than US$1 a day, is likely to be reached, due in large part to sustained economic growth in China and India.
14. Total plan investment outlay on health, family welfare and water supply and sanitation (Central, States and UTs – union territories) has increased from 3.9 per cent in the First Five-Year Plan to 7 per cent in the Eighth Five-Year Plan. Source: Ministry of Family Welfare and Planning Commission.
15. In 1938, Jawaharlal Nehru declared that the social objective should be 'to ensure an adequate standard of living for the masses, in other words, to get rid of the appalling poverty of the people'.

REFERENCES

Agarwal, M. (1997), 'India', in P. Desai (ed.), *Going Global: Transition from Plan to Market in the World Economy*, Cambridge, MA: MIT Press, pp. 473–96.

Agarwal, M. and Sudip Ranjan Basu (2005), 'Development strategy and regional

inequality in India', in A. Barua (ed.), *India's Northeast: Development Issues in a Historical Perspective*, New Delhi: Manohar Publishing.
Ahluwalia, M.S. (1999), 'India's economic reforms: an appraisal', in J. Sachs, A. Varshney and N. Bajpai (eds), *India in the Era of Economic Reforms*, Oxford: Oxford University Press.
Basu, Sudip Ranjan (2002), 'Does governance matter? Some evidence from Indian states', paper presented at the VIIth Spring Meeting of Young Economists, 17–19 April, Paris, France.
Basu, Sudip Ranjan (2003), 'The determinants of economic well-being: an application in the Indian states', paper presented at the VIIIth Spring Meeting of Young Economists, 3–5 April, Leuven, Belgium.
Basu, S.R., S. Fan and X. Zhang (2006), 'Welfare comparison beyond GDP', paper presented at the International Conference on the Dragon and the Elephant: China and India's Economic Reforms, 30 June–2 July 2006, China Executive Leadership Academy Pudong, Shanghai, China.
Basu, S.R. and J. Krishnakumar (2005), 'Spatial distribution of welfare across states and different socio-economic groups in rural and urban India', paper presented at first meeting of the Society for the Study of Economic Inequality (ECINEQ), Palma de Mallorca, 20–22 July 2005.
Bhagwati, J.N. (1998), 'The design of Indian development', in I.J. Ahluwalia and I.M.D. Little (eds), *India's Economic Reforms and Development: Essays for Manmohan Singh*, Oxford: Oxford University Press, pp. 23–39.
Government of India (2002), *National Human Development Report 2001*, Planning Commission of India, New Delhi.
Government of India (various years), *Planning Commission* reports.
Government of India (various years), *Statistical Abstract of India*, Central Statistical Organisation, New Delhi.
Klein, L.R. and S. Özmucur (2002–03), 'The estimation of China's economic growth rate', *Journal of Economic and Social Measurement*, **28**, 187–202.
Klein, L.R. and J.Y. Park (1993), 'Economic forecasting at high frequency intervals', *Journal of Forecasting*, **12**(3–4), 301–19.
Klein, L.R. and R.M. Young (1980), *Introduction to Econometric Forecasting and Forecasting Models*, Lexington, MA: Lexington Books.
Nagar, A.L. and S.R. Basu (2002), 'Weighting socio-economic indicators of human development: a latent variable approach', in A. Ullah et al. (eds), *Handbook of Applied Econometrics and Statistical Inference*, New York: Marcel Dekker.
Nagar, A.L. and S.R. Basu (2004), 'Infrastructure development index: an analysis for 17 major Indian states (1990–91 to 1996–97)', *Journal of Combinatorics, Information and System Sciences*, **27**(1–4), 185–203.
Sachs, J., N. Bajpai and A. Ramiah (2002), 'Understanding regional economic growth in India', CID WP no. 88, Harvard University.
Stone, J.R.N. (1947), 'On the interdependence of blocks of transactions', Supplement to *Journal of the Royal Statistical Society*, **VII**(pt 1), 317–22.
UNDP (2003), *Human Development Report*, New York: Oxford University Press.
World Bank (2006), *The World Development Indicators*, CD-ROM.

4. High-frequency forecasting model for the Russian economy

Vladimir Eskin and Mikhail Gusev

1. RUSSIAN ECONOMIC DEVELOPMENT AND DATABASE ANALYSIS

Comprehensive analysis, econometric modeling and forecasting require reliable and comparable data sets for a long enough historical period to establish dynamic properties. Econometric modeling and forecasting in modern Russia still face a lack of adequate and consistent historical statistics, which makes modeling the national economy complicated.

Only 13 observations (1993–2006) are available for the development of the macroeconomic models with yearly frequency. Additionally, the instability of time series during the period 1993–98 makes econometric modeling and forecasting even more difficult. The instability of time series during 1993–98 is the result of two economic crises for the Russian economy in the 1990s. The first crisis was the collapse of the Soviet Union in 1991. During 1991–96, Russian GDP decreased more than 40 percent.

The main economic changes that took place during that period were liberalization of foreign trade, liberalization of domestic prices and general development of the market economy. The first two resulted in mutual comparability of domestic and world prices, especially for crude oil, gas and primary metals. Increases in the domestic prices of crude oil and other basic commodities increased production costs for domestic manufacturing industries. The poor quality of domestically produced commodities, the increase of production costs and severe competition with imports resulted in a decline of manufacturing production, unemployment growth, and producer and consumer price inflation.

Reduced output in all Russian industries, hyperinflation, unemployment growth and income decreases during 1991–96 reflected the instability of statistical information for that period. It should be mentioned that all major demand-side components of Russian GDP fell during the first seven years after the collapse of the USSR (see Table 4.1).

Russian economists note that the economic recession in the 1990s

Table 4.1 Russian GDP and its main demand-side components (all figures are in 1990 prices, index 1990 value = 100)

	1992	1993	1994	1995	1996	1997	1998	1999	2000	2001	2002	2003	2004	2005	2006
Russian GDP	77	70	62	60	55	55	52	55	61	64	67	72	77	82	88
Household consumption	83	85	86	83	81	82	79	77	83	90	98	105	118	133	147
Government consumption	78	72	66	57	56	56	57	58	59	59	61	62	63	65	68
Investment	55	51	41	37	32	31	17	16	28	32	32	36	40	43	49
Exports	74	69	71	73	76	74	75	84	92	96	106	119	133	141	151
Imports	43	42	49	55	54	58	48	40	53	62	72	84	104	122	146
US GDP	103	106	110	113	117	123	128	133	138	139	142	146	153	157	162

was more serious for Russia than was the Great Depression in the USA, which resulted in a 27 percent decline in US GDP. In 1997, the Russian economy expanded 1.4 percent; this was followed by a financial crisis in 1998. The Russian government could no longer support the existing level of consumption by fixing the exchange rate because central bank reserves decreased to the critical level of US\$11–12 billion as a result of the drop in world oil prices. Consequently, the Russian government had to stop fixing the exchange rate and temporarily halt the servicing of external debt. The financial crisis led to a 5.3 percent decrease of GDP, a surge in inflation, and decline in the exchange value of the Russian ruble. Nevertheless, the financial crisis of 1998 led to a favorable influence on Russia's subsequent economic development. The depreciation of the ruble has been one of the most substantial factors for economic growth since 1999. Domestic goods could be substituted for imports, stimulating manufacturing production growth (see Table 4.2).

It should be noted that the growth of the Russian economy after the 1998 financial crisis was based on using idle productive capacities and a relatively cheap but highly qualified labor force, which was not fully employed in the 1990s. According to expert estimates, at the beginning of 1999, 30 percent of productive capacities were not involved in production and 25 percent of able-bodied citizens were unemployed. Reversing the estimates of these two factors allowed for increased domestic production without investment and other expenditure related to production expansion. Domestic production expansion has been both extensive and intensive, due mainly to import substitution.

After their jump in 2003, world prices of source commodities contributed fundamentally to economic development in Russia. The country became a very large global exporter of crude oil, natural gas, metals and

Table 4.2 Contribution of main demand-side components to GDP growth (%)

	2000	2001	2002	2003	2004	2005	2006
GDP growth	10	5.1	4.7	7.3	7.2	6.4	6.7
Contribution to GDP growth of:							
Household consumption	34	85	86	51	83	103	92
Government consumption	4	−3	10	6	5	6	10
Investment	68	66	−15	36	35	25	44
Net exports	−17	−38	8	5	−19	−36	−58
Exports	31	26	70	57	58	37	39
Imports	−47	−64	−62	−53	−77	−73	−98

wood. In 2006, these commodities accounted for more than 70 percent of total Russian exports.

After 2004, the influence of exports on economic growth decreased; however, the inflow of export earnings from natural resources continued to support domestic household consumption. In 2006, household consumption accounted for 58 percent of total GDP and was the main contributor to economic expansion. At the same time, the share of imports in total GDP rose to 43 percent as a result of growing domestic demand and appreciation of the Russian ruble. In that way, development of the Russian economy became highly dependent on the competitiveness of domestic industrial production. Otherwise, growing domestic demand would have been taken up by imports, leading to deceleration of Russia's economic expansion.

Recently, industrial production growth decelerated from 8.7 percent in 2003 to 4.0 percent in 2005 and 2006. Besides the weak competitiveness of domestic manufacturing production, the slowing of industrial production is explained by two factors: exhausted productive capacities of the fuel and metallurgy industries, and an undeveloped infrastructure, restraining the expansion of manufacturing production. On this point, the 14 percent growth demonstrated by construction in 2006 is important, as evidenced by ongoing infrastructure modernization and expansion or improvement of residential real estate.

The weakest production sector of the Russian economy is agriculture, which had very low growth rates during 2003 to 2006 (see Table 4.3). In the next several years, agriculture will continue to demonstrate low growth rates as a result of a declining population. According to Russia's statistical service, the country's population reached a peak of 148.3 million in 1996; during the next ten years, the population decreased by 0.55 million per year, and in 2006 stood at 142.8 million.

Table 4.3 Russian GDP structure from the supply side

Sector	GDP structure – supply side (%)				Supply-side components – growth rates (%)			
	2003	2004	2005	2006	2003	2004	2005	2006
Agriculture	6	5	5	5	5.5	3.0	1.5	1.7
Industrial production	25	25	25	24	8.7	6.5	4.0	4.0
Construction	5	5	5	6	13.0	10.3	10.6	14.0
Retail and wholesale trade	21	22	23	23	13.2	9.2	9.9	8.7
Transportation and communication	9	9	9	10	7.2	10.9	6.8	9.4
Other services and net taxes	33	33	33	33	2.9	5.8	7.0	7.0
Total GDP	100	100	100	100	7.3	7.2	6.4	6.7

From the supply side, retail and wholesale trade continues to be the driving force of the Russian economy. At the same time, low industrial production growth rates imply that increasing domestic demand is again being satisfied by imports.

High oil prices will support the growth of domestic demand, and in the medium term the Russian economy will likely experience 5–6 percent growth rates. At the same time, stable long-term growth should be based on modernization of productive capacities and enhancement of the ability of manufacturing producers to compete successfully with imports.

Economic growth during 1999–2006 achieved decreased inflation and unemployment, with solid income growth, all evidence of economic stabilization. Consequently, monthly economic indicators have demonstrated favorable behavior since 1999. The analysis of statistical information collected and published by the Federal Statistics Service of Russia shows that it is possible to form a database that covers a large set of monthly indicators, describing different sectors of the economy. The analysis of monthly indicators led to the conclusion that, since 1999, time series have had acceptable stability and enough observations for high-frequency forecasting.

Economic analysis and forecasting should be based on reliable and complete data. Although Russia has met international standards in the field of statistics and data collection, the existing system of indicators needs to be brought up to the best world standards for model building and forecasting. Econometric modeling should be based on data that meet the following requirements:

- the set of indicators should reflect the main changes in the economy of the country;
- the set of indicators should be broad enough to represent all sectors of the economy;
- the methodology of data treatment and of calculation of relevant ratios and indices should be understandable and should allow for carrying out historical calculations of absolute values if needed;
- time series should have enough observations to provide reliable estimates of key statistical properties;
- statistical indicators should reflect the relationships among various sectors of the economy; and
- statistical indicators should meet the required balance between production and consumption.

Russia's statistical database does not meet all the listed requirements. Lack of comparability and methodological mistakes in formation of basic economic indicators are its main problems.

In the 1990s, econometric modeling and forecasting of the Russian economy were limited mainly by abrupt changes in basic economic regularities and by the impossibility of relying on statistical information from the Soviet period. Time series that correctly reflect economic development should have started long before the 1990s in order for the application of econometric methods to be plausible. However, there is still no developed methodology that allows for use of statistical information collected for comparability purposes before and after the collapse of the Soviet Union. The statistical database applied in model building cannot be extended on the basis of data collected in the Soviet period for structural and statistical reasons. There have been radical changes in the conditions of economic development since the collapse of the Soviet Union. These changes covered all sectors of the economy and social life, and are reflected in property rights, the role of the financial sector, foreign trade, the limitation of labor mobility, price and wage formation, and international currency exchange regulations.

The collapse of the Soviet Union resulted in substantial changes in the use of resources and GDP structure. Consequently, the relationships between economic variables in the period of market reforms are essentially different from those of the Soviet period. For example, the financial sector to a large extent restrained the growth of the Soviet economy since the ability of economic agents to obtain fixed and working capital was not linked to financial resources. The income of the population had little or no influence on production of consumer goods and services, since the volume of output was planned by the government and did not correspond to existing demand.

The second reason is determined by changes that took place in the system of statistical indicators, in general, and in the estimation of key economic indicators such as GDP. The Soviets viewed GDP in the context of Marxist theory. According to this theory, a national economy consists of productive and unproductive parts. The productive part comprises industries that provide material goods and services, such as freight transportation, directly connected with material production. The unproductive part includes services such as education, medical care, entertainment and passenger transportation. Marxist economists assert that GDP is produced only in the productive part of the economy; consequently, GDP estimated by Soviet statisticians reflected only the product of the materialistic part the economy. Additionally, estimation of GDP in the Soviet statistics system was based on gross value-added instead of net value-added, which resulted in substantial distortions and double counting.

Prices were also a problem for GDP estimation. According to the centralized plan system, prices were generally underestimated and set by the government; hence established prices of commodities did not reflect the real market interrelationships of these commodities. After the collapse of the Soviet Union, the time period between purchasing of raw materials and the sale of finished products – which is usually determined by the period of production – represented a serious problem for estimating price indicators in an environment of high levels of inflationary pressures.

The Soviet economy produced many low-quality commodities because industrial production had not been oriented to consumer satisfaction. At the same time, many necessary commodities were not produced at all. Due to market reforms, the structure of manufacturing production in Russia changed substantially and became oriented to satisfy growing market demand. Consequently, the decrease of Russian GDP in the 1990s does not adequately reflect the scale of economic decline, which is usually overestimated because plausible changes in the GDP structure are not considered.

The system of statistical measurement and reasons for possible data distortion have changed in comparison with the Soviet period. For example, in the Soviet period there was a tendency to overestimate industrial production; now it is rather underestimated. At the time of the centralized plan economy, industrial producers often overestimated their output because the success of managers was dependent on executing the output plan. After the majority of enterprises became private, managers began to underestimate production results in order to evade paying taxes. As time goes by and the tax structure improves, underestimation of output becomes less attractive due to inevitable fines. That is how official statistical information becomes more and more reliable and applicable for analysis and econometric modeling. However, statistical information from the Soviet period remains biased and uninformative.

The statistical database underlying principal components estimation contains more than 100 monthly indicators. Most indicators have more than 168 observations, starting from January 1993. The statistical database is formed from three information sources: Federal Service of State Statistics of Russia, Central Bank of Russia, and Federal Customs Service of Russia.

2. CURRENT QUARTER MODEL OF THE RUSSIAN ECONOMY

The initial effort of building the current quarter model (CQM) for Russia started in 2002. At that time, although the limitations on building an econometric system were clear (inadequate time-series history, limited number of monthly indicators, structural changes in the economy, etc.), the decision was made to start experimenting with monthly indicators. During the initial stage, equations for GDP and GDP deflator only were created. By 2004, with more indicators and more available data points, the first statistical regularities of the Russian economy were starting to appear. Gradually, the system of equations was put into a formal modeling framework. By mid-2004, the initial version of the model was in place. Since then, the model has been estimated every month. The historical accuracy check for the model is available at the end of this chapter.

At present, the Russian CQM (see Figure 4.1) consists of 66 equations: 48 equations for monthly indicators using principal components and 18 equations for forecasting quarterly indicators. Such key indicators as GDP and GDP deflator are forecasted two quarters ahead on the basis of the Russian CQM. Additionally, separate equations were developed in order to forecast such monthly indicators as CPI inflation, PPI inflation, real average wage, real disposable income, real industrial production, real retail sales, investment in production capacity, unemployment rate, exports and imports.

As mentioned, most monthly indicators have been published starting from January 1993; however, some monthly indicators have been published only since January 1995. Consequently, the time series used for GDP forecasting starts from February 1996 because all monthly indicators are expressed as differences of the logarithms of the year-over-year indices. This is a crude way of handling seasonal factors, in short samples that are presumed to have strong seasonal properties.

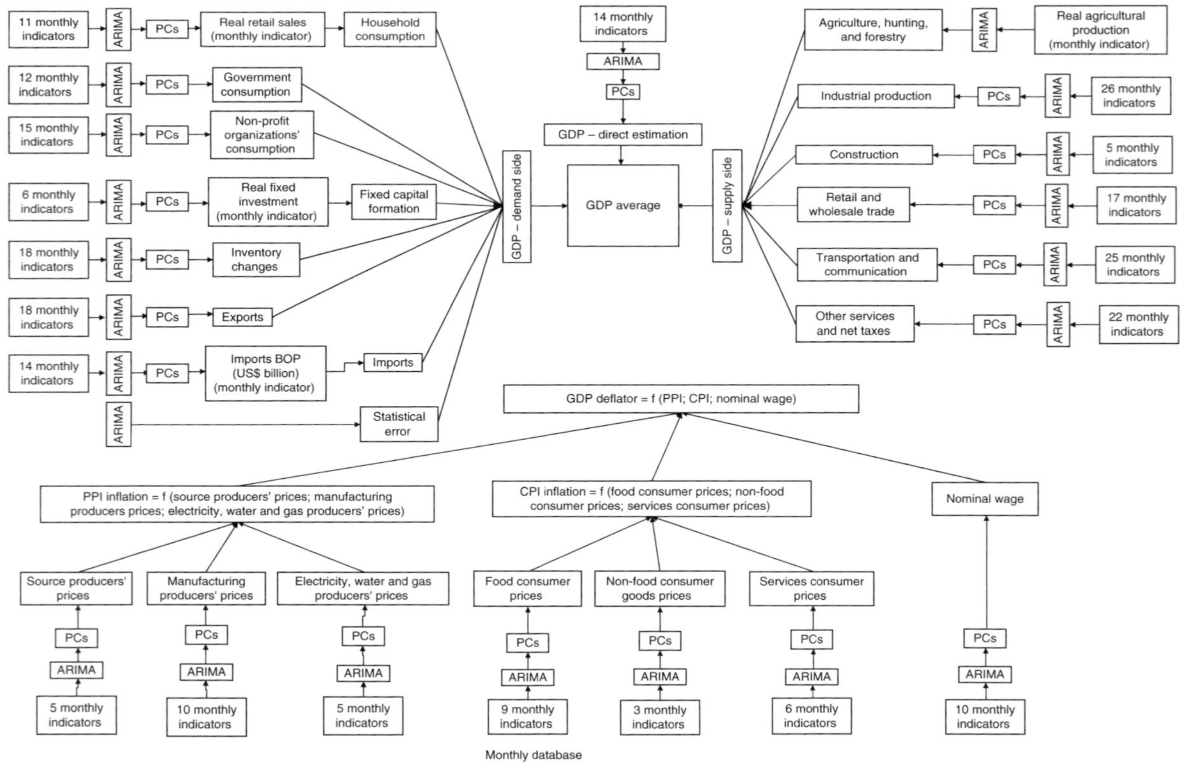

Notes:
ARIMA: autoregressive integrated moving average.
PC: principal component.

Figure 4.1 Structure of the Russian current quarter model (monthly database)

1. Initial monthly indicators are transformed into logarithmic differences of indices as shown below:

$$DLOGX_t^* = LN\left(\frac{X_t}{X_{t-12}}\right) - LN\left(\frac{X_{t-1}}{X_{t-13}}\right),$$

   where:

$$X_t^* = \frac{X_t}{X_{t-12}}$$

   X is the initial monthly indicator,
   LN is a natural logarithm, and
   t is a point-of-time series.
2. Every monthly indicator represented in the differences of the logarithms of the year-over-year indices is forecasted six months ahead when needed, by the ARIMA (autoregressive integrated moving-average) technique.
3. The monthly indicators, out of sample, are transformed into time series at quarterly frequency in order to obtain quarterly indicators of the differences of the logarithms of the year-over-year indices.
4. Quarterly figures such as GDP, GDP deflator, and supply- and demand-side components of GDP represented in the differences of the logarithms of the year-over-year indices are forecasted two quarters ahead from estimated regressions, where independent variables are the principal components built out of the set of selected indicators.

2.1 GDP Forecasting

The Russian CQM features the combination of GDP forecasts from three approaches: bridge equations of both the supply side and demand side of the system of national accounts (SNA) and regression of GDP on the principal components of selected major indicators.

Direct estimation of GDP

Direct estimation is carried out on the basis of regression of GDP on the principal components of selected major indicators. Selected indicators should, as completely as possible, represent the development of the Russian economy. Direct estimation of GDP is carried out on the basis of the following 14 monthly indicators:

- Real agricultural production, Jan. 93 = 100
- Bread and bread products, thousand tons
- Cars, thousands
- Cement, million tons

- Coal, million tons
- Short-term credit interest rate
- Real industrial production, Jan. 93 = 100
- Commercial lumber, million cubic meters
- Crude oil export price, $/ton (as reported by the Customs Office, total US$ value/tons)
- Pig iron, thousand tons
- Real construction, Dec. 94 = 100
- Retail trade inventories, billion current rubles
- Textiles, million units
- Commercial freight transportation, billion ton-kilometers

Results of the estimation of the GDP equation are shown below, p. 103. The regression coefficient of a principal component is accepted as statistically significant if the standard error of this coefficient is lower than the value of the coefficient.

It is important to mention that before an equation is used in forecasting, a calculating experiment should be carried out in order to examine its forecasting ability. This is checked on the basis of historical simulation, where the time period is reduced by two quarters and all independent variables represent actual data. In this case, the discrepancy between actual and forecasted values of a dependent variable will be a residual error. Where discrepancies between actual and computed values of a dependent variable fall within the limits of one standard error, an equation is accepted for forecasting.

In a sense, this approach is a statistical refinement of the way many 'Sovietologists' used to try to interpret what was taking place in the Soviet Union. They studied the time shape of important physical variables measured in units such as tonnage, kilometers, employees, and other key attributes of factors that would be important for Soviet economic activity, and then used combined estimates of the dynamics of such estimated factor impacts for judging the time paths of important 'dependent' variables in the USSR. By using principal components, we employ mutually uncorrelated linear combinations, which can then be used as regressors in equations that aim to be statistically representative of general factors that influence Russia's economic performance. Many more data inputs are used in the present context, and of course the whole pattern of availability of such explanatory data is now entirely different. Sovietologists would not generally have had such abundance and frequency of information about Soviet economic operations. In a sense, we are taking advantage of strides in information technology and openness in reporting to the world at large. In principle, we should have much more success in frequent tracking of Russia than Sovietologists had in tracking the Soviet Union.

Estimation of DLog(GDP)

$$
\begin{aligned}
\text{DLogGDP*} = {} & \underset{(2.250502)}{0.002288319715} + \underset{(24.79353)}{0.01091978048*A1} \\
& - \underset{(-4.425627)}{0.003605561474*A2} + \underset{(2.889773)}{0.003003819739*A6} \\
& - \underset{(-2.677891)}{0.003580829694*A8} + \underset{(2.823277)}{0.00402697752*A9} \\
& + \underset{(2.266216)}{0.00490560403*A12}
\end{aligned}
$$

t-statistic ratios for significance testing are in parentheses below each coefficient.

Sample (adjusted): 1996Q2–2007Q1
Adjusted R^2 = 0.939003 DW = 2.033739

Note: In all our equations, the Ai term represents the principal components, with the i term being the ordering of the principal components themselves. For example, A1 refers to the first principal component, and A2 refers to the second principal component, etc.

Figure 4.2 demonstrates the residual graph (a) and the forecast (b) for GDP for 2007Q2 (107.5 percent) and 2007Q3 (108.2 percent) and their standard errors transformed into year-over-year indices.

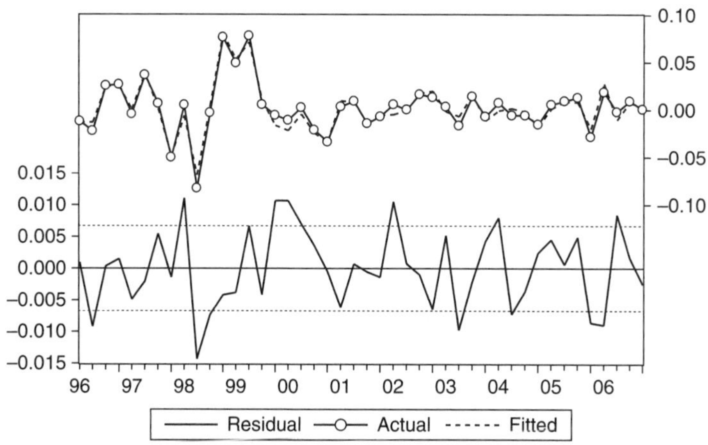

Figure 4.2(a) DLogGDP regression: residual plot*

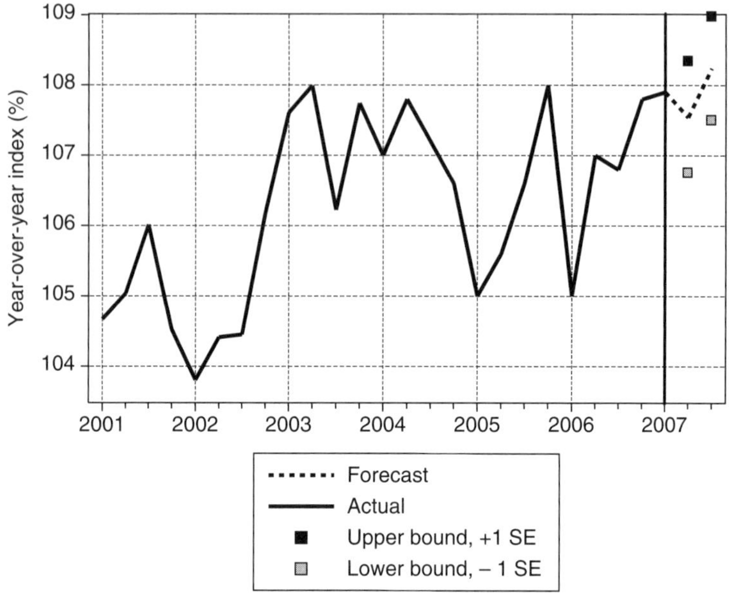

Figure 4.2(b) *DLogGDP* regression: 2007Q2 and 2007Q3 forecast, +/– one standard error confidence interval*

Partial derivatives are computed and used to form a 'confidence' interval about extrapolation values as forecasts. Values of partial derivatives for DLogGDP are shown in Table 4.4. They are estimated using the coefficients in the computation of principal components and in the regression equation, providing the joint influence on the dependent variable, in this case the transformed GDP value.

Demand-side estimation of GDP

The second approach to GDP estimation is from a bridge equation of the demand side of the SNA. The structure of Russian GDP in the context of demand-side components is shown in Figure 4.3.

Every major component of the demand side of GDP should be forecasted separately in order to obtain the GDP forecast. Demand-side GDP estimation can then be obtained by summing estimates of each component. Summation of GDP components from the demand and the supply side may be difficult. The Federal Statistics Service of Russia estimates GDP from the supply side first and then from the demand side. If the demand-side estimation of GDP is not equal to the supply-side estimation, the demand-side estimation is adjusted to equal the supply-side estimate.

*Table 4.4 Partial derivatives of DLogGDP**

With respect to	Value	Rank of significance
Real agricultural production, Jan. 93 = 100	0.007127	1
Bread and bread products, thousand tons	0.001426	9
Cars, thousands	0.000568	12
Cement, million tons	0.002012	8
Coal, million tons	0.000292	13
Short-term credit interest rate	−0.00251	14
Real industrial production, Jan. 93 = 100	0.004569	4
Commercial lumber, million cubic meters	0.00083	10
Crude oil export price, $/ton	0.002262	6
Pig iron, thousand tons	0.004373	5
Real construction, Dec. 94 = 100	0.006684	2
Retail trade inventories, billion current rubles	0.005969	3
Textiles, million units	0.000768	11
Commercial freight transportation, billion ton-kilometers	0.002022	7

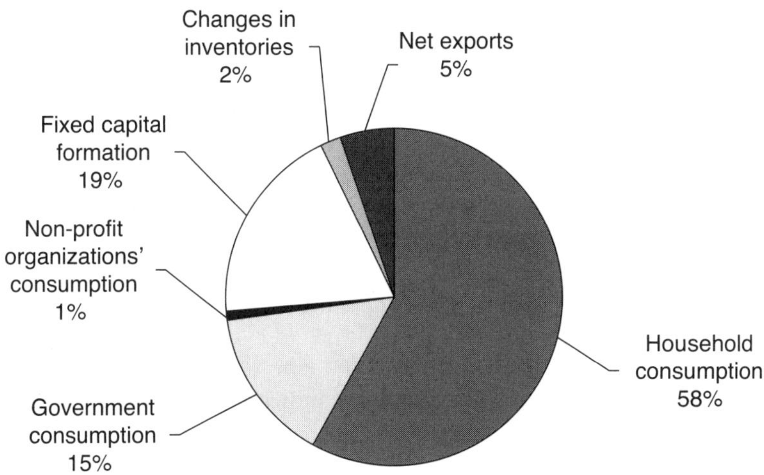

Figure 4.3 Russian GDP structure from demand side in 2006

The statistical error can amount to 1 percent of total GDP. The statistical error should also be incorporated into the estimation of the demand side of GDP. The estimation of statistical error is obtained on the basis of the ARIMA technique.

Although the applied approach of forecasting is equal for all demand- and supply-side components of GDP, initial indicators used for their forecasting are selected on the basis of the special features of each component.

Furthermore, in addition to principal components, some equations can include an external variable that can significantly determine the value of certain GDP components. The world price of crude oil, at the present time, is such a variable of great importance to Russia. Its use should lead to elimination of the crude oil export price for the computation of principal components.

Household consumption Household consumption is the largest and the most substantial component of GDP from the demand side. Household consumption accounts for more than half of Russian GDP. The share of household consumption in total GDP will likely continue to increase due to the inflow of export revenues.

Estimation of household consumption is obtained on the basis of an equation with one exogenous variable – retail sales in constant prices. The retail sales indicator is estimated on the basis of regression of retail sales on the principal components of selected monthly indicators, as follows:

- Real retail sales of food products, Jan. 93 = 100
- Saw timber, million cubic meters
- Real agricultural production, Jan. 93 = 100
- Bread and bread products, thousand tons
- Car imports, thousands
- Total imports (BOP), billion $
- Real fixed investment, Dec. 94 = 100
- Real disposable income, Dec. 92 = 100
- Televisions, thousand units
- Real official ruble/dollar exchange rate, end-month
- Arrears of wages, billion rubles

Government consumption The following indicators are selected for estimation of government consumption:

- Car imports, thousands
- Cell phone imports, thousands
- Defense nominal spending/consolidated budget spending (percent)
- Diesel fuels industry producer prices, index Dec. 1992 = 100
- Employment, millions
- Total exports (BOP), billion $
- Nominal federal budget expenditures, billion rubles

- Nominal federal budget revenues, billion rubles
- Natural gas, billion cubic meters
- Nominal monthly average wages, rubles
- Real monthly average wages, index Jan. 1993 value = 100
- Window glass, million square meters

Fixed capital formation Fixed capital formation is a very important component of GDP. It accounts for almost 20 percent of total GDP and covers activities that are crucial for Russia's post-Soviet economic expansion. The equation for fixed capital formation includes fixed capital investment as the only variable because this monthly indicator reflects the dynamics of fixed capital formation and is released in advance of fixed capital formation. The fixed capital investment indicator is estimated on the basis of regression of fixed capital investment on the principal components of selected monthly indicators. These monthly indicators are:

- Total imports (BOP), billion $
- Buses, thousands
- Real construction, Dec. 94 = 100
- One day interbank credit interest rate, percent per annum
- Real manufacturing production index, Jan. 01 = 100
- Manufacturing producer prices, Dec. 98 = 100

Inventory changes Changes in inventories account for 3 percent of total GDP. It is evident that changes in inventories can have negative values, which do not allow for variations in the differences of logarithms for year-over-year indices. To avoid this obstacle, percentage changes in stock levels were used.

The following indicators were selected for estimating changes in inventories:

- Car imports, thousands
- Chemical producer prices, index Dec. 1998 value = 100
- Construction prices/industrial producer prices
- Eggs, millions
- Electricity producer prices, index Dec. 1992 value = 100
- Employment, millions
- Equipment producer prices, index Dec. 1998 value = 100
- Total exports/imports (BOP)
- Total imports (BOP), billion $
- Meat imports, million $
- Metal-cutting equipment imports, thousands

- Paper, thousand tons
- Railroad freight transportation, million tons
- Real disposable income, index Dec. 1992 value = 100
- Real retail trade inventories, billion rubles
- Services consumer prices/consumer price index ratio
- Sugar, thousand tons
- Freight transportation prices, index Dec. 1993 value = 100

Exports The estimate of exports is based on the following monthly indicators:

- Cement, million tons
- Coal exports, million tons
- Copper exports, million $
- Employment, millions
- Total exports (BOP), billion $
- Real fixed investment, Dec. 94=100
- Natural gas exports, million tons
- Nickel exports, million $
- Real official ruble/dollar exchange rate, end-month
- Freight transportation prices, Dec. 1993=100
- Urals, $/barrel, average

Imports The equation for imports includes imports BOP as the only variable. This indicator is published in US dollars, whereas total imports as a component of GDP is released in rubles. This monthly indicator reflects the dynamics of total Russian imports. In addition, imports BOP are known in advance of GDP components release. We use the following monthly indicators for principal components analysis for imports BOP:

- Real retail sales, Jan. 93 = 100
- Car imports, thousands
- Cell phone imports, thousands
- Short-term credit interest rate, percent per annum
- Real fixed investment, Dec. 94 = 100
- Real industrial production index, Jan. 93 = 100
- Residential dwellings completed, million square meters
- M2, million rubles
- Gross real monthly incomes, rubles per capita, Jan. 93 prices
- Arrears of wages, billion rubles
- Official ruble/dollar exchange rate, end-month
- Refrigerators, thousand units

- Medicine imports, thousand tons
- Meat imports, thousand tons

Non-profit organizations' consumption Non-profit organizations' consumption accounts for 1 percent of total GDP. Estimates are based on the following monthly indicators:

- Butter, thousand tons
- Nominal consolidated budget revenues, billion rubles
- Crude oil production, million tons
- Mineral fertilizers, thousand tons
- Flour, thousand tons
- Gasoline producer prices, index Dec. 1992 value = 100
- Heating oil, thousand tons
- Meat, thousand tons
- Medicines import price, $/ton
- Milk, thousand tons
- Nominal retail trade inventories, billion rubles
- Paper, thousand tons
- Freight railroad cars production, units
- Real construction, index Dec. 1994 value = 100
- Real retail trade inventories, billion rubles

Statistical error Statistical error, like changes in inventories discussed previously, can be a negative value. Therefore statistical error values cannot be simply transformed into logarithmic units. To handle this problem, statistical error was increased by 1000 at every point of the time series. The estimation of the statistical error is carried out on the basis of the ARIMA technique.

Finally, the estimation of the demand side of GDP is carried out by summation of its components. Table 4.5 demonstrates the estimations of the components of GDP from the demand side. The GDP forecast for 2007Q2 is 5.8 percent and for Q3 is 7.2 percent (Figure 4.4).

Changes in inventories are treated by Russia's Federal Service of State Statistics (Rosstat) as a balancing item. Similar to a statistical discrepancy, changes in inventories are used to balance the demand and supply sides of GDP. As a result, changes in inventories are expected to fluctuate greatly, which leads to the difficulty in forecasting this component.

Supply-side estimation of GDP

The third approach to obtain a GDP estimation is a bridge equation of the supply side of the SNA. In 2005, Russia's Federal Service of State

Table 4.5 Estimation of GDP from the demand side

Year-over-year indices of:	Actual		Forecast	
	06Q4	07Q1	07Q2	07Q3
Household consumption	112.6	111.9	112.1	112.8
Government consumption	103.1	104.4	102.0	100.8
Non-profit organizations' consumption	89.8	99.6	103.2	95.4
Fixed capital formation	117.4	119.8	122.9	123.1
Changes in inventories	65.1	280.5	94.2	99.7
Exports	107.4	103.4	103.9	103.5
Imports	123.2	125.5	125.3	124.2
GDP – demand-side estimation	107.8	107.9	105.8	107.2

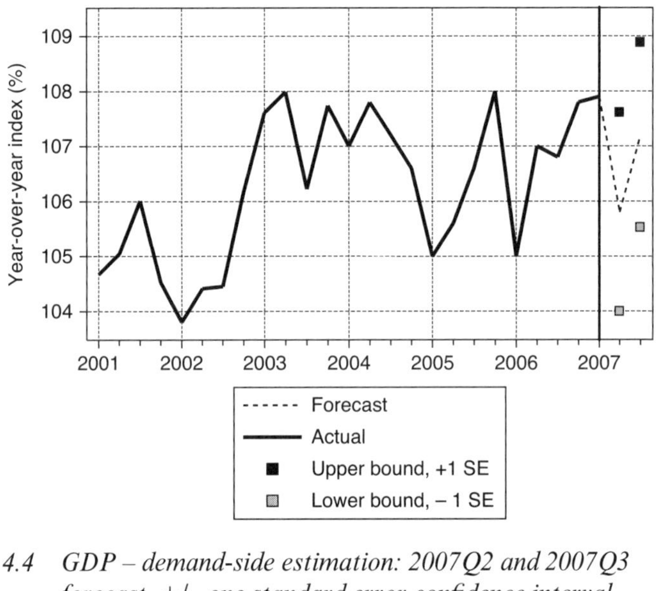

Figure 4.4 GDP – demand-side estimation: 2007Q2 and 2007Q3 forecast, +/– one standard error confidence interval

Statistics (Rosstat) changed the industry classification method. Thus the supply side of GDP is now calculated according to division of the Russian economy by type of economic activity. The GDP supply-side figures by industry have not been published since 2005.

Table 4.6 demonstrates changes in GDP components from the supply side that have taken place since 2005. At first, the decision was taken to develop Russian CQM according to GDP division by kinds of economic

Table 4.6 GDP, supply side

GDP division by industry (before 2005)	GDP division by type of economic activity (since 2005)	Share of GDP (in 2005 %)
Agriculture	Agriculture, hunting and forestry	3.8
	Fisheries, fish farming	0.4
Industrial production	Mining operations	6.0
	Manufacturing production	14.8
	Electricity, gas, and water production and distribution	3.0
Construction	Construction	6.0
Wholesale and retail trade	Wholesale and retail trade	27.7
Transport and communications	Transport and communications	11.1
Other services	Hotels and restaurants	0.8
	Finance activities	3.0
	Operations with immovable property, lease and services	9.3
	Public management and military security, obligatory social insurance	4.5
	Education	2.2
	Public health and social services	2.6
	Other utility, social, and personal services	1.8
	Indirect measured financial mediation	−1.9
	Net products taxes	4.8
	Total	100

activity, since figures of GDP division by type of economic activity only are published by Rosstat.

It should be mentioned that Rosstat has maintained GDP figures according to the new classification only since 2002, and it did not publish official figures for the period 1995–2001. Thus the GDP component values for 1995–2001 were obtained by extrapolating from 2002–04 data, since the official values for the GDP components for the two classifiers are available for that period. The artificial calculation of GDP components for 1995–2001 resulted in a decrease in the quality of the equations and resulted in low predictive power. As a result, we had to return to the old structure of the GDP supply-side classification.

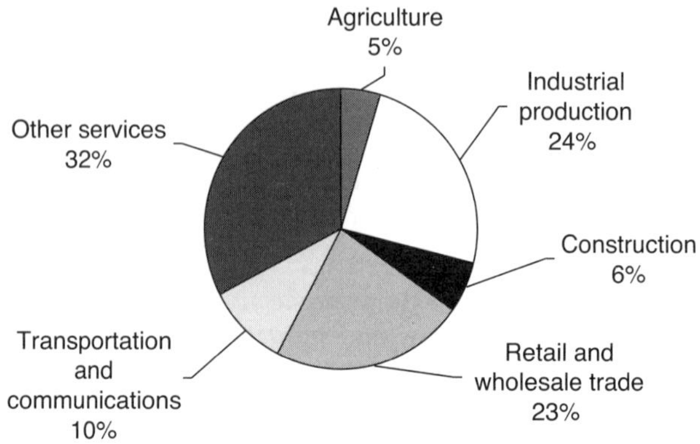

Figure 4.5 Russian GDP structure from supply side in 2006

The supply side of GDP comprises the following six major sectors, and we construct principal components analysis for each sector separately.

1. Agriculture, hunting and forestry
2. Industrial production
3. Construction
4. Wholesale and retail trade
5. Transport and communications
6. Other services including net taxes

Eventually, it will be possible to turn to a new classification of supply-side GDP, when enough observations are accumulated. The structure of Russian GDP from the supply side is shown in Figure 4.5.

As in the demand-side estimation of GDP, every component of the supply side should be forecasted separately in order to obtain a supply-side GDP forecast. Estimation of total supply-side GDP is carried out by summing up the components of GDP from the supply side. The monthly indicators used to forecast the supply-side components of GDP are selected by taking into account the specificity of each component.

Agriculture, hunting and forestry Estimation of agriculture, hunting and forestry is carried out on the basis of regression of agriculture, hunting and forestry on agricultural production in constant prices. Agricultural production in constant prices is a monthly indicator which is available in advance of GDP components release. Also, the equation for agriculture, hunting and forestry contains four dummy variables for 1999Q1, 1999Q3, 1999Q4 and 2000Q1.

Construction Construction accounts for 6 percent of total GDP in 2006. The following monthly indicators were selected for estimation of construction:

- Bulldozers, units
- Coal, million tons
- Pig iron, thousand tons
- Real construction index, Dec. 1994 = 100
- Saw timber, million cubic meters

Industrial production Industrial production accounts for 24 percent of total GDP in 2006. The equation for industrial production was based on the following components:

- Real agricultural production index, Jan. 93 = 100
- Bread and bread products, thousand tons
- Cars, thousands
- Short-term credit interest rate, percent per annum
- Electricity, billion kWh
- Nominal federal budget revenues, billion rubles
- Chemical fibers and threads, thousand tons
- Real fixed investment index, Dec. 94 = 100
- Gasoline, thousand tons
- Commercial lumber, million cubic meters
- Metal-cutting equipment, thousands of units
- Nominal monthly average wages, rubles
- Nominal retail trade inventories, billion rubles
- Industrial price index, Dec. 92 = 100
- Passenger railroad stock, number of wagons
- Semi-processed wood, thousand cubic meters
- Real construction index, Dec. 94 = 100
- Synthetics, resin and plastic, thousand tons
- Shoes, million pairs
- Caustic soda, thousand tons
- Steel pipes, thousand tons
- Steel, thousand tons
- Textiles, million of units
- Tractors, thousands
- Commercial freight transportation, billion ton-kilometers

The estimate for industrial production includes, besides principal components, industrial production in constant prices as a separate variable because this monthly advance indicator reflects the dynamics of quarterly figures of value-added of industrial production. (The industrial production monthly indicator is estimated on the basis of regression of industrial production on the principal components of selected monthly indicators.)

Retail and wholesale trade Retail and wholesale trade accounts for 23 percent of total GDP in 2006. The following indicators were selected for estimation of this sector:

- Animal husbandry producer price index, Dec. 1993=100
- Urals, $/barrel, average
- Buses, thousands
- Cell phone imports, million $
- Nominal consolidated budget revenues, billion rubles
- Copper export, million $
- Diesel fuels, thousand tons
- Meat (industry), thousand tons
- Meat (agriculture), thousand tons
- Crude oil export, billion $
- Printing, pulp and paper producer price index, Dec. 1998=100
- Real official ruble/dollar exchange rate, end-month
- Steel pipes, thousand tons
- Steel, thousand tons
- Saw timber, million cubic meters
- Sunflower and vegetable oil, thousand tons
- Commercial freight transportation, billion ton-kilometers

Transportation and communication Transportation and communication accounts for 10 percent of total GDP in 2006. The forecast for this category is based on the following monthly indicators:

- Real agricultural production index, Jan. 93 = 100
- Bread and bread products, thousand tons
- Bricks, billions
- Bulldozers, units
- Cars, thousands
- Short-term credit interest rate, percent per annum
- Fabric, million square meters
- Nominal federal budget revenues, billion rubles
- Mineral fertilizers, thousand tons
- Fish and fish products, thousand tons

- Real fixed investment index, Dec. 94 = 100
- Gasoline, thousand tons
- Gross nominal monthly incomes, rubles per capita
- Metal-cutting equipment, thousands of units
- Nominal retail trade inventories, billion rubles
- Crude oil extraction industry producer price index, Dec. 92 = 100
- Paper, thousand tons
- Pig iron, thousand tons
- Passenger railroad stock, number of wagons
- Railroad freight transportation, million tons
- Real construction index, Dec. 94 = 100
- Synthetics, resin and plastic, thousand tons
- Shoes, million pairs
- Tractors, thousands
- Commercial freight transportation, billion ton-kilometers

Other services and net taxes Other services account for 33 percent of total GDP. Net taxes are defined as taxes on commodities, net of all subsidies. Net taxes are included as a component in the supply side of GDP estimation. The total for other services and net taxes is calculated as a difference between the GDP estimation and all other components, which are forecasted separately.

Estimation of other services is based on the following monthly indicators:

- Real agricultural production index, Jan. 93 = 100
- Cement, million tons
- Nominal consolidated budget expenditures, billion rubles
- Short-term credit interest rate, percent per annum
- Diesel fuels, thousand tons
- Electricity, billion kWh
- Chemical fibers and threads, thousand tons
- Real fixed investment index, Dec. 94=100
- Total imports (BOP), billion $
- Real industrial production index, Jan. 93 = 100
- Commercial lumber, million cubic meters
- Nominal retail trade inventories, billion rubles
- Crude oil extraction industry producer price index, Dec. 92 = 100
- Paper, thousand tons
- Pig iron, thousand tons
- Railroad freight transportation, million tons
- Real construction index, Dec. 94=100
- Real M2, Jan. 93 prices, million rubles

Table 4.7 Estimation of GDP from the supply side

Year-over-year indices of:	Actual		Forecast	
	2006Q4	2007Q1	2007Q2	2007Q3
Agriculture, hunting and forestry	107.1	102.9	102.3	102.2
Industrial production	104.5	106.6	105.4	106.4
Construction activities	123.9	123.2	126.7	126.2
Retail and wholesale trade	106.0	109.1	107.3	106.8
Transportation and communication	109.4	107.9	104.5	103.4
Other services and net taxes	107.9	106.5	106.6	107.1
GDP – supply-side estimation	107.8	107.9	107.3	107.4

- Real retail trade inventories, billion rubles
- Caustic soda, thousand tons
- Steel pipes, thousand tons
- Saw timber, million cubic meters

Estimation of the supply-side GDP is calculated by summing up the components of GDP from the supply side. Table 4.7 shows the estimations of year-over-year indices of GDP and its components from the supply side, the GDP forecasts for 2007Q2 (107.3) and 2007Q3 (107.4). See also Figure 4.6.

Final GDP estimation

Finally, we obtained three estimates of Russian GDP: direct aggregate estimation, demand-side estimation, and supply-side estimation.

Final estimation of GDP is calculated as a simple average of the three aforementioned estimates. Table 4.8 contains the results of total GDP forecasting. It shows that the Russian economy will be expected to expand 6.9 percent year over year in 2007Q2 and 7.6 percent in 2007Q3.

3. PRICE FORECASTING

The ability to forecast price changes one or two quarters ahead is very important, as this information reveals existing tendencies for inflation or deflation, and leads to an understanding about problems to be expected.

A high level of inflation was a serious issue for Russia after the collapse

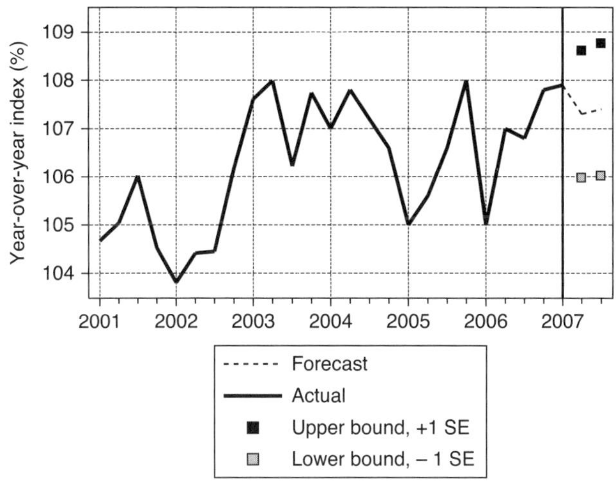

Figure 4.6 *GDP – supply-side estimation: 2007Q2 and 2007Q3 forecast, +/– one standard error confidence interval*

Table 4.8 *Final GDP estimation (2007Q2 and 2007Q3)*

GDP estimations	Actual		Forecast	
	2006Q4	2007Q1	2007Q2	2007Q3
Direct estimation			107.5	108.2
Demand-side estimation	107.8	107.9	105.8	107.2
Supply-side estimation			107.3	107.4
Absolute difference between the highest and lowest estimates			1.6	1.0
Average			106.9	107.6

of the Soviet Union. Despite the Russian government's subsequent success in reducing inflation, CPI inflation remains at 9–10 percent per year. High inflation impacts the main indicators represented in nominal prices; and the expected level of inflation influences economic policy, for stability of the changed Russian state.

One of the main summary indicators reflecting price changes and their effect on the economy is the GDP deflator. The GDP deflator is forecasted on the basis of a regression equation, in which the independent variables are PPI inflation and real average wage. At the same time PPI inflation and real average wage are estimated from a principal components analysis with regression equations, where independent variables are principal components of relevant indicators. The regression equation for PPI inflation includes such exogenous variables as source producers' price indexes; manufacturing producers' price indexes; and electricity, water and gas producers' price indexes. The regression equation for the real average wage is built on the basis of CPI inflation and the nominal average wage as exogenous explanatory variables. The nominal average wage for the previous quarter is an indicator for business and public sector officials to set wages.

Estimation of LogGDP deflator*

LOGDEFGDP = 0.6843*LOGPPI + 0.2901*LOGCPI
(12.53) (8.06)

+ 0.0707*LOGNOMWAGE (t − 1) + 0.3049*AR(1)
(1.92) (2.08)

Sample (adjusted): 1996Q3–2007Q1
Adjusted R^2 = 0.9619 DW = 1.904823

Figure 4.7 demonstrates the residual graph (a) and estimates (b) for the GDP deflator in 2007Q2 (114.8 percent) and 2007Q3 (112.7 percent) within the limits of +/– one standard error.

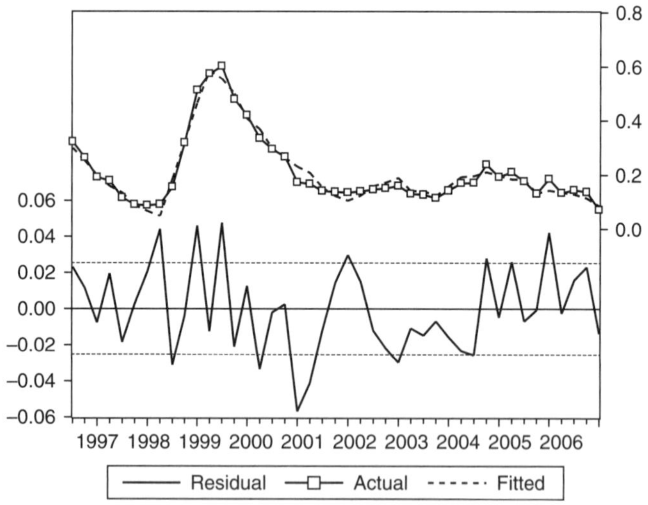

Figure 4.7(a) LogDEFGDP regression: residual plot*

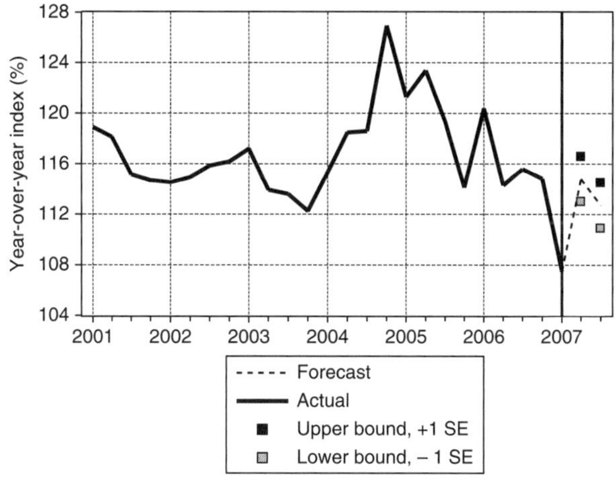

Figure 4.7(b) *LogDEFGDP regression: 2007Q2 and 2007Q3 forecast, +/– one standard error confidence interval*

Table 4.9 *GDP, actual and forecast*

Date	Real GDP (%)									Official release (in bold)
	05Q3	05Q4	06Q1	06Q2	06Q3	06Q4	07Q1	07Q2	07Q3	
Sep. 05	6.4	6.6								≤ 2005Q2
Oct. 05	6.3	6.4								
Nov. 05	6.2	6.1								
Jan. 06	**6.5**	7.2	6.9							≤ 2005Q3
Mar. 06		**8.0**	6.7							≤ 2005Q4
Apr. 06			5.0	4.5						
May 06			6.3	7.0						
Jun. 06			**5.0**	6.7	6.2					≤ 2006Q1
Jul. 06				6.5	6.1					
Aug. 06				6.0	6.1					
Sep. 06				**7.0**	6.3	7.6				≤ 2006Q2
Oct. 06					7.2	5.9				
Nov. 06					6.5	6.7				
Dec. 06					**6.8**	7.3	7.1			≤ 2006Q3
Jan. 07						6.6	7.9			
Feb. 07						6.9	7.9			
Mar. 07						**7.8**	7.8	6.3		≤ 2006Q4
Apr. 07							7.4	5.8		
May 07							7.7	6.0		
Jun. 07							**7.9**	7.1	7.5	≤2007Q1
Jul. 07								7.2	7.2	
Aug. 07								6.9	7.6	

Table 4.10 GDP deflator, actual and forecast

Date	GDP deflator (%)									Official release (in bold)
	05Q3	05Q4	06Q1	06Q2	06Q3	06Q4	07Q1	07Q2	07Q3	
Sep. 05	16.9	16.6								≤ 2005Q2
Oct. 05	17.2	17.0								
Nov. 05	17.1	16.7								
Jan. 06	**19.5**	18.4	17.1							≤ 2005Q3
Mar. 06		**11.1**	18.1	16.8						≤ 2005Q4
Apr. 06			18.8	16.4						
May 06			**20.4**	20.4						≤ 2006Q1
Jun. 06				22.6	23.1					
Jul. 06				21.2	20.7					
Aug. 06				21.1	20.4					
Sep. 06				**14.3**	19.2	20.8				≤ 2006Q2
Oct. 06					18.1	17.3				
Nov. 06					17.5	15.2				
Dec. 06					**15.6**	14.7	10.4			≤ 2006Q3
Jan. 07						14.8	14.4			
Feb. 07						11.6	12.0			
Mar. 07						**14.8**	9.7	10.8		≤ 2006Q4
Apr. 07							9.7	11.5		
May 07							11.8	13.5		
Jun. 07							**7.5**	15.8	16.5	≤ 2007Q1
Jul. 07								14.8	12.7	

Note: GDP deflator was calculated as a DLOG equation through January 2008, and as a LOG equation after that.

4. HISTORY OF FORECAST ACCURACY

Tables 4.9 and 4.10 demonstrate the comparison of actual reported and forecasted values for GDP and the GDP deflator.

The GDP deflator is measured as a year-over-year index. We incorporate the PPI, CPI and nominal wage variables for forecasting the GDP deflator. However, it should be noted that the weights for the year-over-year PPI, CPI and nominal wage are not synchronized to the weights for the quarterly deflators. Consequently, this difference could cause the accuracy of the forecast to be volatile, as seen in our forecast for 2005Q4 and 2006Q2 in Table 4.10.

5. Short-term forecasting of key indicators of the German economy

Andrei Roudoi

1. ECONOMIC GROWTH

The German economy was the third largest in the world in 2006, behind those of the USA and Japan. In 2007, it is likely to be surpassed by China. German GDP, which reached 2.3 billion euros in 2006, was larger than GDP in any other economy that is now in the European Union (EU), accounting for 20.1 percent of total EU GDP.[1] This high share is a result of both the advanced development of the German economy and the large size of the German population, which in 2006 stood at 82.4 million, or 16.1 percent of the total population in the EU-27.

Germany contributes significantly more to EU GDP than the share of its population in the EU population. This is a sign of the high productivity of the German economy. However, it also reflects the fact that many EU countries are transition economies, still catching up with more advanced West European countries.

While Germany's per capita GDP is relatively high by EU-27 standards, it is not that impressive when compared with per capita GDP in other West European countries. In these terms, Germany ranks only eleventh in the EU-27, lagging behind most countries in the more advanced EU-15 (see Table 5.1). Germany's ranking improves by just one notch if per capita GDP is measured in purchasing power parity (PPP) terms.

The economy of the Federal Republic of Germany (FRG, or West Germany) grew at a moderate pace during the decade prior to the country's reunification in October 1990. West German GDP rose 2.2 percent a year on average in 1980–90, not a very strong rate, but still faster than economic expansion in six other EU-15 countries (see Table 5.2).

After reunification, the growth of the unified German economy slowed significantly. In 1991–2006, German GDP increased just 1.67 percent a year on average. In the EU-15, only Italy had a slower growth rate during that period.

The reunification is, to some extent, the cause of Germany's lagging

Table 5.1 EU-27: per capita GDP, 2006

	Current euro		PPP
EU-27	23 500	EU-27	23 500
Luxembourg	71 500	Luxembourg	65 300
Ireland	41 300	Ireland	33 700
Denmark	40 500	Netherlands	31 000
Sweden	33 700	Austria	30 200
Netherlands	32 700	Denmark	29 700
Finland	31 700	Belgium	28 700
United Kingdom	31 500	Sweden	28 200
Austria	31 100	United Kingdom	27 900
Belgium	29 800	Finland	27 300
France	28 400	**Germany**	**26 700**
Germany	**28 200**	France	26 500
Italy	25 100	Italy	24 300
Spain	22 300	Spain	24 000
Cyprus	18 900	Cyprus	21 900
Greece	17 600	Greece	20 800
Slovenia	14 800	Slovenia	20 400
Portugal	14 700	Czech Republic	18 600
Malta	12 400	Malta	17 700
Czech Republic	11 100	Portugal	17 500
Estonia	9 800	Estonia	15 900
Hungary	8 900	Hungary	15 300
Slovakia	8 200	Slovakia	14 700
Latvia	7 100	Lithuania	13 600
Poland	7 100	Latvia	13 100
Lithuania	7 000	Poland	12 400
Romania	4 500	Romania	8 800
Bulgaria	3 300	Bulgaria	8 700

behind many West European countries in terms of GDP growth rates and current per capita GDP. To some extent, Germany made a deliberate decision to expedite reunification despite risks to economic growth. The German Democratic Republic (GDR, or East Germany) was significantly less productive than West Germany and had lower per capita national income. It is often claimed that support for the eastern part of the country was a tremendous burden on West Germany. Another problem was that East German industrial enterprises were frequently unable to compete in the new economic environment, which led to large-scale deindustrialization, and labor relocation from East to West Germany.

While growth in transition economies of Eastern and Central Europe

Table 5.2 EU-15: real GDP growth rate, %

	Average annual		2005	2006	Year over year	
	1980–90	1991–2006			2007Q1	2007Q2
Austria	2.12	2.25	2.0	3.3	3.6	3.3
Belgium	2.24	2.11	1.1	3.2	3.3	2.8
Denmark	1.84	2.27	3.1	3.5	2.7	0.6
Finland	3.21	2.37	2.9	5.5	5.5	4.4
France	2.28	1.87	1.7	2.0	1.8	1.1
Germany	**2.2**	**1.67**	**0.8**	**2.9**	**3.3**	**2.5**
Greece	0.68	3.11	3.7	4.3		
Ireland	2.85	6.53	5.5	6.0	8.1	5.4
Italy	2.06	1.32	0.1	1.9	2.3	2.0
Luxembourg	4.94	5.35	4.0	6.2	4.9	5.0
Netherlands	2.09	2.54	1.5	3.0	2.5	2.6
Portugal	4.03	2.47	0.5	1.3	2.0	1.6
Spain	2.79	3.15	3.6	3.9	4.3	3.9
Sweden	2.43	2.3	2.9	4.2	3.0	3.5
UK	2.18	2.47	1.8	2.8	4.2	1.9

Note: For 1980–90 and for 1991 the figures are for West Germany only.

started to gain momentum after a production decline at the early stage of market transformation, growth in Germany's eastern states (known in German as *Länder*), the transition part of the country, remained sluggish. Table 5.3 shows that in 2000–04 the real GDP average annual growth rate ranged from 0.4 percent to 1.6 percent in the five East German states. In Berlin, which includes both West and East Berlin, the former capital of East Germany, real GDP actually declined during that period. During the same period, GDP growth in the Czech Republic and Poland, transition economies neighboring Germany, averaged 3.2 percent a year. Table 5.3 illustrates a significant population loss in most of the East German states between 1990 and 2006. Despite this loss, the unemployment rates in each of the East German states and Berlin were higher than the unemployment rate in any of the West German states. In 2005, the unemployment rate ranged from 17.2 percent to 20.4 percent in East Germany, far exceeding the national average of 11.2 percent.

The German economy rebounded in 2006, with GDP growth accelerating to 2.9 percent from 0.8 percent in 2005. However, growth improvement was widespread throughout Western Europe. In fact, GDP expansion accelerated in every EU-15 country in 2006. As a result, the German economy remained one of the slowest-growing economies in the EU-15, even though

Table 5.3 Germany: regional economic growth, population growth, and the unemployment rate

	Real GDP average annual growth rate, 2000–04, %	Population, 2006; 1990 = 100	Unemployment rate, 2005, %
Germany total	1.1	104.2	11.2
Baden-Württemberg	1.0	111.6	7.1
Bayern	2.4	111.1	7.1
Berlin	*−0.9*	*99.8*	*19.4*
Brandenburg	**1.1**	**96.9**	**18.2**
Bremen	1.6	98.5	16.6
Hamburg	1.5	107.2	10.5
Hessen	1.0	107.6	8.5
Mecklenburg-Vorpommern	**0.4**	**86.9**	**21.4**
Niedersachsen	0.5	109.7	10.5
Nordrhein-Westfalen	0.7	105.6	10.5
Rheinland-Pfalz	0.9	109.6	8.8
Saarland	1.4	98.6	10.8
Sachsen	**1.6**	**87.2**	**18.7**
Sachsen-Anhalt	**1.0**	**83.3**	**20.4**
Schleswig-Holstein	0.8	109.2	10.3
Thüringen	**1.5**	**87.0**	**17.2**

Note: East German states are in bold.

its ranking improved. In 2005, in only two EU-15 economies was GDP growth slower than in Germany. In 2006, Germany outpaced only four. At the same time, since it was the second-, third- and fourth-largest EU economies (the UK, France and Italy) that grew slower than Germany in 2006, German GDP growth caught up with the average weighted growth in the EU-14 (see Figure 5.1). In the first half of 2007, German economic expansion remained moderate, marginally faster than growth in the EU-14.

Forecasters have often failed to predict accurately fluctuations in German economic growth. For example, in April 2003, the IMF (International Monetary Fund) forecasted that German GDP would grow 1.9 percent in 2004 (see Figure 5.2). The forecast was later revised down, but then, in September 2004, the forecast was upgraded to 2.0 percent. The latest officially reported figure for that year is 1.0 percent, almost a full percentage point lower than the September 2004 forecast. The forecast for 2005, which was too high in 2004, was correctly revised down in 2005.

The IMF underestimated the regained strength of the German economy

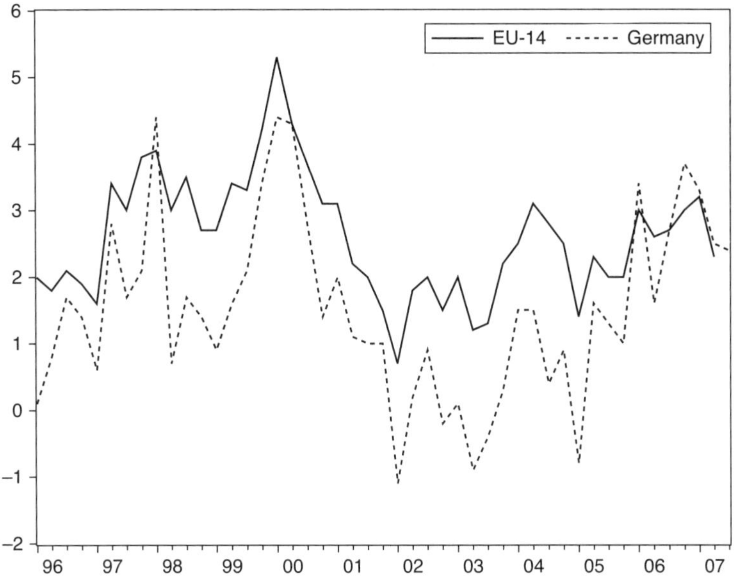

Figure 5.1 EU-14 (EU-15 minus Germany) and Germany: real GDP growth rate, year over year, %

in 2006. In September 2006, the IMF predicted that German GDP would increase 2.0 percent in 2006, significantly below the officially reported growth rate of 2.9 percent. The IMF has been revising upward its forecast for German economic expansion in 2007, which was initially a meager 1 percent. The latest forecast for this year, released in October 2007, is 2.4 percent. This is slightly less than the 2.7 percent reported year-over-year growth rate of the German economy in the first three quarters.

2. GDP STRUCTURE

End-use Breakdown

The key feature of the end-use composition of the German economy is that it is much more export-oriented than the other four largest EU economies (see Table 5.4). German exports of goods and services surged 147.9 percent from the first half of 1995 through the first half of 2007 (Table 5.5). Between 1995 and 2006, the share of exports in Germany's GDP almost doubled, rising from 24.0 percent to 47.5 percent, significantly exceeding

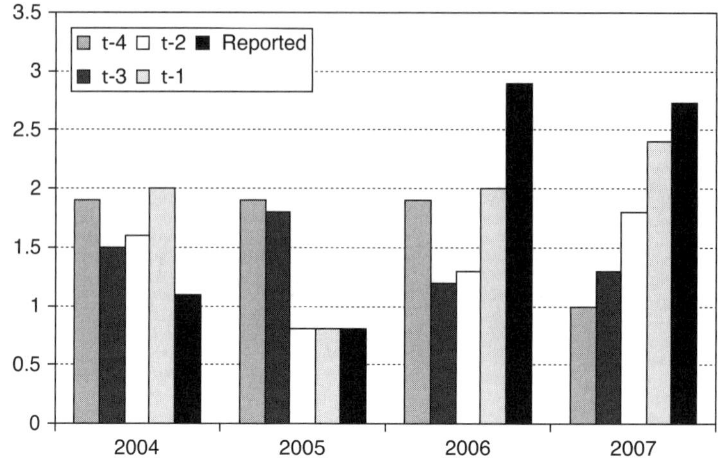

Notes:
t–1 represents the forecast released in September of the respective year; *t*–2 represents the forecast released in April of the respective year; *t*–3 represents the forecast released in September of a year earlier; and *t*–4 represents the forecast released in April of a year earlier. The reported 2007 figure is for the first three quarters of this year.

Figure 5.2 Germany: real GDP growth rate, IMF forecasts and reported, %

that in any of the other four major EU economies. Germany was the only one of the five major EU economies that posted a surplus (8.1 percent) on the balance of external trade in goods and services in 2006. At the same time, German household consumption and gross fixed investment growth rates were meager.

This year's relatively strong economic growth was also driven primarily by exports, which contributed 155.6 percent to the GDP increase in the first half of 2007 with respect to the first half of 2006. Another important factor in the recent GDP rebound was a recovery in fixed investment, whose contribution amounted to 49.4 percent. Household consumption remains subdued. In fact, it inched down 0.2 percent year over year in the first half of 2007.

Value-added Structure

As for all developed countries, Germany's economy is dominated by services (see Table 5.6). At the same time, Germany's value-added breakdown is different from those in the other four major EU countries in several important ways:

*Table 5.4 End-use GDP categories in five largest EU economies: share in total country GDP at market prices, %**

	Germany		France		Italy		Spain		UK	
	1995	2006	1995	2006	1995	2006	1995	2006	1995	2006
Total	100.0	100.0	100.0	100.0	100.0	100.0	100.0	100.0	100.0	100.0
Domestic demand	99.5	92.9	98.9	101.5	96.2	100.7	100.0	108.0	100.4	105.5
Household consumption	57.7	55.2	56.6	58.0	58.4	59.7	60.0	60.6	63.3	66.7
Government consumption	19.6	18.3	23.7	21.8	18.0	18.0	18.1	18.9	19.8	18.7
Gross capital formation	22.2	19.0	18.6	21.4	19.8	22.7	21.9	28.3	17.4	21.9
Gross fixed capital formation	21.9	20.4	18.1	20.6	19.1	21.2	21.5	28.0	16.8	20.8
External balance	0.5	8.1	1.1	−1.5	3.8	−0.5	0.0	−9.1	−0.4	−8.5
Exports of goods and services	24.0	47.5	22.8	31.0	25.7	25.4	22.4	30.2	28.2	38.2
Imports of goods and services	23.5	39.4	21.6	32.5	21.9	25.9	22.4	39.2	28.7	46.6

Note: * In constant 1995 prices.

*Table 5.5 Germany: end-use GDP categories, growth and contribution to total GDP**

	Index, 2007H1		Share of category in GDP increase in 2007H1 with respect to	
	1995H1 = 100	2006H1 = 100	1995H1	2006H1
Total	119.7	102.9	100.0	100.0
Domestic demand	110.2	101.3	51.4	40.7
Household consumption	111.1	99.8	32.3	−3.7
Government consumption	113.8	102.1	13.4	13.2
Gross capital formation	104.4	105.6	5.1	37.3
Gross fixed capital formation	111.8	107.4	12.9	49.4
External balance	1771.5	123.0	55.1	64.1
Exports of goods and services	247.9	109.7	179.8	155.6
Imports of goods and services	205.4	106.9	−124.7	−91.5
Statistical discrepancy			−6.6	−4.8

Note: * In constant 1995 prices.

- In Germany, industry plays a much more important role than in the other four major EU countries. In 2006, the share of industry in German value-added was 26.4 percent. In Italy, the country with the second-largest share of industry among the major EU countries, industry amounted to only 21.5 percent of total value-added. The primacy of industry is related to the export orientation of the German economy.
- German industrial value-added grew with respect to total value-added between 1995 and 2006. In Italy and in the UK in particular, the share of industrial value-added sharply declined.
- Construction plays a less important role in Germany than in the other four major EU economies, reflecting the relative weakness of investment.
- Germany was the only country of the major five where construction value-added declined (by 18.0 percent) between 1995 and 2006. The share of construction in total German value-added dropped significantly, from 6.8 percent in 1995 to 4.1 percent in 2006. In the other four countries, the share of construction either decreased less substantially than in Germany or rose.

*Table 5.6 Sectoral value-added in five largest EU economies: share in total country value-added, %**

	Germany		France		Italy		Spain		UK	
	1995	2006	1995	2006	1995	2006	1995	2006	1995	2006
Total	100.0	100.0	100.0	100.0	100.0	100.0	100.0	100.0	100.0	100.0
Agriculture, hunting, forestry and fishing	1.3	1.2	3.4	2.9	3.3	3.0	4.5	3.9	1.8	1.5
Industry	25.4	26.4	19.0	19.7	25.0	21.5	21.9	20.3	25.7	18.8
Construction	6.8	4.1	5.6	4.6	5.3	5.6	7.5	9.0	5.0	4.5
Wholesale and retail trade, repair of motor vehicles, motorcycles and personal and household goods; hotels and restaurants; transport, storage and communication	18.0	18.8	19.5	20.1	24.2	26.0	26.9	24.6	21.4	24.3
Financial intermediation; real estate, renting and business activities	26.4	28.6	28.1	29.9	22.4	23.7	17.9	20.7	24.5	31.6
Public administration and defense, compulsory social security; education; health and social work; other community, social and personal service activities; private households with employed persons	22.2	21.1	24.4	22.3	19.8	20.1	21.3	20.8	21.5	18.7

Note: * In constant 1995 prices.

The current relatively strong GDP growth has been driven mostly by goods production. The growth of industrial value-added accounted for 43.5 percent of the year-over-year increase in total value-added in the first half of 2007, substantially exceeding the share of industry in total value-added (see Table 5.7). Construction rebounded, posting 7.4 percent growth in January–June 2007, faster than growth in any of the five other major production sectors. The growth of services was dragged down by continued sluggishness in the sector, which includes such items as public administration, health and education. It expanded by a mere 0.5 percent in the first half of 2007.

3. INFLATION

Germany is a founding member of the Eurozone, a group of EU countries that adopted the euro currency union. The Eurozone came into existence in January 1999 and initially included ten countries in addition to Germany: Austria, Belgium, Finland, France, Ireland, Italy, Luxembourg, the Netherlands, Portugal and Spain. Greece and Slovenia joined the Eurozone in January 2002 and January 2007, respectively. Monetary policy in the Eurozone is governed by the European Central Bank (ECB).

The ECB's attitude to inflation is hawkish, for which it has been frequently criticized. The Bank states that the primary objective of its monetary policy is to maintain price stability, which, in turn, 'is the best contribution monetary policy can make to economic growth and job creation'. The ECB sets its inflation target at 'below, but close to, 2 percent over the medium term'.

Since January 1999, the monthly Eurozone Harmonized Consumer Price Index (HCPI) has often exceeded 2 percent year over year, but only once, in May 2001, was it higher than 3 percent (see Figure 5.3); i.e. the ECB has kept inflation under control. During this period, the German HCPI was usually below the ECB target of 2 percent. However, it accelerated in 2007, reaching 2.7 percent in September and October 2007. Also, 2007 was the first year since the creation of the Eurozone in which Germany posted higher HCPI rates than the Eurozone as a whole.

The ECB started its recent tightening cycle in December 2005 after the production situation improved, and the latest interest rate hike occurred in June 2007. Overall, during this period, the ECB marginal lending facility rate – the rate at which the ECB offers overnight credit to banks – was raised from 3 percent to 5 percent. Whether this increase is justified is questionable, given that Eurozone GDP growth, though accelerated, is not particularly strong.

*Table 5.7 Germany: value-added by sector, growth and contribution to total value-added**

	Index, 2007H1		Share of sector in value-added increase in 2007H1 with respect to	
	1995H1 = 100	2006H1 = 100	1995H1	2006H1
Total	122.8	103.2	100.0	100.0
Agriculture, hunting, forestry and fishing	105.8	99.1	0.3	−0.3
Industry	129.2	105.3	32.8	43.5
Construction	72.0	107.4	−8.3	8.8
Wholesale and retail trade, repair of motor vehicles, motorcycles and personal and household goods; hotels and restaurants; transport, storage and communication	127.4	103.0	21.5	17.3
Financial intermediation; real estate, renting and business activities	134.2	103.2	39.4	28.5
Public administration and defense, compulsory social security; education; health and social work; other community, social and personal service activities; private households with employed persons	114.8	100.5	14.5	3.5
Discrepancy			−0.2	−1.2

Note: * In constant 1995 prices.

4. METHOD OF PRINCIPAL COMPONENTS

Multivariable macroeconomic magnitudes (such as GDP, inflation, the unemployment rate etc.) are usually affected by a large number of factors. The problem is that the number of independent variables (factors) that can be included in a regression is significantly limited. This problem becomes

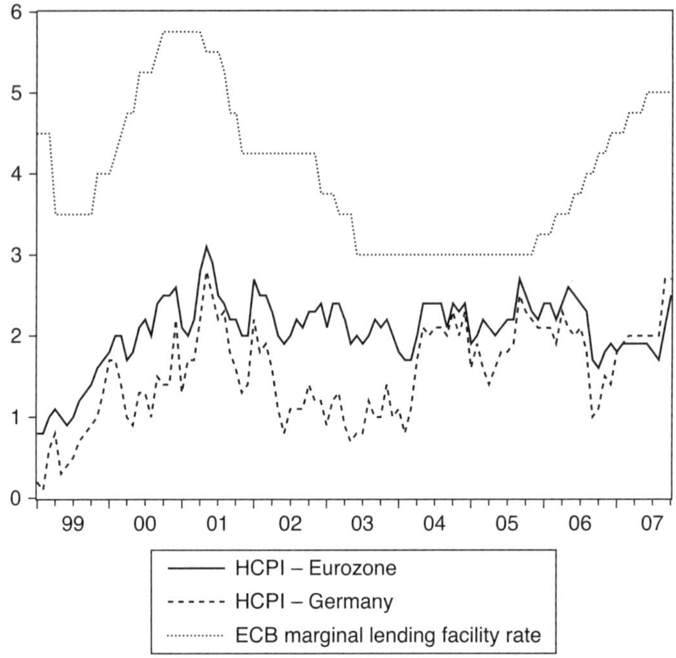

Figure 5.3 Eurozone and Germany: consumer price inflation and Central Bank interest rate

even more serious when time series of consistent data are relatively short. Another difficulty is that variables used as independent influences in regressions are often mutually correlated. This causes the well-known multicollinearity problem. To avoid these problems, forecasters often use a small number of indicators in regressions that are designed to forecast complex macroeconomic variables, while ignoring many other important factors. Fortunately, other, advanced techniques have been developed that are likely to improve forecast accuracy.

One such method is the method of principal components, which is utilized in this chapter. Suppose we have a set of n indicators (for example, 40) that are likely to affect GDP. The forecaster cannot include them all in one regression. However, this set can be transformed into an n-dimensional set of principal components, some of which will be used in the regression. Since the principal components can be ranked according to how much variation in the original indicators they explain, only the most important principal components (for example, three or four) may be used in the regression.

The method of principal components has two main advantages. First, it allows for a reduction in the number of independent variables (and, consequently, permits an increase in the degrees of freedom) that retains the most valuable information about the original indicators. Second, since the principal components, by design, are not linearly correlated with each other, the multicollinearity problem is avoided. The method of principal components allows for utilizing only relatively important information, while disregarding 'excess baggage'.

5. SELECTION OF INDICATORS AND INDICATOR-RELATED TRENDS

This section is an example of how we select indicators used in the extraction of principal components. To forecast German real GDP we have selected 48 monthly indicators:

- Industrial production index – mining
- Industrial production index – food products; beverages and tobacco
- Industrial production index – textiles and textile products; leather and leather products
- Industrial production index – wood and wood products
- Industrial production index – pulp, paper and paper products; publishing and printing
- Industrial production index – coke, refined petroleum products and nuclear fuel
- Industrial production index – chemicals, chemical products and man-made fibers
- Industrial production index – rubber and plastic products
- Industrial production index – other non-metallic mineral products
- Industrial production index – basic metals and fabricated metal products
- Industrial production index – machinery and equipment n.e.c. (not elsewhere classified)
- Industrial production index – office machinery and computers
- Industrial production index – electrical machinery and apparatus n.e.c.
- Industrial production index – radio, television and communication equipment and apparatus
- Industrial production index – medical, precision and optical instruments, watches and clocks

- Industrial production index – motor vehicles, trailers and semi-trailers
- Industrial production index – other transport equipment
- Industrial production index – manufacturing n.e.c.
- Industrial production index – electricity, gas and water supply
- Construction – production index
- Construction – new orders received index
- Retail trade index – food
- Retail trade index – textiles
- Retail trade index – household goods
- Wholesale trade index
- Sale, maintenance, and repair of motor vehicles index
- Hotel and restaurant turnover index
- Unemployment rate
- Employment
- Real pay rate
- Indicator of the German economy's price competitiveness
- Export volume index – to Eurozone – intermediate goods
- Export volume index – to Eurozone – capital goods
- Export volume index – to Eurozone – consumer goods
- Export volume index – to countries other than Eurozone – intermediate goods
- Export volume index – to countries other than Eurozone – capital goods
- Export volume index – to countries other than Eurozone – consumer goods
- Import volume index – from Eurozone – intermediate goods
- Import volume index – from Eurozone – capital goods
- Import volume index – from Eurozone – consumer goods
- Import volume index – from countries other than Eurozone – intermediate goods
- Import volume index – from countries other than Eurozone – capital goods
- Import volume index – from countries other than Eurozone – consumer goods
- Ratio of consumer price index to industrial producer price index
- Ratio of total industrial producer price index to intermediate goods industrial producer price index
- Ratio of total industrial producer price index to utilities producer price index
- Ratio of consumer price index to stock price index
- Real 10-year government bond yield

Almost all of these indicators are available monthly for a full quarter before an estimated value of GDP is released for the same quarter. A regression that includes lag values of missing indicators in principal components allows for the forecasting of GDP.

To compile a set of monthly indicators from which principal components for the GDP equations are computed we consider several criteria. First, monthly indicators should represent key aspects of the economy, namely the supply side, the demand side and market-clearing forces. Second, these indicators should be significant for GDP. This significance may be verified statistically, through a regression of GDP on the explanatory variables in question and correlation coefficients, or indicator selection may be judgmental. Judgmental does not mean arbitrary. For example, we may want to include all major branches of a key sector, such as manufacturing, regardless of the magnitude of the correlation coefficients between manufacturing branch indicators, on the one hand, and GDP, on the other hand. Third, the compilation of the monthly indicator set depends on data availability. For example, as for most economies of the world, the production of goods in Germany is much better represented in monthly statistics than is the production of services. Finally and most importantly, the inclusion of an indicator into a set from which principal components are computed or the removal from this set is ultimately based on whether this helps to improve the explanatory value of the respective regressions, including the properties of the regression residuals, the goodness of fit, and the accuracy of out-of-sample extrapolations.

We believe that the forecasting methodology applied here has certain advantages over business cycle indicator approaches based on a system of lagging, coincident and leading indicators. For example, our approach considers the impact of a broader set of indicators than are in the US Conference Board approach, which uses seven leading and four coincident indicators for Germany. While focused on identifying business cycle turning points, the Conference Board approach does not assume that the indices should be constructed in such a way that would maximize the predictive power of the original indicators. Klein (2000) notes that the focus of the Conference Board approach is on the forecasting of the direction of movement, rather than on its quantitative magnitude (p. 31). The approach presented in this chapter is designed to increase the explanatory power of the original indicators and is concentrated on the forecasting of the GDP quantitative magnitudes. However, it is not intended specifically to determine business cycle turning points. While predicting an increase or a decline in GDP, it does not say that this is a business cycle peak or trough.

At the same time, a number of monthly indicators applied in this study are also used within the framework of the US Conference Board approach. Principal components extracted from these monthly indicators may be used contemporaneously and with lags. Thus some principal components may act as coinciders, some as leaders, and some as both coinciders and leaders or laggards.

The US Conference Board uses industrial production and manufacturing sales as two of the four coincident indicators for Germany. In general, the Board stresses that the importance of industrial production in capturing GDP fluctuations is greater than can be explained based on the sector's size. Industrial production does appear to be an important coincident indicator for German GDP. The correlation coefficient between quarterly GDP and quarterly industrial production was 0.93 between 1995Q1 and 2007Q2. Only to some extent can this high correlation be explained by the size of the industrial sector. To some extent such high correlation may be a result of similarities in the seasonality patterns for the two variables. However, correlation between the quarterly year-over-year GDP and industrial production indices, which eliminates most of the seasonality effect, was also a high 0.77.

In our model, industrial production indicators also play a major role. Of the major production sectors, industry has the most detailed monthly statistics. It is divided into mining, manufacturing and utilities (electricity, gas and water supply). Given data availability and the importance of the industrial category, especially of manufacturing, for the German economy we include 19 industrial production indicators in our set of the original indicators for German GDP. These industrial production indicators are mining, utilities and 17 manufacturing indicators.

Eurostat divides manufacturing into 14 major sectors. The set of manufacturing production indicators utilized in the extraction of principal components for the GDP equation covers all these sectors. At the same time, based on their weight, some sectors were aggregated, while some were disaggregated. The share of the leather and leather products sector (which mostly includes footwear production) in total manufacturing production is minuscule; in 2004[2] it stood at 0.2 percent. Therefore we combined it with textiles and textile products, another small sector, which is close to the leather and leather products sector in terms of the purposes that its goods serve.

On the other hand, we break down the two largest manufacturing sectors of the 14 into subsectors. The electrical and optical equipment sector is divided into four subsectors: (1) office machinery and computers; (2) electrical machinery and apparatus n.e.c.; (3) radio, television and communication equipment and apparatus; and (4) medical, precision and optical instruments, watches and clocks. The transport equipment

Table 5.8 Germany: manufacturing production

	Share of sector in manufacturing production, 2004	Manufacturing production index, 2007H1	
		1995H1 = 100	2006H1 = 100
Manufacturing – total	100.0	137.2	106.9
Food products; beverages and tobacco	11.5	119.8	103.1
Textiles and textile products; leather and leather products	1.8	55.6	100.9
Wood and wood products	1.4	95.7	101.9
Pulp, paper and paper products; publishing and printing	5.5	112.9	102.2
Coke, refined petroleum products and nuclear fuel	6.7	116.1	99.7
Chemicals, chemical products and man-made fibers	9.1	135.2	105.2
Rubber and plastic products	4.0	132.4	**107.6**
Other non-metallic mineral products	2.5	92.3	**114.5**
Basic metals and fabricated metal products	11.5	132.7	**108.2**
Machinery and equipment n.e.c.	12.0	**143.7**	**110.2**
Office machinery and computers	0.9	**358.9**	**135.3**
Electrical machinery and apparatus n.e.c.	6.1	**151.5**	**108.6**
Radio, television and communication equipment and apparatus	2.3	**339.9**	**112.4**
Medical, precision and optical instruments, watches and clocks	2.7	**164.5**	103.9
Motor vehicles, trailers and semi-trailers	17.7	**182.2**	106.7
Other transport equipment	2.0	126.4	97.1
Manufacturing n.e.c.	2.2	88.8	104.9

Note: Figures for sectors that grew faster than average are in bold.

sector is divided into two subsectors: (1) motor vehicles, trailers and semi-trailers; and (2) other transport equipment. The latter subsector produces boats, locomotives, aircraft, street cars or tramways and related items.

Table 5.8 shows that in the first half of 2007, as, in general, over the last 12 years, the fastest-growing sector in our set of manufacturing indicators was office machinery and computers. However, because of its small size, it did not have a major impact on overall manufacturing production. In January–June 2007, German manufacturing was driven mostly by such heavy industry sectors as motor vehicles, metals and machinery n.e.c. (which includes machinery for power generation and machine tools, among other types of machinery).

On the services side, the most detailed set of monthly indicators is available for trade. To forecast German GDP we use five trade indicators: retail trade – food; retail trade – textiles; retail trade – household goods; wholesale trade; and sale, maintenance and repair of motor vehicles. Retail sales is also one of the four indicators that the US Conference Board considers coincident for Germany.

Beyond trade, the only services indicator included in our set of indicators to forecast GDP is hotel and restaurant turnover, which has not been a strong dynamic growth sector. We did not introduce explicit treatment of other service activities for projection of future estimates of German economic growth. For example, transportation and communication expanded 39.7 percent between 1995 and 2006, and the health and social work sector surged 45.8 percent during the same period, the fastest growth rate of the 17 sectors by the Eurostat classification.

Table 5.9 shows that the selected services sectors have either been growing slowly or have even been contracting. One problem with these indicators is that they underrepresent the growth of value-added in trade and hotels and restaurants, which rose respectively 19.8 percent and 7.8 percent from 1995 through 2006. Nevertheless, as regression analysis shows, the exclusion of these indicators from the list of indicators from which we derive principal components results in lower accuracy of GDP out-of-sample forecasts.

We include three key labor market indicators in the set of indicators that we use to extract principal components to forecast German GDP: the

Table 5.9 Germany: services production

	Services production indices, 2007H1	
	1995H1 = 100	2006H1 = 100
Retail trade – food	109.9	97.6
Retail trade – textiles	96.3	100.9
Retail trade – household goods	96.7	100.0
Wholesale trade	106.4	101.4
Sale, maintenance and repair of motor vehicles	97.9	93.6
Hotel and restaurant turnover	73.1	97.9

unemployment rate, employment and the real wage rate. Employment is also used by the US Conference Board as a coincident indicator for Germany.

The recent revival of economic growth in Germany has been accompanied by a drastic decline in the unemployment rate. In the unified Germany, the seasonally adjusted harmonized unemployment rate, which conforms to the methodology of the International Labor Organization (ILO), dropped from its highest point of 10.0 percent in May 2005 to 6.4 percent in July 2007 (see Figure 5.4).[3] It approached its historical low of 5.9 percent, observed in May 1992 (the first month of the German unemployment rate series published by Eurostat).

The reduction of the unemployment rate has been accompanied by an acceleration in the growth of employment. After inching up 0.3 percent per year, on average, between 1995 and 2006, employment rose 1.8 percent year over year in the first half of 2007 (see Table 5.10). These improvements in the unemployment and employment rate have not led to a rebound in household consumption, which, in fact, declined year over year during the same period (see Table 5.5). The consumption weakness was, to a great extent, a result of a 0.5 percent drop in the real average wage rate, whose growth was subdued for most of the period between 1995 and 2006. Apparently, the recent revival of hiring has been skewed toward relatively

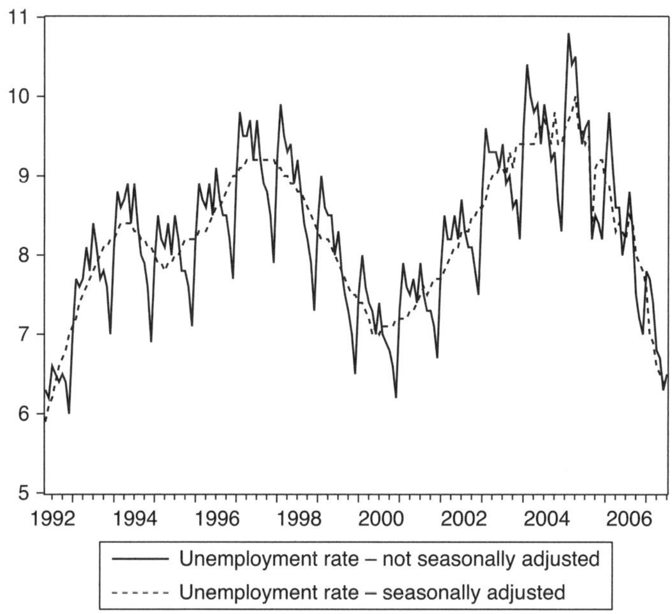

Figure 5.4 Germany: harmonized unemployment rate, %

Table 5.10 Germany: employment and real average wage growth

	2007H1	
	1995H1 = 100	2006H1 = 100
Employment	105.3	101.8
Real average wage rate	106.3	99.5

low-paying jobs and/or salary increases for existing workers have not caught up with inflation.

Although it is a cause of the weakness in household consumption, the sluggish growth of the wage rate (or, more generally, of labor cost[4]) has helped German exports, improving their relative competitiveness. In the first half of 2007, German real labor cost in industry and services, excluding public administration, was only 6.2 percent higher than in the first half of 1996, and compared to the corresponding period of 2006, it actually fell 1.2 percent. In France and Spain this indicator rose, respectively, 19.6 percent and 20.5 percent during the same period.

Because of the growing importance of foreign trade for Germany we include *disaggregated* merchandise foreign trade indicators in the set of indicators from which we extract principal components for GDP regressions. Both exports and imports are divided into Eurozone and non-Eurozone. Then we show separately intermediate goods, capital goods and consumer goods.

Table 5.11 demonstrates that between the first half of 1995 and the first half of 2007 Germany posted substantial increases across all selected trade categories. The growth of consumer goods exports (this category includes cars) was especially significant.

In all categories the growth of trade with countries outside the Eurozone was more buoyant than the rise in trade with the Eurozone. To a great extent, this resulted from the increasing importance of transition and developing countries. For example, between 1995 and 2006, the shares of Poland, China and Russia in German exports increased, respectively, from 1.7 percent to 3.2 percent,[5] from 1.4 percent to 3.1 percent, and from 1.4 percent to 2.6 percent. Despite the weakening of the US dollar, the share of the USA also rose – from 7.3 percent to 8.6 percent. In 2006, the USA was the second major destination for German exports, up from fifth place in 1995. France remains the most important export destination, but its share dropped two percentage points to 9.7 percent.

The regressions for the other five key macroeconomic variables – the consumer price index, the industrial producer price index, exports of goods and services (in euros), imports of goods and services (in euros),

Table 5.11 Germany: growth in foreign trade

	Share in trade flow category, 2006, %	Volume index, 2007H1	
		1995H1 = 100	2006H1 = 100
Exports	100.0		
to Eurozone	42.3	190.2	107.4
Intermediate goods	20.0	155.7	106.8
Capital goods	7.1	211.8	110.0
Consumer goods	11.6	225.0	108.9
outside Eurozone	57.7	228.7	110.4
Intermediate goods	27.2	208.8	109.4
Capital goods	14.0	250.7	110.9
Consumer goods	13.2	238.9	112.1
Imports	100.0		
from Eurozone	43.9	154.2	107.1
Intermediate goods	23.6	160.4	107.0
Capital goods	4.9	192.4	115.0
Consumer goods	10.8	122.2	103.6
from outside Eurozone	56.1	182.6	106.1
Intermediate goods	32.5	170.3	107.5
Capital goods	9.2	262.4	98.7
Consumer goods	11.5	156.8	105.9

and the unemployment rate – are based on their own sets of monthly indicators. For example, the indicator sets from which we extract principal components to forecast the consumer and industrial producer price indices include a large number of disaggregated price series.

Unlike the real GDP regression, these regressions are monthly. In order to be able to forecast the two price indices, exports, imports and the unemployment rate when all the necessary monthly indicators are already known, we do not use any contemporaneous principal components in these regressions.

Since exports and imports are highly volatile, for the respective regressions we smoothed both the dependent variables and the monthly indicators by transforming them into three-month moving averages.

6. REGRESSION SPECIFICATION SELECTION

The selection of regression specifications was based on the analysis of (1) t-statistics, (2) regression residual properties, (3) the accuracy of in-sample forecasts, and (4) the accuracy of out-of-sample forecasts. The fourth criterion is the most important since the goal of the development of these models is to forecast what will happen to the key German macroeconomic indicators in the future.

The coefficient of a right-hand-side variable was considered statistically insignificant if the absolute value of the respective *t*-statistic equaled less than one. Sometimes, the coefficients of variables that are expected to be important, such as principal components that account for a substantial portion of the variance in the original monthly indicators, were found to be insignificant. Variables with insignificant coefficients were not used in these models. However, as economic conditions change, the coefficients of such variables may become statistically significant and may be used in future calculations.

The selected regressions exploit identified trends and patterns in the residuals to increase regression predictive power. The residuals in the selected regressions are random. This is another way of saying that we have built models that lead to a separation of 'signal' from 'noise'. To ensure that regressions are statistically sound, we conducted several residual tests, including the Breusch–Godfrey Lagrange multiplier test for serial correlation, the White heteroskedasticity test, and the normality test.

In-sample forecast accuracy, or goodness of fit, is measured by adjusted R^2. In a quarterly or monthly model that includes seasonal dummy variables, adjusted R^2 may be relatively high even when no other right-hand-side variables are included. This happens because seasonality often accounts for a large portion of the variation in macroeconomic variables. Thus, in such regressions, a high adjusted R^2 should not, by itself, lead the forecaster to accept the tested regression.

Out-of-sample forecasts are obtained by reducing the historical sample by a certain number of quarters or months (depending on whether the regression is quarterly or monthly) and by forecasting the dependent variable using the actual values of the independent variables for the quarters or months that were dropped from the historical sample. Which forecasts should be considered sufficiently accurate can be determined on the basis of the volatility of the forecasted variable.

We prefer the dynamic out-of-sample forecasting approach to the static approach, which differ from one another when lagged dependent variables and/or ARMA (autoregressive moving-average) terms are present in the regression. The dynamic approach assumes that the previously forecasted values of the lagged dependent variables (but not the actual values of the lagged dependent variables) are used to calculate the forecast of the current values. This means that the forecasts for subsequent periods are computed using only the information on the forecasted variable that was available at the start of the forecast exercise.

We have selected the following specification for a real GDP regression:

$$GDP = C(1) + C(2)*DUMMYEURO + C(3)*DUMMY1 + C(4)*DUMMY3 + C(5)*PC1 + C(6)*PC2 + [AR(1)=C(7)],$$ [6]

where *DUMMYEURO* is an intercept structural break dummy variable reflecting the introduction of the euro (*DUMMYEURO* = 0 through 1998Q4; = 1 otherwise); *DUMMY*1 and *DUMMY*3 are quarterly intercept dummy variables for the first and the third quarters, respectively; *PC*1 and *PC*2 are, respectively, the first and the second principal components; and *AR*(1) is the first-order autoregressive term. Real GDP is measured in billion 1995 euros.

The adjusted R^2 for this regression is a high 0.979. The impressive in-sample forecast accuracy can be also observed from Figure 5.5, which shows how close the fitted values are to the reported values.

To test the regression for out-of-sample forecast accuracy we reduced the historical sample by four quarters, re-estimated the regression for the reduced sample, and forecasted GDP using the reported values of the independent variables for the out-of-sample quarters.

We can see from Table 5.12 that the forecasted GDP growth rates were very close to the reported growth rates. On average, for the four out-of-sample quarters, in absolute terms, the forecast error, measured as the

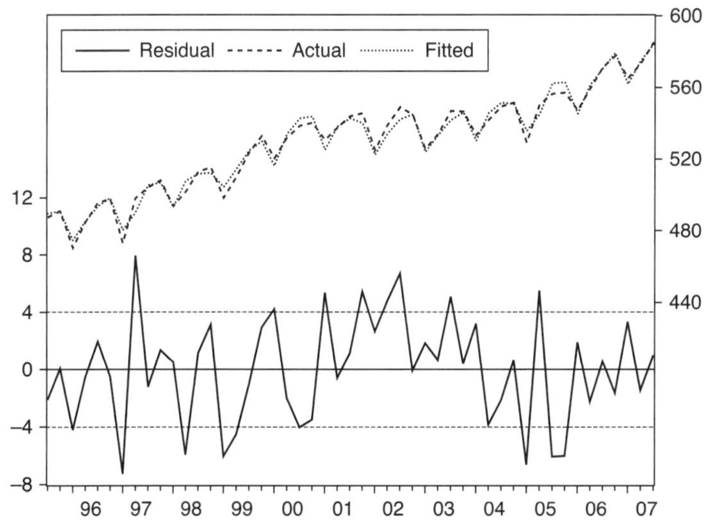

Figure 5.5 Real GDP regression residual plot

Table 5.12 Real GDP year-over-year growth rates (%) and forecast error

	Reported	Forecast	Forecast error
2006Q4	3.7	4.0	−0.3
2007Q1	3.3	2.7	0.6
2007Q2	2.5	2.5	0.0
2007Q3	2.4	2.2	0.2

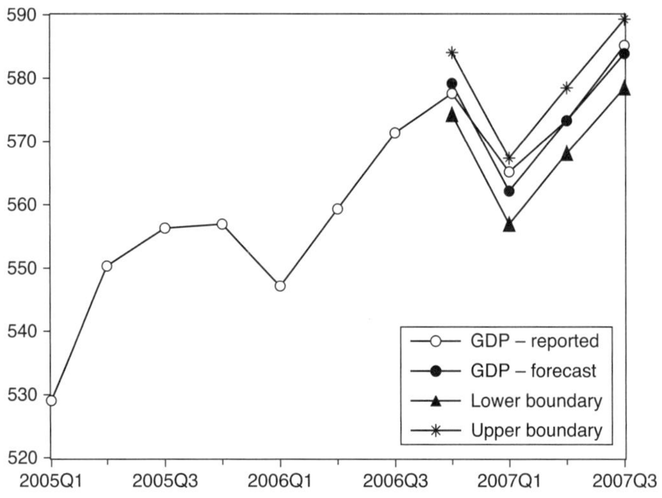

Figure 5.6 Out-of-sample forecast accuracy testing: +/– one standard error confidence interval

difference between the forecasted and reported growth rates, was 0.27 percentage points. This is low given the observed volatility of the German GDP growth rate. In 1996–2007, the average of the absolute values of the difference between growth rates in two consecutive quarters was 0.97 percentage points. The high level of the out-of-sample forecast accuracy of the GDP regression can also be demonstrated by Figure 5.6.

For the other five key macroeconomic variables the selected regression specifications are as follows:

Consumer Price Index

$$CPI = C(1) + C(2)*DUMMY1 + C(3)*DUMMY2 + C(4)*DUMMY3 + C(5)*DUMMY4 + C(6)*DUMMY5 + C(7)*DUMMY6$$

$$+ C(8)*DUMMY7 + C(9)*DUMMY8 + C(10)*DUMMY9$$
$$+ C(11)*DUMMY10 + C(12)*DUMMY11 + C(13)*CPI(-1)$$
$$+ C(14)*PC1(-1) + C(15)*PC1(-3) + [AR(1) = C(16)]$$

Industrial Producer Price Index

$$IPPI = C(1) + C(2)*DUMMY1 + C(3)*DUMMY4$$
$$+ C(4)*DUMMY7 + C(5)*IPPI(-1)$$
$$+ C(6)*IPPI(-2) + C(7)*PC1(-1)$$
$$+ C(8)*PC2(-7) + [AR(1) = C(9), AR(2) = C(10)]$$

Exports of Goods and Services

$$EXPORTS = C(1) + C(2)*DUMMY1 + C(3)*DUMMY3$$
$$+ C(4)*DUMMY4 + C(5)*DUMMY7$$
$$+ C(6)*DUMMY8 + C(7)*DUMMY10$$
$$+ C(8)*DUMMY11 + C(9)*DUMMY2000\_10$$
$$+ C(10)*DUMMY2006\_10 + C(11)*EXPORTS(-1)$$
$$+ C(12)*EXPORTS(-2) + C(13)*EXPORTS(-3)$$
$$+ C(14)*PC1(-1) + C(15)*PC2(-2)$$
$$+ [AR(2) = C(16), AR(7) = C(17), MA(1) = C(18)]$$

Imports of Goods and Services

$$IMPORTS = C(1) + C(2)*DUMMY1 + C(3)*DUMMY2$$
$$+ C(4)*DUMMY6 + C(5)*DUMMY10$$
$$+ C(6)*DUMMY11 + C(7)*IMPORTS(-1)$$
$$+ C(8)*IMPORTS(-2) + C(9)*IMPORTS(-12)$$
$$+ C(10)*PC1(-1) + C(11)*PC2(-2) + C(12)*PC2(-3)$$
$$+ C(13)*PC4(-3) + [AR(1) = C(14), AR(2)$$
$$= C(15), AR(7) = C(16), AR(9) = C(17), MA(3) = C(18)]$$

Unemployment Rate

$$UR = C(1) + C(2)*DUMMY1 + C(3)*DUMMY2 + C(4)*DUMMY3 + C(5)*DUMMY4 + C(6)*DUMMY5 + C(7)*DUMMY6 + C(8)*DUMMY7 + C(9)*DUMMY8 + C(10)*DUMMY9 + C(11)*DUMMY10 + C(12)*DUMMY11 + C(13)*DUMMY1997\_01 + C(14)*DUMMY2005\_01 + C(15)*UR(-1) + C(16)*PC1(-1) + C(17)*PC2(-1) + [AR(1) = C(18), AR(2) = C(19), AR(3) = C(20)]$$

The right-hand-side variables include seasonal intercept dummy variables (*DUMMY*1 = 1 in January; = 0 otherwise, *DUMMY*2 = 1 in February; = 0 otherwise; etc.), intercept dummy variables reflecting the presence of outliers (e.g. *DUMMY*2000_10 = 1 in October 2000; = 0 otherwise), lagged dependent variables, principal components, autoregressive (AR) terms and moving average (MA) terms.

Table 5.13 shows the high levels of both in-sample and out-of-sample forecast accuracy for the five regressions. To test out-of-sample forecast accuracy we reduced the historical sample by six months. For the price indices and the foreign trade variables, the average out-of-sample forecast error is the average absolute value of the difference between the reported and forecasted year-over-year growth rates in the six out-of-sample months. Volatility is measured as the average absolute value of the difference between the year-over-year growth rates in two consecutive months during the respective historical periods. For the unemployment rate forecast accuracy testing, we used levels instead of the year-over-year growth rates.

Table 5.13 Forecast accuracy testing

Regression	Adjusted R^2	Average out-of-sample forecast error, percentage points	Volatility, percentage points
Consumer price index	0.998	0.06	0.20
Industrial producer price index	0.998	0.10	0.27
Exports of goods and services	0.998	0.43	1.65
Imports of goods and services	0.997	0.32	1.76
Unemployment rate	0.986	0.02	0.29

7. CONCLUSION

We have identified regressions that provide short-term forecasts of six key variables of the German economy: real GDP; the consumer price index; the industrial producer price index; exports of goods and services; imports of goods and services; and the unemployment rate. The estimated regressions include principal components as right-hand-side variables. For each dependent variable, the principal components are extracted from sets that include a large number of indicators that we believe have a substantial impact on the respective variable.

The constructed model cannot answer the question whether the improvement in German economic growth observed in 2006–07 is sustainable. Neither can it predict whether the recent acceleration of consumer price growth will continue. However, these regressions can provide initial conditions for structural models, which, in turn, may be utilized to forecast medium-term and long-term developments of these and other macroeconomic variables of the German economy. The contribution in this volume by Fyodor Kushnirsky (Chapter 11) shows how high-frequency models and forecasts can be used as initial input values for lower-frequency (longer-run) forecasts.

NOTES

1. Germany is one of the six countries that in 1951 founded the European Coal and Steel Community, a predecessor organization to the EU. In 1957, the same countries created the European Economic Community. By 1995, the EU consisted of 15 countries. This group of mostly highly developed West European countries is referred to as the EU-15. In May 2004, the EU was joined by ten East European and Mediterranean countries, most of which had been in the Soviet bloc until the late 1980s or the early 1990s. The EU-15 countries and the countries that entered the EU in 2004 are jointly referred to as the EU-25. Finally, two more countries, Bulgaria and Romania, became EU members in January 2007, bringing the total number of EU countries to 27 (the EU-27).
2. This is the latest year for which Eurostat provides data for the sectoral breakdown of German industrial production.
3. The unemployment rate calculated on the basis of the official German methodology is higher than the ILO-defined unemployment rate. Also, the recent decline is less pronounced if the rate is calculated according to the German definition. The seasonally adjusted unemployment rate based on the German definition fell from 11.9 percent in May 2005 to 9.0 percent in July 2007.
4. Labor cost is a quarterly indicator and, therefore, cannot be included in the set of indicators from which we extract principal components.
5. The shares are provided in current prices and exchange rates.
6. We use autoregressive (AR) and moving average (MA) terms for the historical sample, but not for forecasting.

REFERENCE

Klein, Lawrence R. (2000), 'An essay on the accuracy of economic prediction', *International Journal of Applied Economics and Econometrics*, **9**(1), 29–69.

6. Mexico: current quarter forecasts

Alfredo Coutiño

1. THE MEXICAN ECONOMY

Mexico is a relatively open economy, but with some degree of regulation, particularly in sectors considered strategic by the government. The country has made important efforts in its transition from a state-regulated to a more open market economy in the past two decades. However, even though the benefits of the changes implemented have been evident, the pace of structural reform has been slow in the past ten years.

The country set out on its openness path just a few years after the last episode of nationalization measures occurred in 1982, undertaken in connection with the arrival of the world debt crisis. The financial and economic collapse, and its devastating effects, left the country with few options other than the path of economic openness and deregulation, in order to deal with the stubborn inflation and persistent economic imbalances. The first step in that direction was taken in the mid-1980s, with the country joining the General Agreement on Tariffs and Trade (GATT). A few years later, that measure was followed by an intensive process of privatization of state-owned companies, including the previously nationalized banking system. The next step was the deepening of economic openness through the implementation of the North American Free Trade Agreement (NAFTA) in 1994, followed by a series of bilateral trade agreements. At the end of the 1990s, the banking system openness was accelerated by allowing foreign investors to participate more in the financial sector. Other minor reforms were also undertaken in the 1990s, including in the political area, with the reform of the electoral system.

Undoubtedly, all these changes gave the Mexican economy more flexibility and removed important bottlenecks. Economic performance improved significantly, and society increased its participation in an environment of more political openness. The economy was less regulated, but not totally deregulated. The external sector developed to become one of the main engines of growth; exports diversified; and the country's dependence on oil output was reduced. However, the link between Mexico and the USA strengthened to the extent of making the Mexican business cycle highly dependent on US economic performance, for better or worse. On the one hand, Mexico benefited from the partnership with the USA not only when the northern neighbor was in expansion, but also when the USA could provide financial rescue for the Mexican economy when there was a case of potential default during the peso crisis at the end of 1994 and beginning of 1995.[1] On the other hand, it was adversely affected by the US recession in 2001.

Tourism has been an important source of foreign income for the country not only because of its closeness to the USA but also because of its competitive prices. In fact, since the implementation of a more flexible exchange rate system in 1995, the depreciation of the peso has made the country more attractive to foreign tourists. But also the trade agreement in 1994 gave an extra impulse to the country as a vacation destination. Thus tourism revenues multiplied by 150 percent during the first ten years of NAFTA, and doubled from 1993 to 2006, giving the country a positive net balance that increased four-fold during those 13 years.

Another important feature of Mexico during the 14 years of NAFTA has been the increasing role played by remittances sent home by Mexican workers abroad. During just the first ten years of NAFTA, remittances multiplied by 4.5 times, surpassing the amount of foreign direct investment in 2003. Thus, from 2003, remittances became the second source of foreign income for Mexico, after oil revenues. Since most of the remittances are received by low-income families in Mexico, with a marginal propensity to consume close to one, this explains the strong dynamic reported by household consumption and also the marginal effects on domestic saving. The increase in remittances reflects not only the efficiency gained by the banking sector and authorities in tracking those financial activities, but also the important contribution of those income flows to the whole economy.[2]

In general, it is possible to say that the Mexican economy has benefited greatly from the openness measures undertaken in the last two decades of the twentieth century. The openness of trade and capital accounts generated not only a boom in Mexican exports but also an enormous increase of capital flow into the country, particularly in the form of foreign direct investment. Foreign investors brought more financial resources for Mexican partners but also provided better technology to Mexican industry, thus making production processes more efficient. With NAFTA, physical investment also increased in the form of new plants, buildings and construction activity. In order to take advantage of the trade agreement, not only local industries had to expand and modernize, but also foreign companies established themselves in the country, particularly US subsidiaries. Thus Mexico had to increase investment in infrastructure.

In this way, the accumulation of capital increased and multifactor productivity advanced. As a result, the country gained some ground in international competitiveness. Mexican exports gained market share in the USA, and the country's surplus with its main trade partner increased significantly. Mexican consumers found not only a wider supply of goods but also access to less costly merchandise. Mexico restored its international reputation and respect by showing macroeconomic discipline and paying off its debt (from the financial rescue package) in advance of the original maturity. Mexico gained qualification as an investment-grade country for the first time.

Unfortunately, in the past six years (2001–06) the country did not continue deepening the structural reforms. The arrival of the first government from an opposition party (PAN – National Action Party), after 71 years of the PRI (Institutional Revolutionary Party) in power, introduced a pause in the process of structural change. The lack of political leadership meant that the new government failed to get the approval of the main reform proposals sent to Congress. By then, the country was in need of a second round of reforms such as fiscal, labor, energy, pensions and state (for more details, see Coutiño, 2006b). It was also necessary to reinforce public policies to reduce poverty and promote social progress. Given the lack of political skills of the new government, those measures were not implemented and the country lagged behind international competitors.

The absence of new reforms not only restricted the country's potential; it also reduced production capacity. Mexico lost attractiveness for foreign investors. Investment from abroad did not stop, but did not increase significantly. The national private sector preferred either to send its savings abroad or to choose speculative investments. Hence the country suffered a disinvestment process. In fact, the fundamental sources of growth weakened during those six years. The investment–output coefficient fell from 24 percent of GDP in 2000 to 22 percent in 2006; productivity advanced at only a modest rate, and technological change was practically absent. Thus Mexican exports lost ground in the US market and the country lost ground in its world ranking. All these factors explain the poor performance of the Mexican economy during the 2001–06 period, with growth averaging only 2.3 percent.

In fact, the past administration (2001–06) was not able to sustain the growth path at rates similar to those at the end of the previous administration (6 percent), precisely because a disinvestment process occurred. President Fox was not able to fulfill one of the main economic promises: growth of 7.0 percent. During his campaign and at the beginning of the administration, his economic team proposed an average growth rate of 7 percent during the six-year term. Later on, and after repetitive failure in Congress with rejection of various fiscal proposals, the administration

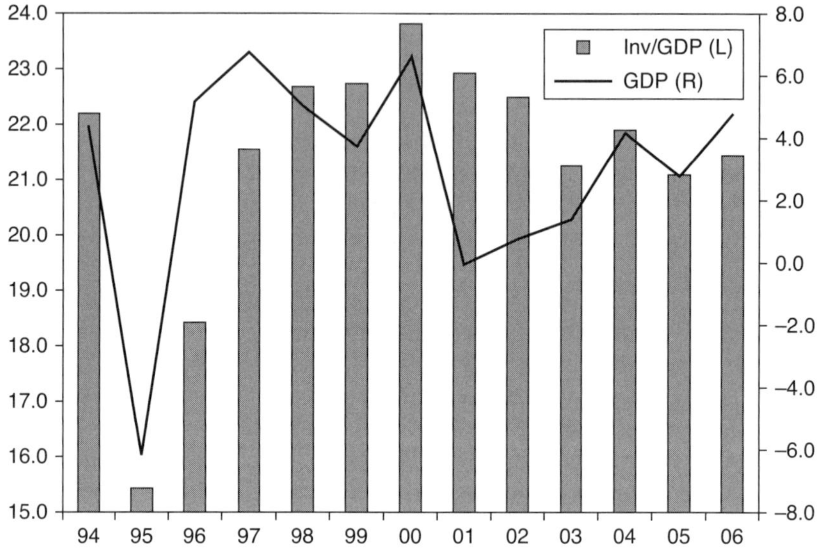

Source: INEGI.

Figure 6.1 Investment–output ratio and GDP growth, %

recognized the economy's difficulties and switched the 7 percent growth target to the end of the period, which, finally, was also unattained. It was clear to a small group of analysts, with respectable econometric models, that the Mexican economy was not going to be able to expand at rates above 5 percent during the period, since the fundamental sources of permanent growth were weakening instead of strengthening.

At present, Mexico is certainly a wide-open economy, but it is not deregulated enough. There still exist some rigid markets and sectors that are becoming obstacles to economic progress. The degree of competition is still too low in some strategic sectors, because there is either government protection or monopoly power of big corporations. Thus state monopoly still exists in the energy sector; there is some monopoly power in telecommunications, and oligopoly in the banking system. Certainly, the country has made some progress in structural change, but it has been insufficient. Monetary policy is highly independent of the executive authorities, with an autonomous central bank. Fiscal policy has been immunized from populism, and fiscal discipline has been institutionalized (for a detailed analysis, see Coutiño, 2006a). One component of the government pension system has been recently reformed, but this is not the case of pensions in other public institutions (see Coutiño, 2007a). A minimal tax reform was also approved in 2007 (see Coutiño, 2007c, 2007d). However, a more profound fiscal reform is still needed, as well as the opening up of the energy sector to private participation. The labor market needs to be more flexible in order to allow labor mobility. Political and justice institutions need to be reinforced and respected, with stricter law enforcement.

Thus the lack of reforms in the previous six years made the Mexican economy less competitive and a weaker player in the international league. The road to reform is still long for the country, but it will become even longer if Mexico continues to be unable to deepen structural change (see Coutiño, 2007c). In that regard, the present administration (Calderón 2007–12) has recognized the structural weakness of the Mexican economy, and has consequently proposed more modest economic growth for its presidential period.

In these circumstances, the process of modeling and forecasting the Mexican economy will continue to include some challenges, since market behavior is not fully guided by free competition, and the flow of information is not yet totally efficient. In this situation, markets can sometimes react quite differently from the predictions of economic theory. Some prices will behave in such a way that would not lead to optimal resource allocation in the economy. Other than that, given the well-defined structure of the Mexican economy and the development of a national system of statistics, the economy can be modeled in great detail, not only by a structural model but also by a high-frequency model. This is precisely our methodology for the analysis of the Mexican economy.

2. THE HIGH-FREQUENCY FORECASTING MODEL

The development of a quarterly system of national accounts and the publication of monthly strategic indicators related to production activity, financial markets and prices allow us to develop a system of high-frequency forecasts in order to anticipate the quarterly GDP well in advance of official publication. It also allows us to respond more efficiently to an increasing user demand for short-term forecasts. The main purpose of the high-frequency forecasting (HFF) model is to provide analysts with an anticipation of the current quarter GDP by replicating, as closely as possible, the methodology used by the statisticians in charge of the national accounts, but executed earlier. The model for Mexico[3] follows the methodology developed at the University of Pennsylvania for the current quarter model (CQM) of the US economy (Klein and Park, 1993, 1995).

The HFF model predicts the quarterly GDP using monthly information on economic activity, financial market transactions, and readings on futures, forwards and expectations. The methodology combines the use of high-frequency indicators, time-series equations and regression analysis. The GDP forecast is generated by three different approaches: production (supply); expenditure (demand); and a canonical form (principal components) (see Coutiño, 2004, 2005a) of many advance indicators. Since the model is a purely econometric forecasting system, it does not rely on personal adjustment. It is automatically re-estimated every month (weekly for the US and China models), when new pieces of information are publicly available and incorporated into the system. The three different approaches generate three independent forecasts of GDP, which are averaged to produce a single quarterly estimate.

In Mexico, the quarterly GDP is computed by the National Institute of Statistics and Geography (INEGI) using the production side. It states that GDP is estimated as the value-added of production sectors. The official release is announced six weeks after the end of each quarter. GDP by the demand side is released one month later (ten weeks after the end of each quarter), but it does not include revisions of the total since the discrepancy is always part of inventory change. INEGI does not produce quarterly figures for GDP by the income side. Thus the first two approaches in our HFF model for Mexico include the production and the expenditure sides. The third approach is built using the principal components methodology, which is also called the aggregative approach. The first two methods try to estimate quarterly GDP using monthly indicators similar to those INEGI uses to compute the quarterly national accounts aggregates. For example, the volume of retail sales is one of the relevant indicators to compute private consumption from the national income and product accounts (NIPA). The quarterly private consumption aggregate is then linked to the monthly retail sales indicator through a bridge equation, as explained later in this chapter.

The first approach in our model is the production side. INEGI collects information on the value-added of production for all types of economic activities, and then computes the corresponding sector aggregate. Thus the monthly information on production of each of several industrial activities generates the quarterly industrial GDP. The same occurs with agriculture and services. Hence, in order to replicate what INEGI does, we could survey the industrial sector, and then compute the aggregate industrial value-added. Fortunately, we do not have to do that, since INEGI already does it. Thus, every month, INEGI computes the approximate value-added of agriculture, industry and services. With this sectoral information, it also computes an aggregate index of production for the whole economy, which is called the general index of economic activity (IGAE). The IGAE represents a little more than 85 percent of the total production of goods and services in the economy, including agriculture, industry and services. In this sense, the IGAE is considered a measure of the monthly GDP.

The existence of the monthly IGAE makes our life much easier, since we can use it as the best single monthly indicator to predict the quarterly GDP by the production-side analysis. The IGAE is published six weeks after the end of each month. For example, by the middle of March we know the observed GDP for January; by the middle of April we know the observed GDP for February, and so on. Hence the first approach (production side) generates the quarterly GDP through two basic equations: the quarterly IGAE based on the monthly IGAE, and the bridge equation.

$$\text{IGAE\%qt} = \text{pch(IGAEqt)} \tag{6.1}$$

$$\text{GDP\%qt} = \text{f(IGAE\%qt)} \tag{6.2}$$

where IGAE%qt is the annual percentage change of the quarterly IGAE; pch(IGAEqt) is the annual percentage change of the three-month average of monthly IGAE; GDP%qt is the annual percentage change of the quarterly GDP, with q = 1, 2, 3, 4 representing the quarter of the year, and $t = 1, 2, \ldots n$ indicating the year. Thus equation (6.1) computes the quarterly IGAE using the three-month average of the monthly IGAE, while equation (6.2) estimates the quarterly GDP as a function of the quarterly IGAE, both equations in percentage changes.

The OLS (ordinary least squares) estimation of equation (6.2), using a sample from 1993Q1 to 2006Q4, is as follows:

Total GDP by production:

$$\underset{}{\text{GDP\%qt}} = \underset{(0.6)}{-\,0.01015} + \underset{(175.5)}{1.0054} * \text{IGAE\%qt} \tag{6.3}$$

$$R^2 = 0.99, \text{DW} = 2.75$$

Since the intercept is not statistically significant, the quarterly GDP is almost fully explained by the quarterly IGAE, in terms of percentage changes.

In addition, we also estimate GDP for the three main production divisions: primary, secondary and tertiary. Equations for primary and tertiary GDP (agriculture and services) are estimated as functions of the IGAE, as shown below.

Meanwhile, the equation for secondary GDP (industry) comes from the principal components section as an ARIMA (autoregressive integrated moving-average) equation. In this case, we use the bridge equation linking the quarterly industrial production (IPI%qt) to the three-month average of the monthly indicator (IPIqt) obtained from the ARIMA equation, both variables in percentage changes.

Primary sector GDP:

$$\begin{aligned} \text{GDP1\%qt} = {} & \underset{(3.0)}{5.22} - \underset{(1.1)}{0.23} * \text{IGAE\%q}_{t-1} - \underset{(2.9)}{0.22} * \text{IGAE\%q}_{t-4} \\ & - \underset{(1.4)}{0.23} * \text{GDP1\%q}_{t-1} - \underset{(0.1)}{0.021} * \text{GDP1\%q}_{t-2} \\ & - \underset{(0.7)}{0.16} * \text{GDP1\%q}_{t-3} - \underset{(2.9)}{0.48} * \text{GDP1\%q}_{t-4} \end{aligned} \tag{6.4}$$

$R^2 = 0.55$, DW = 1.98

Tertiary sector GDP:

$$\text{GDP3\%qt} = \underset{(0.8)}{0.30} + \underset{(18.5)}{0.88} * \text{IGAE\%qt} \tag{6.5}$$

$R^2 = 0.98$, DW = 1.85

Secondary sector GDP:

$$\text{IPI\%qt} = \text{pch(IPIqt)} \tag{6.6}$$

Since these three divisions of GDP (by the production side) are only for distributional purposes, the discrepancy between the total GDP obtained from them and the total from equation (6.3) is called taxes and subsidies.

The second approach computes GDP through the estimation of the quarterly aggregates of domestic demand linked to the corresponding monthly indicators similar to those used by INEGI. Here, we also use the two basic equations: the monthly indicator linked to its quarterly figure and the bridge equation:

$$\text{N\%qt} = \text{pch(Nqt)} \tag{6.7}$$

$$\text{DA\%qt} = \text{f(N\%qt)} \tag{6.8}$$

where N%qt stands for the annual percentage change of the quarterly indicator, pch(Nqt) is the annual percentage change of the three-month average of the monthly indicator, and DA%qt is the quarterly demand aggregate as a function of the quarterly indicator, both in percentage changes.

The following list shows the corresponding monthly indicators linked to the quarterly demand aggregates:

Quarterly demand aggregates (NIPA):	*Monthly indicators:*
Private consumption (Cp)	Retail sales volume (RSI)
Government consumption (Cg)	Primary gov. spending (CGS)
Fixed investment (IF)	Gross fixed investment (GFI)
Export of goods and services (X)	Export of goods (EXP)
Import of goods and services (M)	Import of goods (IMP)
Inventory change (ΔS)	Lagged inventory change ($\Delta St - i$)

Estimation results are as follows, for a sample beginning in 1993 and ending in the last quarter of 2006. A dummy variable was included from 1994 to 2003 to capture the ten-year NAFTA effects on trade (DUM9403). No dummy variable was necessary for the peso crisis in 1995.

Private consumption:

$$\underset{}{\text{Cp\%qt}} = \underset{(4.5)}{1.95} + \underset{(12.5)}{0.62}\ \text{RSI\%qt} \tag{6.9}$$

$$R^2 = 0.94,\ \text{DW} = 2.18$$

Government consumption:

$$\text{Log(Cg)qt} = \underset{(2.2)}{0.25}\ \text{Log(CGS/PDGDP)qt} - \underset{(1.9)}{0.15}\ \text{Log(CGS/PDGDP)q}_{t-4} \tag{6.10}$$

$$+ \underset{(250.2)}{0.92}\ \text{Log(Cg)q}_{t-4}$$

$$R^2 = 0.89,\ \text{DW} = 1.76$$

Fixed investment:

$$\text{IF\%qt} = \underset{(4250.3)}{0.99}\ \text{GFI\%qt} \tag{6.11}$$

$$R^2 = 1.00,\ \text{DW} = 1.67$$

Export of goods and services:

$$\text{X\%qt} = \underset{(2.2)}{5.65} + \underset{(7.5)}{0.72}\ \text{EXP\%qt} - \underset{(2.5)}{3.87}\ \text{DUM9403} \tag{6.12}$$

$$R^2 = 0.98,\ \text{DW} = 1.58$$

Import of goods and services:

$$\underset{}{M\%qt} = \underset{(2.6)}{-\,3.85} + \underset{(15.5)}{0.95\ IMP\%qt} + \underset{(2.6)}{5.75\ DUM9403} \qquad (6.13)$$

$$R^2 = 0.96,\ DW = 1.66$$

Inventory change:

$$\Delta Sqt = \underset{(2.3)}{-\,0.24\ \Delta Sq_{t-1}} - \underset{(1.6)}{0.12\ \Delta Sq_{t-2}} - \underset{(1.4)}{0.11\ \Delta Sq_{t-3}} \qquad (6.14)$$

$$+ \underset{(8.2)}{0.78\ \Delta Sq_{t-4}} + \underset{(2.6)}{42550\ DUM9403}$$

$$R^2 = 0.78,\ DW = 2.05$$

At the end, total GDP is computed as the sum of all the demand components estimated with the previous equations.

Total GDP by expenditure:

$$GDP = Cp + Cg + IF + \Delta S + X - M \qquad (6.15)$$

The third approach is given by the principal components method. The first step is the selection of a set of strategic indicators known to be strongly related to GDP. These monthly indicators come from industrial activity, expenditure, financial and monetary sectors, labor and trade. Then we extract the main independent sources of variation from this set of 15 monthly indicators, which are called the principal components. These new mutually uncorrelated variables are used as independent variables in the explanation of the quarterly GDP (see also Coutiño, 2004, 2005a). Hence we regress the quarterly GDP on the three-month average of the principal components. The following is the list of strategic monthly indicators selected:

- Manufacturing production index (IMI)
- Construction industry index (ICI)
- Industrial production index (IPI)
- Gross fixed investment index (GFII)
- Wholesale sales index (WSI)
- Retail sales index (RSI)
- Man-hours worked in manufacturing (HOUR)
- Real average wages in manufacturing (RAW)
- Employment rate (EMR percent)
- Maquiladora real exports (RMAQ)

- Volume of crude oil exports (VOX)
- Real money supply (RM1)
- Real interest rate (RIR)
- Real exchange rate (RER)
- Real tourism balance (RTOU)

After removing seasonality and trend from those monthly series, we compute the principal components (PC), and then estimate the equation for the quarterly GDP as a function of the vector of independent sources of variation.

Total GDP by principal components:

$$\underset{(850.5)}{\text{GDPqt} = 0.98} + \underset{(32.4)}{0.028\ \text{PC1}} - \underset{(0.8)}{0.00035\ \text{PC2}} + \underset{(2.6)}{0.0022\ \text{PC3}} + \underset{(2.8)}{0.0024\ \text{PC4}} \tag{6.16}$$

$$+ \underset{(1.8)}{0.0034\ \text{PC5}} - \underset{(3.2)}{0.0032\ \text{PC6}} - \underset{(0.9)}{0.0004\ \text{PC7}} + \underset{(3.6)}{0.006\ \text{PC8}}$$

$$R^2 = 0.99,\ \text{DW} = 1.94$$

With equations (6.3), (6.15) and (6.16) we compute three different values for GDP, and then average them to get a single forecast for quarterly GDP. It is important to note that these three equations for total GDP generate three independent estimates of GDP, since they use different approaches and also different sets of source variables.

Finally, in order to compute the nominal value of GDP, we need to have an equation for the price deflator (PGDP). We build this equation using the principal components methodology again. We select a set of ten monthly indicators and extract the main sources of variation. These indicators are different from those used previously for GDP estimation. Then we estimate the equation for the quarterly GDP price deflator as a function of the principal components. We include the dummy for the NAFTA effect.

GDP price deflator:

$$\underset{(202.4)}{\text{PGDPqt} = 0.98} + \underset{(48.5)}{0.11\ \text{PC1}} + \underset{(4.4)}{0.0096\ \text{PC2}} + \underset{(4.8)}{0.018\ \text{PC3}} - \underset{(1.8)}{0.0032\ \text{PC4}} \tag{6.17}$$

$$+ \underset{(2.8)}{0.0082\ \text{PC5}} + \underset{(2.0)}{0.0036\ \text{PC6}} - \underset{(2.6)}{0.0063\ \text{PC7}} + \underset{(1.4)}{0.0038\ \text{DUM9403}}$$

$$R^2 = 0.99,\ \text{DW} = 2.06$$

3. FORECAST SUMMARY

The three different approaches generate three independent estimates of quarterly GDP, which are averaged to obtain only one quarterly result. Table 6.1 summarizes the forecast process. The forecast is made every month for the current-quarter GDP and for the next three quarters. Thus the first column in the table indicates the month in which the forecast was done. We usually compute the forecast at the beginning of the month, after all the indicators are collected in the previous month. Thus the first number in the second column represents our GDP forecast of 3.8 percent for the first quarter of 2005, which was made at the beginning of November 2004. This means that our first forecast for the first quarter was made five months before the end of the first quarter, but seven months before the official release of GDP values by INEGI. Then we keep forecasting the first quarter until the beginning of May, just two weeks before the official release is announced (mid-May). The official figure is indicated at the end of the third column in brackets. We do the same for the second quarter GDP, with the first forecast made at the beginning of February 2005, seven months before the government releases the official figure in mid-August, and so on.

Table 6.1 Monthly forecasts of quarterly GDP (% change, year before)

Month	2005Q1		2005Q2		2005Q3		2005Q4	
	Fcst	Obsv.	Fcst	Obsv.	Fcst	Obsv.	Fcst	Obsv.
Nov. 04	3.8							
Dec. 04	3.6							
Jan. 05	3.8							
Feb. 05	4.2		4.3					
Mar. 05	3.8		4.1					
Apr. 05	3.1		4.0					
May 05	2.8	[2.4]	3.9		3.4			
Jun. 05			3.9		3.4			
Jul. 05			3.6		3.4			
Aug. 05			3.4	[3.1]	3.0		3.9	
Sep. 05					2.5		4.0	
Oct. 05					2.7		3.8	
Nov. 05					2.8	[3.3]	3.8	
Dec. 05							3.5	
Jan. 06							3.1	
Feb. 06							3.0	[2.7]

Note: Numbers in brackets are official releases.

Table 6.2 Monthly forecasts of GDP price deflator (% change, year before)

Month	2005Q1		2005Q2		2005Q3		2005Q4	
	Fcst	Obsv.	Fcst	Obsv.	Fcst	Obsv.	Fcst	Obsv.
Nov. 04	5.6							
Dec. 04	6.0							
Jan. 05	5.6							
Feb. 05	5.2		4.8					
Mar. 05	5.5		5.0					
Apr. 05	5.4		5.0					
May 05	5.4	[5.6]	5.1		4.8			
Jun. 05			5.2		4.8			
Jul. 05			5.4		4.9			
Aug. 05			5.5	[5.9]	5.0		4.5	
Sep. 05					5.2		4.6	
Oct. 05					5.2		4.6	
Nov. 05					5.2	[5.0]	4.7	
Dec. 05							4.8	
Jan. 06							5.0	
Feb. 06							5.1	[5.4]

Note: Numbers in brackets are official releases.

In Table 6.2, we summarize the same forecast process for the GDP price deflator, with the first forecast for the first quarter of 2005 made in November 2004, seven months before the official release.

4. FORECAST ACCURACY

In order to test the forecast accuracy, we perform repetitive forecasts for the first and second quarters of 2006, including the consecutive observed monthly information as it becomes available. Thus we evaluate the precision of the forecast every month as we use more observed information, but we can also assess the convergence direction of the forecast to the official figure.

The official figures for the quarterly GDP are released six weeks after the end of each quarter. Thus GDP for the first quarter of 2006 was released in mid-May. Also, most of the monthly indicators used in the computation of GDP by the three different approaches are released between four and six weeks after the end of the month. Based on that lead time, we test the model accuracy by performing three repetitive forecasts for the same

Table 6.3 GDP forecasts, 2006 (% change, year before)

Month	2006Q1		2006Q2	
	Fcst	Obsv.	Fcst	Obsv.
Mar. 06	5.1			
Apr. 06	5.2			
May 06	5.3	[5.5]		
Jun. 06			4.9	
Jul. 06			4.9	
Aug. 06			4.8	[4.7]

Note: Numbers in brackets are official releases.

quarter in three consecutive months. The first forecast is generated at the beginning of March 2006, which includes observed monthly information up to January, the first month of the first quarter. The second forecast is generated at the beginning of April, with observed monthly information up to February, the second month of the first quarter. Then the third forecast is performed at the beginning of May, with observed information up to the third month of the first quarter (March). We expect that the third forecast will be more precise and closer to the official figure, since it includes more relevant and complete information for the three months of the quarter.

In Table 6.3 we see that our first GDP forecast of 5.1 percent, for 2006Q1, was generated at the beginning of March. This first forecast includes two types of information-observed monthly indicators for the first month of the quarter and estimated indicators for the second and third months. Then the second forecast was done one month later, at the beginning of April, including two months of observed information (January and February) and estimated indicators for only the third month. The second forecast increases the estimate to 5.2 percent. The third forecast was done at the beginning of May (two weeks prior to the official release), and includes most of the observed information for the three months of the quarter. This third forecast raises the estimate to 5.3 percent. The official figure was released two weeks later, at the middle of May, and was 5.5 percent (as indicated by the third column), very close to our latest forecast.

We do the same exercise for 2006Q2, as illustrated by the fourth column of Table 6.3. The first forecast (generated at the beginning of June), with only one month of observed information for the second quarter, estimated the quarterly GDP growth at 4.9 percent. The second forecast, one month later, maintained the estimate at 4.9 percent, indicating that the new monthly information simply reconfirmed the previous forecast. Then the

Table 6.4 GDP price deflator forecasts, 2006 (% change, year before)

Month	2006Q1		2006Q2	
	Fcst	Obsv.	Fcst	Obsv.
Mar. 06	5.0			
Apr. 06	4.8			
May 06	4.8	[4.7]		
Jun. 06			5.8	
Jul. 06			6.2	
Aug. 06			6.6	[8.6]

Note: Numbers in brackets are official releases.

third forecast (made two weeks before the official release) indicated that the new relevant monthly information for the third month of the second quarter suggested a downward revision of our previous estimate to 4.8 percent. The official figure announced two weeks later was 4.7 percent, even closer to our previous forecast.

These two exercises show a quite good degree of accuracy of our HFF model. The model generates not only reasonably precise forecasts but also a well-defined convergence. In both quarters, the forecast convergence is always from either below or above, but not erratically such as one time up and another down. In other words, the HFF converges asymptotically to the official figure.

The same accuracy test is performed for the model of the GDP price deflator. The forecasts obtained are shown in Table 6.4. Again, the forecast precision is fairly good, and the convergence appears in both quarters of 2006.

Even though the estimates for the second quarter are less precise than those for the first quarter, the model shows a forecast improvement as soon as new relevant monthly information is added. Indeed, the forecast that was made two weeks prior to the official release is much more accurate than the forecast generated three months in advance. This suggests that any new single piece of information is relevant and adds some extra value, either to confirm or to correct the forecast.

5. A HIGH-FREQUENCY PREDICTION FOR 2007

The HFF model for Mexico has been actively in use since 2002, and the results are summarized in a monthly publication entitled *The*

Report on Mexico,[4] which is available at the website of Project LINK–United Nations at: www.chass.utoronto.ca/link/mexicocqm/mexicocqm.htm.

The latest version of the model generates forecasts for four quarters ahead. At the beginning of 2007, the model was used to forecast the four quarters of the year. Thus, from the end of 2006, the model was anticipating a slowdown of economic activity in Mexico for the calendar year 2007. Monthly economic indicators for the last quarter of 2006 already signaled slower activity, which was extrapolated to 2007 by using ARIMA equations for model input.

The main economic indicators at the end of 2006 were showing a slower Mexican economy, probably affected by a contractionary phase of the political business cycle. In 2006 there were elections and 2007 was the beginning of the new administration. The political business cycle has two well-defined phases every six years with the change of the presidential administration. The first is an expansionary phase, which covers the first six months of the last year of the outgoing government. In this phase, fiscal policy is used to spur the economy in order to produce a sentiment of well-being, which in turn might induce voters to maintain the status quo. The second is a contractionary phase, in which the fiscal stimulus is withdrawn after the election (beginning of July), and it extends until the first half of the first year of the new administration. Thus the effects of the political cycle are reflected in both an economic expansion in the last year of the outgoing government and a slowdown in the first year of the new government. This is precisely the case of 2006 and 2007. Thus GDP strongly expanded by 4.8 percent in 2006, with activity showing the two phases mentioned above: expansion in the first half and deceleration in the second half of the year.

Since the fiscal stimulus started to decelerate during the second half of 2006, and was expected to remain low during the first semester of 2007, monthly indicators were replicating that trend. This explains why the HFF model was anticipating an extended slowdown during the first half of 2007 (see Coutiño, 2007b). Hence our latest forecast for 2007Q1 was estimated at the beginning of May, two weeks before the official release, and it indicated that GDP would grow 2.3 percent, a rate lower than 4.3 percent in the previous quarter and 5.5 percent one year before. This is illustrated in Table 6.5 in the row 'average real GDP'. The forecast of 2.3 percent for 2007Q1 is the average of the three estimates obtained by different approaches: 2.8 percent from principal components, 2.2 percent from production, and 1.8 percent from expenditure.

The model also anticipated that the economy would continue to decelerate in the second quarter, with growth falling to 1.0 percent. In the third

Table 6.5 GDP forecasts, 2007

	2006 Q1	2006 Q2	2006 Q3	2006 Q4	2007 Q1	2007 Q2	2007 Q3	2007 Q4
	Observed				Estimated			
Real GDP (1993 billion pesos)								
Principal components	[1793.6	1851.7	1802.9	1900.9]	1844.4	1876.8	1845.1	1964.2
(%) change, year ago	5.5	4.9	4.5	4.3	2.8	1.4	2.3	3.3
Production side	[1793.6	1851.7	1802.9	1900.9]	1833.8	1869.1	1836.1	1954.9
(%) change, year ago	5.5	4.9	4.5	4.3	2.2	0.9	1.8	2.8
Expenditure side	[1793.6	1851.7	1802.9	1900.9]	1825.2	1862.8	1828.7	1946.1
(%) change, year ago	5.5	4.9	4.5	4.3	1.8	0.6	1.4	2.4
Average real GDP	[1793.6	1851.7	1802.9	1900.9]	1834.4	1869.5	1836.6	1955.1
(%) change, year ago	5.5	4.9	4.5	4.3	2.3	1.0	1.9	2.9
Model forecast (one month before the official release)	5.3	4.8	4.4	4.2	–	–	–	–

Note: Numbers in brackets are official figures.

quarter it was estimated that economic activity would start to recover with growth of 1.9 percent, and then would continue to grow at a rate of 2.9 percent in the fourth quarter. Thus, the model predicted that the Mexican economy would report a deceleration in 2007, with growth of only 2.0 percent in the year, after 4.8 percent in 2006.

Observed data showed that growth effectively decelerated to 2.6 percent in the first quarter, stayed decelerated at 2.8 percent in the second quarter, and started to recover in the third quarter (3.7 percent), precisely as the model predicted. Thus, even though growth did not continue to fall in the second quarter, the HFF model accurately anticipated that in 2007 Mexico would not escape from the traditional deceleration that characterizes the beginning of each new administration.

Finally, by 2006Q2 the economy was showing signs of having reached its maximum growth (see Table 6.5); then it was evident that the goal of 7 percent growth was unattainable. In fact, by then, the disinvestment process was confirmed. But since 2004, our model was showing an economy facing capacity restrictions given the fall of the investment–output ratio to 21 percent at the end of 2003 from 24 percent in the year 2000.

6. THE FORECAST FOR 2008

At the end of 2007, information on Mexican trade (non-oil) started to reflect some weakness of the US economy in the last quarter of the year. At the same time, Mexican economic activity was facing disruptions caused by supply restrictions generated by unfavorable weather conditions. Hence some moderation of the Mexican economy could be expected not only for the end of 2007 but also for the beginning of 2008.

These preliminary pieces of information, incorporated in our model, generate forecasts that indicate moderation of growth for the beginning of the year. However, since monthly indicators on domestic absorption show a continuous strengthening, given the normalization of the fiscal stimulus and the materialization of private decisions on consumption and investment, the model also predicts an acceleration of growth for the second half of the year.

Hence the high-frequency forecasts for 2008 indicate GDP growth of 2.9 percent in the first quarter, followed by 2.8 percent in the second quarter, 3.8 percent in the third, and 4.3 percent in the last quarter, as shown in Table 6.6. In this way, the model is predicting growth of 3.5 percent for 2008, indicating that the Mexican economy will be back to the expansion path, after leaving behind the traditional deceleration in the first year of the new administration (2007) and overcoming the potential weakness of the US economy in the first half of 2008.

Table 6.6 also contains the estimates generated by the model for the different aggregates of GDP (production and demand sides), GDP price deflator, and nominal GDP for 2008.

In Table 6.7, we present the forecasts for the main monthly indicators used in the three approaches of the HFF model. These are generated by ARIMA equations.

7. CONCLUSION

We can see the HFF model as a valuable and important economic instrument not only to anticipate the current-quarter GDP but also to adjust the short-term forecasts of larger-scale econometric models by providing initial values for projections from the latter. Each single piece of new high-periodicity information is extremely relevant to correct the short-term forecast. In the case of Mexico, the importance of the HFF model is demonstrated not only by its six years of use but also by its accuracy and prediction power.

This new generation of HFF models has the virtue of automatic

Table 6.6 Quarterly aggregate forecasts

	2007 Q1	2007 Q2	2007 Q3	2007 Q4	2008 Q1	2008 Q2	2008 Q3	2008 Q4
	Observed				Estimated			
Real GDP (1993 billion pesos)								
Principal components	[1839.4	1903.6	1870.5]	1982.6	1901.9	1968.3	1950.9	2077.8
(%) change, year ago	2.6	2.8	3.7	4.3	3.4	3.4	4.3	4.8
Production side	[1839.4	1903.6	1870.5]	1973.1	1890.9	1955.0	1939.7	2056.0
(%) change, year ago	2.6	2.8	3.7	3.8	2.8	2.7	3.7	4.2
Expenditure side	[1839.4	1903.6	1870.5]	1967.4	1883.6	1949.3	1932.2	2042.2
(%) change, year ago	2.6	2.8	3.7	3.5	2.4	2.4	3.3	3.8
Average real GDP	[1839.4	1903.6	1870.5]	1974.4	1892.1	1957.5	1940.9	2058.7
(%) change, year ago	2.6	2.8	3.7	3.9	2.9	2.8	3.8	4.3
Real GDP by sectors (1993 bp)								
Total GDP (production side)	[1839.4	1903.6	1870.5]	1973.1	1890.9	1955.0	1939.7	2056.0
(%) change, year ago	2.6	2.8	3.7	3.8	2.8	2.7	3.7	4.2
Primary sector	[88.3	96.7	82.6]	109.3	90.2	99.6	85.8	114.0
(%) change, year ago	0.2	3.8	5.3	2.8	2.2	3.0	3.8	4.3
Secondary sector	[445.2	465.0	469.4]	471.8	457.7	476.6	486.3	492.5
(%) change, year ago	0.6	0.8	1.8	3.2	2.8	2.5	3.6	4.4
Tertiary sector	[1157.5	1188.2	1167.8]	1232.8	1190.3	1220.7	1211.3	1283.5
(%) change, year ago	3.5	3.5	4.4	4.1	2.8	2.7	3.7	4.1
Real GDP by demand (1993 bp)								
Total GDP (expenditure side)	[1839.4	1903.6	1870.5]	1967.4	1883.6	1949.3	1932.2	2042.2
(%) change, year ago	2.6	2.8	3.7	3.5	2.4	2.4	3.3	3.8
Private consumption	[1323.0	1414.5	1466.8]	1449.7	1373.2	1473.9	1531.3	1522.2
(%) change, year ago	3.5	4.6	5.0	4.8	3.8	4.2	4.4	5.0
Public consumption	[146.0	172.0	137.8]	197.3	149.5	176.8	142.2	204.8
(%) change, year ago	−3.9	−1.6	0.7	1.8	2.4	2.8	3.2	3.8

Table 6.6 (continued)

	2007 Q1	2007 Q2	2007 Q3	2007 Q4	2008 Q1	2008 Q2	2008 Q3	2008 Q4
	Observed				Estimated			
Gross fixed investment	[405.4	422.7	428.9]	448.8	434.2	449.7	458.1	479.8
(%) change, year ago	4.9	6.9	6.0	8.1	7.1	6.4	6.8	6.9
Exports	[737.2	778.7	808.6]	840.9	760.8	798.2	839.3	875.4
(%) change, year ago	4.3	3.6	7.4	5.8	3.2	2.5	3.8	4.1
Imports	[789.8	885.3	927.6]	944.8	816.7	919.0	987.9	1012.8
(%) change, year ago	5.6	7.5	9.8	6.5	3.4	3.8	6.5	7.2
GDP price deflator (1993 = 100)								
GDP deflator	[511.9	507.0	511.4]	515.5	538.5	532.3	533.9	537.2
(%) change, year ago	4.2	−1.1	3.1	4.5	5.2	5.0	4.4	4.2
Nominal GDP (billion pesos)								
Total GDP	[9415.0	9650.6	9566.3]	10178.0	10188.5	10420.2	10363.4	11058.1
(%) change, year ago	6.9	1.7	7.0	8.5	8.2	8.0	8.3	8.6

Note: Numbers in brackets are official figures.

re-estimation of coefficients, as soon as a new piece of information becomes available, which also represents an advance with respect to the generation of structural models. In addition, the HFF is useful since it is the result of repetitive forecast analyses through time.

Finally, since these new econometric models are mechanical systems, they avoid forecast manipulation or subjective data adjustment. Professor Klein has said: 'economists are not musicians to tune up econometric models'. Hence the HFF is the result of the interaction and power of economic information and not the output of the economist's mind. In this sense, the HFF methodology teaches that 'the wind should not be an explanatory variable in the econometric model; therefore, the forecast should not change with the wind direction'.

Table 6.7 Monthly indicator forecasts

	2007						2008		
	Jul.	Aug.	Sep.	Oct.	Nov.	Dec.	Jan.	Feb.	Mar.
Production activity									
General indicator of eco.act.	[152.0	151.8	146.2	157.1]	158.9	155.9	149.7	146.2	152.2
(%) change, year ago	4.5	4.3	2.7	4.7	3.8	3.2	3.0	3.0	2.7
Industrial production index	[149.9	155.5	148.6	155.7]	153.7	147.7	148.0	142.5	154.0
(%) change, year ago	2.2	2.8	0.2	3.0	3.2	3.7	3.2	3.3	3.2
Gross fixed investment	[186.9	192.1	172.7	189.3]	188.3	199.8	192.8	175.8	189.8
(%) change, year ago	7.7	7.5	2.7	8.3	8.2	7.9	7.1	7.8	6.3
Wholesale sales index	[115.3	118.9	113.5	123.9]	127.9	126.9	112.9	107.9	121.9
(%) change, year ago	1.7	0.4	−0.9	7.6	6.9	6.6	5.9	6.0	4.3
Retail sales index	[117.6	119.7	113.8	119.4]	122.4	154.9	121.9	110.9	116.9
(%) change, year ago	4.2	3.7	2.8	4.1	4.6	4.8	3.9	3.9	2.8
Employment and wages									
Open unemployment rate									
(% of AEP)	[3.95	3.92	3.87	3.93	3.46]	3.31	3.89	3.95	3.80
Real wages in manufacturing	[98.4	100.2	96.8	98.8]	99.1	131.1	98.1	97.1	101.1
(%) change, year ago	1.1	1.7	0.9	2.4	2.3	2.0	1.9	2.0	1.8
Prices (1994 = 100)									
Consumer price index	[122.2	122.7	123.7	124.2	125.0	125.6]	126.6	127.2	127.7
(%) change	0.42	0.41	0.78	0.39	0.71	0.41	0.79	0.49	0.38
Producer price index	[122.5	123.6	124.9	125.4	126.4	126.2]	126.9	127.4	127.8
(%) change	0.71	0.90	1.02	0.37	0.80	−0.09	0.56	0.38	0.26
Oil price mex. mix ($)	[64.54	63.04	67.32	71.78	80.05	77.77]	78.59	73.59	68.77
(%) change	7.6	−2.3	6.8	6.6	11.5	−2.9	1.1	−6.4	−6.6
Financial sector									
Exchange rate (peso/$)	[10.80	11.04	11.05	10.84	10.87	10.85]	10.93	10.98	11.01
(%) change	−0.3	2.2	0.1	−1.8	0.2	−0.2	0.7	0.5	0.3
Interest rate (Cetes 28)	[7.19	7.20	7.21	7.20	7.44	7.44]	7.50	7.50	7.50

Table 6.7 (continued)

	2007						2008		
	Jul.	Aug.	Sep.	Oct.	Nov.	Dec.	Jan.	Feb.	Mar.
Stock exchange index	[31703	29486	30406	31908	29298	30043]	30164	30109	30074
External sector									
Exports (billion $)	[22.632	24.462	23.097	26.135	24.415]	22.569	20.411	21.378	23.045
(%) change, year ago	14.1	7.1	12.7	12.7	17.1	12.2	7.4	9.0	6.4
Imports (billion $)	[23.405	25.644	23.809	27.782	25.175]	23.813	21.295	22.171	23.874
(%) change, year ago	15.9	8.6	8.3	13.3	12.0	11.9	2.9	10.7	8.2
Trade balance (billion $)	[−0.773	−1.182	−0.713	−1.647	−0.760]	−1.244	−0.884	−0.793	−0.829

Note: Numbers in brackets are official figures.

NOTES

1. Also known as the tequila crisis. Details can be found in Klein and Coutiño (1996).
2. For a detailed analysis on remittances see Coutiño (2005b).
3. This model constitutes the first HFF model for the Mexican economy, and it was developed by the author as his doctoral dissertation under the supervision of Lawrence R. Klein. See Coutiño (2004), and Klein and Coutiño (1999).
4. Monthly publication by the Center for Economic Forecasting of Mexico (CKF). See CKF (2007).

REFERENCES

CKF (2007), *The Report on Mexico*, Center for Economic Forecasting of Mexico (CKF), Philadelphia, PA, www.ckf-forecasting.com, May.

Coutiño, A. (2004), *A High-Frequency Forecasting Model for the Mexican Economy*, Ph.D. dissertation, University of Madrid.

Coutiño, A. (2005a), 'On the use of high-frequency economic information to anticipate the current quarter GDP: a study case for Mexico', *Journal of Policy Modeling*, **27**, 327–44.

Coutiño, A. (2005b), 'Remittances: a new source of income for Mexico', *Dismal Scientist: LatAm*, June, Moody's Economy.com.

Coutiño, A. (2006a), 'Mexico's new law ensures fiscal discipline', *Dismal Scientist: LatAm*, March, Moody's Economy.com.

Coutiño, A. (2006b), 'An economic strategy for Mexico (2007–2012)', *Dismal Scientist: LatAm*, December, Moody's Economy.com.

Coutiño, A. (2007a), 'Winds of potential reforms in Mexico', *Dismal Scientist: LatAm*, April, Moody's Economy.com.

Coutiño, A. (2007b), 'On the accuracy of our forecast for Mexico', *Dismal Scientist: LatAm*, May, Moody's Economy.com.

Coutiño, A. (2007c), 'Can reform succeed in Mexico?', *Dismal Scientist: LatAm*, June, Moody's Economy.com.

Coutiño, A. (2007d), 'The relevance of Mexico's fiscal reform', *Dismal Scientist: LatAm*, August, Moody's Economy.com.

Klein, L.R. and Park, J.Y. (1993), 'Economic forecasting at high-frequency intervals', *Journal of Forecasting*, **12**, 301–19.

Klein, L.R. and Park, J.Y. (1995), 'The University of Pennsylvania model for high-frequency economic forecasting', *Economic and Financial Modeling*, Autumn, 95–146.

Klein, L.R. and Coutiño, A. (1996), 'The Mexican financial crisis of December 1994 and lessons to be learned', *Open Economies Review*, **7**, 501–10. Reprinted in G. Tavlas (ed.), *The Collapse of Exchange Rate Regimes: Causes, Consequences and Policy Responses*, The Netherlands: Kluwer Academic Publishers, 1997.

Klein, L.R. and Coutiño, A. (1999), 'A high-frequency model for the Mexican economy', Ciemex-Wefa, Inc., July. Reprinted in *Essays on Macroeconomic Aspects of Mexico*, Instituto Lucas Alamán de Estudios Económicos, Mexico, November 2000.

7. A high-frequency forecasting model and its application to the Japanese economy

Yoshihisa Inada

INTRODUCTION

The purpose of this chapter is to evaluate the weekly forecast performance of the Japanese economy by a high-frequency forecasting model that the author developed at the Department of Economics at Ritsumeikan University. In the following pages we first explain the development of the postwar Japanese economy for better understanding of the current Japanese economy. Then we explain the features of our high-frequency model and the forecast method in Section 2. We introduce the application to the Japanese economy of high-frequency model building based on the history of the method of estimating the preliminary figures of quarterly GDP in Section 3, followed by the presentation of a forecasting model. The forecast accuracy of the Japanese high-frequency model is evaluated in Section 4. Recent examples of forecasts based on the high-frequency model are shown in Section 5. Finally, the development of the high-frequency model forecast in the future is discussed.

1. DEVELOPMENT OF THE POSTWAR JAPANESE ECONOMY

The Japanese economy in the postwar era can be divided roughly into five periods. First, the era from the end of the war to a full-fledged high growth period is explained in 'Postwar recovery, 1945–55'. It was in 1955 that the industrial output exceeded the peak of prewar days. The second is the 'High-growth period, 1956–73' that continued, and ended with the first world oil crisis. The third period is an 'Adjustment period after the collapse of high growth, 1974–91', followed by a shift from high growth to low growth. The fourth period is the 'Long-term slump period, 1992–2001' from the bursting of the economic bubble to January 2002, the trough of the thirteenth business cycle in postwar Japan. The fifth period is the 'Gradual recovery period, 2002–present'. The above-mentioned classification is rough, in terms of the real GDP growth rate (see Figure 7.1).[1] Official business cycle dating is shown in Table 7.1.

1.1 Postwar Recovery, 1945–55

The Japanese economy in postwar days faced a chronic demand deficiency, as in prewar days, and began to build domestic demand-oriented economic growth. This was because the political and economic regime of prewar days had collapsed, and the introduction of the Constitution of Japan together with a series of economic democratization policies based on it played an important role.

The feature of economic democratization policies was based on the implementation of (1) dismissal of the financial clique (*zaibatsu*), (2) land reform, and (3) establishment of labor's primary rights. The dismissal of *zaibatsu* removed the economic base that promoted aggression and eliminated the negative effects of the monopoly firm. The democratization of the market was promoted so that a price adjustment mechanism might work. Moreover, land reform liberated the peasant people from non-democratic conditions of prewar days, based on the absentee farmer, and promoted the conversion to the landed farmer. This resulted in improving the farmer's purchasing power. The establishment of labor's primary rights guaranteed that the worker and the manager aimed at the improvement of working conditions, including pay based on fair distribution.

A series of economic democratization policies remedied the chronic demand deficiency that prevailed in prewar days, and contributed to achieving domestic demand-led growth. Additionally, the generation of external demand due to the outbreak of the Korean War in 1950, that was served by the USA as a supply base from Japan, accelerated the economic growth rate. Thus the output level of prewar days was recovered, and the Japanese economy aimed at high economic growth by 1955.

1.2 High-growth Period, 1956–73

The average economic growth rate was 9.2 percent from 1956 to 1973; this is the high-growth period. The average growth rate was 7.7 percent for the first term of the high-growth period that started in 1956 and ended in 1959, and that accelerated to 9.7 percent for the later term, that started in 1960 and ended in 1973. Looking at the real GDP growth contribution in the high-growth period, private final consumption expenditure explains 5.4

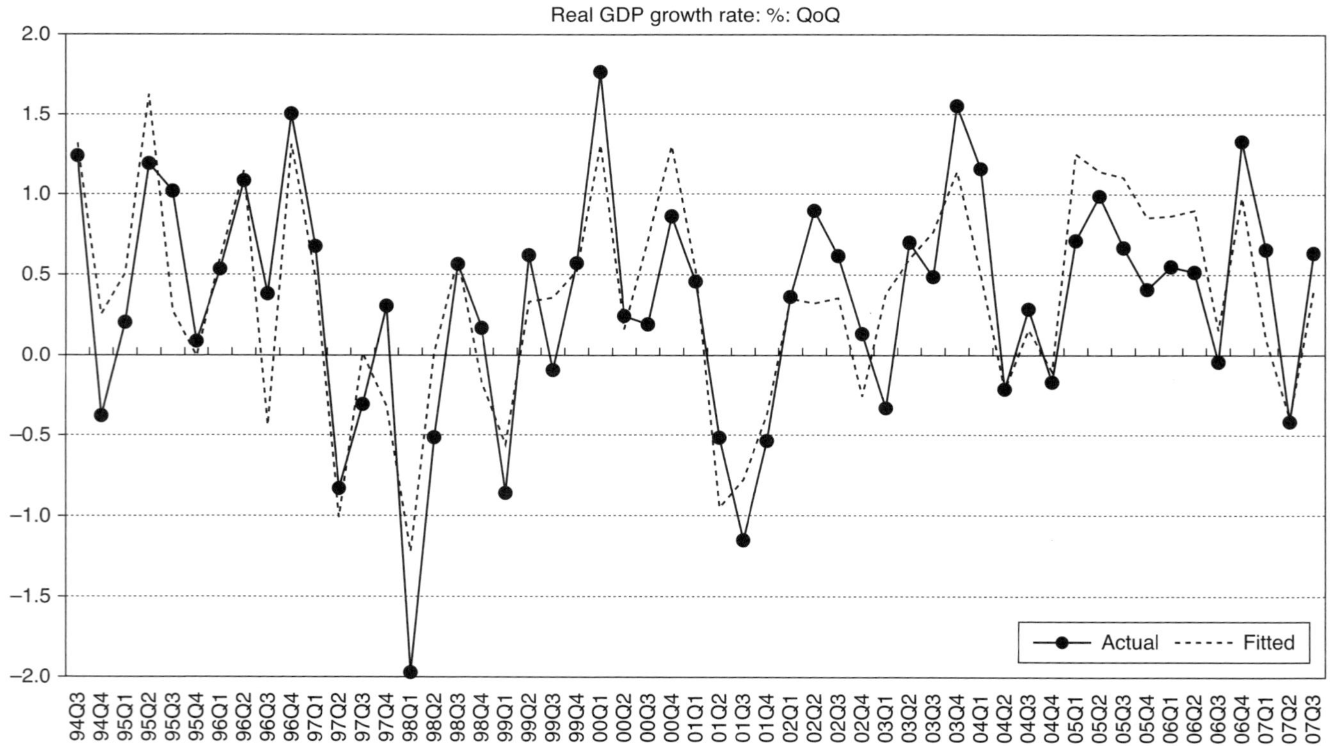

Figure 7.1 Tracking history of real GDP growth rate: regression on principal components

Table 7.1 Japan's business cycle dating

	Peak		Trough		Expansion	Contraction	Cycle	
	Year	Month	Year	Month	T to P	P to T	T to T	P to P
1st	1951	6	1951	10		4		
2nd	1954	1	1954	11	27	10	37	31
3rd	1957	6	1958	6	31	12	43	41
4th	1961	12	1962	10	42	10	52	54
5th	1964	10	1965	10	24	12	36	34
6th	1970	7	1971	12	57	17	74	69
7th	1973	11	1975	3	23	16	39	40
8th	1977	2	1977	10	22	9	31	38
9th	1980	2	1983	2	28	36	64	37
10th	1985	6	1986	11	28	17	45	64
11th	1991	2	1993	10	51	32	83	68
12th	1997	5	1999	1	43	20	63	75
13th	2000	11	2002	1	22	14	36	42
Ave. month					33.2	16.1	50.3	50.1

percentage points in overall growth. Private capital formation (residential investment, non-residential investment and changes in private inventory) was responsible for 2.6 percentage points. While public demand (government final consumption expenditure, public investment and changes in public inventory) contributed 1.5 percentage points, net exports of goods and services explained –0.3 of a percentage point. The contribution ratios to the growth rate are 58.9 percent for private final consumption expenditure, 27.7 percent for private capital formation, 16.3 percent for public demand and –2.9 percent for net exports, respectively. All the domestic demand items such as private final consumption expenditure, private capital formation, and public demand contributed to the overall growth.

As multiplier theory teaches, GDP will change only to the extent that autonomous expenditure such as private capital formation, public demand and exports changes. Exports were not yet an engine of economic growth at this time. The growth contribution ratio of private final consumption expenditure narrowed from 67.1 percent in the first term of high growth to 57.0 percent in the second term. While that of private capital formation expanded from 23.8 percent in the first term to 28.6 percent in the second term, that of public demand also increased from 11.6 percent in the first term to 17.3 percent in the later term. It is understood that private investment for plant and equipment and public investment contributed greatly to the achievement of high growth in the second term. It should be noted that the expansion of public investment supported the enhancement of productivity (the supply-side effect) through the maintenance of society's infrastructure, while having improved the growth rate through the multiplier effect (the demand-side effect). Moreover, these improved the growth expectations of enterprise. It was the adoption of a peace constitution, instead of one based on military expenditure, that enabled public investment expansion to continue as the fiscal expenditure of Japan expanded in the postwar days.

After the Bretton Woods policies collapsed in 1971, the exchange rate system shifted from a fixed rate to a floating rate. This change brought about a sharp appreciation of the yen, and the foreign price-competitiveness of Japanese products weakened. The aggregate demand support through export expansion in the recession period became difficult. Japanese corporations could not help giving priority to streamlining the efforts for the recovery of global competitiveness, and their motivation to invest weakened. Additionally, the first oil crisis occurred in October 1973, and the increasing uncertainty about the acceleration of inflation caused the decrease in corporate expectations of Japanese economic growth.[2]

1.3 Adjustment Period after Collapse of High Growth, 1974–91

The high growth of the Japanese economy was restrained by the world oil crisis. The period from 1974 to 1991, after the collapse of high growth, was an adjustment period. It might be appropriate to divide this adjustment period into the first half (1974–85) and the second half (1986–2001) after the Plaza Accord in 1985. The first half contains the peaks of the seventh business cycle (November 1973) through the tenth business cycle (June 1985), and the latter half contains the peak of the eleventh business cycle (February 1991). A gradual long-term economic recovery continued in the latter half, although a short-lived business cycle continued in the first half.

The economic growth for the first half is 3.4 percent, and that for the latter half is 4.5 percent, although the average economic growth rate for the entire adjustment period is 3.8 percent. Comparing the growth contribution of GDP items between the first half and the second half, private final consumption expenditure expanded slightly from 2.0 percentage points to 2.4 percentage points. Private capital formation recovered from 0.3 percentage points to 2.0 percentage points. The growth rate contribution of private sector demand rose in the latter half, although in the first half it declined sharply from the previous period. The contribution of public demand remained unchanged at 0.5 of a percentage point in both periods. As for the net exports of goods and services, the growth contribution in the latter half decreased to –0.4 of a percentage point from 0.6 of a percentage point in the first half. Thus it was the domestic demand-led economic growth in the first half and the domestic demand-led growth in the latter half that centered on private capital formation.

To overcome the stagflation caused by the oil crisis, the government, while tightening monetary policy with the aim to control inflation, also attempted to bring the economy out of negative growth by issuing deficit-covering bonds for the first time after the war, and expanding public works investment. Exports of autos and electric equipment increased rapidly, which turned out to be a major help in reducing inflation, but it was not expected that fiscal policy reform in 1980 would be needed. Exports have a significant impact on economic growth, and export-led economic growth continued in the first half of the period. In fact, net exports explain 19 percent of the overall growth rate for this period.

However, this export-led economic growth did not last long. Rapid increases in the trade surplus with the USA caused Japan–US trade friction, and the USA urged Japan to convert to domestic demand-led economic growth for the resolution of trade problems. The US trade deficit soared and many advanced economies had a sense of impending crisis that the dollar might suddenly fall, and the world economy would then suffer a tremendous shock. This sense of crisis caused the major powers to agree on cooperation in achieving an exchange rate adjustment to the dollar, and led to the Plaza Accord in 1985. A weak dollar and strong yen were rapidly established, and export-led economic growth became difficult. In coping with the trade friction and appreciation of the yen, the big export enterprises established the system of local production by expanding direct investments in the USA.

To avoid recession caused by the super-strong yen, the government implemented an ultra-loose monetary policy. Moreover, aggressive public works investment was expanded based on an agreement with the USA (Japan–US Structural Impediments Initiative). Excess demand for land was generated by the expansion of the demand for office building by private companies, land-use promotion, deregulation policy, and an increase in public works investment. As a result, real-estate prices soared. Escalating real-estate prices spread to other financial assets, and a bubble was generated.

The hike of asset values caused a wealth effect, stimulated household consumption, residential investment, and investment for more plant and equipment. Actually, private capital formation in the second half of the adjustment period explains 44.5 percent of the economic growth rate. Obviously the strength of this influence was very large compared with 9.7 percent in the first half of the period.

1.4 Long-term Slump Period, 1992–2001

The rise of real-estate values became abnormal from the latter half of the 1980s to the beginning of the 1990s, and inflated asset values had become a problem that could no longer be ignored. The government implemented a vigorous tightening of monetary policy. This meant a great increase in the cost of borrowing for real-estate dealers. The supply and demand condition of the real-estate market collapsed all at once, and prices fell sharply. The asset-inflated (bubble) economy collapsed. Financial institutions that had loaned money to the real-estate sector had incurred huge losses. As a result, it became imperative for the financial institutions to write off bad loans and improve management; thus full-scale restructuring started. The Japanese economy fell into a protracted slump that was called the 'lost decade'. This long-term slump period actually lasted 11 years, from February 1991 to January 2002, making it the bottom of the thirteenth business cycle.

The average real GDP growth rate from 1992 to 2001 was only 0.9 percent, which shows the realities of the protracted slump. The contribution to the overall growth of private final consumption expenditure decreased to 0.7 of a percentage point, and private capital formation posted a negative contribution of –0.4 of a percentage point. While public demand contributed 0.6 of a percentage point, net exports made no contribution to growth. Private final consumption expenditure explained 77.4 percent of the overall growth rate, and the contribution ratio rose greatly from the previous period. A sharp rise in the marginal propensity to consume suggests that households in this period consumed largely through dissaving.[3] We can easily understand why the expansion of household income was small. Private capital formation reduced the economic growth rate by 42.9 percent. Private companies gave priority to disposal of bad loans, froze capital investment, and executed a bold restructuring. On the other hand, public demand explained 60.2 percent of the overall growth. The Japanese economy would have fallen into long-term negative growth without public demand support.

1.5 Gradual Recovery Period, 2002–Present

A substantial increase in fiscal expenditure was not able to overcome the long-term slump, although it had some effect in controlling recession. The fiscal conditions of Japan deteriorated greatly, and it became an important subject of financial policy in a low-growth situation.

The Koizumi Cabinet was launched in April 2001. It cleared up the structural reform route that does not depend on financial policy, under the slogan, 'There is no economic recovery without structural reform'. The structural reform includes policies to promote the disposal of bad loans to encourage capital investment, deregulation aiming at gearing up market competition, and liquidation of the labor market, while, on the other hand, adopting belt-tightening financial policy. These supply-side policies enhance economic efficiency and aim at achieving the target of fiscal reconstruction and economic growth simultaneously.

In the early days of the government, business conditions deteriorated further because the policy included austerity measures. It was in January 2002 that the economy hit bottom. The supply-side policy strengthened the financial position of enterprise and led to the improvement of profits. Additionally, aggregate demand recovered by increasing exports, thanks to China's high economic growth. Capital investment for plant and equipment began to increase, and the economic growth rate started to rise. However, it was a gradual economic recovery that did not lead to a hike in wages, even if the financial position of enterprises improved, and the recovery of private final consumption expenditure was not taking place. A series of deregulations caused structural change in the labor market. The jobless rate fell because of an increase in the number of part-timers. As a result, the average wage per person decreased.

The average economic growth rate from 2002 to 2006 registered a modest recovery rate of 1.7 percent, higher than in the previous period. The contribution of private final consumption expenditure was 0.7 of a percentage point, and its contribution ratio decreased to 41.4 percent. The contribution of private capital formation rose to 0.5 of a percentage point, and the contribution ratio became 31.0 percent. On the other hand, the contribution of public demand was –0.2 of a percentage point, and the contribution ratio decreased to –12.6 percent. It should be noted that the contribution of net exports jumped in this period. The contribution became 0.7 of a percentage point, and the contribution ratio rose to 37.9 percent. This time the contribution and the contribution ratio of net exports rose most strongly. It can be said that a gradual economic recovery after 2002 was effected by exports and corporate capital investment.

At the time when the Koizumi Cabinet was succeeded by the Abe Cabinet in September 2006, the government announced a new economic policy. It was the so-called 'Rising tide policy' scenario. The basic idea of this growth scenario is due to Professor L.R. Klein, of the University of Pennsylvania, and Dr Yuzo Kumasaka, of ITeconomy Advisors. It is a challenging attempt to improve the potential growth rate to 3 percent or more by a bold introduction of information technology policy. Whether the Japanese economy can improve the growth rate again in conditions of a population decrease depends on whether a growth strategy can be followed or not.

2. METHOD OF THE HIGH-FREQUENCY FORECASTING MODEL

2.1 What is the High-frequency Forecasting Model?

Forecasting models are classified according to a future time horizon as follows: (1) high frequency; (2) short term; (3) medium term; and (4) long term, or super long term. In this section, we discuss the high-frequency forecasting model. High-frequency forecasting deals with prediction of official data releases. In general, data are at higher frequency than quarterly. For example, the most-watched data by the market are industrial production, jobless rate, household consumption, new housing starts, private machinery orders, consumer price index, corporate goods price index, trade data, etc. They are released at monthly frequency. Recently forecasts have been made on a daily basis (using exchange rate, interest rate and commodity prices). We cannot talk about making forecasts at higher frequency without improvements in the speed of data services.

Diffusion indices are used in a diagnosis of the current state of the economy. Diffusion indices calculate data that are compared with those of three months ago, and judge the expansion and the contraction of business. Additionally, monthly survey data such as the 'consumer confidence survey' and 'the economy watcher survey' are used for quick economic diagnosis. Data sets that can inclusively diagnose the economy are GDP accounts. However, to our regret, the frequency of publication of GDP is quarterly, at most, and the release comes with a time lag. The quarterly frequency is still the most frequent, but some countries (Canada and the UK) make monthly GDP available too.

The high-frequency forecasting model mentioned in this chapter makes the best use of news flashes and monthly data to change the forecast frequently, even at a quarterly rate. The basic idea of this model was shown by L.R. Klein of the University of Pennsylvania at the end of the 1980s, and put into practice in the 1990s (see Klein and Sojo, 1989, and Klein and Park, 1993). Since then, this idea has been applied in a number of countries. The high-frequency forecasting model, or release of the current quarter model (CQM) forecast, is made for China, South Korea, Hong Kong, Thailand, India, Mexico, Russia, France, the USA and Japan. The reports for countries can be seen on the Project LINK website (www.chass.utoronto.ca/LINK).

2.2 Key Determinants of Forecasting Accuracy

Generally speaking, (1) an accurate, stable model and (2) accurate initial conditions are necessary to achieve high-accuracy forecasts. Especially when the forecasting model is nonlinear, later versions become extremely important.

As mentioned above, the CQM establishes the statistical relations between monthly data and main entries of quarterly GDP and its composition. It is a pure econometric technique, and personal data adjustment should not enter this system. We revise current and next-quarter forecasts every week on a forward-rolling basis.

Let us think about the accuracy of the forecast by using the CQM as an example. As is generally known, GDP statistics (preliminary quarterly estimates (QE) of gross domestic expenditures (GDE)) are secondary data that are estimated from basic monthly data. QE is estimated according to a manual by the staff of the national accounts calculation unit of the Cabinet Office's Economic and Social Research Institute. If we follow their method, we can reproduce QE from the basic monthly data. The CQM contains this process in the forecast, and, in that sense, an accurate, stable model will serve the CQM.

Let us think about another condition, the setting of an accurate initial value. For instance, the first preliminary QE for the July–September quarter was released on 13 November 2007. After almost one week, the main private think-tanks announced the short-term forecast that reflected the preliminary QE. Each think-tank will decide upon the forecast values for July–September using the model. In that case, to bring the forecast value as close to the current state of the economy as possible, constant adjustments are often used (add factors). It is extrapolated arbitrarily as a way of a general constant adjustment based on past prediction error. However, some monthly data in September and October can be used. Based on these data, we can calculate add factors that exclude arbitrariness if we can decide that the current-quarter forecast value is more accurate:

$$y_t = f(x_t, \theta) + a_t$$

where y_t: explained variable,
x_t: explanatory variable,
θ: estimated parameter,
a_t: constant adjustment

The idea of the CQM by Klein stems from the need to request constant adjustments that are not arbitrary or subjective.

2.3 Forecast Procedure

The CQM incorporates information from new monthly data announced every week, and forecasts GDP weekly. Let us look more carefully at an example of CQM, the expenditure-side model approach. The CQM forecast is done in the following four steps:

1. *Preprocessing of monthly data* The data used for the model are first selected and the data are tested for a unit root. Next, a regular data-filtering process is applied, such as transforming the data to first differences to secure stationarity conditions. The monthly data actually used for the Japanese CQM (expenditure-side model) consist of about 50 variables.[4]
2. *An auto-regressive moving average (ARMA) model estimate of monthly data and forecasts six months ahead is made, setting accurate initial conditions* The ARMA is estimated for each data series that explains GDP components after conversion so that original data may retain stationary conditions, and using the data for (y_t).

$$y_t = a_1 y_{t-1} + a_2 y_{t-2} + \ldots + \varepsilon_t$$

   where ε_t: error term
   Next, the best model (or degree of the variable) is selected, for forecasts six months ahead. For the forecast performance of the ARMA model, six months or so are likely to provide very good forecasts. The forecast values of the basic data for two quarters are generated with the conversion of these forecast values for six months into quarters.
3. *Estimation of the equation, bridging the basic data that are converted quarterly and the GDE components, yielding an estimate of an accurate and stable model* Let us take residential investment as an example. We regress residential investment on construction work expenses for the dwelling. Both data are on a quarterly basis. It should be noted that these expenses, originally at monthly frequency, are now converted to quarters. This regression is called a bridge equation. If the number of basic monthly data that estimate the GDP component is one, the coefficient of the explanatory variable becomes almost one usually. The variable is transformed to first differences (*DIFF*). Bridge equations of all GDP components are estimated. The monthly data requirements for bridge equations are listed in Box 7.1 for GDP and for the GDP deflator.

BOX 7.1 DATA USED IN THE BRIDGE EQUATIONS

Monthly data explaining GDP

Household consumption, household number, retail sales
New car sales, new housing starts' floor space
Activity index for public sector
Dwelling construction works expense in schedule
Sales of information services, private machinery orders
Non-dwelling construction works expense in schedule, capital goods shipment
Public works construction in schedule
Inventory index (overall, final goods)
Foodstuff control
Customs clearance (goods export), balance of payments (transportation, tourism, other)
Balance of payments (income receipts)
Customs clearance (goods import), balance of payments (transportation, tourism, other)
Balance of payments (income payment)
Total cash earnings, employment number

Monthly data explaining GDP deflator

CPI (goods, services)
CPI (auto, imputed rental, overall)
CPI (services)
Construction cost deflator (dwelling)
Corporate service price index (software)
Input/output price index (electro machinery), CGPI (capital goods)
Construction cost deflator (public works)
Export price index, CPI (overall)
CPI (overall), import price index
Import price index, CPI (overall)

$$DIFF(JP\_IFR) = f(DIFF(w_i * \Sigma ICVDW/PCDWELL00))$$

where:

JP_IFR: real residential investment
w_i: weights for construction progress

ICVDW: construction work expense for dwelling
*PCDWELL*00: construction cost deflator

4. *Forecasts by using the bridge equation two quarters ahead: the CQM forecast* By substituting the values of two quarter estimates made in step (2) into the estimated bridge equations of GDE components, we can generate two quarter forecasts of each item of GDE and also total GDE.

Steps (2) through (4) are repeated every week, although step (1) is done quarterly. Therefore, information with new monthly data that explain GDP can be used at each forecast update every week on a forward-rolling basis. In general, the accuracy of the GDP forecast rises when fresh data can be acquired. This process is repeated until the first preliminary QE is released. Therefore the forecast value of GDP will change not only once each quarter but also every week. On a weekly basis, an appropriate judgment about the direction in which the economy is heading can be obtained by seeing the direction of the change of the forecast value. The CQM forecast gives valuable information for market economists and traders.

3. APPLICATION TO THE JAPANESE ECONOMY

The work of the CQM forecast is divided into two parts: (1) the estimation of the ARMA model and the forecast, and (2) the estimation of the relevant bridge equations. For the estimate of the bridge equation, available to the public, the estimation manual of GDP is indispensable. The estimation method of national income statistics in Japan according to the so-called 'system of national accounts'[5] in the 1970s was recommended by the United Nations. The available material concerning GDP data creation before 1998 was from the Economic Planning Agency. However, this manual was difficult for the users, and almost a black box concerning the sources that the National Income Statistics Division was using for estimation of the GDP data. The CQM for the Japanese economy started in 1993 with this difficult manual, and the method of estimating the bridge equations hardly changed until 1998, because there was little change in the method of estimating QE.

After 1998 a substantial change occurred. Each ministry and agency began to enhance their home pages, and we were able to download data more easily. The wave of data opening to the public surged, and advanced further, distributing the method of estimating GDP to the public. Additionally, the government set a goal for a quicker release of QE data. Next we explain the change in the method of estimating QE after 1998.

3.1 Changes in QE Estimation

In Japan the former QE estimation method required two months, or more, for the release of the first preliminary GDP after the end of a current quarter. However, QE is made public about one month after the end of a quarter in a number of advanced countries. Therefore, it used to take a long time for us to diagnose the Japanese economy, and this was not a desirable situation for the policy-makers. Also economists in private organizations had asked the government to speed up the release time of QE. Then the government decided to start discussing quicker release of QE.

3.1.1 The advisory committee for quicker release of GDP

This advisory committee was set up in the Economic Planning Agency in July 1998, and compiled a report concerning tentative preliminary figures of GDP in May 1999. The conclusion of the report was the following: (1) It is difficult to announce the preliminary figure at an early date by using the same basic statistics, such as former QE. (2) If a part of the demand component, for instance, gross fixed capital formation, is estimated by using other statistics, it can reduce the required time by a month or more in comparison with the use of preliminary figures. (3) However, the mean absolute difference between a tentative value estimated by such a technique and QE was a relatively large 0.7 of a percentage point (or 2.8 percent at the annualized rate) in a recent span of 12 quarters. The committee decided to set a trial period for reason (3). Concretely, the tentative value is additionally made public when QE is announced, and this practice started in the January–March quarter 1999.

3.1.2 The GDP preliminary figure exploratory committee

This committee was set up in the Economic Research Institute of the Economic Planning Agency in April 2000 after a one-year trial period for the tentative estimation values for January–March 1999 through October–December 1999. The purpose of setting up this committee was to continue to examine the strategy for estimating QE as well as the tentative preliminary figure by a new approach, reflecting the discussion about recent GDP statistics, the improvement of consumption-related statistics, and a shift to 93 SNA. The first report of this committee was announced in October 2000. Moreover, the estimation method shifted from 68 SNA to 93 SNA after the release of QE for the July–September quarter 2000. The committee produced a second report in June 2001, and unveiled a review of the tentative estimated value and an examination of the estimation method for public capital formation.

3.1.3 The new estimation method of QE

When the first preliminary GDP figure for April–June 2002 was made public, QE was revised according to the present estimation method (see Department of National Accounts, 2006) through the development of the above-mentioned reports. The present estimation method has the following features: (1) Corresponding to an environmental change that affects statistics, information mainly from supply-side statistics to estimate QE was greatly expanded, and, as a result, an economic trend can be captured more adequately. (2) Contributing to a prompt economic assessment, the release time of QE was reduced to one month plus about two weeks, and it compares favorably with timing for the world's industrialized countries. (3) Consistency is improved in estimating annual and quarterly GDP series. (4) Additionally, an estimation technique that puts more emphasis on quarter-to-quarter change than year-on-year change was adopted. (5) A flexible execution of retroactive revision was made, and (6) the method of seasonal adjustment was changed and improved. After 1998, the estimation method of private final consumption expenditure and private investment for plant and equipment was frequently changed. The biggest change was that for the chain-linking method, applied to Japan's SNA from the second preliminary GDP for July–September 2004, and the annual revision for fiscal year 2003. Japan shifted from the familiar fixed-base-year method to the chain-linking method. It should be noted that additivity of GDP components is not compatible with the chain-linking method.

As briefly summarized above, the method of estimating QE has become unstable in the short term although these changes will improve the estimation accuracy of GDP in the long term. Therefore, securing the accuracy of the forecast for the person who takes charge of the forecast becomes very difficult. From the viewpoint of reform of QE, it was really the age of *Sturm und Drang* after 1998.

3.2 NIPA versus SNA

While the USA did not adopt the SNA system and instead has its own method, called the national income and product accounts (NIPA), Japan has adopted SNA and began to maintain national income statistics from the 1970s.

All expenditure, production and income sides of GDP are released at annual frequency in both Japan and the USA. At quarterly frequency, the data for only the expenditure and income sides of GDP for Japan and the USA are made public. Although only employee remuneration is made public every quarter for Japan, the data release frequency of other income-side GDP components is once a year. As for the production-side GDP, neither Japan nor the USA makes data public at quarterly frequency. While the first and the second preliminary figures are unveiled for the expenditure-side GDP in Japan, three versions of advance, preliminary and final expenditure-side GDP are released in the USA.

The data on expenditure, production and income-side GDP are not estimated at monthly frequency for Japan. Monthly data of private consumption and capital investment are made public for the USA as well as the base of the quarterly data. Also, some income-side GDP items, such as household income, etc., are made public.

3.3 Alternative Approach: Principal Components Analysis Model

As the methodology of the US forecast, Klein advocates a three-sided approach for (1) the expenditure side, (2) the income side, and (3) the production side. Moreover, the mean value of the growth rate forecast from three models is recommended as the best single growth rate forecast.

Expenditure-side approach:

$$\text{GDP} = \text{C(Consumption)} + \text{I(Fixed investment)} + \Delta\text{H(Inventory change)} + \text{G(Government expenditure)} + \text{E(Exports)} - \text{M(Imports)}$$

Income-side approach:

$$\text{GDP} = \text{W(Wage income)} + \text{YF(Corporate income)} + \text{IN(Interest)} + \text{R(Rental)} + \text{TI(Indirect tax)} - \text{S(Subsidy)}$$

Production-side approach:

$$\text{GDP} = \text{GP(Gross output)} - \text{IP(Intermediate products)} = \text{VA(Value-added)}$$

Which model is actually used depends on the release frequency of GDP data, although it is natural that three approaches to explain GDP are recommended by the principle of the three-sided equivalence of GDP as the forecasting model. Three-sided GDP data are not released at the same frequency, as seen in the previous section.

In the first two forecasting models, the bridge equations that tie monthly data to each item of quarterly GDP are used. However, the forecast by the third approach, the production-side model, cannot be made at quarterly frequency because production-side GDP data (value-added) are released only at annual frequency in Japan. Therefore, an alternative approach has been adopted for a production-side model, using principal components analysis to forecast the aggregate data such as real GDP, and the GDP deflator based on production-related monthly data. As a result, the CQM forecast for the USA is done by three models: (1) expenditure side, (2) income side, and (3) principal components analysis.

For the Japanese CQM, the expenditure-side approach plays a central role, while the income-side approach is not adopted. The frequency is once a year, when the quarterly series of income-side GDP items are released. It is only employee remuneration among the income-side data that is made public in every quarterly report as a part of QE. Due to such constraints, we do not have an income-side model in the Japanese CQM. Instead, we adopt a principal components approach as in the US CQM. See Klein and Özmucur (2007) for forecasting by the principal components analysis model in detail. We explain the approach in the next section. The mathematical statistics used for the principal components approach are explained in detail in the chapter by Özmucur and Klein in this volume (Chapter 10).

3.3.1 Variables in principal components analysis model

Fifteen monthly variables used for the principal components calculation of real GDP are:

- index of industrial production,
- index of industrial inventories,
- household consumption expenditures in real terms,
- retail sales in real terms,
- real construction work expense for dwellings,
- real private machinery orders,
- real public investment,
- export volume,
- import volume,
- number of employees,
- ratio of job offers to seekers,
- monthly case earnings,
- terms of trade,
- exchange rates, and
- interest rate differentials.

These variables correspond to those used to calculate the principal components of the US model.

Six variables used for the principal components calculation of the GDP deflator are as follows:

- nationwide CPI (overall),
- domestic CGPI,
- construction cost deflator for dwellings,
- construction cost deflator for public works construction,
- import price index, and
- monthly cash earnings.

To remove the seasonality and the trend, all monthly variables except interest rate differentials are seasonally adjusted, and are divided by the trend. Interest rate differentials are deviations from trends. Such filtering is done beforehand.

Corresponding monthly data are converted into quarterly values as the next step, and the principal components are calculated based on the adjusted variables. We regress real GDP and the GDP deflator on the principal components as explanatory variables.

3.3.2 Estimation of principal components

Principal components analysis is a well-known technique in sociology and psychology. In the field of econometrics, it is often used as a technique of variable selection to avoid multicollinearity (see Maddala, 1992). Here, we provide a basic explanation.

If we use k explanatory variables, we can estimate the following linear functions.

$$z_1 = a_{1,1}x_1 + a_{1,2}x_2 + \ldots + a_{1,k}x_k$$

$$z_2 = a_{2,1}x_1 + a_{2,2}x_2 + \ldots + a_{2,k}x_k$$

We choose the as so that variance of z_1 is maximized subject to the condition that $a_{1,1}^2 + a_{1,2}^2 + \ldots + a_{1,k}^2 = 1$. Then z_1 is said to be the first principal component. It is the linear function of the xs that has the highest variance. Next, we consider the linear function z_2 such that it is uncorrelated with z_1 and has maximum variance subject to the condition that $a_{2,1}^2 + a_{2,2}^2 + \ldots + a_{2,k}^2 = 1$. Then z_2 is said to be the second principal component. Following this procedure, we find k linear functions $z_1, z_2, \ldots, z_k$. We can also show that

$$\text{var}(z_1) + \text{var}(z_2) + \ldots + \text{var}(z_k) = \text{var}(x_1) + \text{var}(x_2) + \ldots + \text{var}(x_k).$$

But unlike $x_1, x_2, \ldots, x_k$, which may be highly intercorrelated, $z_1, z_2, \ldots, z_k$ are mutually orthogonal or uncorrelated. Instead of regressing y on $x_1, x_2, \ldots, x_k$, we regress y on $z_1, z_2, \ldots, z_k$. In doing this we obtain a relationship between y and $x_1, x_2, \ldots, x_k$, because the x variables are directly related to the z variables. This is an appealing point in using principal components and we regress y on only a subset of the principal components, namely that subset that shows a significant relation to the dependent variable y.

The first principal component (z_1) is computed as a linear combination of the series in the group with weights given by the first eigenvector (Vector 1). The second principal component (z_2) is the linear combination with weights given by the second eigenvector (Vector 2) and so on.

The eigenvalues are characteristic roots of successive correlation matrices. If we divide an eigenvalue by the total number of variables, this is equal to the fraction of the variance of the original variables accounted for by the principal component. The cumulative proportion means that if we use all 15 principal components for prediction of GDP, we can account for the total variation of the main indicators. If we use component 1, however, we can account for only 36 percent of the total variation of the 15 representative indicators in the case of the Japanese data. If we use the first two components, then we can explain almost 57 percent of the total variation, and so on. The first nine components explain 96 percent of the total variation. We have used these nine components to search for statistically significant variables to explain GDP.

3.3.3 Estimated equation: real GDP

The regression of percentage change in real GDP on six (first-difference) principal components of the 15 indicators is the choice for estimating Japan's output. An autoregressive moving average (ARMA) correction of residuals is also included. The principal components used account for 96 percent of the total variation of the original set of 15 indicators. The regression covers the period 1994Q3 to 2007Q3, including 53 observations and is estimated using ordinary least squares (OLS).

In the estimation, we select the first, third, fourth, sixth, eighth and ninth principal components in the equation. The multiple correlation coefficient shows that the variation in all six principal components accounts for 70 percent of the variation of real GDP. There is no significant serial correlation in error terms of the regression. Figure 7.1 shows the estimated growth rate of quarterly real GDP.

3.3.4 Estimated equation: GDP deflator

In a similar analysis of the GDP deflator, we find that five principal components explain 98 percent of the total variation of the original set of variables, but in the final estimate, we select first, second, third and fifth principal components to explain the GDP deflator. A regression of the percentage change of the GDP deflator on the first difference of four components with moving average residual variation reveals that the regression equation approximately reproduces the historical values of the GDP deflator (see Figure 7.2). As Figure 7.2 shows, Japan's economy entered a deflationary phase except during April–June 1997, when the government raised the consumption tax rate.

4. ACCURACY OF HIGH-FREQUENCY FORECASTING MODEL: THE JAPANESE CASE

For the estimation method of QE in the 68 SNA period, the following problems occur: (1) The final version of the GDP estimate uses supply-side statistics, while QE uses mainly demand-side statistics. Thus the final estimate of QE might be revised. (2) There is a possibility that adequate accuracy cannot be reached by mainly using demand-side statistics when QE is estimated because such statistics are from sample surveys. (3) The timing of the QE release is much slower than that of major advanced countries.

Problems (1) and (2) are related to estimation of private consumption expenditure and non-residential investment that have big weights in GDP. Additionally, a problem has occurred in the method of estimating public investment.

From the viewpoint of forecast accuracy of GDP, the estimation model is very stable and the CQM forecast is expected to show high performance in the period of 68 SNA because there was little change in GDP estimation, but some problems in the estimation methods are pointed out.

In the transition period to 93 SNA, further improvement of the GDP forecast accuracy was expected because a detailed estimation manual was completely open to the public. But the stability of the method of estimating GDP was frequently modified. After the shift to 93 SNA, the forecast accuracy is seen over the whole sample period when the accuracy of the CQM is evaluated separately for the time of 68 SNA and of 93 SNA.

On a weekly basis, the CQM forecast for the Japanese economy, which began at Ritsumeikan University in December 1993, was transferred to Konan University from April 1995 onwards.[6] At 3 December 2007, the number of weekly forecast reports was 707. The forecast record, in machine-readable format, has been preserved from July–September 1994 until the present time. Summary accuracy results are in Table 7.2.

Now the CQM announces the forecast result of both models, from the expenditure side and from principal components analysis. However, only the forecast value of the expenditure-side model is indicated in Table 7.2 because the forecast by principal component analysis started from 2004, and the sample size is small.

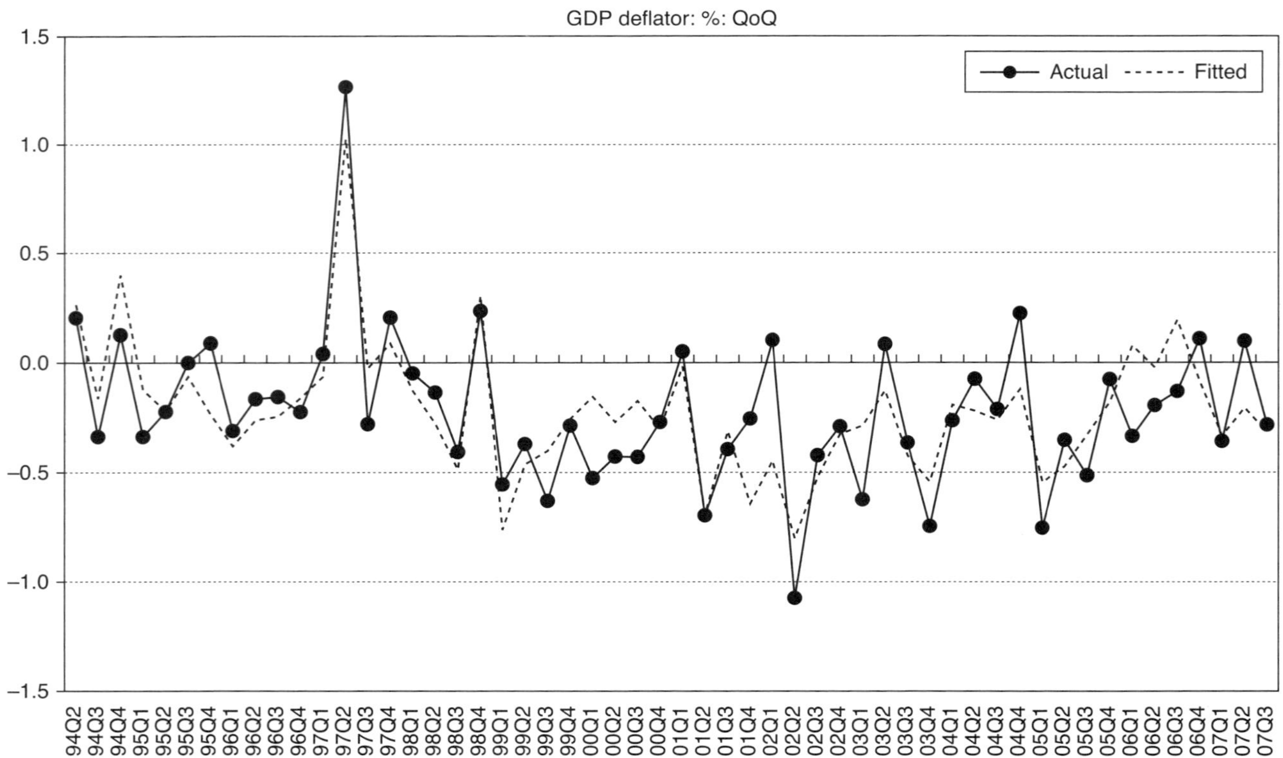

Figure 7.2 *Tracking history of GDP deflator inflation: regression on principal components*

Table 7.2 Mean absolute error (%) current quarter model GDP (1994Q3–2007Q3)

	Fourth week after initial estimate	Eighth week after initial estimate	Final week
Total period	2.3	1.9	1.7
93 SNA	1.8	1.4	1.6
68 SNA	2.8	2.5	2.0
GDP deflator (2000Q4 – 2007Q3)			
93 SNA (only)	0.3	0.3	0.4

After the first QE release, it takes three months until the first QE of the next quarter is made public. It takes 11 weeks at the earliest and 15 weeks at the latest, due to the release schedule. When entering the 93 SNA period, it takes 12 or 13 weeks, on average, because the release time is shortened. The forecasts of real GDP growth at the fourth week, the eighth week and the final week during the corresponding quarter are listed respectively in tabulations for computing the weekly forecast records. Specifically, the first QE for July–September 2007 was released on 13 November. The forecast of GDP for the corresponding quarter had already started in the following week, when the first QE for January–March was made public (17 May). The following week, when the first QE for April–June was made public (on 13 August), is assumed to be the first week of the forecast. Following the fourth and eighth week, the last week prior to when the first QE for July–September was released is assumed to be a final week forecast. Here, we count the forecast number from when QE in the previous quarter was made public to when the QE was released in the current quarter.

Figures 7.1 and 7.2 show the tracking history of the Japanese CQM from the July–September 1994 period to the July–September 2007 period including the fourth week, the eighth week, and the final week in all 53 quarters.

The correlation coefficient of the forecast value of the real GDP growth rate at the fourth week and QE is 0.472 when using the whole sample period. The correlation coefficient of the forecast value at the eighth week and QE is up to 0.65, when new information for another four weeks is added. The correlation coefficient rises to 0.680 at the final week. It is a feature of the CQM forecast that the accuracy of the forecast rises clearly as new monthly indicators are included. Thus the CQM forecast reacts to the dynamism of the economy on a weekly basis.

4.1 Forecast Accuracy of Real GDP Growth in the Period of 68 SNA

Next, let us evaluate the forecast performance separately for the 68 SNA period and the 93 SNA period (through July–September 2007). The forecast values of the real GDP growth rates for 68 SNA correlate 0.52 at the fourth week, at the eighth week 0.69 and at the final week 0.76. The corresponding correlations are 0.35, 0.56 and 0.46 for 93 SNA.

On two occasions the direction of the change (plus or minus) was forecast by mistake among 25 forecasts in the 68 SNA period. In this period the correlation coefficient of forecast at the fourth week and QE was 0.521. It can be said that the forecast accuracy at the final week is far higher than the mean accuracy value of a private think-tank.[7]

Looking at the differences between the forecast value and QE, the mean absolute value of difference between the final week CQM forecast and QE is a small 2.0 percentage points. As mentioned before, the Economic Planning Agency developed a tentative estimate of GDP that can reduce release time by one month or more. According to this simulation, estimates differ from QE by 0.7 of a percentage point (or 2.8 percentage points at the annualized rate). This equals the forecast performance of the fourth week (2.8 percentage points) in the CQM. The fourth week's forecast is available about two months earlier than QE is released. That is, the CQM forecast has shown the same performance as the accuracy of the tentative simulation at an early stage by about two months. In our experience, the CQM forecast advances the market consensus by one or two months. Accurate prediction of economic growth one or two months earlier from the market consensus becomes a big advantage of the CQM forecast.

4.2 Transition to 93 SNA and Forecast Accuracy of Real GDP Growth

Next, let us see the forecast performance after the period of introduction of 93 SNA. In Table 7.2, as expected, the forecast performance in the 93 SNA period seems to improve (lower mean absolute error) compared with the 68 SNA period. It is thought that there are frequent changes in the GDP estimation method.

Among 28 forecast quarters, the number of incorrect forecasts of the direction of the change (plus or minus) increased to five times in the 93 SNA period. However, it should be noted that there is a reason for a mistake in the direction of the change, because the growth rate is quite low, and the differences between actual and forecast are not large. At the fourth week, the correlation coefficient of the forecast and QE is 0.36. At the eighth week, it is 0.56. But at the final week, it falls to 0.45, lower than that of the eighth week. There is still room for improvement in that the forecast accuracy at the final week was lower than the eighth week's forecast.

After 1998, the estimation method of QE was frequently changed, especially as regards private final consumption expenditure with the highest share in GDP. For instance, the consumption data of the single-person families of 'the household survey' are temporarily used to improve the estimated accuracy for overall household consumption; however, the use of the data was frozen in one year. And 'the survey of the household economy' was newly invoked to improve the estimate accuracy of expenditures for consumer durable goods. Such a change in estimation is frequently introduced. In that sense, it can be said that the decrease in predictive power cannot be avoided.

The feature of the CQM forecast is a combination of the bridge equation with the ARMA model forecast. A frequent change in the estimation method means that a stable estimate of the bridge equation becomes difficult.

Still, the mean absolute value of the difference between the growth rate forecast and QE is 1.6 percentage points and lower than the result of the tentative simulation of the final week, and forecast errors shrink from the 68 SNA period.

5. A RECENT EXAMPLE OF THE CQM FORECAST

The CQM forecast has been used not only for the weekly analysis but also for the quarterly forecast. The macroeconomic analysis project team of the Kansai Institute for Social and Economic Research (KISER) has been regularly commenting on the business climate analysis as 'Business Trend Analysis and Forecast'.[8] This project team is composed of researchers at KISER, academic people, and young corporate persons who participate from the member companies of KISER. It has a history of 30 years or more as a joint research group of young employees and academic circles in the Kansai area, and the forecast result is used widely. I succeeded to the chair of this project in 2005, although it had been established under Professor Emeritus Chikashi Moriguchi and Professor Kanemi Ban of Osaka University.

This project was also formed as a new attempt to combine the forecast from conventional macroeconometric models with the CQM forecast. Actually, the CQM's latest forecast is used as an input to the current and next quarter forecast for the quarterly econometric model, and this contributes to the more accurate forecasts of quarterly growth patterns. Also, the quarterly forecast of KISER is used for the Pacific Economic Outlook (PEO) project of the Pacific Economic Corporation Council (PECC).

The CQM forecast forum for Japan, the USA and China[9] is established at KISER and, on a monthly basis, economic outlooks for the three major economies are announced, and information is offered to the member companies. The CQM forecast has been positively used not only for weekly but also for monthly and quarterly analysis.

6. CONCLUDING REMARKS

The CQM, an idea of Professor Klein, is the forecasting model that combines time-series analysis (the ARMA model) and the national accounts system (GDP) or NIPA. It is somewhat different from familiar econometric models that include structural equations in the system. The Konan University CQM, which applies this idea to the Japanese economy, has shown a very good forecast performance for more than ten years. However, frequent changes in the national method of estimating GDP after 1998 has reduced the forecast accuracy of the model. However, the CQM forecast is about one or two months earlier than the market consensus, and information obtained from the dynamics of the CQM is very useful for market participants. Future tasks are to extend the forecast horizon from two quarters at present to four quarters, while maintaining forecast accuracy.

NOTES

1. The real GDP growth rate, 1956 through 1988, is calculated from GDP at 1990 prices and based on a fixed-base-year method. The real GDP growth, 1994 through 2006, is at 2000 prices and based on the chain-linking method. The real GDP growth rate including the long-term slump period is in terms of a fixed-base-year method for 1992 through 1994 and in terms of a chain-linking method for 1995 through 2006. Consistent data for 1988–94 are supplied by the author.
2. For corporate expectations of Japanese economic growth, see Economic Social Research Institute of the Cabinet Office (ESRI's) *Annual Survey of Corporate Behavior*. Time-series data for growth expectation of the corporate sector can be downloaded from http://www.esri.cao.go.jp/en/stat/ank/ank-e.html.
3. For the estimation of the propensity to consume in a salaried worker's household, see Inada (2004).
4. See Department of National Accounts (2006) for the basic monthly data used to estimate QE. Only typical, indispensable data are used in the CQM, although a great number of data are used in an actual GDP estimate.
5. In 1968, the United Nations developed the national income calculation method or system of national accounts (hereafter, SNA) to measure the economic power of every country in the world quantitatively and made the estimation manual public. It was recommended to estimate GDP based on this manual. Each country shifted to SNA based

on this recommendation. They are known as 68 SNA. As the social economic climate changed, a new estimation manual was made public in 1998 (hereafter, 93 SNA).

6. The CQM forecast continues to be made at Konan University. The forecast report is announced every other week in Japanese and in English. An English report can be downloaded from the website of Project LINK: http://www.chass.utoronto.ca/LINK.
7. For the market consensus, see the ESP forecast survey that started in May 2004 by the Economic Planning Association. Data can be downloaded from the website http://www.epa.or.jp/.
8. The report can be downloaded from http://www.kiser.or.jp/research/project_old.html.
9. The forum was set up in cooperation with Dr Yuzo Kumasaka and Wendy Mak, visiting researcher of the University of Pennsylvania.

REFERENCES

Department of National Accounts, Economic and Social Research Institute, Cabinet Office (2006), *The Estimation Method of Quarterly GDP (QE)*, 5th edn.

Economic Planning Agency (1978), *View and How to Use the New SNA*, Tokyo: Government Printing Office.

Inada, Yoshihisa (2004), 'Japanese household consumption and survey data', *Konan Economic Papers*, **45** (3).

Inada, Yoshihisa (2005), 'High-frequency forecasting model for the Japanese economy: an application of the principal components approach', *Konan Economic Papers*, **45** (4).

Inada, Yoshihisa (2007), 'Konan University current quarter model forecast for the Japanese economy', Project LINK website: www.chass.utoronto.ca/LINK.

Klein, L.R. and S. Özmucur (2007), 'The University of Pennsylvania models for high-frequency macroeconomic modeling', Project LINK website: http://www.chass.utoronto.ca/LINK.

Klein, L.R. and J.Y. Park (1993), 'Economic forecasting at high-frequency intervals', *Journal of Forecasting*, **12**, 301–19.

Klein, L.R. and E. Sojo (1989), 'Combination of high and low frequency data in macroeconometric models', in L.R. Klein and J. Marquez (eds), *Economics in Theory and Practice: An Eclectic Approach*, Dordrecht/Boston, MA: Kluwer, pp. 3–16.

Maddala, G.S. (1992), *Introduction to Econometrics*, 2nd edn, New York: Macmillan.

8. The making of national economic forecasts: South Korea

You Chan 'Kevin' Chung

OVERVIEW OF SOUTH KOREA (SEE BOX 8.1)

South Korea's economy, according to the 2008 World Bank report, is ranked fourteenth in the world in terms of gross national income.[1] In terms of per capita gross national income, South Korea is ranked as forty-ninth in the world.[2] It is an impressive statistic considering that this was achieved in a little over half a century, after the devastating aftermath of the Korean War in 1953, which resulted in the separation of the peninsula into two nations with virtually no infrastructure left. This rapid

BOX 8.1 SOUTH KOREA AT A GLANCE

- Full name: The Republic of Korea
- Population: 48.4 million (UN, 2006), still growing
- Capital: Seoul
- Area: 99 sq. km (38 345 sq. miles)
- Major language: Korean
- Major religions: Buddhism, Christianity
- Life expectancy: 75 years (men), 82 years (women) (UN)
- Monetary unit: won
- Main exports: Electronic products, machinery and transport equipment
- Gross national income per capita: US$17 690 (World Bank, 2008, p. 15)
- Internet domain: .kr
- International dialling code: +82

Source: BBC.com (http://news.bbc.co.uk/1/hi/world/asia-pacific/country_profiles/1123668.stm)

development of South Korea is exemplified by its membership in OECD in 1996 and its becoming one of the world's largest producers of semiconductors by conglomerates, such as Samsung and LG, while Hyundai and Kia and Daewoo (Now GM–Daewoo) have become significant automobile producers and exporters. South Korea is also known for heavy industry, producing steel and other basic products. In construction, Korean workers have lent their know-how to the Middle East. This rapid development came after the Korean War as an impressive achievement.

Economic reform in South Korea after the Korean War was led by General Park Jung Hee, who took power through a military *coup* in 1961. Starting with a large investment in education, the country's first five-year economic development plan (1962–66) was a success in which the country was transformed from a predominantly agricultural society into a modern manufacturing society, where vast arrays of consumer products were made and exported. Transportation and communication infrastructure were built to keep up with the country's rapid industrialization. Within a decade, South Korea added capital-intensive heavy industry. By the 1980s, South Korea had become a major steel-producing nation. POSCO (Pohang Iron and Steel Company) is ranked second in terms of size for the production of iron and steel.[3] Income per capita increased from $87 to $5199 in a span of 27 years (from 1962 to 1989). As a result, South Korea joined the per capita income ranking shared by Israel, Hong Kong, Singapore and Taiwan, overtaking countries such as Mexico, Argentina and Hungary (Harvie and Lee, 2003). Coupled with this, and the successful Olympic Games in Seoul in 1988, the 1990s saw continued progress in South Korea's per capita income. It exceeded $10 000 for the first time. The 35-year period of extraordinary growth gave hope to many developing countries.

While the country's economic performance prior to 1996 is often referred to as the 'Miracle on the Han River', by no means did South Korea's economy follow a smooth path after that date. Underlying the miracle of growth, there were structural as well as political weaknesses. In the midst of strong economic growth, the assassination of General Park Jung Hee in 1979 brought about political turbulence, and General Chun Do Hwan's *coup* followed in a rise to power that led to an uprising at Gwangju City in 1980, where hundreds died as troops fired into a crowd of people, and brought about political instability. Furthermore, the revelation of corruption in government was made public, and two past presidents, Roh Tae Woo and Chun Do Hwan, were charged with bribery in 1993. Structurally, government-backed policy that often regulated and controlled the economic environment in the period after the Korean War inevitably led to close relationships between government officials and conglomerates. This resulted in improper business practices, where loans often lacked proper risk assessment. By the mid-1990s, a substantial accumulation of non-performing loans was evident, and in January 1997, a *chaebol* (conglomerate), the Hanbo Steel Company, went bankrupt, followed by Sammi Steel in March 1997, Kia Motors, and other troubled conglomerates, which went bankrupt or entered a bailout program administered by banks.[4] By the end of the year, South Korea requested a bailout package of $58.3 billion from the International Monetary Fund.

Many citizens thought that the cause of South Korea's economic crisis in 1997 was due to Thailand's baht currency crisis, which happened in August 1997. It is suggested that Asia as a whole struggled, and one fall led to another; thus a Korean crisis was inevitable in a timeframe that was too short for any prediction. However, closer study of the events in 1997 shows that, even before Thailand's baht currency crisis in the summer of 1997, where Thailand would turn to IMF for relief, South Korea was experiencing events that contributed to the snowballing of a crisis. The Hanbo collapse in January 1997, and labor unrest at Kia in February 1997,[5] are all signals or indications of what was to unfold in the next ten months, namely, the full East Asian financial crisis.

Possibly a functioning economic policy model might have been able to forecast trouble ahead as soon as fresh information became available. The advantage of a high-frequency economic forecasting model, featured in many national economies in this volume, is that it is designed so that indicators are often available before bankruptcy is declared, thus allowing one to peer into the future. For example, modeling South Korea's GDP, using 31 monthly indicators, could have enabled one to forecast GDP in a quarterly timeframe. The choice of monthly indicators is broadly based on knowledge of the structure of the economy. We seek indicators that represent and influence short-run economic performance. For example, as can be seen from the data, the historic time series of South Korea's GDP (Figure 8.1) follows a pattern similar to those of the monthly data sets that are readily available (Figure 8.2). More specifically, since South Korea is known for its automobile, steel and construction industries, it is appropriate to model the GDP of South Korea by using these three indicators (along with others) that have similar behavior as shown in Figure 8.2.

All three industries in Figure 8.2 show that their data-series movements resemble the movement of GDP. These data sets are available in monthly form, and are published before the quarterly output of GDP becomes available. They are the basis for the high-frequency forecasts that anticipate what lies ahead for the economy of South Korea.

This volume specifically tackles this problem and emphasizes the

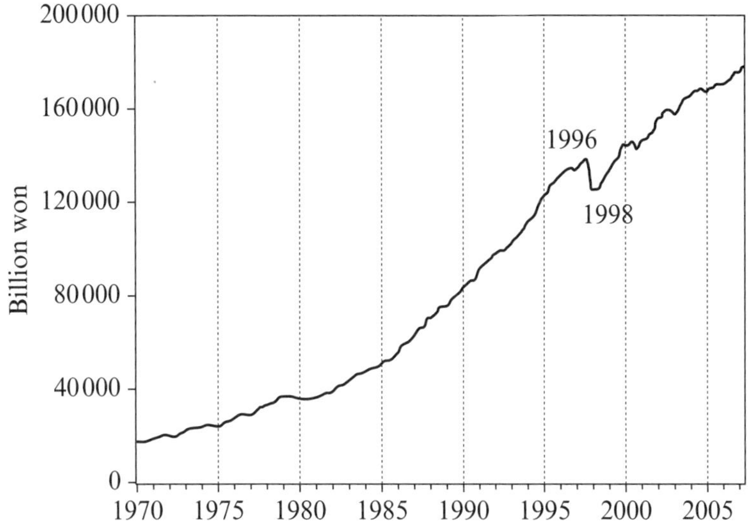

Figure 8.1 South Korea's GDP (2000 constant price, SA)

feasibility of using the frequent information that is constantly being updated to help forecast what might happen tomorrow, next month or next year. The high-frequency model takes advantage of the wide availability of data sets that are updated every day, month or quarter. In the twenty-first century, data gathering of different indices is constantly being improved. High-frequency model building takes advantage of the wealth of readily available information.

This chapter on South Korea presents high-frequency models of GDP, consumer/producer price indices (C/PPI), employment/unemployment and imports/exports. Each model consists of different indicators ranging in number from 30 to 39, chosen based on the specific knowledge of the market as well as the availability of data sets from both the National Statistical Office[6] and the Bank of Korea.[7] Efforts were made to study the indicators in real terms. For example, if there were manufacturing indices in volume and in current prices, the volume index was preferred. In situations where current price data, alone, were available, prices in US dollars were preferred over those in won. The employment/unemployment and import/export models are relatively new, over a shorter historic time period. However, for GDP, CPI and PPI, the track record for testing performances reaches close to two years in their respective frequencies. Each subsection begins with an introduction followed by the summary forecast.

(a) Automobile industry

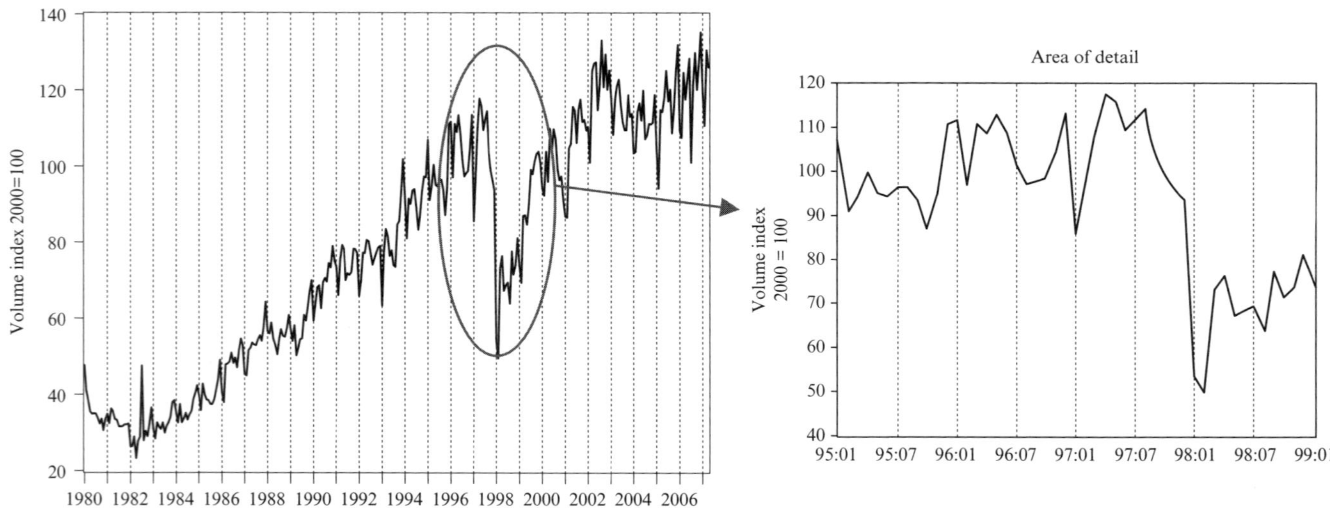

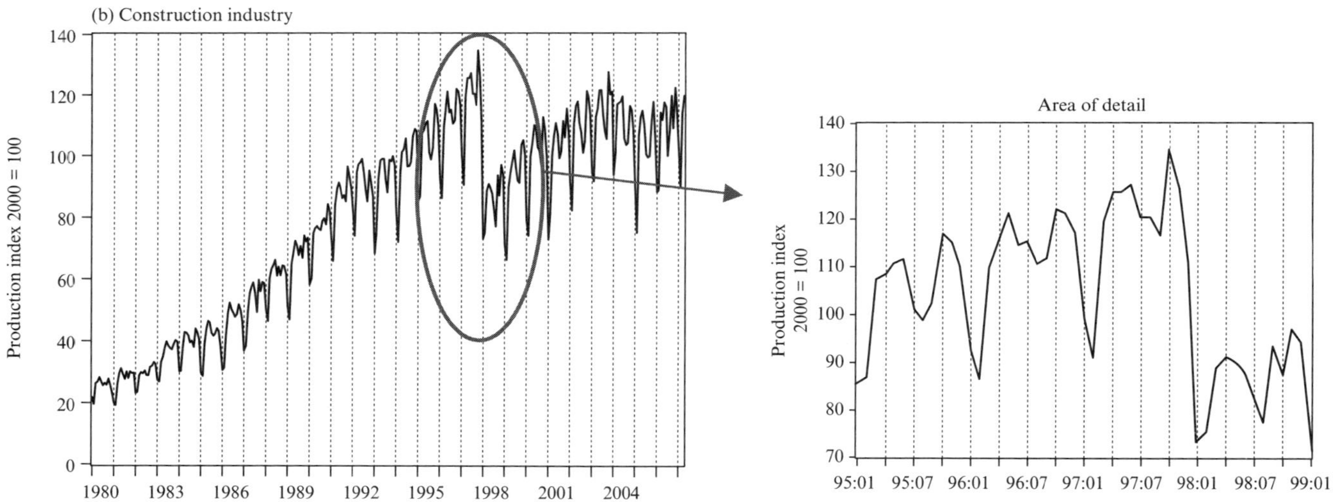

Figure 8.2 South Korea's automobile, construction and steel industries

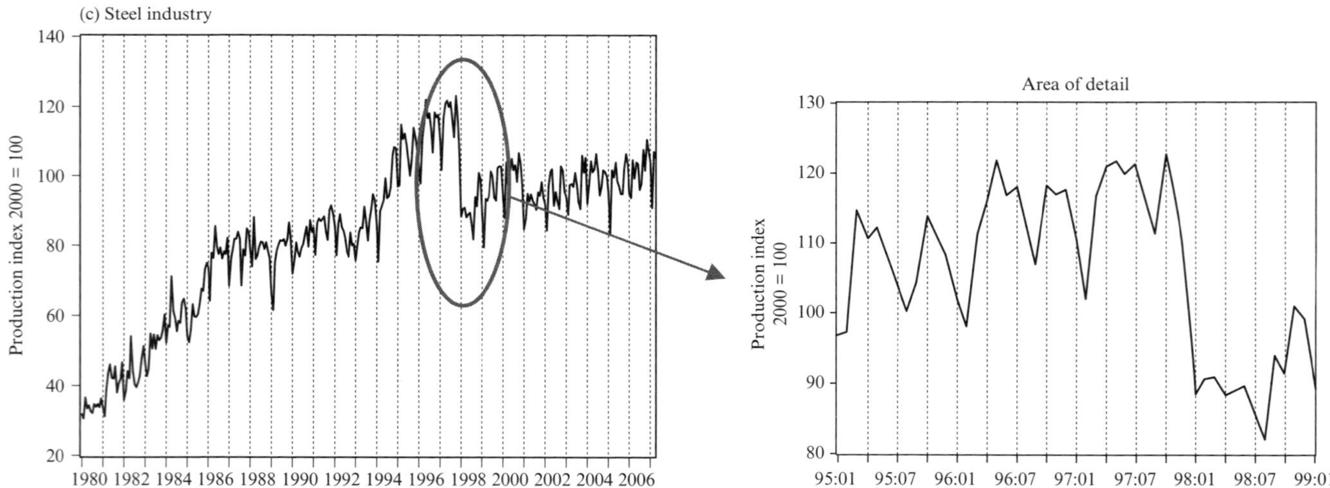

Figure 8.2 (continued)

What follows are the updated versions of the forecasts for GDP, CPI, PPI, employment/unemployment rate end, export/import volume index for South Korea, made in September 2007.

Updates were done in two steps. First, previous forecasts were compared with the actual values that were published by the National Statistical Office after extrapolations. If the forecast turned out to be satisfactory, i.e. with the forecast confidence intervals encompassing the actual realized values, then the model's specifications were kept and further extrapolations were made for the next six months by updating the monthly indicators of the model. If the result turned out to be unsatisfactory, where the forecast value did not perform according to requirements, then the model was revised. This revision assessed the model and the indicators to see if something had been left out that resulted in skewing of the forecast result. After the revision, the revised model was tested by assuming that the realized values were not available. By comparing the realized value and the forecast of the revised model, we were able to assess the revised model.

Prior forecasts for GDP, CPI and PPI did not measure up to historical performances. Therefore, in our revision, while the total number of indicators was not altered, for this update, ARIMA (autoregressive integrated moving average) extrapolation was done in a different manner. In previous ARIMA extrapolation, each indicator was extrapolated and the principal components analysis was estimated using the extrapolated indicators to obtain the values of the six-months-ahead extrapolated component values. However, for this update, six months' extrapolations were done directly for each component that was obtained from the principal components analysis. (All the ARIMA extrapolations were done this way for the September update.) The results show that the models for this update, in general, require fewer autoregressive and moving-average adjustments to achieve random errors. While revision was necessary for GDP, CPI and PPI, the historic performances show that the models with the chosen indicators are robust. Especially given the fact that the revision did not alter the existing monthly indicators, the equations that represent South Korea's economy still show that it is working well and progressing.

For the models on employment/unemployment rate and export/import volume index, track records are non-existent. However, from *ex-post* estimation these four models have provided *ex-ante* estimation for the first time on such an update. Extrapolation six months ahead was done for these new models. These models should be looked at carefully over the next few months to assess their performance.

GROSS DOMESTIC PRODUCT (AGGREGATE APPROACH)

In order to model South Korea's GDP, 31 monthly indicators were chosen based on knowledge of the Korean economy. Taking an aggregate approach, indicators were chosen in three categories: supply, demand and market-clearing. Monthly indicators such as automobiles and semiconductors were included along with exchange rates and imports of crude oil, which play a major role in each quarter's GDP (see Table 8.1 for the full list of 31 indicators).

As shown in Figure 8.1, South Korea developed economically along a rising path until 1996; the financial crisis hit in December 1997. South Korea's GDP showed a large drop in 1998 before it continued its development in the twenty-first century.

The model spans the period January 2001 to June 2007. While the original model ranged from January 1990 to June 2007, the monthly sample size was shortened to 2001–07, in order to include two important indicators: (1) semiconductors; and (2) information and communications equipment. This matches the data sets available from the National Statistical Office.

Using principal components analysis, which deals with the multicollinearity problem that might arise among the indicators, within-sample estimates both *ex post* and *ex ante* were made before the final model was chosen for extrapolation. Once the final model was chosen, six months' extrapolation was made by using ARIMA estimates for each component (different from previous practice) obtained from the principal components analysis. Since the components were estimated in monthly frequency, they were averaged into quarterly frequency to match the frequency of the dependent variable GDP at 2000 constant prices (seasonally adjusted). Both AR error transformation and MA error transformation were added if necessary to achieve random residuals.

$$GDP = 3.836 + 0.1195Comp1 - 0.0402Comp4$$

$$+ 0.0374Comp5 + 0.05235Comp7$$

$$R^2 = 0.9926, \text{DW} = 1.9815$$

where: $Compi$ = ith principal component, AR = autoregressive error transformation and MA = moving average error transformation.

The result shows that out of eight components that were first included in the regression model, four components, 1, 4, 5 and 7, turned out to

Table 8.1 GDP aggregate approach (31 monthly indicators)

Indicator	Index/volume/unit of measurement
Agriculture	Volume index
Commercial	Floor area
Communication	Dollar
Computers and office machinery	Seasonally adjusted index
Construction	Production index
Dwellings	Floor area
Production: electricity seasonally adjusted	Production index
Electrical machinery and apparatus n.e.c.	Seasonally adjusted index
Total exports	Dollar
Factory	Floor area
Fisheries	Volume per weight
Intermediate goods	Production index
Manufacturing equipment	Production index
Manufacturing	Seasonally adjusted index
Mining	Seasonally adjusted index
Motor vehicles, trailers and semi-trailers	Seasonally adjusted index
Textiles (except sewn wearing apparel)	Seasonally adjusted index
Passenger cars (export)	Volume index
Information and communication equipment (export)	Dollar
Semiconductors (export)	Dollar
Fabricated metal	Production index
Crude oil and petroleum products import	Volume
Retail trade	Volume index
Sales of motor vehicles and automotive fuel	Volume index
Wholesale trade	Volume index
(Deposits: corporate)/PPI	Inflation adjusted
(Deposits: household)/CPI	Inflation adjusted
Exchange rate	Won/US$
Exchange rate	Won/Japan yen (100 yen)
Real M2 (M2/CPI)	Inflation adjusted
Overseas direct investment	Dollar basis

be significant. AR and MA error transformation were not necessary to achieve white-noise residuals. This could be verified by both the Durbin–Watson statistic of 1.98 above and the residual plot (Figure 8.3), where the residuals show a random movement in the time-series graph.

Table 8.2 is a summary of the updated forecast as well as prior forecasts. As mentioned, revision was made to the prior model by employing

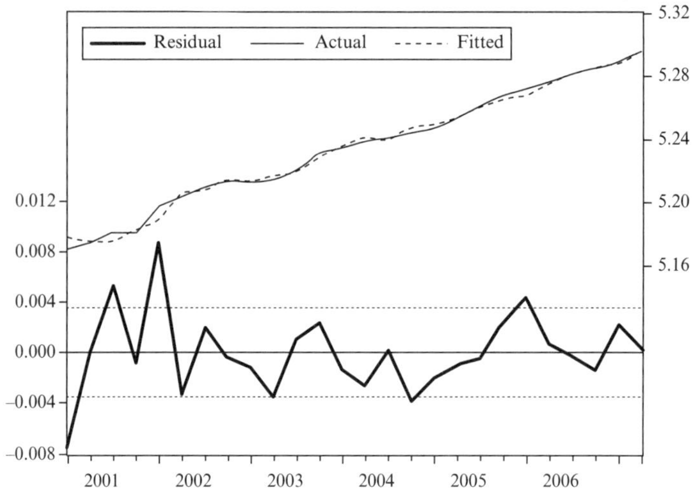

Figure 8.3 Residuals plot

a different ARIMA extrapolation method. The revised model was tested by verifying estimates and performance against published values. (Revised models were extrapolated by assuming that the published data were not available.) As can be seen on the right-hand side of Table 8.2, the revised model performs better than the prior model where the 95 percent confidence interval encompasses the actual values. Furthermore, the forecast for the next four quarters, the upper bound and the lower bound are tabulated and the predicted GDP growth rates are calculated in Table 8.3. The new model predicts that GDP will grow on average 4.1792 percent for this coming year. The average of quarter-to-quarter growth rates is predicted to be 1.1849 percent for the next four quarters. The period between 2007Q4 and 2008Q1 is expected to show a slowing of GDP growth in South Korea.

A graph of GDP growth since 2001 and the extrapolation four quarters ahead are shown in Figure 8.4. The boundaries of all the GDP projections encompass all the actual values except that for 2006Q4. This can be seen in the right-hand panel (b) of Figure 8.4.

The historic performance of the GDP model is promising. With the out-of-sample forecast values following closely the later realized values, this model could potentially be used by those interested in peering into South Korea's future.

Table 8.2 GDP (aggregate approach) forecasts

Forecast**	Forecast (GDP)			Forecast – 2SE	Forecast + 2SE	Actual* (GDP)	Within 95% CI?	
	Prior	Revision*	Latest	Latest	Latest		Prior	Revision*
2007Q1	192328.10	193174.65				194446.44	No	Yes
2007Q2	195351.05	197567.52				197915.59	No	Yes
2007Q3	195568.58	197899.76	198218.84	194505.09	202003.49			
2007Q4			201784.36	198059.93	205578.83			
2008Q1			200549.06	196813.33	204355.69			
2008Q2			204730.20	200914.27	208618.59			

Notes:
* Revision: see page 205.
** Forecast: Prior – April 2007 (ARIMA of indicators).
Latest – September 2007 (ARIMA of components).

Source: * Statistical Office of South Korea (http://kosis.nso.go.kr).

Table 8.3 Predicted GDP growth rate

	Log(GDP)	GDP	Quarterly (%)	Annualized rate (%)
2007Q3	5.2971449	198 218.8362	1.4680	4.0506
2007Q4	5.3048875	201 784.3602	1.7988	4.7171
2008Q1	5.3022206	200 549.0568	−0.6122	3.1480
2008Q2	5.3111819	204 730.1954	2.0848	4.8012
Forecast		Avg	1.1849	4.1792

CONSUMER PRICE INDEX (YEAR 2000 = 100)

The 34 monthly indicators for the CPI consist mainly of export, housing and import prices (see Table 8.4). Indicators similar to those used for GDP forecasts are used to represent the quoted movement of CPI. Export prices, such as those for passenger cars, steel, wireless telephone sets and semiconductors, were included. The import price for crude petroleum, and housing prices as well as education expenses, were taken into account. Two export prices were added to the CPI indicators: (1) semiconductors; and (2) information and communications equipment. Because data for these two indicators start from 2001M01, the sample size was shortened from 1990M01–2007M03 to 2001M01–2007M03.

Principal components analysis with seasonal indicators, autoregressive, and moving average error correction constituted a forecast equation. Out-of-sample extrapolation of components was made for six months using estimates of independent variables by ARIMA methods for forecasting the CPI of South Korea. Both autoregressive: AR(2), and moving average: MA(1), MA(3) and MA(4) were necessary in order to isolate white-noise error. Since the dependent variable, in this case the CPI, is reported monthly, the entire analysis of this case uses a larger sample of observations. The residual variation, after accounting for the three principal components of monthly indicator variables plus some lagged effects for autocorrelation moving average terms (ARIMA and MA), tests out as a random series using Durbin–Watson statistics. This could be verified through the equation table and the graph of the residuals that has a random movement. (See Appendix for equation and graphs.)

The result reveals that the older model has not performed well for the period May to August 2007. While the prior model had the predicted range of the index as 121.00 to 122.00, the revised version had a range of 123.00 to 124.00, closer to the actual realized values. With a revised model, we perform six-months-ahead forecasts of South Korea's CPI.

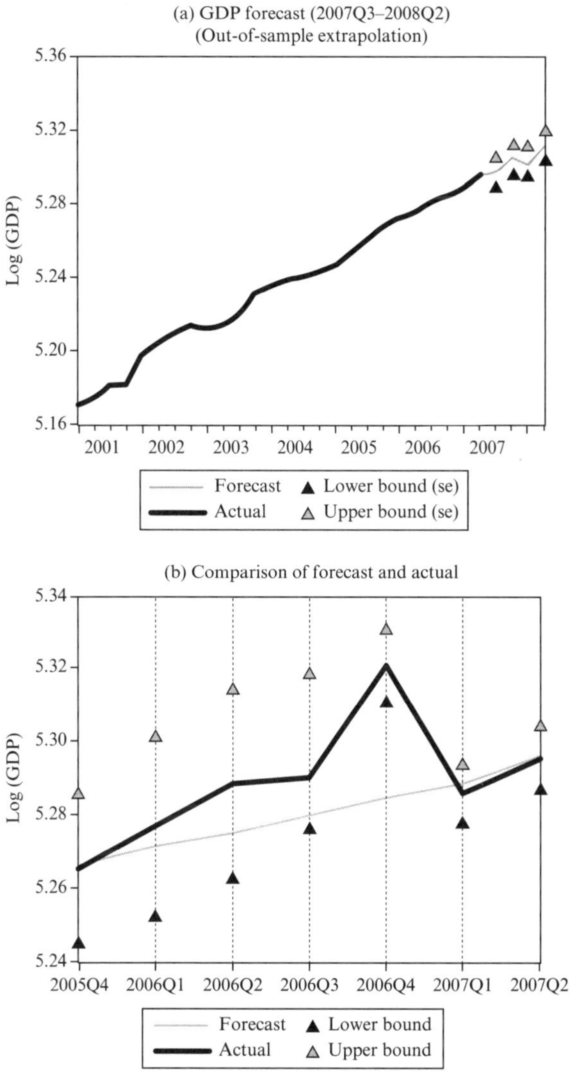

Figure 8.4 GDP growth since 2001 (a) and extrapolation four quarters ahead (b)

The summary of the forecast from August 2007 to January 2008 suggests that the average annual growth rate for the CPI is 3.6710 percent for the six months until January 2008. In other words, our CPI model predicts that inflation will increase on average by 3.6710 percent over the next six months from the previous year. On a month-to-month basis, it shows

Table 8.4 Consumer price index (34 monthly indicators)

Indicator	Index/volume/unit of measurement
Passenger car, medium	Dollar basis
Cement	Dollar basis
Shape steel	Dollar basis
Aluminum foil	Dollar basis
Wireless telephone set	Dollar basis
Passenger car, large	Dollar basis
Container for transportation	Dollar basis
Agricultural, forest and marine products	Dollar basis
Textile, apparel and leather products	Dollar basis
Food and live animals	Dollar basis
Crude materials, inedible, except fuels	Dollar basis
Information and communication equipment	Dollar basis
Semiconductors	Dollar basis
Passenger cars	Dollar basis
Public transport	Price index
Food price, domestic	Price index
Education (school fees and others)	Price index
Apartment	Price index
Apartment (Seoul)	Price index
Terraced house	Price index
Livestock products	Dollar basis
Crude petroleum and natural gas	Dollar basis
Petroleum products	Dollar basis
Synthetic rubber and plastic materials	Dollar basis
Durable and semi-durable consumer goods	Dollar basis
Non-durable consumer goods	Dollar basis
Capital goods	Dollar basis
Consumer goods	Dollar basis
Adjusted M2: (M2/CPI)	Won
Production: electricity seasonally adjusted	Production index
Production capacity index	Volume index
Operation ratio index (original index)	Volume index
Deposit at deposit money bank	Won

that the growth rate of CPI will be 0.3543 percent. The six-months-ahead forecast also suggests that CPI would increase steadily with a slight sign of slowdown in December 2007. This is consistent with the result we have obtained from GDP. Overall, the index is expected to range from 124.4 to 126.4 over a six-month period. Lastly, the bandwidths for each point forecast are approximately the same.

Recently the Bank of Korea announced that the inflation target has been set for the period 2007–2009 in a range of 2.5~3.5 percent in terms of the three-year average annual consumer price inflation.[8] This range is exceeded by our prediction. In fact, our forecast shows, on average, that inflation would be 17 basis points higher than the highest targeted inflation of South Korea.

The historical track records show that the estimated CPI has been performing well over the last 18 months. The bandwidth of ±2SE encompassed the actual values in all but two cases out of 19 that were announced after the forecast was made six months in advance.

PRODUCER PRICE INDEX (YEAR 2000 = 100)

In total, 30 monthly indicators were chosen to represent South Korea's PPI model (see Table 8.5). The sample span, ranging from 2001M01 to 2007M03, consists mainly of prices of raw, intermediate and finished goods. Prices of raw materials, construction, manufacturing and intermediate materials, processed fuel, and energy were included. To take into account the transportation cost, which plays a major role in the PPI, prices for transportation of both rail and other freight were included. Likewise, the import price of crude petroleum, as well as investment from abroad and circulation of money in the economy, were taken into account as indicators of movement in the PPI. Similar to the cases of CPI and GDP, two indicators, railroad and other freight prices, were used, thus necessitating an adjustment of the sample span from 2001M01 to 2007M03 instead of 1990M01 to 2007M03.

Using principal components analysis, as in the previous cases, deals with the multicollinearity problem that might arise among the indicators. In-sample estimates, both *ex post* and *ex ante*, were examined before the final model was chosen for extrapolation. Autoregressive error transformation and moving average error transformation were added as explanatory variables to achieve white noise in the residuals. Additionally, monthly dummy variables for seasonality were added.

An out-of-sample extrapolation was made for six months (using ARIMA) for forecasting the PPI. For the final equation, five principal components, a dummy seasonal variable, plus an ARIMA term were needed. (See Appendix for equation and graphs.)

The same analysis that was shown in detail for the CPI was used, with equally good results. The forecast of the PPI shows that over the span of six months, the price is expected to increase sharply and then level off during the months of August and September before moving up steadily and slowing down once again in November. From August 2007 to January

Table 8.5 Producer price index (30 monthly indicators)

Indicator	Index/volume/unit of measurement
Stage-of-processing price index	Price index
Raw materials	Price index
Raw materials for manufacturing	Price index
Raw materials for construction	Price index
Raw materials for crude fuels	Price index
Other raw materials	Price index
Intermediate materials	Price index
Intermediate materials for manufacturing	Price index
Intermediate materials for construction	Price index
Interm. materials for processed fuels and energy	Price index
Other intermediate materials	Price index
Finished goods	Price index
Capital equipment	Price index
Consumption goods	Price index
Durable consumption goods	Price index
Non-durable consumption goods	Price index
Raw and intermediate materials (raw+intermediate)	Price index
Raw and intermediate materials for construction	Price index
Raw and intermediate materials for fuels, energy	Price index
Other raw and intermediate materials	Price index
Freight transportation price	Price index
Railroad freight charges	Price index
Crude petroleum and natural gases	Dollar basis
Petroleum products	Dollar basis
Synthetic rubber and plastic materials	Dollar basis
Real M2	Won
Production capacity index	Index
Operation ratio index (original index)	Index
Deposit at deposit money bank	Dollar basis
Overseas direct investments	Dollar basis

2008, the average annual growth rate for the PPI is 2.9486 percent for the six months until January 2008. On a month-to-month basis, it shows that the growth rate of PPI would be 0.1872 percent. The forecast predicts that the PPI will hover around the value of 116 until it breaks 117 in January 2008 (see Appendix).

The track record above is impressive. The actual values are well within the confidence interval of the predicted values, and the movement of the forecast follows a pattern similar to that of the actual values.

LABOR FORCE (EMPLOYMENT/UNEMPLOYMENT RATE)

The labor force in South Korea has shown an increasing participation rate. *World Bank 2007* reports that for both the male and female population in South Korea, the participation rate has increased, by 2 percent and 4.5 percent, respectively. In terms of economic activity and industrial composition, participants are heavily involved in the service sector. The World Bank reports that the service industry accounts for 56 percent and 68 percent of the employment of males and females, respectively. From the aftermath of the Korean War, South Korea has progressed from an agricultural society to one of manufacturing (light and heavy industry) and services. Therefore, in order to model the labor force of South Korea, these patterns in labor force participation were taken into account.

For labor force, both the employment and unemployment rate indicate that they move in quite different directions but in similar ways (see Appendix). Initially, 37 monthly indicators were chosen for modeling the labor force of South Korea (see Table 8.6). These include sales of motor vehicles and automotive fuel, restaurant meals, hotel volume index as well as health, recreational and sporting activities. The production index of manufacturing was considered as well, since manufacturing remains a large part of South Korea's economy. Permits authorized for building and construction were included since these indicators forecast future employment of construction workers, which is largely a male occupation.

On review, two major aspects of the labor market were covered by including indicators of 'benefit/insurance' and 'wage/number of hours worked'. Both types of indicators are important in predicting the labor force since its trends have direct influence on total employment in the economy. The present version of indicators uses a total of 39 monthly indicators for the labor force model.

Employment Rate

Both lags of each component as well as dummy variables for each month were examined as regressors in the estimation process for significance, but none turned out to be significant, and the above regression equation turned out to be the model used with a white-noise residual. A Durbin–Watson statistic of 1.99 is quite acceptable for guarding against serial correlation of the errors. The principal component variables are significant, with t-statistics all greater than 2. Visually the residual graph shows a white-noise property. (See Appendix for equation and graphs.)

Both residual and out-of-sample extrapolations six months ahead for

Table 8.6 Employment and unemployment (39 monthly indicators)

Indicator	Index/volume/unit of measurement
Sales of motor vehicles and automotive fuel	Wholesale and retail sale index
Wholesale trade	Wholesale and retail sale index
Retail trade	Wholesale and retail sale index
All groups	Service industry activities index
Wholesale and retail trade	Service industry activities index
Hotels and restaurants	Service industry activities index
Transport	Service industry activities index
Post and telecommunications	Service industry activities index
Financial institutions and insurance	Service industry activities index
Real estate and renting, leasing	Service industry activities index
Business activities	Service industry activities index
Education	Service industry activities index
Health and social work	Service industry activities index
Recreational, cultural, sporting activities	Service industry activities index
Other community, repair and personal service activities	Service industry activities index
Number of registered motor vehicles	Number of registered motor vehicles
All industries	Production index by industry
Mining	Production index by industry
Manufacturing	Production index by industry
Electricity, gas	Production index by industry
Pop.15 years old and over	Economically active population
Dwellings	Permits authorized for building
Commercial	Permits authorized for building
Factory	Permits authorized for building
Educational and social	Permits authorized for building
Others	Permits authorized for building
Manufacturing production index by special classification	Production index by industry
Manufacturing operation ratio	Macroeconomic analysis
Manufacturing inventory rate	Macroeconomic analysis
Export price (% change)	Macroeconomic analysis
Import price (% change)	Macroeconomic analysis
Compensation for accident	Industrial accident compensation insurance
Compensation for accident in manufacturing industry	Industrial accident compensation insurance
Wages in manufacturing	Monthly earnings
Wages in textiles	Monthly earnings
Wages in motor vehicles	Monthly earnings

Table 8.6 (continued)

Indicator	Index/volume/unit of measurement
Work days textiles (except sewn wearing apparel)	Working days
Work days motor vehicles, trailers and semi-trailers	Working days
Work days manufacturing	Working days

the employment rate predict that the rate is estimated to be steady. The employment rate will be expected to be in the range of 59.69 percent to 59.82 percent. The actual values, which were presented after the forecast, show that the first two months of our forecast model do well in capturing the interval pattern. The 95 percent confidence interval shows a small and steady increase in size, subject to indication of more uncertainty of the forecast further ahead in time (see Appendix).

The predicted employment growth rate shows that over six months, month-to-month estimates of future employment changes are negative, on balance; however, the average employment rate change from the previous year is 0.1 percent. This shows that overall, in the next six months, the employment rate may yet rise on average, although there may be a decline in July, August and December 2007.

Unemployment Rate

Unemployment is an economic magnitude of unusual importance. The rate of unemployment is a small and exceptionally difficult variable to measure accurately. It is not easy to determine the precise meaning and measurement of the unemployment rate, yet it is so important that we are led to try to make forecasts of this elusive concept.

Similar to the employment rate estimation, output shows a lagging tendency for each principal component, and dummy variable indicators of each month are used as regressors in the estimation process for the unemployment rate, but none of the latter was statistically significant. The residual output turned out to be white noise. Principal component 3 was kept as an explanatory variable, although it carried a *t*-statistic just under 2. Unlike the case of the employment rate, AR(1), alone, was necessary for obtaining white-noise residual error. Even though we recognize difficulties of measuring and explaining the unemployment rate, the estimated equation provides a reasonable fit to the data. The residual variation is quite small and random. (See Appendix for equation and graphs.)

Results show that six-months-ahead forecasts predict that the unemployment rate will be steady, in the range of 3.34 percent to 3.39 percent. The estimated confidence interval spreads as we extrapolate further ahead in time. In checking the two values that were made available after the forecast, it can be seen that both fall well within the upper bound and the lower bound of the confidence interval for the forecast (see Appendix).

Overall, the model predicts that the unemployment rate will show a monthly average growth of 0.382 percent for the next six months. The expected rise of the unemployment rate during December 2007 is consistent with the previous models, where it showed an expected slowdown in the economy. On average, the unemployment rate shows a yearly decline of 1.572 percent. This suggests that in the short run, unemployment is likely to go up, but in comparison to previous years it is on a slight decline.

EXPORT VOLUME INDEX (YEAR 2000 = 100)

South Korea's exports consist mainly of manufacturing, amounting to 91 percent of total exports. Manufacturing includes passenger cars, semiconductors and heavy industry products. South Korea's manufacturing has evolved from producing light-industry products such as textiles and moving on to heavy-industry products. Domestic, i.e. non-export, industry is dominated by the service industry. South Korea is still considered in the outside world as a developing country with heavy emphasis on manufacturing. The automobile volume index, the iron and steel production index and the semiconductor production index are just a few examples of chosen indicators. China, the USA and Japan have consistently been the three most important destinations for South Korea's exports. Exchange rates of each major destination country versus South Korea's won were chosen as a separate indicator of export activity. Transport costs of both air and water volume indices also were taken into account.

An initial 28 monthly indicators for South Korea's export activity were modified by including three important indicators. West Texas crude oil price and interest rates of both the USA and Europe were included, expanding the monthly indicators from 28 to 31 (see Table 8.7).

For each principal component, lags were introduced (up to two lags) to compensate for time consumption that often arises in the export process. The selected principal components were statistically significant, while lags were not. For monthly dummy variables, January and July indicators were introduced but showed no significance in the model. Lastly, an autoregressive and a moving average error transformation were included to achieve small white-noise residuals. The output equation shows that

Table 8.7 Export (31 monthly indicators)

Indicator	Index/volume/unit of measurement
Foods and direct consumer goods	Volume index
Fish and shellfish	Volume index
Crude material and fuels	Volume index
Petroleum products	Volume index
Light-industry products	Volume index
Textile yarn and thread	Volume index
Woven and textile fabrics	Volume index
Clothing	Volume index
Tires and inner tubes	Volume index
Gold	Volume index
Paper and paperboard	Volume index
Heavy-industry products	Volume index
Chemicals	Volume index
Iron and steel products	Volume index
Machinery and precision equipment	Volume index
Precision equipment	Volume index
Electric/electronic machines	Volume index
Electric machines for domestic purposes	Volume index
Information and communication equipment	Volume index
Semiconductors	Volume index
Passenger cars	Volume index
Information and communication equipment (excluding semiconductors)	Volume index
Won per US$	Closing rate
Won per Japan yen (100 yen)	Closing rate
Won per Saudi riyal	Closing rate
Won per China yuan	Closing rate
Water transport	Volume index
Air transport	Volume index
West Texas crude	Dollars per barrel
Interest USA	Bank prime loan rate
Interest euro	Money market interest rate

out of eight principal components, the first six are significant. To achieve white-noise error, it required using AR(1), AR(2) and AR(3), along with MA(2). The Durbin–Watson statistic is 2.1129. (See Appendix for equation and graphs.)

The six-months-ahead forecast predicts that the export volume will show a decline in the months of July and August. However, with a large increase in volume of exports estimated for the month of September, the data show a steady increase until the end of the year, before they show a decline in December. Both the monthly and annual growth rates of export volume are positive, and this suggests that both, in the short and long term, on average, will increase in the next six months. The export volume index is predicted to be approximately 221 in July 2007, and is expected to increase up to 231 by December. On average, the forecast suggests an annual growth rate at 6.566 percent in export volume for the coming six months. An average of 0.133 percent is the predicted month-to-month change of export volume for the third and fourth quarter. (See Appendix for table and graph.)

IMPORT VOLUME INDEX (YEAR 2000 = 100)

South Korea's imports have been examined and tested for extrapolative accuracy in the same way that exports were tested. Imports of manufactures include direct consumer goods such as electronics and clothing. No longer does South Korea rely heavily on inexpensive clothing and shoes, which are mostly imported from China. To estimate a good import equation, the model computed indices of durable and non-durable consumer goods, machinery and electronics, as well as capital goods. Also, to account for fuel imports at 25 percent, a volume index of crude oil and fuel was included. Imports into South Korea consist mainly of manufactures, while fuel accounts for the next largest amount of imports.

Origins of import show that Japan, China and the USA are the three major countries that supply South Korean imports. While Japan has been the leading origin source of imports, China has been catching up in recent years, surpassing the USA in 2003–04. (See Appendix for graphs.) To take this into account, these three countries' exchange rates were selected as indicators in the import model. Also, most oil imports come from Saudi Arabia (fourth in origin of imports). Therefore the exchange rate of the riyal was taken into account as an indicator. Similar to the export model, an air and water transport volume index, which tracks the movement of goods, was included.

There are 27 monthly indicators for imports, and the model has been modified by including three important extra indicators (see Table 8.8). West Texas crude oil price and the world interest rates of both the USA and Europe were included (Japan's interest rate time series ended short of 2004, so it was not included). Initially, among 30 indicators, four indicators, West Texas crude, exchange rate of yen versus won, yuan versus won and US dollar versus won, were considered as separate variables since

Table 8.8 Import (30 monthly indicators)

Indicator	Index/volume/unit of measurement
Consumer goods	Volume index
Cereals	Volume index
Direct consumer goods	Volume index
Non-durable consumer goods	Volume index
Durable consumer goods	Volume index
Electric machines for domestic purposes	Volume index
Crude material and fuel	Volume index
Fuel	Volume index
Crude oil	Volume index
Mineral	Volume index
Light-industrial crude material	Volume index
Textile yarn and thread	Volume index
Chemicals	Volume index
Iron and steel products	Volume index
Non-ferrous metal	Volume index
Capital goods	Volume index
Machinery precision equipment	Volume index
Precision equipment	Volume index
Electric and electronic machines	Volume index
Information and communication equipment	Volume index
Semiconductors	Volume index
Water transport	Volume index
Air transport	Volume index
Interest USA	Bank prime loan rate
Interest euro	Money market interest rate
Won per US$	Closing rate
Won per Japan yen (100 yen)	Closing rate
Won per Saudi riyal	Closing rate
Won per China yuan	Closing rate
West Texas crude	Dollar per barrel

these four variables were influential in the import pattern of South Korea. For the September revision, however, all 30 variables were included in the principal components analysis.

For each principal component, lags were introduced (up to two lags) to compensate for lags in the import processes that often arise. Of six components, components 1, 3, 4 and 5 were significant, while lags were not significant. Monthly seasonal dummy variables were not statistically significant. Compared to a prior model, where four indicators were considered separately, since all 30 indicators were included in the principal components analysis, this revised model did not have to go through the process of deciding models based on four separate variables. This simplified our process of modeling a parsimonious import volume model for South Korea. Lastly, in order to realize white-noise residuals, only AR(1) was effectively necessary. As shown in the Appendix, all the independent variables are significant, with a Durbin–Watson statistic of 1.92, which suggests no serial correlation in error terms. (See Appendix for equation and graphs.)

The forecast of import volume six months ahead suggests that South Korea will experience sharp growth before it shows a slowdown during November 2007. The import volume index (year 2000 = 100) is predicted to exceed 170 in September 2007, before a slowdown in November. The 95 percent confidence interval shows, over time, that the size of the bandwidth does not increase but remains constant for six months (see Appendix).

On average, the forecast suggests an 8.209 percent annual growth rate in import volume for the coming six months. An average of 1.136 percent is the predicted month-to-month change of import volume for the third and fourth quarters. (See Appendix for table and graph.) This goes along with the projected export volume increase and the appreciation of the Korean won over the last few years, which increased South Korea's purchasing power.

SUMMARY OF FORECAST

The most recent estimates (September 2007) using the high-frequency modeling approach forecast the following features for South Korea's economy.

For the next four quarters (2007Q3–2008Q2), our model predicts that GDP will grow on average 4.1792 percent over the previous year. During these four quarters, from 2007Q3 to 2008Q2, it is estimated to grow on average 1.1849 percent from quarter to quarter. It is estimated that GDP will show a slowdown between 2007Q4 and 2008Q1.

The CPI model predicts that inflation will increase on average 3.6710 percent over the next six months from the previous year. On a month-to-month basis, it shows that the growth rate of CPI will be 0.3543 percent. Similarly, the forecast of PPI shows that the average monthly growth in PPI in six months is 0.1872 percent while the average annual growth rate (from the previous year) of PPI is 2.9486 percent over the next six months. Both estimates suggest a slight decline in the indices in November and December for CPI and PPI respectively.

The employment rate in South Korea is expected to growth on average 0.10 percent over the previous year for the next six months. However, within these six months, the average month-to-month change is expected to be –0.006 percent. This suggests that, in the short run, on a month-to-month basis, the employment rate is expected to decline, while average employment will show an increase from the previous year. A large decline is expected between November and December. On the other hand, the unemployment rate model predicts that unemployment will show a monthly average growth of 0.382 percent for the next six months (with a large increase between November and December) while, on average, the growth of the unemployment rate will decline from the previous year (−1.572 percent).

In terms of trade, export volume is expected to increase on average, with the forecast suggesting 6.566 percent annual growth rate in export volume for the coming six months. An average of 0.133 percent is the predicted month-to-month change of export volume for the third and fourth quarters. Consistent with the GDP forecast, the export index is predicted to decline in December 2007. Import volume is also expected to increase on average with the forecast, suggesting 8.209 percent annual growth rate in volume and an average growth rate of 1.136 percent month to month. Imports show a predicted decline during October and November 2007.

Overall, based on these forecasts six months ahead, South Korea is expected to show a slight slowdown during 2007Q4, but will nonetheless make some progress and show steady growth in the economy. These models are 'at the ready' for future usage.

NOTES

1. The World Bank, GNI 2008 (http://siteresources.worldbank.org/DATASTATISTICS/Resources/GNI.pdf).
2. The World Bank, GNI per capita 2008, Atlas Method (http://siteresources.worldbank.org/DATASTATISTICS/Resources/GNIPC.pdf).
3. Reuters, Iron & Steel: Company Rankings (http://www.investor.reuters.com/business/BusRankingsCompanies.aspx?industry=ISTEEL&target=busrankcomp).
4. 'Jinro's Last Minute Loan Highlights Nation's Bailout Ills', *Asian Wall Street Journal*, 4 August 1997.
5. 'Korean Auto Output Falls, Industry Strikes Cut Production in January', *Asian Wall Street Journal*, 10 February 1997.
6. National Statistical Office: http://www.nso.go.kr/.
7. Bank of Korea: http://ecos.bok.or.kr/.
8. Inflation target by Bank of Korea: http://www.bok.or.kr/template/eng/html/index.jsp?tbl=tbl_FM0000000066_CA0000003691.

REFERENCES

Harvie, Charles and Hyun Hoon Lee (2003), *Korea's Economic Miracle: Fading or Reviving?*, Basingstoke: Palgrave Macmillan.
World Bank (2008), *World Development Indicators*, April.

APPENDIX: SUPPORTING EQUATIONS, GRAPHS AND TABLES

Table 8A.1 Output summary

Equations	R^2	DW
$GDP = 3.836 + 0.1195Comp1 - 0.0402Comp4 + 0.0374Comp5 + 0.05235Comp7$	0.993	1.981
$CPI = 1.286 + 0.0587Comp1 + 0.0156Comp3 + 0.0183Comp5 + 0.729AR(2) + 1.190697MA(1) - 0.54891MA(3) - 0.35479MA(4)$	0.997	2.258
$PPI = 0.556 - 0.11671Comp1 + 0.056Comp2 - 0.05623Comp3 + 0.03146Comp4 + 0.05128Comp6 + 0.00126Dummy(9) + 0.2454AR(2) + 0.682MA(1)$	0.998	1.981
$EmploymentRate = 1.7236 + 0.00188Comp1 - 0.0026Comp4 + 0.001168Comp7 + 0.5469AR(3) + 1.0536MA(1) + 0.8868MA(2) + 0.3159MA(3)$	0.910	1.991
$UnemploymentRate = 0.871 - 0.0196Comp1 + 0.0389Comp3 + 0.0323Comp4 - 0.0238Comp5 + 0.8799AR(1)$	0.951	2.071
$Export = 0.2742 + 0.0382Comp1 + 0.0545Comp2 + 0.06147Comp3 - 0.0158Comp4 + 0.0385Comp5 - 0.014658Comp6 + 0.9302AR(1) - 0.8718AR(2) + 0.924AR(3) + 1.099MA(2)$	0.997	2.113
$Import = 0.3699 + 0.0785Comp1 - 0.0504Comp3 + 0.0214Comp4 - 0.0144Comp5 + 0.559AR(1)$	0.996	1.922

Notes:
COMP*i* = *i*th principal component.
AR = autoregressive error transformation.
MA = moving average error transformation.
Dummy*X* = dummy variable of *X*th month of the year.

Consumer Price Index (2000 = 100)

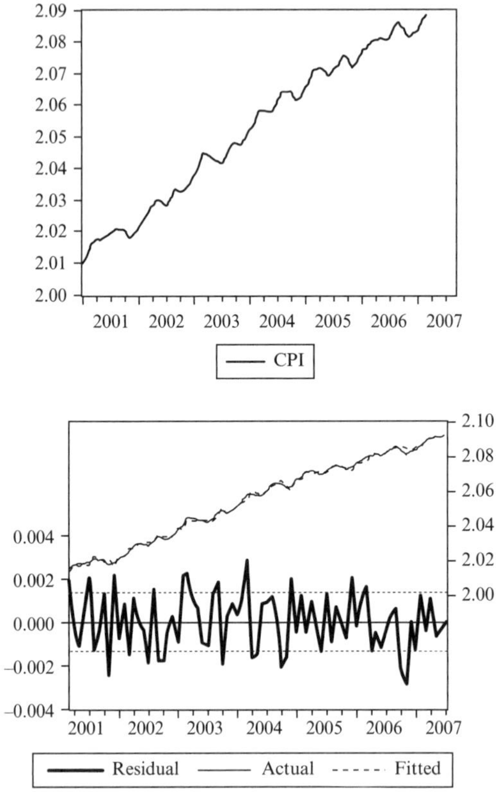

Note: CPI of South Korea has steadily increased over the years in a visible pattern of seasonality.

Source: Bank of Korea (http://ecos.bok.or.kr/).

Figure 8A.1 CPI and residual graph

Table 8A.2 CPI forecasts

Forecast**	Forecast(CPI)			Forecast – 2SE	Forecast + 2SE	Actual * (CPI)	Within 95% CI?	
	Prior	Revision***	Latest	Latest	Latest		Prior	Revision
2007M04	123.1613					123.1845366	Yes	
2007M05	121.8391					123.3027575	No	
2007M06	120.9692	123.3825				123.3027575	No	Yes
2007M07	121.0795	123.7518				123.775641	No	Yes
2007M08	121.0408	124.2261	124.4198	123.5811	125.2641	123.8939***	No	Yes
2007M09	121.0508	124.3211	125.0754	123.8033	126.3606			
2007M10			125.4155	124.009	126.8379			
2007M11			126.1265	124.6843	127.5854			
2007M12			126.2569	124.802	127.7288			
2008M01			126.4287	124.9634	127.9111			

Notes:

* Actual – Statistical Office of South Korea (http://kosis.nso.go.kr).

** Forecast – Prior – April 2007 (ARIMA of indicators).
Latest – September 2007 (ARIMA of components).

*** Revision – revision of prior forecast made by using the ARIMA of each component instead of the indicators.

Table 8A.3 Predicted CPI growth rate

	Log(CPI)	CPI	Monthly (%)	Annual rate (%)
2007M08	2.09489	124.4198	0.5204	2.4780
2007M09	2.09717	125.0754	0.5270	2.7179
2007M10	2.09835	125.4155	0.2719	3.4996
2007M11	2.10081	126.1265	0.5669	4.5967
2007M12	2.10126	126.2569	0.1034	4.3977
2008M01	2.10185	126.4287	0.1360	4.3358
Forecast		Avg of 6M	0.3543	3.6710

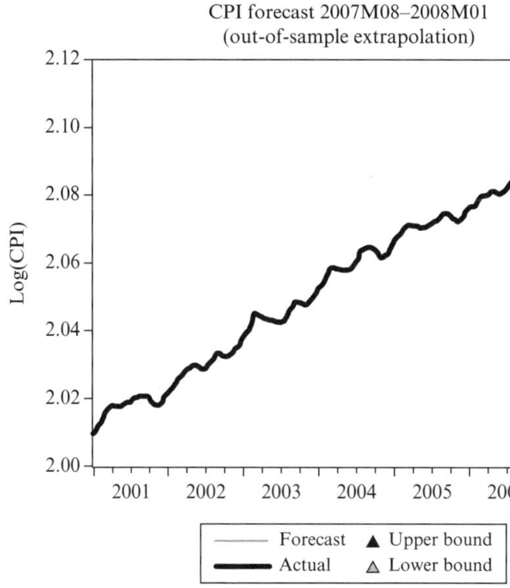

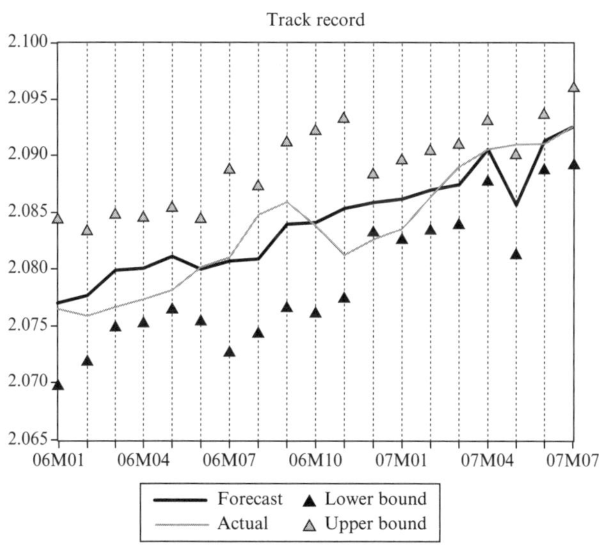

Figure 8A.2 CPI forecast and track record

*Table 8A.4 Track record frequency: monthly; dependent variable: LOGCPI (monthly); independent variable: 33 indicators (monthly)**

	Forecast	Forecast – 2SE	Forecast + 2SE	Actual*	Actual–forecast
2006M01	2.0770	2.06967	2.08434	2.0765	−0.0005
2006M02	2.0777	2.07192	2.08354	2.0759	−0.0019
2006M03	2.0799	2.07497	2.08483	2.0767	−0.0032
2006M04	2.0800	2.07531	2.08469	2.0773	−0.0027
2006M05	2.0810	2.07641	2.08559	2.0781	−0.0029
2006M06	2.0800	2.07546	2.08454	2.0803	0.0003
2006M07	2.0807	2.07259	2.08891	2.0810	0.0002
2006M08	2.0809	2.07445	2.08737	2.0849	0.0040
2006M09	2.0840	2.07664	2.09133	2.0860	0.0020
2006M10	2.0842	2.07616	2.09228	2.0839	−0.0004
2006M11	2.0854	2.07748	2.09329	2.0813	−0.0040
2006M12	2.0859	2.08330	2.08850	2.0826	−0.0033
2007M01	2.0862	2.08277	2.08966	2.0835	−0.0027
2007M02	2.0870	2.08354	2.09052	2.0864	−0.0006
2007M03	2.0875	2.08401	2.09104	2.0890	0.0014
2007M04	2.0905	2.08765	2.09330	2.0906	0.0002
2007M05	2.0858	2.08136	2.09021	2.0911	0.0053
2007M06**	2.0913	2.08885	2.09365	2.0910	−0.0003
2007M07**	2.0926	2.08911	2.09599	2.0926	0.0001

Notes:

* Statistical Office of South Korea (http://kosis.nso.go.kr).

** Revision – revision of prior forecast made by using the ARIMA of each component instead of the indicators.

Producer Price Index (2000 = 100)

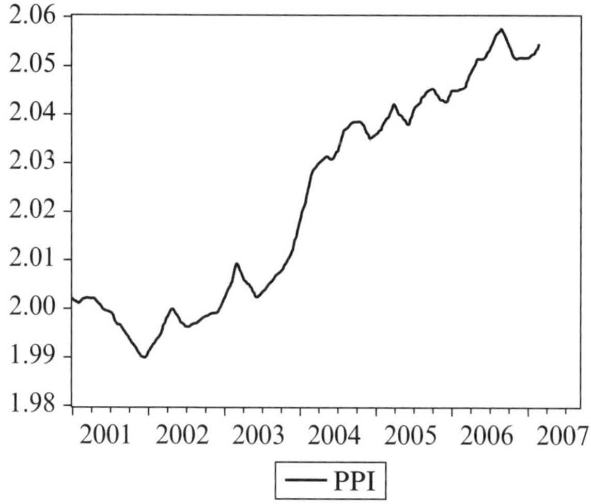

Note: PPI has shown a trend increase over the past 7 years. However, the data suggest that the movement of the PPI is rather more erratic than is the CPI (see Figure 8A.1).

Source: Bank of Korea (http://ecos.bok.or.kr/).

Figure 8A.3 PPI, 2000–2007

Table 8A.5 Predicted PPI growth rate

	Log(PPI)	PPI	Monthly (%)	Annual rate (%)
2007M07	2.06632	116.4980	0.8641	3.0956
2007M08	2.06468	116.0587	−0.3771	1.8953
2007M09	2.06471	116.0672	0.0073	1.6350
2007M10	2.06611	116.4424	0.3232	2.9552
2007M11	2.06612	116.4449	0.0021	3.5065
2007M12	2.06702	116.6871	0.2080	3.6297
2008M01	2.06825	117.0169	0.2826	3.9226
Forecast		Avg of 6M	0.1872	2.9486

*Table 8A.6 Track record frequency: monthly; dependent variable: LOGPPI (monthly); independent variable: 30 indicators (monthly)**

	Forecast	Forecast – 2SE	Forecast + 2SE	Actual*	Actual –forecast
2006M01	2.0459	2.04257	2.04925	2.0450	−0.0009
2006M02	2.0474	2.04367	2.05122	2.0450	−0.0024
2006M03	2.0478	2.04414	2.05152	2.0450	−0.0028
2006M04	2.0475	2.04395	2.05114	2.0480	0.0005
2006M05	2.0479	2.04438	2.05144	2.0511	0.0032
2006M06	2.0486	2.04508	2.05205	2.0512	0.0026
2006M07	2.0521	2.04883	2.05527	2.0531	0.0010
2006M08	2.0522	2.04728	2.05722	2.0565	0.0043
2006M09	2.0531	2.04662	2.05964	2.0577	0.0045
2006M10	2.0535	2.04581	2.06111	2.0535	0.0000
2006M11	2.0508	2.04782	2.05386	2.0512	0.0003
2006M12	2.0490	2.04520	2.05280	2.0515	0.0025
2007M01	2.0522	2.04782	2.05653	2.0515	−0.0006
2007M02	2.0538	2.04892	2.05867	2.0523	−0.0015
2007M03	2.0536	2.04826	2.05889	2.0546	0.0010
2007M04**	2.0552	2.05059	2.05972	2.0592***	0.0040
2007M05**	2.0564	2.05158	2.06124	2.0618***	0.0054
2007M06**	2.0579	2.05219	2.06357	2.0626	0.0047

Notes:
* Statistical Office of South Korea (http://kosis.nso.go.kr).
** Revision – revision of prior forecast made by using the ARIMA of each component instead of the indicators.
*** Statistical Office has published updated values for months April and May.

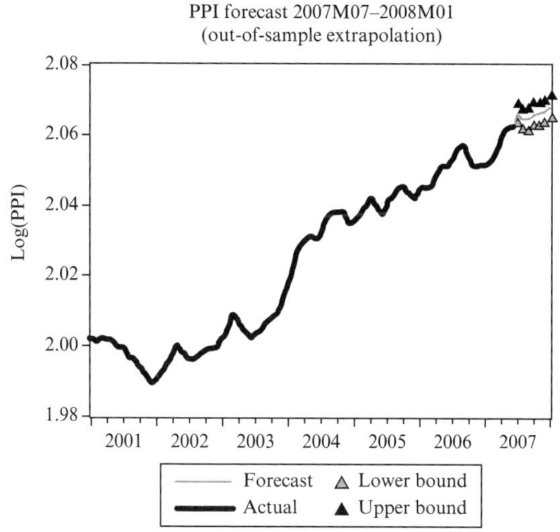

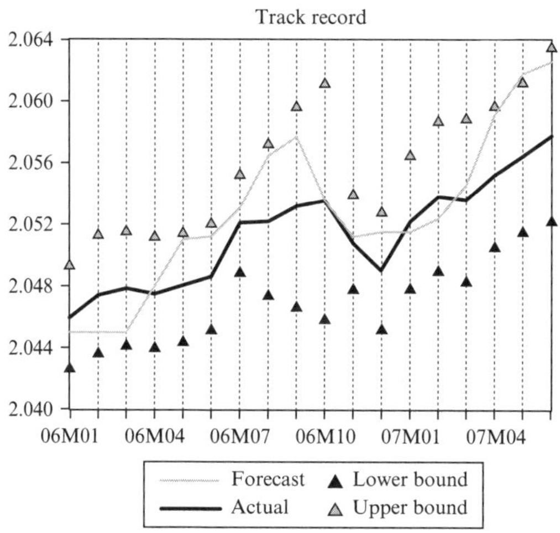

Figure 8A.4 PPI forecast and track record

Labor Force (Employment/Unemployment Rate)

Note: A 5 percentage point increase in the participation rate occurred for women since 1990.

Figure 8A.5 Labor force participation rate for males and females, 1990 and 2005; and employment and unemployment rates, 1999–2007

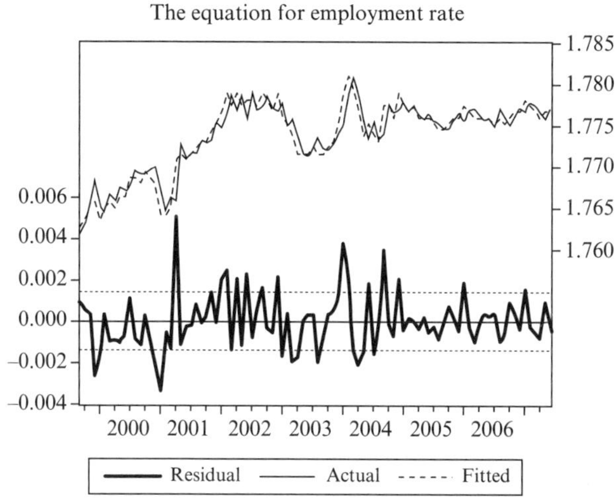

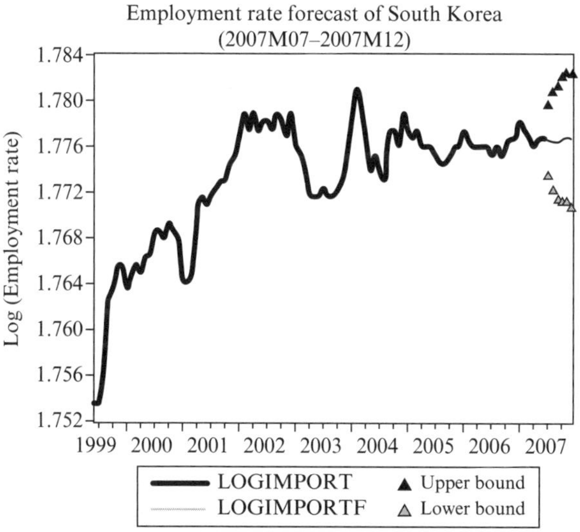

Figure 8A.6 Equation and employment rate forecast

Table 8A.7 Forecast and actual employment growth rate

	Forecast (Employment %)	Upper bound	Lower bound	Actual	Difference
2007M07	59.74	60.21	59.35	59.80**	–0.06
2007M08	59.69	60.35	59.18	59.90**	–0.21
2007M09	59.75	60.43	59.08		
2007M10	59.78	60.54	59.04		
2007M11	59.82	60.60	59.04		
2007M12	59.78	60.58	58.99		

Note: ** Actual value obtained after the forecast.

Table 8A.8 Predicted employment growth rate

	Log(Employment Rate)	Employment rate	Monthly change (%)	Annual change (%)
2007M07	1.7762	59.74	−0.107	0.228
2007M08	1.7759	59.69	−0.080	−0.020
2007M09	1.7763	59.75	0.104	0.252
2007M10	1.7766	59.78	0.053	0.137
2007M11	1.7769	59.82	0.067	0.037
2007M12	1.7765	59.78	−0.072	−0.036
Forecast		Avg 6 months	−0.006	0.100

Unemployment Rate

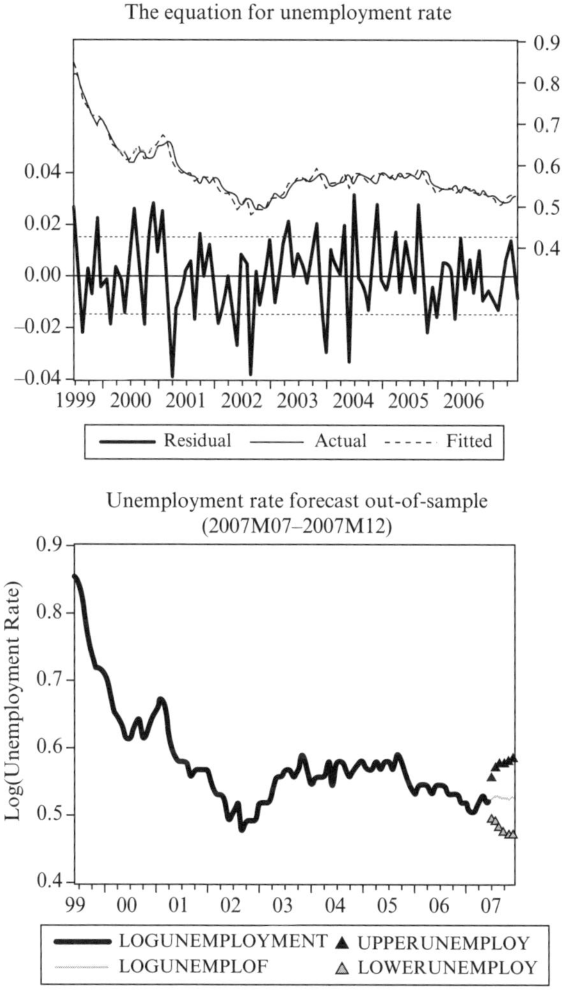

Figure 8A.7 Equation and unemployment rate forecast

Table 8A.9 Forecast and actual unemployment growth rate

	Forecast (Unemployment %)	Upper bound	Lower bound	Actual	Difference
2007M07	3.34	3.59	3.12	3.40**	−0.06
2007M08	3.39	3.72	3.08	3.20**	0.19
2007M09	3.36	3.75	3.02		
2007M10	3.36	3.78	2.98		
2007M11	3.34	3.80	2.95		
2007M12	3.38	3.85	2.96		

Note: **Actual value obtained after the forecast.

Table 8A.10 Predicted unemployment growth rate

	Log(Unemployment Rate)	Unemployment Rate	Monthly change (%)	Annual change (%)
2007M07	0.5244	3.34	1.356	−4.436
2007M08	0.5296	3.39	1.214	−3.276
2007M09	0.5268	3.36	−0.650	−1.078
2007M10	0.5259	3.36	−0.204	−1.280
2007M11	0.5242	3.34	−0.383	−1.658
2007M12	0.5284	3.38	0.960	2.295
Forecast		Avg 6 months	0.382	−1.572

Export Volume Index (2000 = 100)

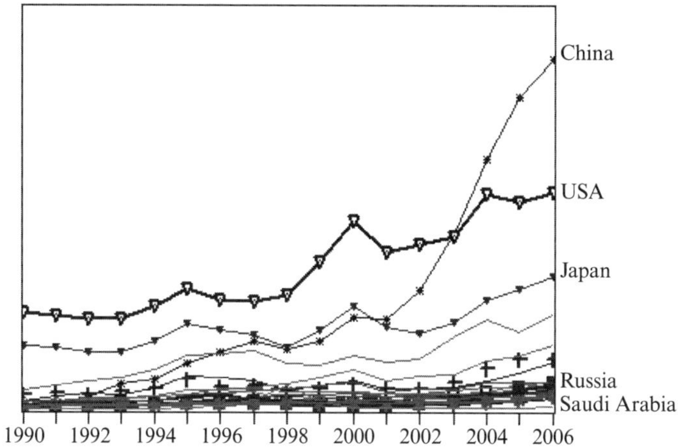

Source: Bank of Korea (http://ecos.bok.or.kr/).

Figure 8A.8 Destination of exports, 1990–2006

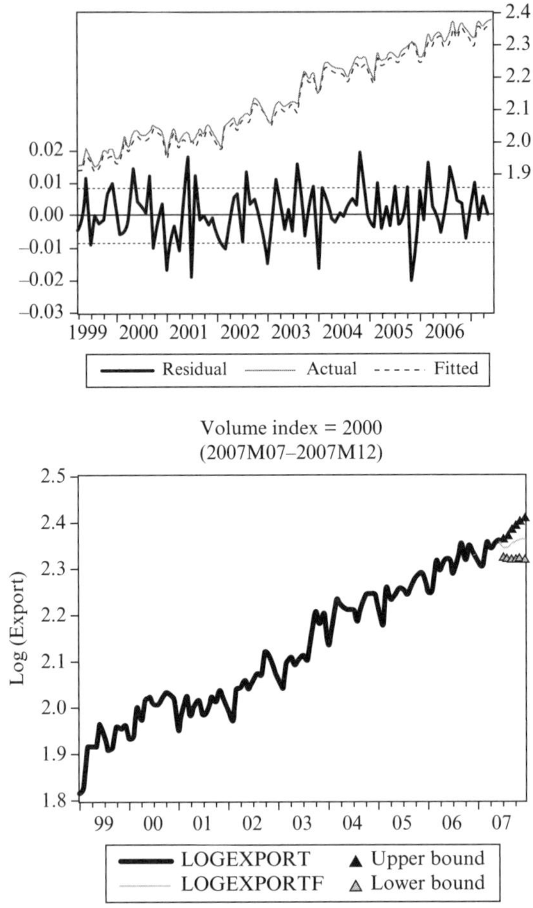

Figure 8A.9 Equation and export forecast

Table 8A.11 Forecast export volume index

	Forecast(Export Volume Index)	Upper bound	Lower bound
2007M07	220.90	230.71	211.51
2007M08	220.78	234.00	208.30
2007M09	226.13	243.04	210.39
2007M10	226.71	246.64	208.39
2007M11	229.94	252.48	209.42
2007M12	230.78	255.17	208.73

Table 8A.12 Predicted export volume growth rate

	Log(Export)	Export	Monthly change (%)	Annual change (%)
2007M07	2.3442	220.90	−3.621	13.632
2007M08	2.3440	220.78	−0.055	6.760
2007M09	2.3543	226.13	2.421	−0.692
2007M10	2.3555	226.71	0.258	9.047
2007M11	2.3616	229.94	1.425	2.196
2007M12	2.3632	230.78	0.367	8.451
Forecast		Avg 6 months	0.133	6.566

Import Volume Index (2000 = 100)

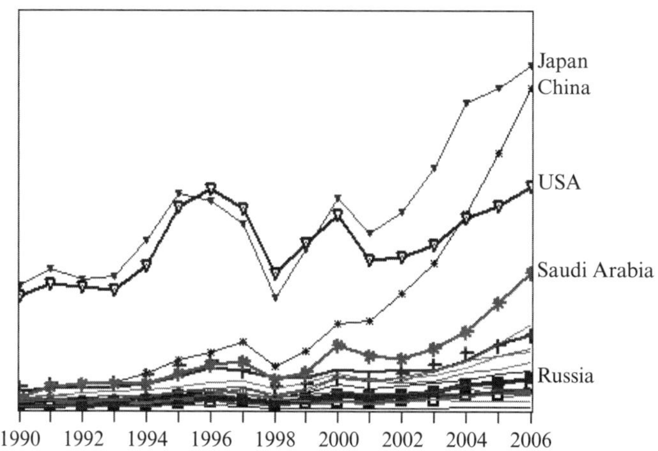

Source: Bank of Korea (http://ecos.bok.or.kr/).

Figure 8A.10 Origin of imports, 1990–2006

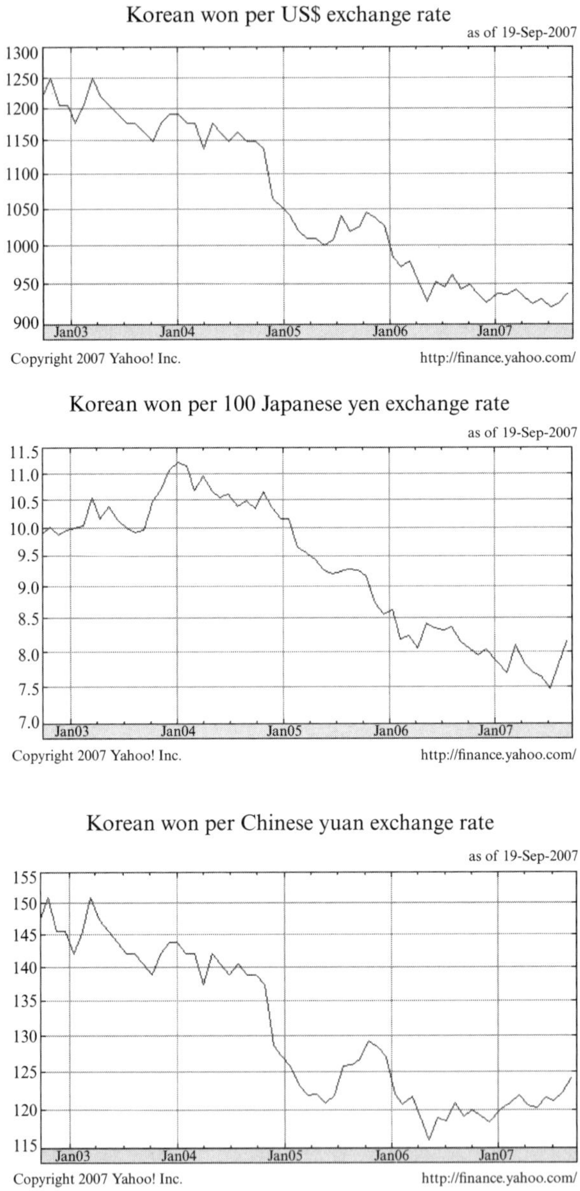

Note: It can be seen that South Korea has been appreciating with respect to the other three currencies.

Figure 8A.11 Korean won exchange rate with respect to other currencies

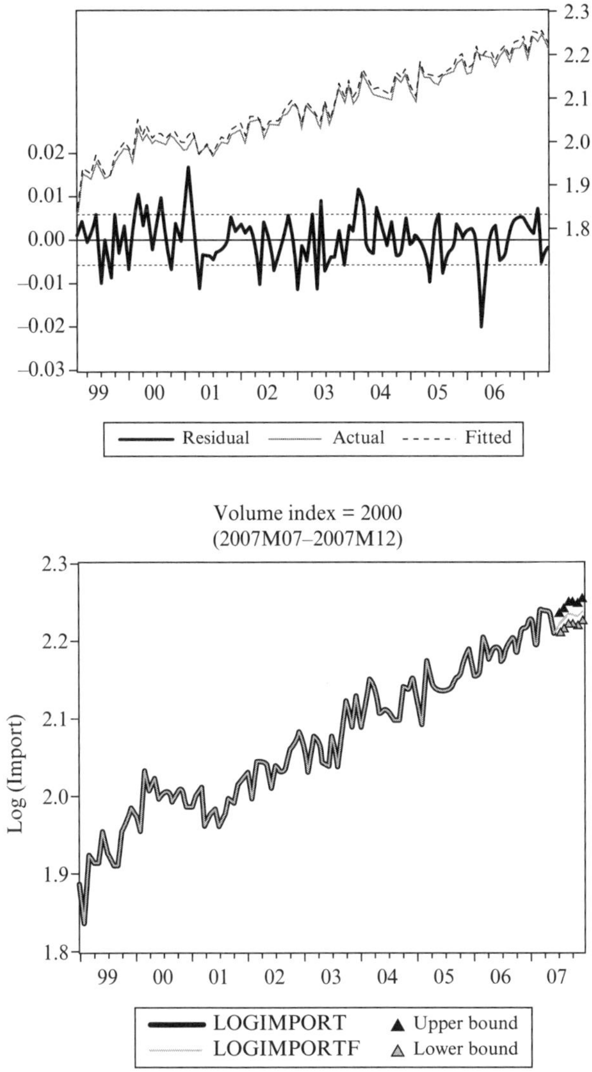

Figure 8A.12 Equation and import forecast

Table 8A.13 Forecast import volume index

	Forecast(Import Volume Index)	Upper bound	Lower bound
2007M07	166.58	171.27	162.02
2007M08	168.65	174.08	163.40
2007M09	171.70	177.43	166.15
2007M10	171.09	176.85	165.51
2007M11	170.58	176.33	165.01
2007M12	173.19	179.04	167.52

Table 8A.14 Predicted import growth rate

	Log(Import)	Import	Monthly change (%)	Annual change (%)
2007M07	2.2216	166.58	2.891	12.175
2007M08	2.2270	168.65	1.245	8.668
2007M09	2.2348	171.70	1.804	6.776
2007M10	2.2332	171.09	−0.355	12.408
2007M11	2.2319	170.58	−0.298	4.137
2007M12	2.2385	173.19	1.530	5.089
Forecast		Avg 6 months	1.136	8.209

9. Current quarter model for Turkey

Süleyman Özmucur

1. INTRODUCTION

Forecasting of economic activity requires the use of all available information. However, key data are collected at different frequencies. This necessitates building models utilizing data at different frequencies, which was the starting point for high-frequency macroeconometric models initiated by Klein and Sojo (1989). Forecasts are useful not only for studying the short-term developments of the economy, but also for adjusting lower-frequency macroeconometric models so that they are solved from up-to-date initial conditions (Klein and Sojo, 1989; Klein and Park, 1993, 1995).

We propose to form principal components of the monthly indicators whose periodic values appear at either different or similar time points of each month. Principal components analysis is based on our general point of view that a country's (any country's) economic growth is highly multivariate. No single measured economic activity can account for anything as complex as a modern economy. We examine many time series, and select those that seem to have *a priori* importance. In order to conserve degrees of freedom, we narrowed the list of explanatory variables in the relevant regression as much as possible. There have been important motivations in adopting the principal components methodology.

The chapter is in six sections. The second section deals with the methodology of principal components. A brief summary of the basic features of the Turkish economy and available monthly data are presented in the third section. Section 4 is devoted to the estimation of the model. Model performance is presented in Section 5, and forecasts based on the model are given in Section 6.

2. THE METHODOLOGY OF PRINCIPAL COMPONENTS

The methodology used in our current quarter model (CQM) is essentially based on Klein and Sojo (1989), and Klein and Park (1993, 1995), but with some modifications due to data limitations.[1] In Turkey, there are few monthly indicators such as an index of retail sales to be related to quarterly personal consumption expenditures on the expenditure side of NIPA (national income and product accounts). Furthermore, there are no reliable indicators on non-wage income on the income side and no such indicators on agricultural value-added on the production side. This motivates the use of principal components.

The principal components method is one in which the components are estimated linear functions of the indicators that we choose to represent the movement of the economy as a whole. This is a short-cut method for a full-scale structural econometric model. It is extremely useful in cases where there are many variables to be considered, but not many observations. This methodology is also very useful in cases where there is significant correlation among explanatory variables (multicollinearity). This data reduction technique captures the information provided by many variables which are highly intercorrelated.

The technique of principal components analysis was first described by Karl Pearson (1901), and about three decades later a description of computing methods was introduced by Hotelling (1933). The objective is to collect data for k variables $X_1, X_2, \ldots X_k$, and find combinations of these to produce principal components, $Z_1, Z_2, \ldots Z_k$, which are mutually uncorrelated (Anderson, 1984; Manly, 1986; Stone, 1947). The lack of correlation among Zs is a useful property because it means that principal components can extract specific information from the data. These are ordered so that Z_1 displays the largest amount of variation, Z_2 displays the second-largest amount of variation, and so on, i.e. $\text{Var}(Z_1) \geq \text{Var}(Z_2) \ldots \geq \text{Var}(Z_k)$. If the original variables are mutually uncorrelated, the method of principal components does not contribute much to the problem of data reduction. The best macroeconometric results are obtained when the original variables are significantly correlated. If that is the case, then information from hundreds of original indicators may be represented by only a few principal components.

The principal components analysis starts with data on k variables for n periods. The first principal component is then that linear combination of the variables $X_1, X_2, \ldots X_k$; $Z_1 = a_{11}X_1 + a_{21}X_2 + \ldots a_{k1}X_k$ that varies as much as possible, subject to the condition that $a_{11}^2 + a_{21}^2 + \ldots a_{k1}^2 = 1$. Thus the variance of Z_1 is as large as possible, given the constraint on the constants. The constraint is introduced because if this is not done, then

$Var(Z_1)$ can be increased by increasing one of the weights, a_{j1}. The second principal component, $Z_2 = a_{12}X_1 + a_{22}X_2 + \ldots a_{k2}X_k$, varies as much as possible, subject to the condition that $a_{12}^2 + a_{22}^2 + \ldots a_{k2}^2 = 1$, and also to the condition that Z_1 and Z_2 are uncorrelated.

It turns out that principal components analysis involves finding the eigenvalues of the sample covariance matrix. The variances of the principal components are the eigenvalues of the covariance matrix. There are k of these, some of which may be zero, but not negative because the covariance matrix is positive definite. Assuming that eigenvalues are ordered as $\lambda_1 > \lambda_2 > \ldots \lambda_k > 0$, then λ_i corresponds to the ith principal component: $Z_i = a_{1i}X_1 + a_{2i}X_2 + \ldots a_{ki}X_k$, where $Var(Z_i) = \lambda_i$, and the coefficients are elements of the corresponding eigenvector, and, a property of the eigenvalues is that they add up to the trace (sum of the diagonal elements) of the covariance matrix (V), i.e. $\lambda_1 + \lambda_2 + \ldots \lambda_k = V_{11} + V_{22} + \ldots V_{kk}$. Since diagonal elements are variances of original indicators (X), the sum of the variances of principal components is equal to the sum of variances of Xs. A reduced number of principal components may account for all the variation in the original data (Manly, 1986).

In order to avoid a variable having large influence on the principal components, it is customary to use standardized variables. In this case, all original variables are transformed to have zero means and unit variances. The matrix of cross-products is the correlation matrix, rather than the covariance matrix. Therefore the sum of eigenvalues is equal to the sum of variables (k). The larger the eigenvalue, the larger the effect of the variable on total variance to be explained. The elements of eigenvectors, which are the coefficients in the principal components, are also the correlation coefficient between the principal component and the original variable.

There are several methods to determine the number of principal components. One of the common approaches is to keep components with variances above one.[2] Another common alternative is to retain principal components which account for a large proportion, say 90 percent, of the total variance. If the correlations between original variables are high, there may be one or a few principal components that account for more than 90 percent of the variance, and there may be one or two eigenvalues that are greater than one. On the other hand, if original variables are only weakly or moderately correlated, there may be quite a few eigenvalues that are greater than or equal to one, and quite a few that are much smaller than one. In that case, there may be a need for a large number of principal components to account for 90 percent of the variance in original data.

A more formal derivation of the method of principal components is given below (Anderson, 1984):

Suppose **X** is a matrix of n observations on k variables, where variables are expressed as deviations from the sample means because the main concern is the variation in data.

The problem is to determine linear combinations of original variables that are pair-wise uncorrelated and of which the first will have maximum possible variance, the second the maximum possible variance among those uncorrelated with the first, and so on:

$$z_{1t} = a_{11}x_{1t} + a_{21}x_{2t} + \ldots + a_{k1}x_{kt},\ t = 1,2, \ldots n$$

In matrix form:

$\mathbf{Z}_1 = \mathbf{X}\mathbf{a}_1$, where $\mathbf{Z}_1$ is an n-element vector and $\mathbf{a}_1$ a k-element vector. The sum of squares of z_1 is: $\mathbf{Z}_1'\ \mathbf{Z}_1 = \mathbf{a}_1'\mathbf{X}'\mathbf{X}\mathbf{a}_1$.

The objective is to choose $\mathbf{a}_1$ to maximize $\mathbf{Z}_1'\ \mathbf{Z}_1$, with a constraint $\mathbf{a}_1'\mathbf{a}_1 = 1$. The constraint is necessary because without the constraint the variance $(\mathbf{Z}_1'\ \mathbf{Z}_1)$ could be made indefinitely large.

$\varphi = \mathbf{a}_1'\mathbf{X}'\mathbf{X}\mathbf{a}_1 - \lambda_1\ (\mathbf{a}_1'\mathbf{a}_1 - 1)$, where λ_1 is a Lagrange multiplier. Taking partial derivatives and equating to zero:

$$(\partial\varphi/\delta\mathbf{a}_1) = 2\ \mathbf{X}'\mathbf{X}\mathbf{a}_1 - 2\lambda_1\mathbf{a}_1 = 0 \text{ gives}$$

$$(\mathbf{X}'\mathbf{X})\mathbf{a}_1 = \lambda_1\mathbf{a}_1$$

Thus $\mathbf{a}_1$ is an eigenvector of $\mathbf{X}'\mathbf{X}$ corresponding to the root λ_1.

Using

$$\mathbf{Z}_1'\ \mathbf{Z}_1 = \mathbf{a}_1'\mathbf{X}'\mathbf{X}\mathbf{a}_1 = \mathbf{a}_1'\ \lambda_1\mathbf{a}_1 = \lambda_1$$

Therefore λ_1 is to be chosen as the largest eigenvalue of $\mathbf{X}'\mathbf{X}$. The $\mathbf{X}'\mathbf{X}$ matrix, in the absence of perfect collinearity, will be positive definite and thus have positive eigenvalues. The first principal component of $\mathbf{X}$ is then $\mathbf{Z}_1$.

To determine the second principal component, define $\mathbf{Z}_2 = \mathbf{X}\mathbf{a}_2$, where $\mathbf{Z}_2$ is an n-element vector and $\mathbf{a}_2$ a k-element vector. The sum of squares of z_2 is: $\mathbf{Z}_2'\ \mathbf{Z}_2 = \mathbf{a}_2'\mathbf{X}'\mathbf{X}\mathbf{a}_2$. The problem is to choose $\mathbf{a}_2$ to maximize $\mathbf{a}_2'\mathbf{X}'\mathbf{X}\mathbf{a}_2$ subject to $\mathbf{a}_2'\mathbf{a}_2 = 1$ and $\mathbf{a}_1'\mathbf{a}_2 = 0$. The reason for the second constraint is that $\mathbf{Z}_2$ must not be correlated with $\mathbf{Z}_1$.

$$\mathbf{a}_1'\mathbf{X}'\mathbf{X}\mathbf{a}_2 = \lambda_1\ \mathbf{a}_1'\mathbf{a}_2 = 0 \text{ if and only if } \mathbf{a}_1'\mathbf{a}_2 = 0$$

$\varphi = \mathbf{a}_2'\mathbf{X}'\mathbf{X}\mathbf{a}_2 - \lambda_2\ (\mathbf{a}_2'\mathbf{a}_2 - 1) - \mu(\mathbf{a}_1'\mathbf{a}_2)$, where λ_2 and μ are Lagrange multipliers. Taking partial derivatives and equating to zero:

$$(\partial\varphi/\delta\mathbf{a}_2) = 2\mathbf{X}'\mathbf{X}\mathbf{a}_2 - 2\,\lambda_2\,\mathbf{a}_2 - \mu\mathbf{a}_1 = 0$$

Premultiply by $\mathbf{a}_1'$:

$$2\mathbf{a}_1'\mathbf{X}'\mathbf{X}\mathbf{a}_2 - 2\lambda_2\,\mathbf{a}_1'\mathbf{a}_2 - \mu\mathbf{a}_1'\mathbf{a}_1 = 0$$

using $\mathbf{X}'\mathbf{X}\mathbf{a}_1 = \lambda_1\mathbf{a}_1$

$$\mathbf{a}_2'\mathbf{X}'\mathbf{X}\mathbf{a}_1 = \lambda_1\mathbf{a}_2'\mathbf{a}_1 = 0$$

Thus $\mu = 0$, and $(\mathbf{X}'\mathbf{X})\mathbf{a}_2 = \lambda_2\mathbf{a}_2$. Therefore λ_2 should be chosen as the second-largest root of $\mathbf{X}'\mathbf{X}$. This process will continue until the last root (kth) is chosen.

3. A BRIEF DESCRIPTION OF THE TURKISH ECONOMY AND DATA ON MONTHLY INDICATORS

Turkey took significant steps towards liberalization of the economy in January 1980, after several economic and financial crises in the 1970s. The goals of the liberalization package were to lower the rate of inflation and ultimately to create an export-oriented and a liberalized economy that would be competitive in world markets.[3]

The program was successful in lowering the rate of inflation and increasing exports (Figure 9.1). Merchandise exports rose from \$10 billion in 1987 to \$110 billion in 2007. Tourism revenues also increased more than ten-fold during that period. These significant developments in exports and tourism revenues reduced the dependence on workers' remittances, which were very critical in the 1970s. However, current account issues continued to be a concern because of parallel increases in imports, largely due to significant reduction in tariffs as part of agreements with the EU and high import content of exported goods. The real GDP growth rate was lower than the levels realized during the import substitution era. It was also very volatile. Foreign debt, which accumulated at a much higher pace, acted as a drag on the public sector. The state sector kept its importance in major fields of the economy such as determination of wages of civil servants and workers in state economic enterprises. Populist policies were adopted before every election. In Turkey, many indicators related to government expenditures must be included to capture macroeconomic developments (Figure 9.1). The economy was vulnerable to another crisis by the end of every decade. In 1989, the capital account was fully liberalized. However,

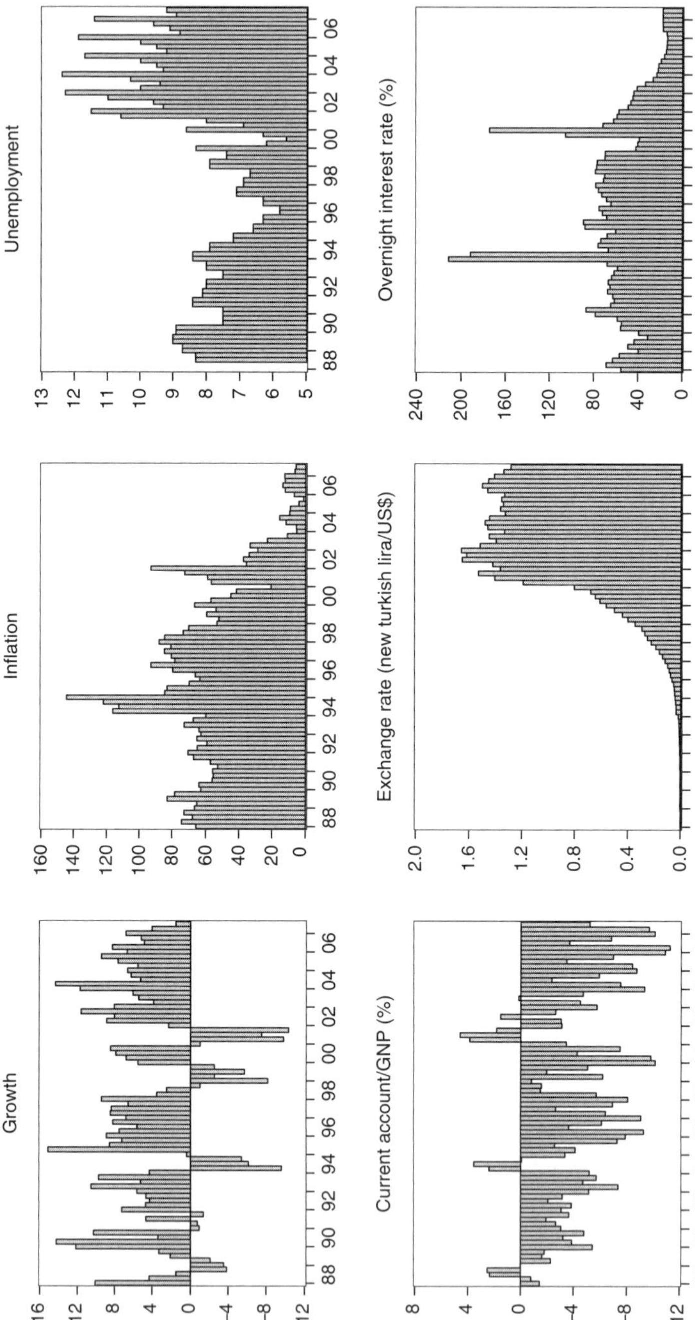
Growth
Inflation
Unemployment
Current account/GNP (%)
Exchange rate (new turkish lira/US$)
Overnight interest rate (%)

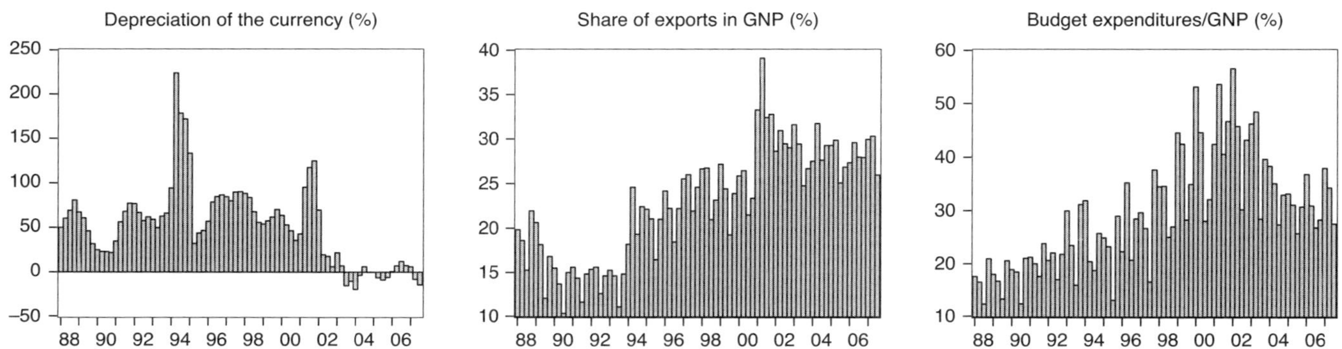

Figure 9.1 Turkey: quarterly indicators, 1988Q1–2007Q3

an attempt to fix the interest rate, despite the large fiscal deficit and high inflation, led to another crisis in 1994. Despite IMF supervision, the economy had a banking crisis in November 2000 and a currency crisis in February 2001, with skyrocketing exchange and interest rates (Figure 9.1).

On the social front, Turkey took very significant steps, largely due to requirements by the EU. Although Turkey's adventure with the EU goes back about 50 years, it is not clear whether Turkey's chance of accession today is higher than its chance in 1957. There are many reasons for the slow process. The most obvious ones are the large size of its population (75 million in 2007, forecasted to be the largest in the EU if Turkey is accepted in 2025), and low income level (per capita GDP of about 25 percent of Europe). Relatively high inflation and volatile growth and exchange rate depreciation are some other important factors when Turkey is compared to other European countries. Historical grievances are slow to disappear. Turks, originally from Central Asia, landed in Asia Minor (Anatolia) in 1071. The Ottoman Empire, which survived from 1299 to the establishment of the Republic of Turkey in 1923, ended the Byzantine Empire in 1543, and occupied and ruled some of the countries that are already members of the EU, with veto powers, until the First World War. Religion is also considered to be an important reason for the possible rejection of the Turkish bid. Policy-makers in Turkey are in the process of changing civil and criminal laws in the direction of European laws. EU accession is seen as a very long process which will help Turkey in the long run, whether it is accepted or not. Turkey's younger population, prosperous natural resources and incomparable historical sites are some positive factors that the country relies on. Most of these factors related to relationships with the EU are important in the long run, but we try to include some of these indicators that are available at high frequency.

There are many data series to be considered for a current quarter model (CQM) of Turkey. Variables were selected from many spheres of economic activity. There are variables on production, exports, imports, government expenditures and revenues, money supply, interest rates, exchange rates, consumer prices, producer prices, and import and export prices. The availability of a long data set (at least covering the post-1987 period when quarterly GDP data are available) is the primary consideration. Some variables may be highly correlated with others. These may be considered for exclusion in order to gain degrees of freedom.

Most of the variables are non-stationary, as suggested by the augmented Dickey–Fuller (ADF) and Phillips–Perron (PP) unit root test. Therefore changes or percentage changes of most of these variables are used in calculations. Indicator variables are forecasted using Box–Jenkins

BOX 9.1 MONTHLY INDICATORS

Industrial production index – (percent change, year over year (yoy))
Industrial production index – manufacturing (percent change, yoy)
Industrial production index – utilities (percent change, yoy)
Industrial production index – textiles (percent change, yoy)
Unemployment (rate change, yoy)
Merchandise exports/CPI (percent change, yoy)
Merchandise imports/CPI (percent change, yoy)
Current account balance/CPI
Trade balance/CPI
Merchandise balance/CPI
Government budget balance/CPI
Central government expenditures/CPI (percent change, yoy)
State budget revenue/CPI (percent change, yoy)
Total tax revenue/CPI (percent change, yoy)
Direct taxation/total taxation
Money supply (M3)/CPI (percent change, yoy)
Monetary base/CPI (percent change, yoy)
M2/M3 (change, yoy)
Turkish lira/US$ (percent change, yoy)
Turkish lira/euro (percent change, yoy)
Consumer price index (CPI) (percent change, yoy)
Producer price index (PPI) (percent change, yoy)
Istanbul stock exchange index/CPI (percent change, yoy)
Overnight interest rate
Discount interest rate
Interest rate on three-month savings deposits
Rate on 12-month deposit – rate on one-month deposit
Rate on six-month deposit – rate on one-month deposit

methodology. Twenty-eight monthly variables are used in the principal components analysis (Box 9.1).

4. ESTIMATION OF THE MODEL

Having formed principal components of the list of relevant indicators, we estimate the regression equation for the important substantive target variables in order to gain understanding of the macroeconomy and use those principal components that show significant relationships to the chosen substantive variables.

If we write, for the *i*th principal component, as a linear function of the indicator variable X_{it}

$$Z_{it} = \sum_{i=1} \gamma_i X_{it}$$

our procedure can be stated as one that estimates regression relationships between the specific economic variables (growth, inflation, unemployment, and current account balance) that we want to project and the principal components, Z_{it}, which, in turn, are based on the primary indicators:

$$Y_{it} = \sum_{j=1}^{n_i} \alpha_{ij} Z_{jt} + e_{it}$$

where $n_i < n$ ($n = 28$) is the subset of principal components that are found to be significantly related to X_{it}, a magnitude that we are trying to project; Y_{it} are the macroeconomic variables that describe the state of the economy, such as the national income and product accounts; and e_{it} = random error.

In estimating the coefficients in the above relationship, e_{it} may be an ARIMA process:

$$e_{it} = \sum_{j=1}^{3} \rho_{ij} e_{it-j} + \sum_{j=1}^{3} \mu_{ij} u_{it-j}$$

where both e_{it} and u_{it} are independent random-error variables. The 'noise' in this process comes from e_{it}.

There are eight quarterly variables to be forecasted:

- Four stochastic equations (equations subject to random errors):
  - growth in real GDP (year on year) (GROWTH)
  - growth in the GDP deflator (year on year) (INFLATION)
  - rate of unemployment (percent) (UNEMPLOYMENT)
  - current account balance/GDP ratio (percent) (CURRENT ACCOUNT)
- Four identities (definitions):
  - real GDP, measured in base period (1987) prices
  - GDP deflator (index of prices)
  - nominal GDP, measured in current prices
  - growth in nominal GDP (year on year)

All four stochastic equations indicate a good fit between the dependent variable and quarterly averages of monthly principal components (Table

Table 9.1 Estimated equations

Variable	Growth	Inflation	Unemployment	Current account
C	4.288	54.374	10.384	−6.630
Z01	−1.239	9.324	0.232	0.823
Z02	1.986	5.115	0.119	−0.703
Z03	1.327	2.044		
Z04	−0.797			
Z06	0.814	−5.587		
Z07		−4.425		
Z08	0.871	4.629	0.225	
Z12	−1.170			
Z14	1.550			
Z17	−1.235			
Z21				1.207
Z22	−2.299			
Z24			0.652	3.220
Z27				4.509
Quarter 2			−1.443	0.897
Quarter 3			−1.403	4.519
Quarter 4			−0.899	1.772
AR(1)			0.799	0.518
AR(2)				−0.247
AR(3)				0.526
AR(4)			0.734	
AR(5)			−0.568	
R^2	0.899	0.922	0.859	0.825
Adjusted R^2	0.883	0.916	0.836	0.795
SE of regression	1.984	9.106	0.660	1.590
F-statistic	56.983	134.776	37.291	27.028
Durbin–Watson statistic	1.783	1.394	1.962	2.114

9.1). The growth equation has ten principal components, with an adjusted R^2 of 0.88, and a Durbin–Watson coefficient of 1.78. All variables are significant at the 1 percent level, with the exception of Z17 and Z22, which are significant at the 5 percent level. The inflation equation has six principal components, with an adjusted R^2 of 0.92. All variables are significant at the 1 percent level. The rate of unemployment equation has four principal components, and three seasonal dummy variables. There are also autoregressive coefficients to correct for serial correlation in residuals. All seasonal dummy variables and autoregressive coefficients are significant at the 5 percent level, and principal component variables are significant at the 10 percent level. This equation has an adjusted R^2 of 0.84, and a Durbin–Watson coefficient of 1.96. The current account equation has also seasonal dummies and autoregressive coefficients. This equation, with five principal components, has an adjusted R^2 of 0.79, and a Durbin–Watson coefficient of 2.11. All variables are significant at the 5 percent level. These four stochastic equations, along with four identities, make up the model to be used in forecasting the eight dependent variables that are generated by the four statistical estimates of stochastic equations and the four definitional equations.

5. PERFORMANCE OF THE MODEL AND COMPARISONS WITH ALTERNATIVE MODELS

The model is estimated for the period 1990Q1–2007Q3 and performance is compared with alternative models.[4] In-sample errors are used in model comparisons.

The model effectively captures recent developments in the economy (Figure 9.2 and Table 9.2). Since data are not seasonally adjusted, growth and inflation are calculated as percentage changes from the same quarter a year ago (year-on-year growth). Since unemployment rate and current account as a percentage of GDP are already measured, no such transformation was used for these two variables. The seasonal factors are clear in these variables. Volatility in growth and seasonality in the current account and unemployment are captured successfully by the model. The significant reduction in rate of inflation, and a higher level of unemployment following crises of 2000 and 2001, are also correctly predicted by the model (Figure 9.2). There are some periods where forecast errors are slightly higher than average. For example, inflation in 1995, 2000 and 2002 was underestimated (Table 9.2). This was largely due to financial crises in 1994, 2000 and 2001.

The model performance is compared with those of alternative models. Random-walk, ARIMA and VAR models are used as alternatives. The model performs significantly better than alternative models. For example, mean absolute error in growth predictions is 1.46 for the model, 3.99 for the random walk, 3.07 for ARIMA and 2.52 for the VAR (Table 9.3). Similar results are obtained in other equations. In addition to mean absolute error, mean absolute percentage error (MAPE) is given for real GDP, deflator and nominal GDP. The MAPE for real GDP is 1.39 for the model, compared with 3.87 for the random walk, 2.97 for ARIMA and 2.43 for the VAR model.

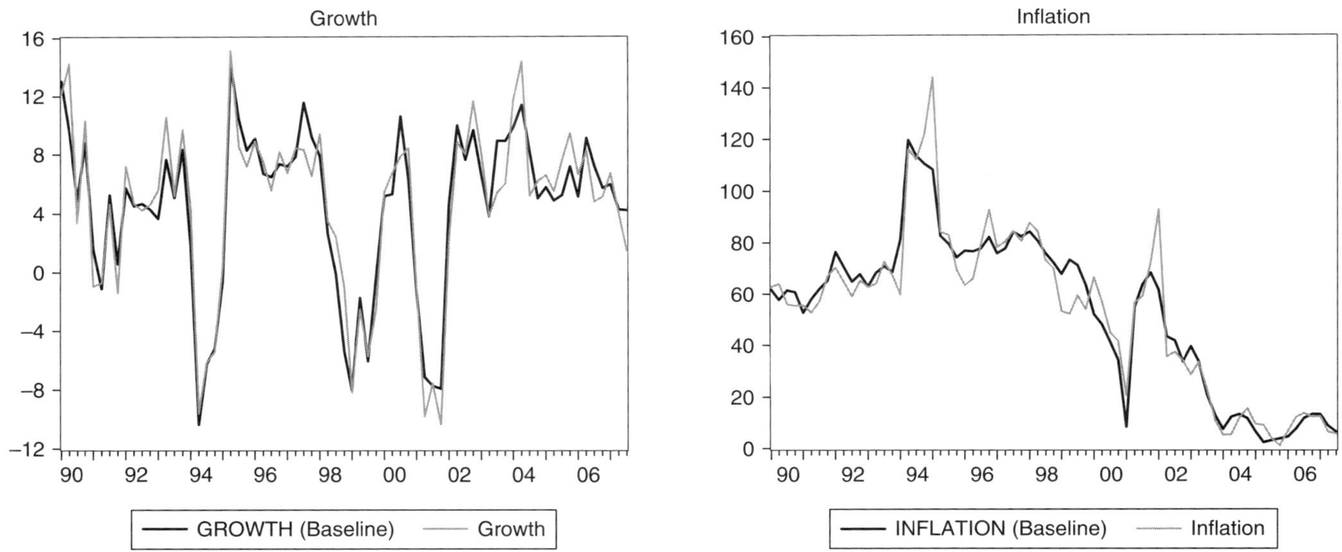

Figure 9.2 Actual and model predictions (one-period-ahead forecasts)

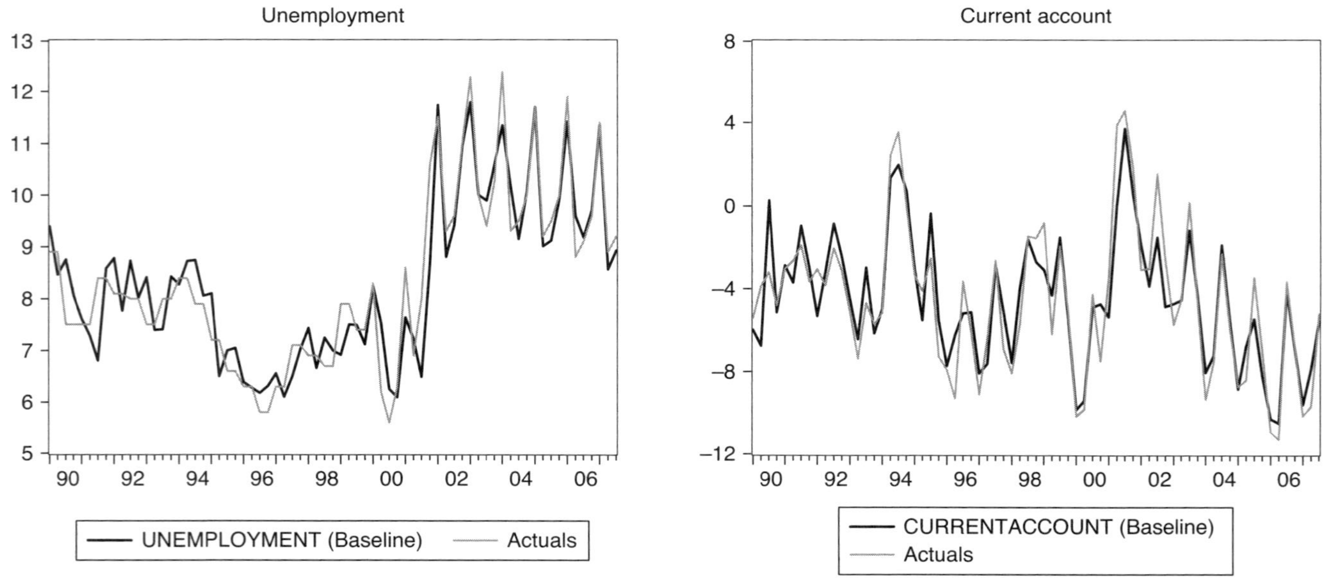

Figure 9.2 (continued)

Table 9.2 Model solution, 1990Q1–2007Q3

	1990	1991	1992	1993	1994	1995	1996	1997	1998
Growth									
Baseline	9.1	1.6	4.8	6.2	−5.0	8.1	7.4	9.0	1.3
Actuals	10.0	0.4	5.2	7.8	−4.2	7.8	7.5	7.5	3.6
Deviation	−1.0	1.2	−0.4	−1.6	−0.8	0.3	−0.1	1.4	−2.3
Inflation									
Baseline	60.4	59.5	69.9	67.7	106.3	86.2	78.4	80.1	78.3
Actuals	59.5	58.1	64.9	66.7	102.5	95.2	75.4	80.9	78.9
Deviation	0.9	1.4	5.0	1.0	3.8	−9.0	3.0	−0.9	−0.6
Unemployment									
Baseline	8.7	7.6	8.3	7.9	8.5	7.2	6.3	6.5	7.1
Actuals	8.2	8.0	8.1	7.8	8.2	6.9	6.1	6.7	6.8
Deviation	0.5	−0.4	0.3	0.2	0.3	0.3	0.2	−0.2	0.3
Current account									
Baseline	−4.4	−2.6	−3.0	−5.0	−0.2	−3.6	−6.1	−5.9	−4.0
Actuals	−4.3	−2.8	−3.0	−5.7	0.2	−4.3	−6.7	−6.3	−4.2
Deviation	−0.1	0.2	0.1	0.7	−0.4	0.7	0.7	0.3	0.2
Real GDP (1987 prices, thousands of new Turkish lira)									
Baseline	20716	21245	22012	23440	22496	24530	26217	28645	28459
Actuals	20860	21010	22068	23757	22648	24432	26235	28223	29135
Deviation	−144	235	−56	−316	−152	98	−18	422	−676
% deviation	−0.8	1.2	−0.4	−1.5	−0.8	0.2	−0.1	1.3	−2.3
GDP deflator (1987 = 100)									
Baseline	468	743	1248	2036	4198	7610	14002	25038	44545
Actuals	464	737	1213	2024	4153	7837	13866	25113	44553
Deviation	4	7	36	12	45	−227	136	−75	−8
% deviation	0.6	0.9	3.1	0.6	2.7	−3.6	2.1	−0.5	−0.2
GDP (nominal, millions of new Turkish lira)									
Baseline	98	160	277	483	959	1899	3710	7314	12765
Actuals	98	157	270	487	957	1935	3695	7207	13080
Deviation	1	4	7	−4	2	−36	15	106	−316
% deviation	−0.2	2.1	2.7	−0.9	1.8	−3.4	2.0	0.8	−2.5

6. FORECASTS (2007Q4–2008Q4)

Forecasts for monthly indicators are obtained using ARIMA equations. All available data are utilized. For example, if data for a variable are available for November, forecasts start from December. If the latest data are for October, forecasts for that variable start in November.

These monthly forecasts of indicators are used to form variables to be used in principal components analysis. Quarterly averages of monthly principal components are calculated to be used in the relationships

Table 9.2 (continued)

	1999	2000	2001	2002	2003	2004	2005	2006	2007
Growth									
Baseline	−4.0	6.9	−6.0	8.0	7.1	8.6	5.8	6.8	4.9
Actuals	−4.7	7.2	−7.2	7.7	5.9	9.4	7.3	6.2	4.1
Deviation	0.7	−0.3	1.2	0.3	1.2	−0.8	−1.5	0.6	0.7
Inflation									
Baseline	68.9	43.8	48.7	45.0	26.7	11.1	4.0	9.2	9.4
Actuals	54.7	52.4	52.1	50.0	24.0	9.5	5.9	11.2	8.1
Deviation	14.2	−8.6	−3.4	−4.9	2.8	1.7	−1.9	−1.9	1.3
Unemployment									
Baseline	7.3	7.0	7.5	10.2	10.6	10.2	9.9	10.0	9.6
Actuals	7.7	6.6	8.5	10.4	10.5	10.3	10.1	9.9	9.8
Deviation	−0.4	0.4	−1.0	−0.1	0.1	−0.1	−0.2	0.1	−0.2
Current account									
Baseline	−3.6	−7.2	−0.3	−3.0	−3.7	−5.7	−7.3	−8.0	−7.7
Actuals	−3.5	−7.9	1.7	−1.8	−3.7	−6.3	−6.9	−8.2	−8.4
Deviation	−0.1	0.7	−2.0	−1.2	0.0	0.6	−0.4	0.2	0.7
Real GDP (1987 prices, thousands of new Turkish lira)									
Baseline	27965	29750	27910	29790	31882	34118	36261	39331	40878
Actuals	27771	29787	27567	29731	31445	34277	36800	39062	40525
Deviation	195	−37	343	59	437	−160	−539	269	353
% deviation	0.7	−0.3	1.3	0.3	1.2	−0.7	−1.4	0.6	0.7
GDP deflator (1987 = 100)									
Baseline	75087	98380	156740	228580	292213	317995	326088	362317	388402
Actuals	68951	104021	159991	232722	286087	313710	331197	368379	383818
Deviation	6136	−5641	−3252	−4142	6126	4285	−5110	−6062	4584
% deviation	9.2	−5.5	−2.7	−1.9	2.2	1.7	−1.7	−1.8	1.2
GDP (nominal, millions of new Turkish lira)									
Baseline	21245	29558	44509	68810	93006	108818	118571	143107	159056
Actuals	19378	31205	44606	69552	90146	107866	122125	144415	155799
Deviation	1868	−1648	−98	−742	2861	952	−3553	−1307	3257
% deviation	10.0	−5.8	−1.4	−1.7	3.3	1.0	−3.1	−1.2	1.9

with growth, inflation, unemployment and current account balance. The growth rate is forecasted to be lower in 2007 and 2008 (Table 9.4). The growth is expected to be 4.31 percent in 2007 and 3.05 percent in 2008, compared to 7.32 percent in 2005 and 6.24 percent in 2006. The difference from the previous year is also given in the table. For example, growth rate is forecasted to be 4.31 percent in 2007, 1.93 less than 6.24 percent (the growth rate in 2006). On the other hand, there is an increase in the predicted rate of inflation (measured by the GDP deflator) and the rate of unemployment. Inflation, which came down from 11.2 percent in 2006 to 7.6 percent in 2007, is predicted to increase to 9.7 percent in 2008. The rate

Table 9.3 Model performance and comparison with alternative models

	Principal components	Random walk	ARIMA	VAR	RW-PC	ARIMA-PC	VAR-PC
Growth	1.46	3.99	3.07	2.52	1.05	2.53	1.61
Inflation	5.84	9.09	8.18	8.04	2.21	3.25	2.34
Unemployment	0.46	0.75	0.47	0.36	−0.10	0.30	0.02
Current account	1.13	2.81	1.97	1.63	0.50	1.67	0.84
Real GDP							
MAE	408	1009	795	662	255	601	387
MAPE	1.39	3.87	2.97	2.43	1.04	2.47	1.58
Deflator							
MAE	4157	6797	6200	6601	2444	2640	2043
MAPE	3.69	5.71	5.15	5.19	1.50	2.02	1.46
GDP (nominal)							
MAE	1430	2072	2002	2033	603	642	572
MAPE	3.86	6.32	5.54	5.01	1.15	2.46	1.68

of unemployment, which improved slightly in 2005 to 2007, is expected to pick up to the 10 percent level in 2008. The current account balance/GDP ratio is expected to improve slightly in 2008 (from a deficit of 8.2 percent of GDP in 2007 to a deficit of 7.7 percent in 2008).

NOTES

1. See Klein and Özmucur (2008) for a more detailed analysis of the CQM for the USA and applications in other countries.
2. See Zwick and Velicer (1986) for comparison of alternative methods and problems associated with them.
3. See Özmucur (2007) for a detailed analysis of the Turkish economy and related references.
4. See Mariano (2002) for alternative tests of model comparisons.

Table 9.4 Model forecasts (2007Q4–2008Q4)

	2005				2006				2005	2006
	Q1	Q2	Q3	Q4	Q1	Q2	Q3	Q4		
Growth	6.62	5.54	7.66	9.45	6.68	8.27	4.83	5.18	7.32	6.24
(year dif)	−5.13	−8.81	2.41	3.20	0.06	2.73	−2.83	−4.27	−2.08	−1.08
Inflation	9.4	9.0	3.9	1.2	6.7	12.1	13.6	12.2	5.9	11.2
(year dif)	4.3	3.6	−7.8	−14.3	−2.7	3.1	9.7	11.0	−3.6	5.3
Unemployment	11.7	9.2	9.5	10.0	11.9	8.8	9.1	9.6	10.1	9.9
(year dif)	−0.70	−0.10	0.00	0.00	0.20	−0.40	−0.40	−0.40	−0.20	−0.25
Current account	−8.7	−8.4	−3.5	−7.0	−10.9	−11.3	−3.7	−6.8	−6.9	−8.2
(year dif)	0.61	−0.89	−1.13	−1.07	−2.19	−2.85	−0.21	0.15	−0.62	−1.27
	2007				**2008**				**2007**	**2008**
	Q1	Q2	Q3	Q4	Q1	Q2	Q3	Q4		
Growth	6.79	4.05	1.51	4.88	4.44	4.26	4.09	3.41	4.31	4.05
(year dif)	0.12	−4.22	−3.32	−0.29	−2.35	0.21	2.57	−1.47	−1.93	−0.26
Inflation	12.4	6.3	5.6	6.1	7.7	8.4	10.1	12.6	7.6	9.7
(year dif)	5.7	−5.8	−8.0	−6.0	−4.7	2.1	4.5	6.4	−3.5	2.1
Unemployment	11.4	8.9	9.2	9.7	11.3	9.2	9.5	9.9	9.8	10.0
(year dif)	−0.50	0.10	0.10	0.14	−0.09	0.30	0.28	0.19	−0.04	0.17
Current account	−10.2	−9.7	−5.2	−7.7	−10.0	−8.7	−4.6	−7.6	−8.2	−7.7
(year dif)	0.78	1.59	−1.52	−0.86	0.11	1.01	0.60	0.14	−0.00	0.47

	2005				2006				2005	2006
	Q1	Q2	Q3	Q4	Q1	Q2	Q3	Q4		
Real GDP	31721	35507	42695	37277	33839	38444	44758	39208	36800	39062
(year % ch.)	6.62	5.54	7.66	9.45	6.68	8.27	4.83	5.18	7.36	6.15
Deflator	315764	317198	328805	363024	336999	355686	373559	407272	331197	368379
(year % ch.)	9.4	9.0	3.9	1.2	6.7	12.1	13.6	12.2	5.6	11.2
GDP (nominal)	100164	112627	140382	135325	114037	136740	167199	159683	122125	144415
(year % ch.)	16.7	15.0	11.8	10.7	13.8	21.4	19.1	18.0	13.2	18.3
	2007				2008				2007	2008
	Q1	Q2	Q3	Q4	Q1	Q2	Q3	Q4		
Real GDP	36137	40002	45436	41123	37743	41708	47292	42526	40675	42317
(year % ch.)	6.79	4.05	1.51	4.88	4.44	4.26	4.09	3.41	4.13	4.04
Deflator	378857	378147	394450	432302	408138	409844	434349	486687	395939	434754
(year % ch.)	12.4	6.3	5.6	6.1	7.7	8.4	10.1	12.6	7.5	9.8
GDP (nominal)	136908	151267	179222	177775	154043	170937	205412	206968	161293	184340
(year % ch.)	20.1	10.6	7.2	11.3	12.5	13.0	14.6	16.4	11.7	14.3

REFERENCES

Anderson, T.W. (1984), *An Introduction to Multivariate Statistical Analysis*, 2nd edn, New York: John Wiley.

Box, G.E.P. and G.M. Jenkins (1976), *Time Series Analysis: Forecasting and Control*, rev. edn, San Francisco: Holden-Day.

Hotelling, Harold (1933), 'Analysis of a complex of statistical variables into principal components', *Journal of Educational Psychology*, **24** (September), 417–41; (October), 498–520.

Klein, L.R. and S. Özmucur (2008), 'The University of Pennsylvania models for high-frequency macroeconomic modeling', in R.S. Mariano and Yiu-Kuen Tse (eds), *High-Frequency Economic Forecasting and High Frequency Data Analysis*, Singapore: World Publishers, pp. 53–91.

Klein, L.R. and J. Yong Park (1993), 'Economic forecasting at high-frequency intervals', *Journal of Forecasting*, **12**, 301–19.

Klein, L.R. and J. Yong Park (1995), 'The University of Pennsylvania model for high-frequency economic forecasting', *Economic & Financial Modelling*, Autumn, 95–146.

Klein, L.R. and E. Sojo (1989), 'Combinations of high and low frequency data in macroeconometric models', in L.R. Klein and J. Marquez (eds), *Economics in Theory and Practice: An Eclectic Approach*, Dordrecht/Boston, MA: Kluwer Academic Publishers, pp. 3–16.

Manly, Bryan F.J. (1986), *Multivariate Statistical Methods, A Primer*, London: Chapman and Hall.

Mariano, R.S. (2002), 'Testing forecast accuracy', in M.P. Clements and D.F. Hendry (eds), *A Companion to Economic Forecasting*, Oxford: Blackwell, pp. 284–98.

Özmucur, S. (2007), 'Liberalization and concentration: case of Turkey', *Quarterly Review of Economics and Finance*, **46** (5), 762–77.

Pearson, K. (1901), 'On lines and planes of closest fit to a system of points in space', *Philosophical Magazine*, **2**, 557–72.

Stone, R. (1947), 'On the interdependence of blocks of transactions', *Supplement to the Journal of the Royal Statistical Society*, **IX** (1), 1–45.

Zwick, William R. and Wayne F. Velicer (1986), 'Comparison of five rules for determining the number of components to retain', *Psychological Bulletin*, **99** (3), 432–42.

10. Estimation of the US Treasury yield curve at daily and intra-daily frequency*

Lawrence R. Klein and Süleyman Özmucur

In this era of gravitation by central banks towards inflation targeting, an examination of its use as a major guide for macroeconomic policy and performance is needed. The main policy instrument is the very short-term interest rate. In the USA, this becomes the federal funds rate, which is an overnight rate for reconciling required reserve balances among private banks.

The Federal Reserve and other central banks are quite accurate in hitting their target values for the operative short-term rate (the federal funds rate in the USA). For other countries different target rates are used, and there is no question that central banks in the main advanced economies can hit their short-run targets with great accuracy.

Control over the operative rate is, however, only the first step in implementation of monetary policy. Economy-watchers attach great importance to the signals given off by announcements of the targets for the operative rates, but do these rates serve well as guides to the state of monetary policy – in the direction of credit tightening, easing, or staying put?

The entire yield curve and the entire span of interest rates are what really matter, not to mention non-monetary policies, and our first step in this study is to examine how good is the control over operative rates for interpreting the dynamics of the whole spectrum of rates in any given economy.

Figure 10.1, depicting some relevant time series of US interest rates from 1990 to early 2006, shows the course of the federal funds rate, some closely allied treasury rates and a medium-term treasury rate – the ten-year rate. After 1990 and the Gulf War period, the Federal Reserve objective was to stimulate the macroeconomy by significantly lowering the federal funds rate, but often not much happened to the ten-year treasury rate, which is much more relevant for judging or lowering private capital costs in order to know what to expect in the form of economic stimulus.

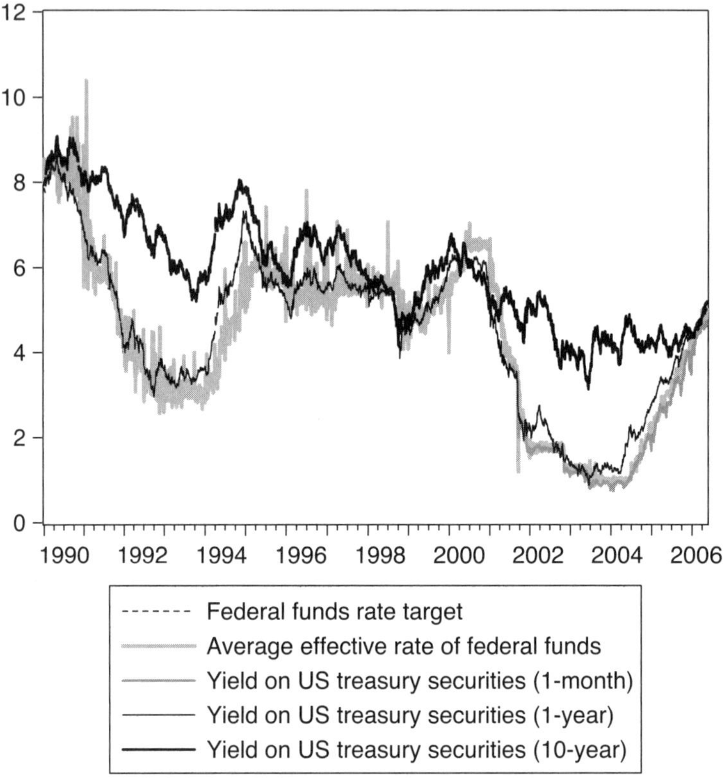

Figure 10.1 The federal funds rate, and yields on US treasury securities

Again, after 2001 and the Iraq War, the federal funds rate was the operative rate and frequently showed hardly any significant relationship to the ten-year treasury rate, either for the downswing in the federal funds rate or for its upswing.

Eventually, large movements in the federal funds rate may percolate through to the market-sensitive rates for actual investment decisions, but the operative rate hardly seems to be a reliable policy tool for influencing real economic activity.

It is evident in Figure 10.1 that some other short-term rates follow the federal funds rate closely, but effective control over this operative rate does not lead to effective control over the more meaningful rates that are used in basic investment decision-making, leading to capital formation.

There are some important institutional reasons why there has been a weak connection between the federal funds rate and a medium-term rate such as

Table 10.1 US macroeconomic statistics, 1990–93

	1990	1991	1992	1993
GDP, % change	1.2	−0.6	2.3	3.1
Unemployment, %	5.5	6.7	7.4	6.8
M2, % change	5.3	3.2	2.1	1.3
Federal funds rate, %	8.1	5.7	3.5	3.0
3-month treasury yield, %	7.5	5.4	3.4	3.0
10-year treasury yield, %	8.6	7.9	7.0	5.9

Source: OECD, *Economic Survey, US*, 1995.

the ten-year treasury rate, namely, that the technical environment for implementation of banking operations has changed drastically in the information age, starting some time in the 1980s. When the federal funds rate was lowered along a steep gradient, plainly visible in 1991 and 1992, following the Gulf War, there was hardly any corresponding movement in M2, because the meaning of money drastically changed in this period, and there was little stimulus for borrowing in order to realize private investment goals.

The graph of the federal funds rate and the ten-year treasury yield is highlighted because the mortgage rate appears to follow this ten-year treasury rate and was particularly important for the recent expansion of residential real-estate investment. The overall economy was sustained significantly by households' attention to their investment in real residential property, at a time when corporate scandals turned many people away from trust in equity markets or other security investments.

Another aspect of the relation between the federal funds rate, and the yield curve in general, is that many monetary authorities favor decisively the concept of inflation targeting. A subtle change has taken place in the USA in this respect.

It used to be the case that the Federal Reserve favored a broader statement about the goal of monetary policy. One of their most important public affairs publications, *The Federal Reserve System, Purposes and Functions* (1994), stated explicitly on p. 1, 'Today, the Federal Reserve's duties fall into four general areas: Conducting the nation's monetary policy by influencing the money and credit conditions in the economy in pursuit of full employment and stable prices.'

This is only the first of four general areas of interest and responsibility, but it differs from a more recent statement of the goals of monetary policy in the 2005 edition, which says (p. 15), 'Stable prices in the long run are a precondition for maximum sustainable output growth and employment as well as moderate long-term interest rates.' There is a very important and subtle distinction between the older and the new statement of the goals of monetary policy. Without declaring that they are formal inflation targeters, it rationalizes their behavior in acting like other advanced industrial economies that are more openly targeting inflation. The 2005 statement makes price stability a precondition, while in 1994 (p. 17) it states that 'a stable level of prices appears to be the condition most conducive to maximum sustained output'.

There is an admission that 'in the short run some tension can exist between the two goals [of sustainable output growth and employment at the same time as achievement of price stability]'. It is our opinion that it is possible to generalize the condition of the optimality region for more than one goal at a time.

The field of control theory is devoted to the optimization of weighted combinations of multiple targets, subject to the constraint of dynamic movement of the multivariate economy, accompanying an equation system of descriptive economic performance. For inflation targeting, the focus is on the path of inflation alone, with some informed attention paid to the other variables that would constitute a control theorist's loss or gain function.

In the USA, attention is directed towards the treasury yield curve, with special emphasis on the ten-year rate at the present time, as well as the shape of the yield curve.

THE MEANING OF THE YIELD CURVE

The yield curve displays interest yields on various treasury securities of different maturity. A normal yield curve begins with the overnight rate and systematically spreads to rates of successive monthly maturity, to yearly maturities of successive length, reaching up to the 30-year treasury bond. The longer the maturity, the higher the yield, is the normal view. As maturity rises, there should be more risk, requiring a higher yield, as long as the risk of repayment remains constant. For this reason, the treasury yield curve is used because all treasury securities are viewed presently as riskless; i.e. the US Treasury has not, in modern times, failed to pay interest when due or principal at maturity.

It is a fact, however, that at various times the treasury yield curve becomes steeper or less steep, and in the most embarrassing situation has inverted – by carrying a higher yield on a short-term treasury than on some long-term treasuries.

Since a yield curve, at any time, might look like most other simplistic economic relationships between two variables, interest level and maturity level, the yield curve moves about, and a fixed relation between the ten-year treasury and the federal funds rate, in Figure 10.1, does not show any simple relationship. In the graph, the federal funds rate and monthly maturity rates (target and realized values) are all grouped together, showing that maturities up to one year do, in fact, move closely with the federal funds rate, making one solid 'blur', while the ten-year rate stands apart, showing no tendency to move to where the Federal Reserve's policy committee would like it to be. There are significant stretches where the federal funds rate is being moved down, to stimulate the economy, and the ten-year treasury rate hardly moves down by a comparable magnitude. Also there are protracted periods when the federal funds rate moves significantly upwards, while the yield on the ten-year treasury pays hardly any attention to the policy rate.

It is because of this conceptual relation between yield and maturity that we have an entirely different perspective on the shape of the yield curve.[1] We define, not one particular relationship between interest rate and maturity, but an entire batch of relationships between yield on the *i*th treasury security and the set of multiple variables that account for the movements over time of that yield. For each maturity, we find a different set of explanatory variables. There are systematic patterns, but not a simple bivariate relationship between a particular yield and the corresponding security's maturity. For us, every strategic point, for a given maturity on the yield curve, is determined by a different set of explanatory variables. Our yield curve is made up of as many multivariate equations as there are major maturities that we are separately considering. For us, however, there are two key maturities, namely the overnight maturity that constitutes the monetary authority's operative rate, and the ten-year treasury because it appears to be so important for the mortgage market. The ten-year maturity carries that significance now, but some other maturity may replace it as a focal point as the economic situation evolves.

Our approach, thus, involves estimation of

$$y_{it} = f_i(x_{1t}...x_{nt}) + \ell_{it} \qquad (10.1)$$

where:

y_{it} = yield of the *i*th treasury security at time *t*

x_{jt} = *j*th explanatory variable for estimating y_{it}

ℓ_{it} = random error for estimating the yield of the *i*th maturity.

Since some of the explanatory variables are outside the sphere of influence of Fed decisions; we emphasize that the Fed does not control the yield curve or should not even be convinced that it can estimate the yields on the various maturities by the methods on which it relies.

Our depiction of the yield curve is presented in Figure 10.2 for days

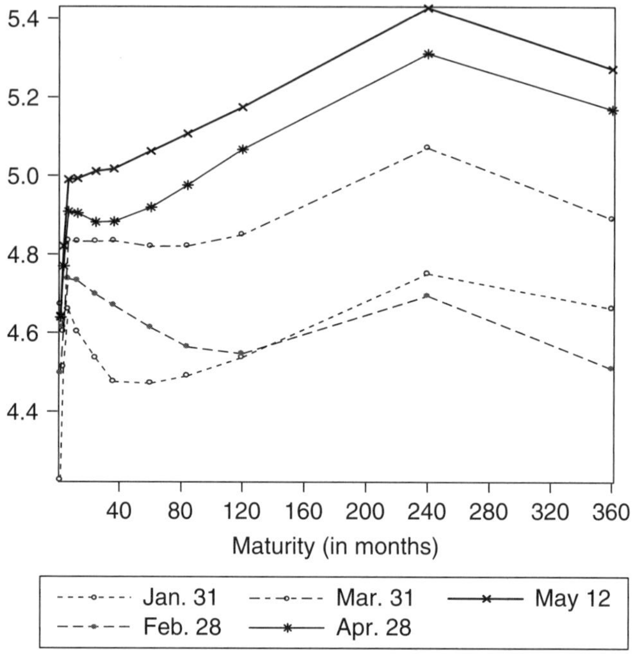

Figure 10.2 Yield curves at five dates in the early part of 2006

in the first five months of 2006. The equations that determine points on this yield curve for a given day are discussed in the next section, for each maturity.

The tendency for the yield curves in Figure 10.2, for different months of 2006, to drop from the 20-year to the 30-year treasury values, is not an inversion in the sense that we are monitoring yields here, because the 30-year treasury was being phased out, but then returned in this period.

The values of y_{it} that determine the shape and position of the yield curve, at any time point, t, must each be estimated from its corresponding function f_i at time t.

Our objective in this chapter is not only to estimate realistic yield curves for the US economy, but also to attempt to do so in essentially real time; i.e. we use variables in the f_i functions that are known in advance so that we can estimate yield curves every working day and also at any time during that working day. We deal mainly with daily market opening time and closing time for the US economy, but in principle the same can be done for other economies and other time periods, no matter how close each time period is to any other time period.

ESTIMATES OF THE DAILY YIELD CURVE EQUATIONS

We start with the (daily data) equation for the one-month-treasury bill rate. All variables preceded by *D* are in first difference form – today's minus yesterday's yield. Also, all dependent variables are measured in daily differences.[2] The one-month yield is significantly related to the federal funds rate, the futures yield for a two-year (the shortest available futures) maturity, the 'Monday' effect and an autoregressive error–moving-average (ARMA) transformation of first- and second-order residuals (Table 10.2).[3]

We can say, of this estimate, that the degree of correlation is quite small and the error term indicates absence of serial correlation. As for all the relevant yields of securities and successive maturities, the explanatory variables must be known before the market opens for daily trading in the USA.

The next equation, for a three-month yield, has mainly the same specification and the degree of correlation is similar. The autoregressive adjustments are for fourth and tenth order.

The equation for the six-month yield has a similar specification, and continues to follow the federal funds rate, as do the equations for the one- and three-month yields, and the overall correlation continues to grow. An autoregressive estimate of third order is significant.

The one-year yield has a similar specification, but adds the Dow Jones futures price, and does not require an autoregressive or moving average transformation of error. The overall correlation continues to grow.

The two-year yield continues to show significant effect of the federal funds rate, but the futures price in this equation is the five-year value. The Monday effect (which is significant in almost all the equations) is retained, as is the Dow Jones futures, but the euro deposit rate is added and the first two autoregressive adjustments are used. The overall correlation continues to rise and there is no residual serial correlation. The eurodollar deposit rate in all equations has a negative coefficient when significant, suggesting a substitution relationship between US treasuries and euro deposits.

The three-year yield shows little relationship to the federal funds rate but is related to the two-year futures and the euro deposit rate, as well as the Dow Jones futures rate and also the Monday effect. It has the same degree of correlation as the two-year rate. Neither the one-year nor the three-year rates appear to need correction for serially correlated disturbances.

The five-year-yield equation moves up to higher overall correlation, but is not significantly related to the federal funds rate. It is strongly related to its own futures price. The euro deposit rate and the Dow Jones futures, together with the Monday effect, round out the relationship. Two autocorrelation terms, AR(1) and AR(2), are significant.

Table 10.2 A summary of estimated treasury yield equations[a]

	1-month	3-month	6-month	1-year	2-year	3-year	5-year	7-year	10-year	20-year	30-year
CONSTANT	0.004*	−0.005*	−0.004*	−0.003*	−0.001	−0.001	−0.001	0.000	−0.001	0.000	0.000
D(FEDERAL FUNDS RATE)	0.108**	0.089**	0.092*	0.036***	0.049**	0.002	0.019	−0.007	−0.019**	−0.017*	−0.018**
D(TREASURY FUTURES (2 YEAR))	0.090*	0.226*	0.351*	0.562*		0.855*					
D(TREASURY FUTURES (5 YEAR))					0.812*		0.908*				
D(TREASURY FUTURES (10-YEAR))								1.082*	1.013*		
D(TREASURY FUTURES (30-YEAR))										0.989*	0.888*
D(EXPECTED INFLATION (T−1))								0.023**	0.042*	0.015**	0.032*
D(EXPECTED EURODOLLAR DEPOSIT RATE)					−0.002**	−0.002***	−0.002***	−0.002**	−0.002**	−0.001	0.000

DLOG(DOW JONES FUTURES)*100				0.001**	0.003*	0.003*	0.003*	0.002*	0.003*	0.001*	
MONDAY	−0.016*	0.027*	0.023*	0.014*	0.005*	0.003***	0.004*	0.002**	0.004*		
DUMMY911	−0.198*	−0.110*	−0.088**								
DUMMY30											−0.059*
AR(1)	0.618*				−0.075***		−0.147*		−0.075**	−0.161*	−0.191*
AR(2)	−0.999*				−0.061***		−0.067*				
AR(3)			−0.095**								
AR(4)		0.041***									
AR(10)		0.128*									
MA(1)	−0.610*										
MA(2)	0.983*										
Adjusted R^2	0.199*	0.193*	0.392*	0.612*	0.759*	0.749*	0.841*	0.880*	0.866*	0.933*	0.819*
Durbin–Watson	1.831	2.023	1.980	2.061	2.001	2.147	2.001	2.226	2.000	2.028	2.037

Notes:
[a] Detailed equations and alternative specifications may be found in Klein and Özmucur (2006a, 2006b). For brevity, they are not repeated here.
* Significant at the 1 percent level.
** Significant at the 5 percent level.
*** Significant at the 10 percent level.

The seven-year-yield equation is negatively and insignificantly related to the federal funds rate and negatively related to the euro deposit rate. It has significant positive relationship with the expected inflation rate, the ten-year treasury futures rate, the Dow Jones futures rate and the Monday effect.[4]

The very important ten-year equation has several significant variables, apart from the constant term. It is negatively associated with the federal funds rate and the euro deposit rate, but positively with inflation expectations, the ten-year futures rate, the Dow Jones futures, the Monday effect, and a negative autoregressive correction factor. The 20-year equation is the first in serial order to show an overall correlation in excess of 0.93. It shows a significant negative relationship to the federal funds rate and the euro interest rate. Inflation expectations, the 30-year futures rate and the Dow Jones futures rate have positive effects. It is not significantly related to the euro deposit rate.

The 30-year bond was withheld (retired on 15 February 2002) from the market when the Clinton Administration was realizing large budget surpluses. The futures yield for the newly introduced treasury bond future is significant, but the euro deposit rate is not. The expected inflation rate shows a significant positive effect and the federal funds rate a negative effect. A first-order autoregressive error correction term is significant.

Each of these displayed equations provides an estimate for one point at a given time period on our yield curve, on the basis of known explanatory variables at the start of each day's trading. At the beginning of each trading day, during the day, and at closing, our system can estimate the whole yield curve, according to our conception of it. Yield curves for each of five separate days are shown in Figure 10.2.

A FORECAST ERROR EXPERIMENT

For every trading day in the interval 23 January 2006 through 12 May 2006, we tested the forecast power of our system for 11 maturities (one month, three months, six months, one year, two years, three years, five years, seven years, ten years, 20 years, 30 years). Average absolute and root mean square errors for closing yields were tabulated daily. At all maturities, our yield estimates had smaller average errors than those of simplistic models.

- simplistic model 1: no daily change; today's yield = yesterday's yield (myopic expectations)
- simplistic model 2: AR equations (autoregressive models in first differences of yields)

For all maturities, from one month to 30 years, our equations performed better than simplistic models, in the sense that average absolute or root mean square error was systematically lower in our model. In particular, the much-studied and popular ten-year treasury yield was consistently (but not for every day) estimated with about two basis points lower error than in the simplistic mechanical or autoregressive models.

We have tried to model the effects of advance indicators that are known prior to trading on each market day. Apart from the finding that we have realized, on average, a smaller absolute error, measured in basis points, by using our model equations in this empirical test, we encountered some market features that are worth pointing out.

In the early days of 2006 we found that using a reading of crude oil price and gold price, both featured as contributing to external inflationary shocks, made our equations perform more poorly. We have no satisfactory explanation for the 'Monday' effect, but it does seem to have some empirical bearing on the market for US treasury securities.

Some major events took place during our test period. The 30-year treasury bond had been retired (15 February 2002) as a result of redemption policy initiated by the US Treasury when the government's fiscal policy produced surpluses instead of deficits – an unusual situation. The financial community protested the absence of a good long-term measuring instrument for inflation, and eventually the 30-year bond was reissued (9 February 2006) during the period of our test. That event redirected activity away from our equations, for a few days, and the observed errors were larger, but corrected in a short time span of a few days.

The transfer of chairmanship at the Federal Reserve took place during our test period (Chairman Ben Bernanke was sworn in on 1 February 2006), and this also brought about market redirection for a few days.

Although gold and oil price changes did not improve the forecasting performance of our equations, they did appear to have monetary influence from time to time. There were periods with relatively large errors: 1, 8 and 10 February and 9, 16 and 28 March for the yield forecasts of the ten-year note. For the 20-year treasury, 1, 2 and 3 February were bad days for yield forecasts. The 30-year bond forecast errors were quite low on 1, 2, 3, 15 and 16 February but large on 9 and 10 February. The long bonds (30-year) had low errors on 17, 20, 21, 22 and 23 March.

Equations were estimated every morning, before 8 am, and forecasts for the end of the day rates were obtained. At the end of the day, these were compared with actual figures. In order to check forecasting ability of the model, various statistics were used, and comparisons with alternative models were made.[5]

Comparisons for the 23 January–12 May period (80 observations) are

Table 10.3 Mean absolute error and root mean square error (basis points) (23 January 2006–12 May 2006)

(a) Mean absolute error (basis points)

	Model	Mechanical	ARIMA	Model minus mechanical	Model minus ARIMA
1-month	2.30	2.61	2.64	−0.31	−0.34
3-month	1.49	1.60	1.63	−0.11	−0.13
6-month	1.36	2.00	2.10	−0.64	−0.74
1-year	1.26	2.32	2.39	−1.06	−1.13
2-year	1.36	3.10	3.15	−1.74	−1.79
3-year	1.13	2.89	2.92	−1.76	−1.79
5-year	1.19	3.39	3.42	−2.20	−2.23
7-year	1.03	3.15	3.19	−2.12	−2.16
10-year	**1.03**	**3.07**	**3.11**	**−2.04**	**−2.07**
20-year	1.17	3.46	3.48	−2.29	−2.32
30-year	1.28	3.21	3.22	−1.93	−1.94

(b) Root mean square error (basis points)

	Model	Mechanical	ARIMA	Model minus mechanical	Model minus ARIMA
1-month	3.95	4.51	4.40	−0.56	−0.45
3-month	1.97	2.02	2.10	−0.06	−0.13
6-month	2.02	2.85	2.87	−0.83	−0.86
1-year	1.92	3.13	3.20	−1.21	−1.28
2-year	2.10	4.08	4.12	−1.98	−2.03
3-year	1.48	3.80	3.80	−2.32	−2.32
5-year	2.51	4.80	4.86	−2.28	−2.34
7-year	1.47	4.03	4.08	−2.57	−2.61
10-year	**1.29**	**3.79**	**3.83**	**−2.50**	**−2.54**
20-year	2.68	4.55	4.63	−1.87	−1.95
30-year	1.84	4.10	4.07	−2.26	−2.23

given in Table 10.3. Mean absolute error and root mean square error based on 80 periods indicate that our model performs better than alternative models (no change, and ARIMA).[6] Mean absolute error for the one-month rate is 2.3 basis points. Errors are much smaller for other maturities. For example, average absolute error is 1.03 basis points for the ten-year and seven-year, and 1.26 basis points for the one-year treasury securities. These errors are much smaller than errors in the alternative models. For example, average absolute error for the ten-year rate is 3.07 basis points for the mechanical model (no change) and 3.11 basis points for the ARIMA (3,1,0) model. Root mean square errors are also smaller for our model. For example, root mean square error for the ten-year treasury is 1.29 basis points. Corresponding figures are 3.79 for the 'no-change' model and 3.83 for the ARIMA. These are significant differences.

It is generally the case that first differences of predictions and realizations are less closely correlated, and again the degree of correlation rises with the length of maturity. Estimated yield curves for selected dates (end of month or data period) indicate that they are very close to actual curves, which are available at the end of the day (Figure 10.3).

The forecasting accuracy of the model can be seen by the correlation between actual and predicted values and the Theil inequality coefficient. Correlations between actual and *ex-ante* forecast lie between 0.971 for the one-month rate and 0.998 for the ten-year rate (Table 10.4, Figure 10.4). Theil inequality coefficients are very close to zero, indicating a close fit (Table 10.4). The decomposition of the inequality coefficient can be very useful to see the source of the error. The bias proportion is very small, less than 0.03 for the one-month rate and less than 0.045 for the ten-year rate. On the other hand, covariance proportion is above 0.90 for the one-month rate, and above 0.93 for the ten-year rate. Prediction and realization diagrams (Figure 10.4) lie very close to a 45-degree line (perfect fit).

It is possible to test if these errors, which are smaller for the model, are statistically significant. This can be done with the use of a Diebold–Mariano statistic, which has several advantages. Forecast errors do not have to be equal to zero on average, and they do not have to be normally distributed. Furthermore, it is also very flexible; the researcher is able to determine the loss function. The statistic has an asymptotic normal distribution.[7] Diebold–Mariano statistics based on 80 forecast periods with five lags are given in Table 10.5. Loss functions, square of forecast errors and absolute value of forecast errors yield the same conclusion. In these tests the model is compared with the 'no-change' model.[8] The model has significantly smaller errors than alternative models at the 1 percent level for all maturities, except one-month and three-month. The model has smaller losses (square of errors or absolute value of errors) for the one-month and three-month rates, but not statistically significant at the 5 percent level.

Another criterion to evaluate the performance of the model is the ability to predict directional change (here, daily changes in treasury yields). This can be done by comparing actual change from a day earlier ($A_t - A_{t-1}$) with the predicted change ($P_t - A_{t-1}$), where P is the predicted, and A is the actual, yield. If both changes are positive or negative, it is a correct

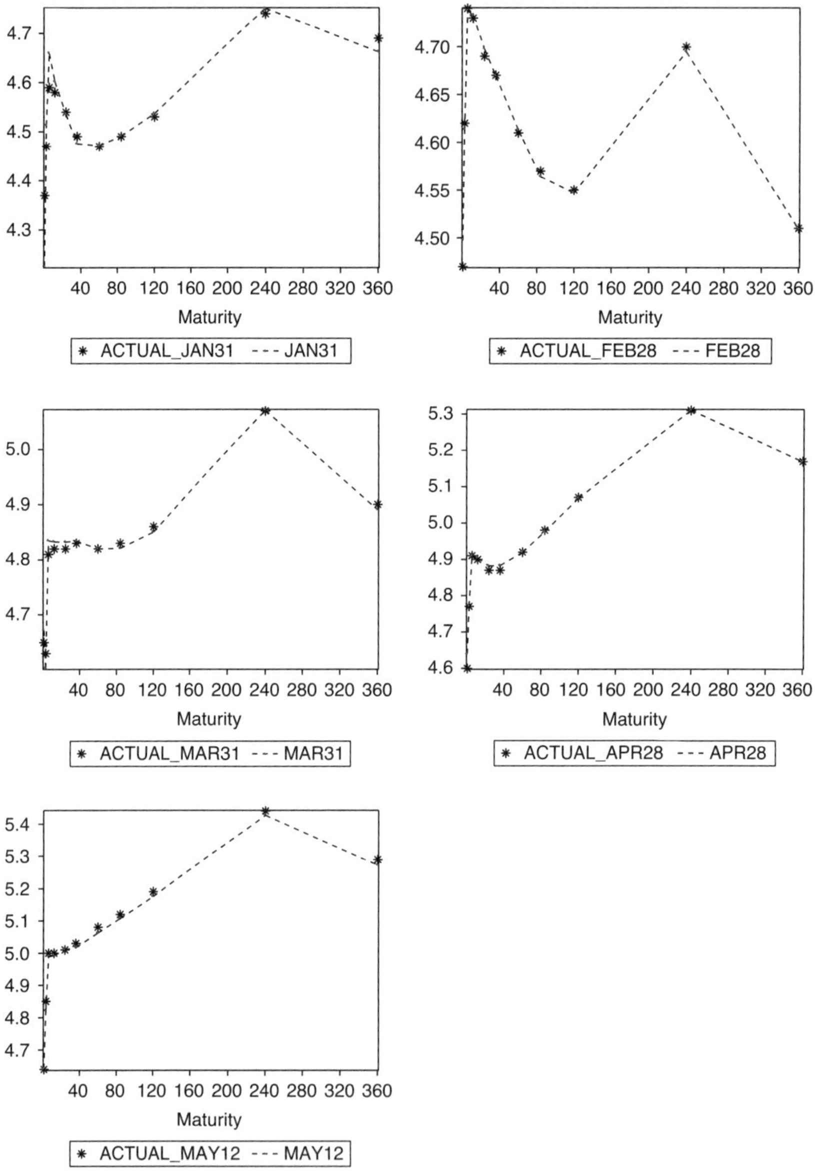

Figure 10.3 Actual and estimated yield curves for selected dates

Table 10.4 Theil inequality coefficients

	Theil inequality coefficient	Bias proportion	Variance proportion	Covariance proportion	Correlation (actual and forecasts)	Correlation (change in actual and forecasts)
1-month	0.0044	0.0280	0.0697	0.9024	0.971*	0.534*
3-month	0.0021	0.0236	0.0130	0.9634	0.987*	0.389*
6-month	0.0021	0.0400	0.0148	0.9452	0.989*	0.710*
1-year	0.0020	0.0181	0.0003	0.9816	0.990*	0.810*
2-year	0.0022	0.0019	0.0003	0.9977	0.990*	0.876*
3-year	0.0016	0.0332	0.0033	0.9635	0.996*	0.946*
5-year	0.0026	0.0088	0.0066	0.9846	0.991*	0.881*
7-year	0.0015	0.0129	0.0023	0.9848	0.997*	0.938*
10-year	0.0013	0.0424	0.0213	0.9363	0.998*	0.951*
20-year	0.0027	0.0107	0.0038	0.9856	0.994*	0.812*
30-year	0.0019	0.0544	0.0126	0.9330	0.997*	0.919*

Note: * Significant at the 1 percent level.

prediction of the change. If the actual change is positive, but the predicted change is negative, or the actual change is negative and the predicted change is positive, it is an error in prediction of the change (Table 10.6). These can be seen in lower correlations between changes in actual and predicted values (Table 10.4). For example, the correlation between changes in actual and changes in the predicted ten-year rate is 0.95, but the correlation is only 0.39 for the three-month rate. There are 45 cases where there is an increase in the yield and the directional prediction of the yield is an increase (correct prediction) in the ten-year treasuries (Table 10.6). In one case, the model prediction is an 'increase', but the actual change is a 'decrease' (incorrect prediction). In five cases, the model prediction is a 'decrease', but the actual change is an 'increase' (incorrect prediction). There are 29 cases where there is a decrease in the yield and the directional prediction of the yield is also a decrease (correct prediction). There are 74 correct (93 percent) and six incorrect predictions out of a total of 80 daily changes in the ten-year yield. The model performs slightly better when rates are decreasing than when they are increasing. For example, the percentage of correct prediction in the ten-year yield is 90 percent (45/(45 + 5)*100) when rates are increasing (actual change is positive) and 97 percent (29/(29 + 1)*100) when rates are decreasing (actual change is negative). The chi-square (χ^2) test for the ten-year yield (Tsay, 2005) indicates that the model outperforms a random-choice model with equal

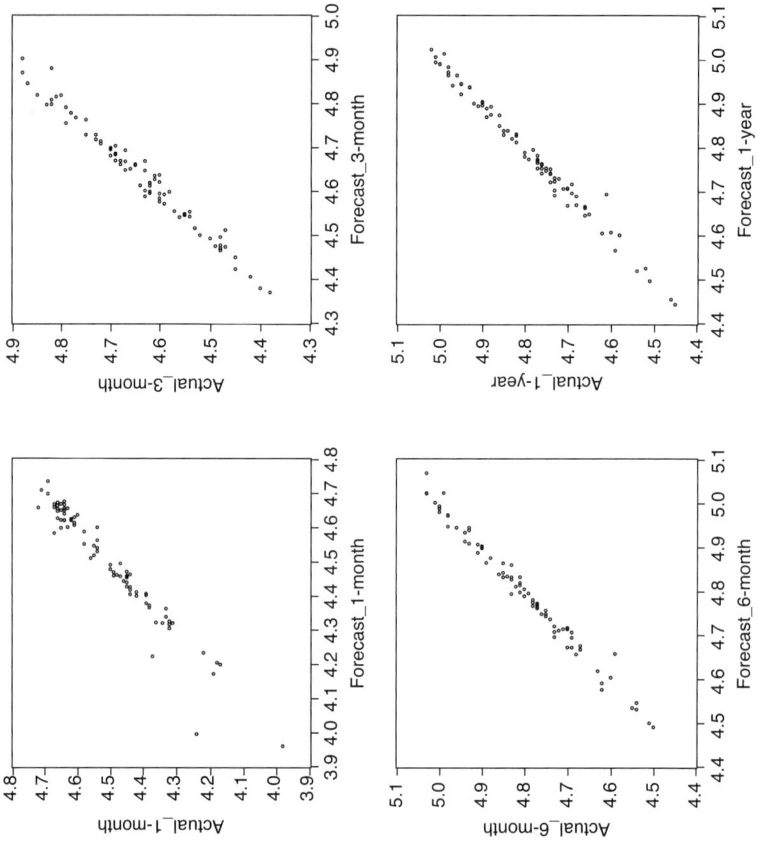
Actual_1-month
Forecast_1-month
Actual_3-month
Forecast_3-month
Actual_6-month
Forecast_6-month
Actual_1-year
Forecast_1-year

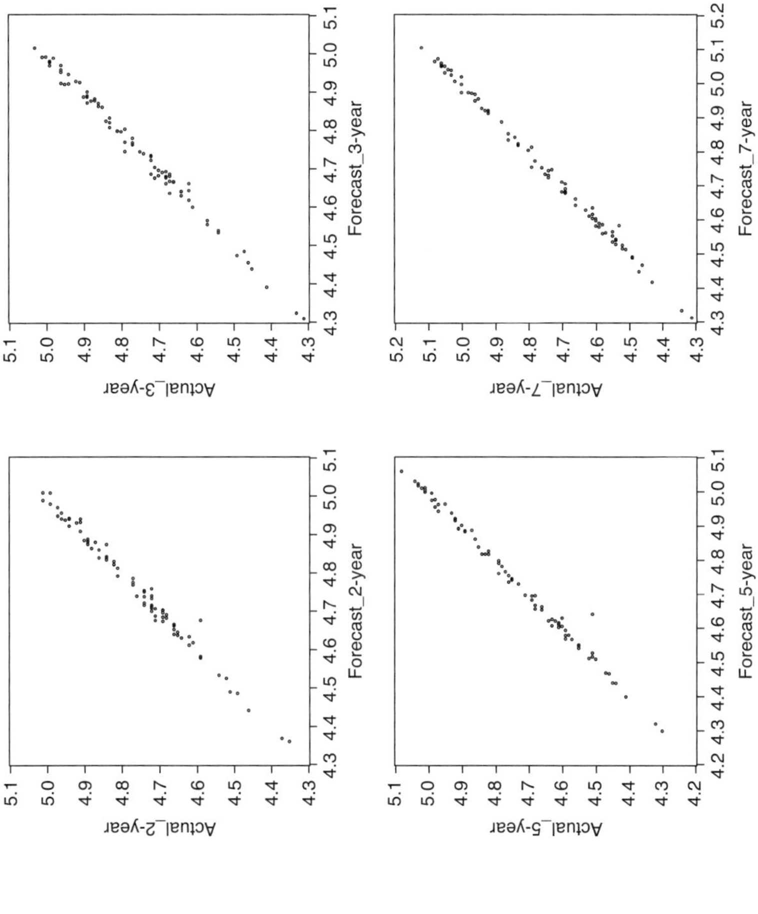

Figure 10.4 Prediction and realization diagrams

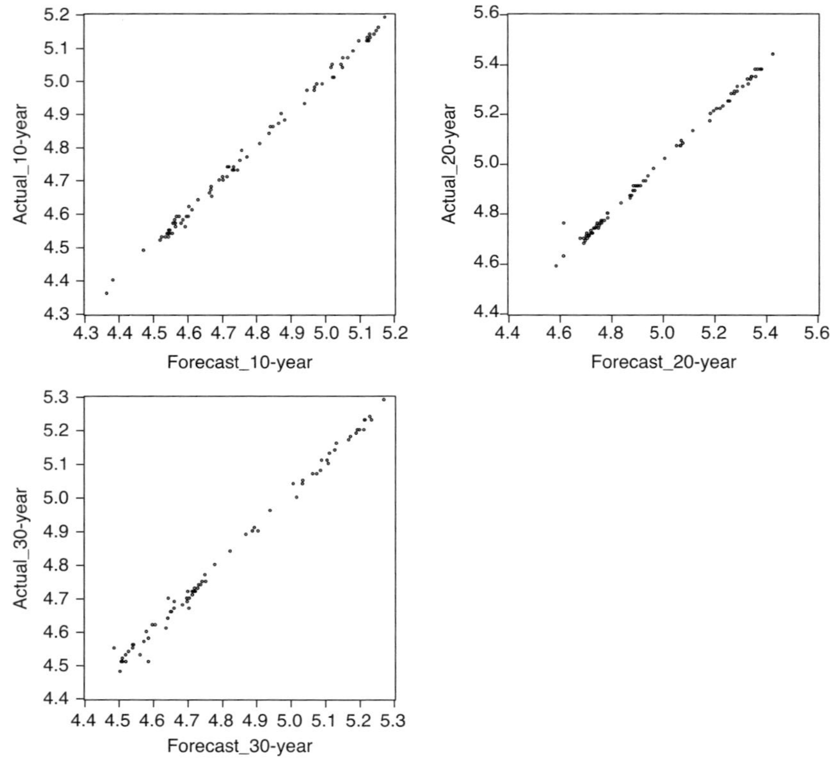

Figure 10.4 (continued)

Table 10.5 Diebold–Mariano statistics with alternative loss functions

	Loss function: square of forecast errors	Loss function: absolute value of forecast errors
1-month	−1.85***	−1.85***
3-month	−0.60	−0.47
6-month	−3.46*	−2.79*
1-year	−3.03*	−4.09*
2-year	−3.82*	−6.18*
3-year	−4.51*	−7.74*
5-year	−2.78*	−5.40*
7-year	−5.41*	−7.05*
10-year	−8.05*	−10.42*
20-year	−3.65*	−11.24*
30-year	−24.61*	−10.89*

Notes:
* Significant at the 1 percent level.
*** Significant at the 10 percent level.

probabilities of upward and downward movements. The model performs very well in terms of prediction of changes with treasury yields of maturities from one year through 20 years. About 90 percent of changes are predicted correctly. The performance is relatively good for the six-month (79 percent) and 30-year (83 percent) maturities. The accuracy of predicting changes is not that good for treasuries with one-month and three-month maturities. Based on directional measure of χ^2 tests the model does significantly better, with the exception of the three-month yield.

A TRADING EXPERIMENT

It is possible to make a simple experiment of daily transactions to see the performance of the model in a trading setting. A simple decision rule exercised at the beginning of the day, and the gain or loss at the end of the day, is easily seen. The same experiment is repeated for all the days to compare the performance of the model against the mechanical model.

The simple rule involves comparison of actual yield (A) at the beginning of the day and its predicted yield (P) at the end of the day. If predicted change in the yield is negative, i.e. $P_t - A_{t-1} < 0$, then the suggested decision is to 'buy'. The gain, which may turn out to be negative also, at the end of the day is $G_t = A_t - A_{t-1}$. If the prediction is correct, there will be a positive gain. If predicted change in the yield is positive, i.e. $P_t - A_{t-1} >$

Table 10.6 Prediction of turning points (80 daily changes)

	Prediction up and actual up (1)	Prediction up and actual down (2)	Prediction down and actual up (3)	Prediction down and actual down (4)	Number of correct predictions (1+4)	Number of incorrect predictions (2+3)	Share of correct predictions (actual up) 1/(1+3)	Share of correct predictions (actual down) 4/(2+4)	Share of total correct predictions (1+4)/(1+2+3+4)	Chi-square (χ^2)
1-month	35	11	12	22	57	23	0.74	0.67	0.71	13.4*
3-month	37	9	23	11	48	32	0.62	0.55	0.60	1.7
6-month	45	3	14	18	63	17	0.76	0.86	0.79	24.8*
1-year	50	2	6	22	72	8	0.89	0.92	0.90	48.4*
2-year	49	1	7	23	72	8	0.88	0.96	0.90	49.8*
3-year	51	3	6	20	71	9	0.89	0.87	0.89	43.6*
5-year	49	1	6	24	73	7	0.89	0.96	0.91	53.1*
7-year	47	0	8	25	72	8	0.85	1.00	0.90	51.8*
10-year	45	1	5	29	74	6	0.90	0.97	0.93	57.6*
20-year	45	2	8	25	70	10	0.85	0.93	0.88	44.3*
30-year	40	2	12	26	66	14	0.77	0.93	0.83	35.5*

Note: * Significant at the 1 percent level.

0, then the suggested decision is to 'sell'. The gain (or loss avoided) at the end of the day is $G_t = A_{t-1} - A_t$, or $G_t = (-1)*(A_t - A_{t-1})$. If the prediction is correct, there will be a gain since the price at the end of the day is lower than the price at the beginning of the day. The sum of these daily gains indicates a higher return for the model (Table 10.7). For example, for the ten-year treasuries, the sum of gains in 80 days is 2.42, compared to a gain of 0.82 for the mechanical model.[9] If the trading cost is 8 cents per $100 par value,[10] the net gain for $1000 in 80 days is $1356 (2.42*1000 − 80*(0.08/100)*1000 − 1000) with a percentage return of 135.6 percent, compared to a loss of $244 (negative 24.4 percent return) in the mechanical model. The returns are even higher for five-year (160.6 percent) and seven-year (139.6 percent) treasuries. Results for other treasuries are also very favorable, with the exception of the three-month treasuries. The unweighted average return is 93.7 percent for the model, and negative 37.2 percent for the mechanical model.

Actual paper trading with eSignal was helpful to refine trading rules. A month of experimentation indicated that it is necessary to consider four important points:

1. Markets are affected by major news, especially if they are very different from the expected ones. A release by the FOMC (Federal Open Market Committee) and a statement by a former Fed chairman are some examples of markets that may be affected by such news. The week of 26 February, which started with a statement by the former Fed chairman on the 30 percent possibility of a recession towards the end of 2007, and negative news regarding developments in the stock market in China, contributed to significant fluctuations in US equity and bond markets.
2. There may be significant movements within a day. It may not be the best strategy to act just once in the morning and wait until the end of the day. It may be better to trade as necessary. For that purpose, the equations are re-estimated during the day and yields are predicted. A set of results is given in Table 10.8. Corresponding estimates are provided in Figures 10.5 and 10.6. The changes during the day may be significant, and much more pronounced than the one given in Table 10.8.
3. Another issue that came up in simulated trading is related to the average absolute error in the forecasted change in the yield. If the average absolute error is less than 1.3 basis points (the average for the estimation period), one should not act. This may reduce the possibility of a loss. If the predicted change is greater than 1.3 basis points, then one can buy or sell as suggested by model results.

Table 10.7 Performance in daily trading

	Gain			Net gain ($1000 value, 8 cents/$100 cost per transaction)			Percent net gain		
	Model	Mechanical	Difference	Model	Mechanical	Difference	Model	Mechanical	Difference
1-month	1.59	0.69	0.90	526	−374	900	52.6	−37.4	90.0
3-month	0.44	0.50	−0.06	−624	−564	−60	−62.4	−56.4	−6.0
6-month	1.44	0.52	0.92	376	−544	920	37.6	−54.4	92.0
1-year	1.80	0.56	1.24	736	−504	1 240	73.6	−50.4	124.0
2-year	2.34	0.64	1.70	1 276	−424	1 700	127.6	−42.4	170.0
3-year	2.21	0.71	1.50	1 146	−354	1 500	114.6	−35.4	150.0
5-year	2.67	0.77	1.90	1 606	−294	1 900	160.6	−29.4	190.0
7-year	2.46	0.80	1.66	1 396	−264	1 660	139.6	−26.4	166.0
10-year	2.42	0.82	1.60	1 356	−244	1 600	135.6	−24.4	160.0
20-year	2.41	0.85	1.56	1 346	−214	1 560	134.6	−21.4	156.0
30-year	2.23	0.75	1.48	1 166	−314	1 480	116.6	−31.4	148.0
Total	22.01	7.61	14.40	10 306	−4094	14 400	93.7	−37.2	130.9

Table 10.8 Real-time forecasting – daily forecast tracking

	1-month	3-month	6-month	1-year	2-year	3-year	5-year	7-year	10-year	20-year	30-year
7:47:08 am	4.79618	4.82926	5.04799	5.03764	4.99643	4.97006	4.94503	4.94965	4.99183	5.20556	5.06829
8:00:00 am	4.79618	4.82926	5.04799	5.03770	4.99692	4.97057	4.94543	4.94791	4.99024	5.20568	5.06833
8:02:06 am	4.79618	4.82926	5.04799	5.03770	4.99709	4.97075	4.94557	4.94807	4.99040	5.20572	5.06835
8:15:00 am	4.79618	4.82926	5.04799	5.03764	4.99940	4.97075	4.94557	4.94807	4.99841	5.20569	5.06835
8:17:08 am	4.79618	4.82926	5.04799	5.03764	4.99944	4.97066	4.94821	4.95668	4.99844	5.20570	5.06835
8:29:58 am	4.79618	4.82926	5.04799	5.03764	4.99704	4.97071	4.94552	4.95239	4.99443	5.20868	5.07102
8:32:08 am	4.79730	4.83273	5.05312	5.04527	5.00051	4.98286	4.94910	4.95537	4.99730	5.20894	5.07106
8:45:00 am	4.79730	4.83273	5.05312	5.04553	5.01050	4.98394	4.95996	4.96490	5.00631	5.21614	5.07732
8:47:07 am	4.79730	4.83273	5.05312	5.04553	5.01042	4.98385	4.95989	4.96482	5.00623	5.21612	5.07732
9:00:00 am	4.79798	4.83486	5.05312	5.05003	5.01254	4.99036	4.96237	4.96482	5.00594	5.21802	5.07906
9:02:07 am	4.79798	4.83486	5.05628	5.05016	5.01288	4.99070	4.96265	4.96478	5.00621	5.21811	5.07906
9:15:00 am	4.79798	4.83486	5.05628	5.05009	5.01275	4.99058	4.96254	4.96470	5.00611	5.21412	5.07551
9:17:08 am	4.79798	4.83486	5.05628	5.05003	5.01007	4.99032	4.95961	4.96016	5.00185	5.21406	5.07550
10:42:10 am	4.79832	4.83593	5.05785	5.05234	5.01025	4.99392	4.95976	4.96246	5.00402	5.21410	5.07550
10:57:10 am	4.79832	4.83593	5.05785	5.05201	5.00975	4.99345	4.95933	4.95566	4.99759	5.20605	5.06842
11:12:07 am	4.79764	4.83379	5.05470	5.04725	4.99760	4.98583	4.94597	4.94855	4.99087	5.20090	5.06396
11:27:12 am	4.79764	4.83379	5.05470	5.04719	4.99980	4.98559	4.94850	4.95486	4.99676	5.20380	5.06662
11:42:12 am	4.79618	4.82926	5.04799	5.03688	4.97849	4.96924	4.92517	4.92536	4.96897	5.17957	5.04528
11:57:12 am	4.79618	4.82926	5.04799	5.03665	4.97797	4.96873	4.92473	4.92498	4.96857	5.17943	5.04529
12:12:13 pm	4.79618	4.82926	5.04799	5.03635	4.96895	4.96782	4.91490	4.91777	4.96175	5.17425	5.04082
12:27:13 pm	4.79618	4.82926	5.04799	5.03684	4.98138	4.96886	4.92851	4.92936	4.97270	5.18146	5.04703
12:42:13 pm	4.79618	4.82926	5.04799	5.03671	4.98116	4.96866	4.92833	4.92923	4.97255	5.18635	5.05148

Table 10.8 (continued)

	1-month	3-month	6-month	1-year	2-year	3-year	5-year	7-year	10-year	20-year	30-year
12:57:12 pm	4.79516	4.82606	5.04325	5.03005	4.98707	4.95862	4.93487	4.92940	4.97273	5.18641	5.05149
1:12:10 pm	4.79516	4.82606	5.04325	5.03023	4.98767	4.95922	4.93537	4.92988	4.97322	5.18656	5.05151
1:27:13 pm	4.79516	4.82606	5.04325	5.03003	4.98154	4.95922	4.93537	4.92988	4.97288	5.18644	5.05151
1:42:13 pm	4.79516	4.82606	5.04325	5.03003	4.97249	4.95865	4.91854	4.92943	4.97276	5.18642	5.05149
1:57:13 pm	4.79516	4.82606	5.04325	5.03054	4.98509	4.95988	4.93229	4.93036	4.97374	5.18674	5.05150
2:12:13 pm	4.79516	4.82606	5.04325	5.03063	4.98530	4.96008	4.93247	4.93051	4.97390	5.18680	5.05150
2:27:13 pm	4.79516	4.82606	5.04325	5.03050	4.98497	4.96008	4.93247	4.93051	4.97364	5.18671	5.05150
2:42:11 pm	4.79516	4.82606	5.04325	5.03056	4.98841	4.95995	4.93599	4.93041	4.97380	5.18676	5.05151
2:57:04 pm	4.79618	4.82926	5.04799	5.03764	4.98914	4.97093	4.93660	4.93095	4.97437	5.18696	5.05150
3:12:13 pm	4.79618	4.82926	5.04799	5.03757	4.99378	4.97070	4.94186	4.93076	4.97417	5.18690	5.05149
3:27:13 pm	4.79653	4.83033	5.04956	5.04054	4.99546	4.97578	4.94327	4.93200	4.97549	5.18735	5.05150
3:42:07 pm	4.79653	4.83033	5.04956	5.04034	4.99500	4.97532	4.94288	4.93166	4.97513	5.18722	5.05150
3:57:13 pm	4.79653	4.83033	5.04956	5.04093	4.99632	4.97661	4.94398	4.93262	4.97614	5.18757	5.05149
4:12:03 pm	4.79653	4.83033	5.04956	5.04030	4.99487	4.97519	4.94277	4.93156	4.97502	5.18719	5.05149
4:27:27 pm	4.79653	4.83033	5.04956	5.04008	4.99436	4.97469	4.94235	4.93118	4.97462	5.18705	5.05149

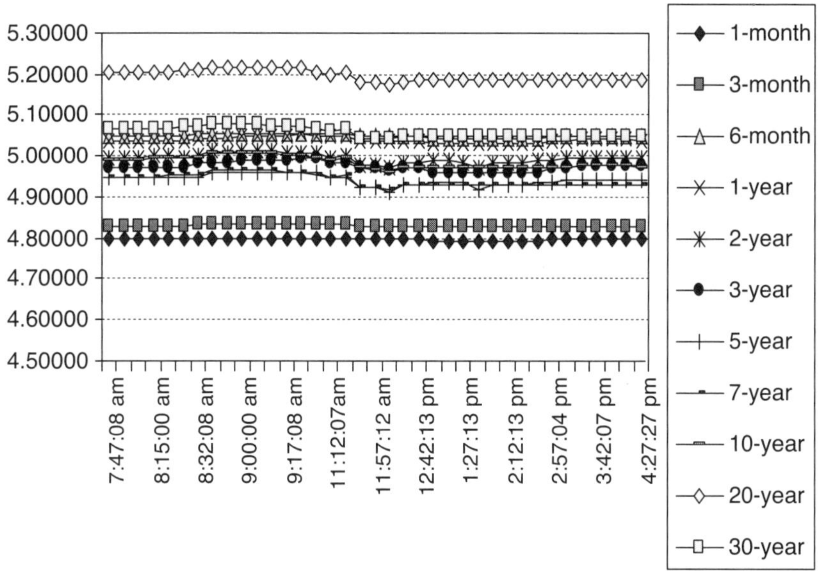

Figure 10.5 Real-time forecasting of treasury yields

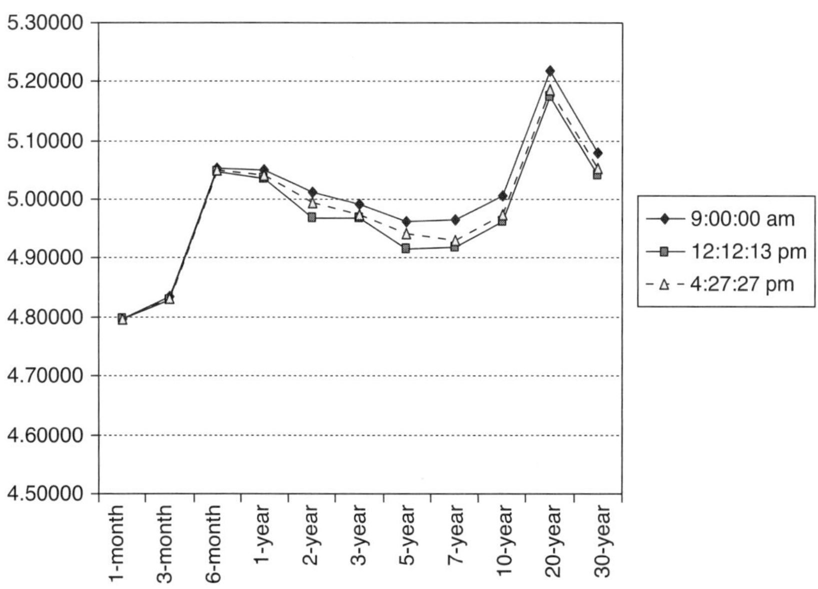

Figure 10.6 Real-time estimation of the yield curve

4. The fourth issue is whether to use the actual or predicted values of the previous period. The adopted rule is based on $P_t - A_{t-1}$ (predicted value is compared with the actual value a day earlier), but the direction of $P_t - P_{t-1}$ (predicted value compared with the predicted value a day earlier) may be different. Although the adopted rule is the preferred one, one cannot ignore the fact that this rule may be a source of a problem in a volatile environment, where model predictions are systematically underestimated or overestimated.

These issues indicate that further experimentation is necessary to come up with a successful trading rule. We have experimented with trading rules, simply as tests for a theoretical model.

CONCLUSION

A model used to estimate points on the yield curve by forecasting treasury yields at different maturities using different explanatory variables is constructed. Once the final structure was established, the 11-equation model was re-estimated every morning to forecast the end-of-the-day treasury yields. The performance of the model is compared with alternative models, such as 'no-change' and ARIMA using several criteria. The model performs significantly better based on the mean absolute error, the mean square error, the Theil inequality coefficient, and Diebold–Mariano statistics. The model is also better, in a statistically significant sense, in predicting directional changes. A simple trading rule adopted also favors the model in all cases, with the exception of the three-month treasury yield. In general, the performance of the model improves with maturity; the performance is much better for yields of longer maturities.

NOTES

* The authors are indebted to Joshua White, of Decision Economics, Inc., for insightful assistance on the presentation of the material, especially for 'real-time' applications, and Giselle Guzmán of Columbia University for comments and suggestions. This paper is intended to be a scholarly contribution and is not intended as an exercise in profit-making investment.

1. There are many attempts to estimate the yield curve, pioneered by McCulloch (1971, 1975), and Nelson and Siegel (1987). For alternative methods of estimation of the yield curve, see Boudoukh et al. (2005), Carr et al. (1974), Cochrane and Piazzesi (2002), Delbaen and Lorimier (1992), Diebold and Li (2006), Diebold et al. (2006), Evans (2005), Ioannides (2003), Jordan (1982), Jordan and Mansi (2003), Linton et al. (2001),

Lustig et al. (2005), Pham (1998), Piazzesi (2005), Shea (1984, 1985), Siegel and Nelson (1988) and Wright (2006).

2. The statistical package EViews 5.1 by Quantitative Micro Software (QMS) is used in estimation of equations. See QMS (2005).
3. Equations given here are based on data up to 12 May 2006. More recent estimates were not very different. In our experiments the ending period was 11 May for the prediction of yields on 12 May. Similarly, the ending period was 20 January for prediction of the 23 January yields. Chow prediction tests indicate that there are no significant changes in coefficients of yield-curve components during the 23 January through 12 May periods.
4. The expected inflation rate is measured as the spread between the unprotected yield on ten-year treasuries and inflation-protected ten-year treasuries (TIPS). High demand for protection would tend to drive down the yield on TIPS and increase the spread, while monetary authorities try to raise the whole yield curve, by talk and action. With a time lag, some positive effect can be expected.
5. For forecast evaluation see Clements (2005), Clements and Hendry (1998, 2002), Diebold (2004), Granger and Newbold (1973, 1986), Klein (2000), Klein and Young (1980), Mariano (2002), Theil (1961) and Tsay (2005).
6. ARIMA (p, d, q) models are identified and estimated using the Box–Jenkins (1976) methodology. See also Hamilton (1994) and Tsay (2005). Orders are different for different maturities. For example, ARIMA (7, 1, 0) is used for the one-month rate, and ARIMA (3, 1, 0) is used for the ten-year rate. These are available from the authors.
7. See Diebold and Mariano (1995). There are small sample modifications of this asymptotic statistic. For a survey, see Mariano (2002), and Clements (2005).
8. Similar results are obtained for comparisons with ARIMA models.
9. The transaction and other fees are not considered in these calculations. This is really not an issue in comparisons with the mechanical model, because the same costs apply to every case.
10. The bid–ask spread figure of 8 cents per $100 par value is obtained from Chakravarty and Sarkar (2001). However, any other possible costs accrued do not change the major conclusion that the model performs better than the mechanical model. It should be noted that for individual investors trading directly at the Treasury website, there is a $45 'penalty' for selling before maturity. See US Treasury (2006).

REFERENCES

Boudoukh, Jacob, Matthew Richardson and Robert Whitelaw (2005), 'Fiscal hedging and the yield curve', National Bureau of Economic Research, Working Paper 11840, December, www.nber.org/papers/w11840.

Box, G.E.P. and G.M. Jenkins (1976), *Time Series Analysis: Forecasting and Control*, rev. edn, San Francisco: Holden-Day.

Carr, J.L., P.J. Halpern and J.S. McCallum (1974), 'Correcting the yield curve: a re-interpretation of the duration problem', *The Journal of Finance*, **29**(4), 1287–94.

Chakravarty, S. and A. Sarkar (2001), 'A comparison of trading costs in the U.S. municipal, corporate, and treasury bond market', Krannert Graduate School of Management, Purdue University, Paper No. 1148, November (mimeo).

Clements, M.P. (2005), *Evaluating Econometric Forecasts of Economic and Financial Variables*, Basingstoke: Palgrave Macmillan.

Clements, M.P. and D.F. Hendry (1998), *Forecasting Economic Time Series*, Cambridge: Cambridge University Press.

Clements, M.P. and D.F. Hendry (eds) (2002), *A Companion to Economic Forecasting*, Oxford: Blackwell.

Cochrane, John H. and Monika Piazzesi (2002), 'The FED and interest rates: a high-frequency identification', National Bureau of Economic Research, Working Paper 8839, March, www.nber.org/papers/w8839.

Delbaen, F. and Sabine Lorimier (1992), 'Estimation of the yield curve and the forward rate curve starting from a finite number of observations', *Insurance: Mathematics and Economics*, **11**, 259–69.

Diebold, F.X. (2004), *Elements of Forecasting*, 3rd edn, Cincinnati, OH: South-Western College Publishing.

Diebold, Francis X. and Canlin Li (2006), 'Forecasting the term structure of government bond yields', *Journal of Econometrics*, **130**(2), 337–64.

Diebold, F.X. and R.S. Mariano (1995), 'Comparing predictive accuracy', *Journal of Business and Economic Statistics*, **13**, 253–65.

Diebold, Francis X., Glenn D. Rudebusch and S. Boragan Aruoba (2006), 'The macroeconomy and the yield curve: a dynamic latent factor approach', *Journal of Econometrics*, **132**(1–2), 309–38.

Evans, Martin D.D. (2005), 'Where are we now? Real-time estimates of the macro economy', National Bureau of Economic Research, Working Paper 11064, January, www.nber.org/papers/w11064.

Granger, C.W.J. and P. Newbold (1973), 'Some comments on the evaluation of economic forecasts', *Applied Economics*, **5**, 35–47.

Granger, C.W.J. and P. Newbold (1986), *Forecasting Economic Time Series*, 2nd edn, New York: Academic Press.

Hamilton, James D. (1994), *Time Series Analysis*, Princeton, NJ: Princeton University Press.

Ioannides, Michalis (2003), 'A comparison of yield curve estimation techniques using UK data', *Journal of Banking & Finance*, **27**, 1–26.

Jordan, James V. (1982), 'Term structure modeling using exponential splines: discussion', *Journal of Finance*, **37**(2), 354–56.

Jordan, James V. and Sattar A. Mansi (2003), 'Term structure estimation from on-the-run treasuries', *Journal of Banking & Finance*, **27**, 1487–509.

Klein, L.R. (2000), 'Essay on the accuracy of economic prediction', *International Journal of Applied Economics and Econometrics*, **9**, 29–69.

Klein, L.R. and S. Özmucur (2006a), 'An approach to estimation of the treasury yield curve in near real time', *Estudios de Economia Applicada*, **24**(1), 11–29.

Klein, L.R. and S. Özmucur (2006b), 'Estimation of the US treasury yield curve at daily and intra-daily frequency', University of Pennsylvania, July (mimeo).

Klein, L.R. and R.M. Young (1980), *An Introduction to Econometric Forecasting and Forecasting Models*, Lexington, MA: D.C. Heath & Company.

Linton, Oliver, Enno Mammen, Jans Perch Nielsen and Casten Tanggaard (2001), 'Yield curve estimation by Kernel smoothing methods', *Journal of Econometrics*, **105**, 185–223.

Lustig, Hunno, Chris Sleet and Sevin Yeltekin (2005), 'Fiscal hedging and the yield curve', National Bureau of Economic Research, Working Paper 11687, October, www.nber.org/papers/w11687.

Mariano, R.S. (2002), 'Testing forecast accuracy', in M.P. Clements and D.F. Hendry (eds), *A Companion to Economic Forecasting*, Oxford: Blackwell, pp. 284–98.

McCulloch, Huston J. (1971), 'Measuring the term structure of interest rates', *Journal of Business*, **44**, 19–31.

McCulloch, Huston J. (1975), 'The tax adjusted yield curve', *The Journal of Finance*, **30**, 811–29.

Nelson, Charles R. and Andrew F. Siegel (1987), 'Parsimonious modeling of yield curves', *The Journal of Business*, **60**(4), 473–89.
Pham, Toan M. (1998), 'Estimation of the term structure of interest rates: an international perspective', *Journal of Multinational Financial Management*, **8**, 265–83.
Piazzesi, Monika (2005), 'Bond yields and the Federal Reserve', *Journal of Political Economy*, **113**(2), 311–44.
Quantitative Micro Software (2005), *Eviews 5.1 User's Guide*, Irvine, CA, www.eviews.com.
Shea, Gary S. (1984), 'Pitfalls in smoothing interest rate term structure data: equilibrium models and spline approximations', *The Journal of Financial and Quantitative Analysis*, **19** (3), 253–69.
Shea, Gary S. (1985), 'Interest rate term structure estimation with exponential splines: a note', *The Journal of Finance*, **40**(1), 319–25.
Siegel, Andrew F. and Charles R. Nelson (1988), 'Long-term behavior of yield curves', *The Journal of Financial and Quantitative Analysis*, **23**(1), 105–10.
Theil, H. (1961), *Economic Forecasts and Policy*, 2nd edn, Amsterdam: North-Holland.
Tsay, R.S. (2005), *Analysis of Financial Time Series*, 2nd edn, Hoboken, NJ: John Wiley & Sons.
US Treasury (2006), *Treasury Direct Investor Kit*, www.treasurydirect.gov.
Wright, Jonathan H. (2006), 'The yield curve and predicting recessions', Federal Reserve Board, Finance and Economics Discussion Series 2006-07, Washington, DC <www.federalreserve.gov>.

11. Using data and models at mixed frequencies in computation and forecasting[1]

Fyodor I. Kushnirsky

1. INTRODUCTION

This chapter considers the use of statistical information at mixed frequencies for estimating economic variables and forecasting. There are two types of problems involved. The first type is interpolation, i.e. the estimation of unknown variables based on related data of higher or lower frequency; this problem has always been of interest in numerical analysis, statistics and econometrics. Depending on the number and type of specified data points, some interpolation procedures are algebraic and others are statistical, resulting in obtaining an average path as an approximation. In other words, econometric estimation can be viewed as an interpolation process in a broader sense than algebraic interpolation; the generalization is caused by the fact that it is not possible to satisfy the interpolation conditions exactly at every point, and a least-squares approximation is performed by minimizing the sum of squared errors.

The second type of problems, the construction of macroeconometric models at mixed frequencies and their joint use for medium- and long-term forecasting, is novel. The methodology of constructing and combining such models – high frequency, with monthly or even more frequent observations, and low frequency, with annual observations – was suggested by Klein and Kushnirsky (2005). This methodology differs from conventional forecasting techniques.

To illustrate, suppose that two models at different frequencies are available in conventional medium-term forecasting. Their use will likely be arranged so that the high-frequency model is applied to the first year or two, and the low-frequency model to the rest of the period. In our approach the high-frequency model plays a much broader role: it is used not only for short-term forecasting but also, and most importantly, for periodic adjustments of key economic variables in the low-frequency model. That is, the structural equations of the low-frequency model are not replaced by the high-frequency equations at the beginning of a forecast period as in a conventional approach, but are modified with the account of information flows from the high-frequency model. Although the low-frequency system remains intact for the rest of the period, the initial adjustment inevitably affects the overall solution, with the amplitude of the effect dying out toward the end of the period.

Philosophically, our methodology of combining high-frequency and low-frequency econometric models is based on the premise that long-term forecasts need to be adjusted for newly emerging trends that could not have been captured because they had not affected the historic data. While the philosophy is not new, we suggest using for such adjustments up-to-date information from a high-frequency model, rather than conventional add factors practiced in applications.[2]

Although computational algorithms differ for high-frequency and low-frequency models, selected variables in their joint solutions can be forced to become as close as possible to each other or even coincide.[3] For this purpose, we use either special loss functions to minimize the discrepancies between high-frequency and low-frequency solutions, or the importation of variables from a high-frequency solution to a low-frequency solution. Moving from one model to another follows an appropriate interpolation rule. In most instances the direction of interpolation is from the high-frequency to the low-frequency solution; as a result, the latter is periodically tuned up to accord with new high-frequency data.

This chapter is organized as follows. In Section 2, we review the estimation of unknown variables based on related data of different frequencies. The restoration of unknown variables, with the use of methods of numerical analysis or statistical aggregation, disaggregation and conversion, is an important problem in applied research. In the challenging case of disaggregation, when a low-frequency time series provides insufficient information to restore an unknown high-frequency series, it is often desirable to look for some additional guidance, such as patterns of growth or increments, as a way to increase the degree of reliability. In Section 3, the methodology of a combined use of high-frequency and low-frequency econometric models for medium- and long-term forecasting is discussed. We give the general specification of the models and methods to obtain their independent solution, procedures to modify the solution of the low-frequency model to force selected key variables to agree with the high-frequency forecast, and the results of application to the Ukrainian and Mexican economies. In Section 4 we generate an *ex-post* Mexican forecast for the period of former President Fox's Administration (2001–06). The purpose is to test the use of models at mixed frequencies for the adjustment of annual forecasts in tune with rapidly changing economic developments, a task that presented a challenge to Mexican officials. Section 5 summarizes major findings and provides concluding remarks.

2. USING DATA AT MIXED FREQUENCIES: RESTORATION OF UNKNOWN VARIABLES

2.1 Interpolation

Interpolation problems were originally developed to specify the value of mathematical and statistical functions from published data. In modern numerical analysis, interpolation is a process of defining a mathematical function that takes on specific values at certain points. Once the function is defined, it can be used both in between the specified points and outside. Thus, in this case interpolation is not limited to its literal meaning. Statistical methods and econometrics are also widely used for calculating interpolated data.

Interpolation is used in both forecasting and in the estimation of missing or unknown data. Observations on economic indicators are given at certain points in time, e.g. at year end. If the researcher is interested in finding values at a higher frequency, say, at the end of month, this is the task of interpolation. Suppose that the variable in question is the GDP. Several types of interpolation problems could be described, depending on whether the bases for annual and monthly GDP measures are different or similar. In all cases, a major link between the time periods is that the annual GDP is the sum of monthly GDP values. The interpolation problem in this case is to split the annual GDP into 12 components that sum to the annual value and follow some other available leads, e.g. similarities in the pattern of growth.

An example of an interpolation problem in estimating missing data is to find GDP values for the second and third quarters given the GDP in the first and the fourth quarters. As another example, let us assume that the quarterly GDP is measured on an accumulation principle; that is, a combined value for the first two quarters is reported at the end of the second quarter, and so on. In this case annual and the last quarter's values coincide, so that the same function that connects annual values can be used to interpolate the unknown quarterly values.

A desired property of curves that economists and other social scientists wish to fit to observed data points (specifying a tabulated function) is the smoothness of these curves (Gerald and Wheatley, 2003). When the tabulated function varies so slowly that first differences between data points are considered constant, it may be approximated by a straight line between adjacent points. For functions with larger variation when, say, differences of order n are constant, an approximation may be performed by a polynomial of degree n. Algebraic polynomials are one of the most useful interpolating functions:

$$P(x) = a_n x^n + a_{n-1} x^{n-1} + \ldots + a_1 x + a_0,$$

where n is a non-negative integer and $a_0, \ldots, a_n$ are real constants. For any function defined and continuous on a closed and bounded interval, it was proven by Karl Weierstrass that there exists a polynomial that is as close as intended to the given function. Given some data points, the aim is to find a polynomial that goes exactly through these points.

A widely used form of interpolation polynomials is the Lagrange polynomial. Given a set of $(n + 1)$ data points $(x_0, y_0), \ldots, (x_n, y_n)$, the Lagrange polynomial is a linear combination of Lagrange polynomials:

$$P(x) = y_0 P_0(x) + y_1 P_1(x) + \ldots + y_n P_n(x) \tag{11.1}$$

The combination in formula (11.1) is made up of $(n + 1)$ terms, and each of the terms is nth degree in x. Lagrange polynomial $P_k(x)$ in formula (11.1) equals zero at all given points but the kth. The pattern of such a polynomial is to form the numerator as a product of linear factors of the form $(x - x_k)$ omitting one x_k in each term; the omitted value is used to form the denominator by replacing x in each of the denominator factors:

$$P_k(x) = \frac{x - x_0}{x_k - x_0} \cdot \ldots \cdot \frac{x - x_{k-1}}{x_k - x_{k-1}} \cdot \frac{x - x_{k+1}}{x_k - x_{k+1}} \cdot \ldots \cdot \frac{x - x_n}{x_k - x_n}$$

Each Lagrange polynomial $P_k(x)$ in formula (11.1) is multiplied by y_k corresponding to x_k, which is omitted in the numerator factors.

A major factor in the widespread use of Lagrange polynomials is their generality. They can be used with functions of unknown form, tabulated at irregular intervals, and are relatively easy to compute. A drawback is that the Lagrange procedure for a polynomial of high degree requires a large number of multiplications and may become very slow. Polynomials of high degree, in general, give an unsatisfactory fit since they tend to generate large fluctuations about the true function. The principle of least squares, in which a polynomial of low degree fits the data points as closely as possible but not exactly, is an alternative to the use of high-degree polynomials.

Another alternative to high-degree polynomials is spline curves, which are piecewise polynomials linked at given data points.[4] The interpolation can be made smooth if the piecewise polynomials have matching derivatives at these points, and the smoothness is enhanced by matching higher-order derivatives. Given $(n + 1)$ values x_k such that $x_0 < x_1 < \ldots < x_n$, with $(n + 1)$ values y_k, the problem is to find a spline function of degree n

$$S(x) = \begin{cases} S_0(x) \; x \in [x_0, x_1] \\ S_1(x) \; x \in [x_1, x_2] \\ \ldots \\ S_{n-1}(x) \; x \in [x_{n-1}, x_n] \end{cases}$$

where each $S_i(x)$ is a polynomial of degree k.

While a polynomial of degree n is uniquely defined by the data points, the spline of degree n, which interpolates the same data set, is not uniquely defined. One has to fill in $(n - 1)$ additional degrees of freedom to construct a unique spline interpolant. The simplest form of spline interpolation is linear when data points are connected by straight lines. Algebraically, each S_i is constructed as

$$S_i(x) = y_i + \frac{y_{i+1} - y_i}{x_{i+1} - x_i}(x - x_i) \tag{11.2}$$

The quadratic spline, constructed as

$$S_i(x) = y_i + z_i(x - x_i) + \frac{z_{i+1} - z_i}{2(x_{i+1} - x_i)}(x - x_i)^2$$

gives a better accuracy because it adds a quadratic term to the linear interpolation formula.

The most popular in applications are cubic splines. The condition for a cubic spline fit is that one passes a set of cubics through the data points, using a new cubic in each interval. Both the slope and the curvature must be the same for the pair of cubics that join at each point. To construct a cubic spline $S(x)$, one starts from a table of points $(x_i, y_i), i = 0, 1, \ldots, n$ for function $y = f(x)$. That makes $n + 1$ points and n intervals between them. The cubic spline interpolation is a piecewise continuous curve, passing through each of the values in the table. A separate cubic polynomial for each interval has its own coefficients:

$$S_i(x) = a_i(x - x_i)^3 + b_i(x - x_i)^2 + c_i(x - x_i) + d_i, \; x \in (x_i, x_{i+1}) \tag{11.3}$$

The spline is formed by these cubic polynomial segments. Since there are n intervals, with four coefficients in polynomial (11.3), a total of $4n$ independent conditions is required to define the spline. Two conditions for each interval are obtained from the requirement that the cubic polynomial match the values of the table at both ends of the interval: $S_i(x_i) = y_i, S_i(x_{i+1}) = y_{i+1}$. These conditions result in a continuous function. One still needs $2n$ more conditions. Since the interpolation is to be made as smooth as possible, the requirement is that the first and second derivatives also be continuous:

$$S'_{i-1}(x_i) = S'_i(x_i), S''_{i-1}(x_i) = S''_i(x_i)$$

These conditions result in $2(n-1)$ constraints for $(n-1)$intervals. The following are two additional standard conditions that completely fix the spline:

a) 'natural' – $S''_0(x_0) = 0,\ S''_{n-1}(x_n) = 0$;
b) 'clamped' – $S'_0(x_0) = f'(x_0),\ S'_{n-1}(x_n) = f'(x_n)$.

Cubic splines are easy to implement, and they produce a curve that appears to be seamless. When constructing interpolating polynomials, there is a tradeoff between having a better fit and having a smooth, well-behaved fitting function. The more data points are used in the interpolation, the greater the accuracy. But the degree of the resulting polynomial rises, which leads to greater oscillation between the data points. Therefore a high-degree interpolation may be a poor predictor of the function between points. Cubic splines avoid this problem, even though they are only piecewise continuous.

Along with other methods, cubic spline interpolation is implemented in the widely used EViews software for the so-called up conversion, from low-frequency to high-frequency data, which we shall illustrate in the next section.

2.2 Disaggregation and Conversion

Switching between data at different frequencies takes place each time aggregation or disaggregation is performed. The high-frequency data to be aggregated contain sufficient information for the conversion so that in this case the issue is just to choose a method of conversion. From the nature of economic variables, the method is clear for some of them, but more than one choice may exist for others. For example, if the variable in question is the GDP, then the summation is the way to move from higher to lower frequency. In case of a price index measured by the GDP deflator or the CPI, everything depends on how monthly indices are represented: (a) if they are reported on an annual basis, the last high-frequency value becomes the low-frequency value for the relevant year; (b) if they are reported with respect to the preceding month or the same month of the previous year, then an appropriate chain index is to be computed for the conversion. In another example, the conversion of monthly employment figures, there are usually two choices for the method, depending on whether the researcher wants to obtain the low-frequency value as a year-end or as an average annual number.

A rule of thumb is that the higher the required frequency of an economic variable, the greater the scarcity of the official statistical information. In other words, the availability of official statistics declines as one moves from annual to quarterly to monthly reporting. Even elaborate national income and product accounts (NIPA) in developed countries do not provide a complete set of monthly data, and for many developing and transition countries, monthly, and often quarterly, statistical reporting is much more limited. A common-sense approach for disaggregating data is to extract as much information as possible on high-frequency patterns embedded in the low-frequency data. However, often the only information available is the sum of the estimated data or their average value.

Disaggregation, such as any numerical problem of subdividing a sum into several components, naturally poses a more serious problem for the researcher than aggregation. Many of the studies on disaggregation of statistical time series follow an approach suggested by Chow and Lin (1971).

Let y_0 be an n-element column vector of low frequency, yearly observations to be divided among q (e.g. quarterly) periods and y an N-element column vector of observations on unknown disaggregate time series ($N = qn$). It is also assumed that for each disaggregate time series there exists a multiple regression relationship with known related indicators:

$$y = X\beta + e,$$

where X is an $(N \times k)$ matrix of observations on k known indicators, and e is an N-element column vector of error terms ($E(e) = 0, E(ee') = V$). The best linear unbiased estimator of y is given by

$$\hat{y} = Xb + VA'(AVA')^{-1}(y_0 - AXb)$$

$$b = [X'A'(AVA')^{-1}AX]^{-1}X'A'(AVA')^{-1}y_0,$$

where A is an $(n \times N)$ aggregation matrix converting high-frequency, quarterly values into low-frequency, annual values.

The illustrated approach to disaggregating statistical data by Chow and Lin has become popular because they use a system of econometric equations that provides an additional characterization of an unknown high-frequency time series. Some other studies limit themselves to the creation of a high-frequency series based only on a set of low-frequency annual data. An example of this type of procedure has been offered by Boot et al. (1967), who decided to trend the estimated series so that the sum of squares of either the first or the second differences was a minimum subject to annual constraints.

Considering the case of adjusting monthly or quarterly time series to make them agree with annual totals, Denton (1971) generalized the method suggested by Boot et al. Denton considers the distribution of m annual totals among k intra-annual periods. The series in question consists of $n = mk$ values and it is represented by two n-element vectors: the original $z = (z_1, \ldots, z_n)$ and a new, adjusted vector $x = (x_1, \ldots, x_n)$. The solution fits the original vector z to the new vector by a method that minimizes quadratic form expression $(x - z)'A(x - z)$, subject to the condition that k values of the new time series within each year sum to the annual total for that year.

Whenever any additional aggregate information on the disaggregated time series is available, researchers use it to adjust appropriately a disaggregation procedure. Such a situation was considered by Rossi (1982), who formulated a procedure when not only annual totals for quarterly values, but also contemporaneous aggregates were available. Specifically, in the estimation of quarterly series for 20 categories of consumer goods, 24 aggregates were known for a given year: 20 yearly totals, one for each category, and four values of total consumer expenditures, one for each quarter. A general formulation of such a problem was provided by Di Fonzo (1990), who derived an optimal, in a least-squares sense, estimator for the disaggregate time series that satisfies both temporal and contemporaneous constraints.

In an applied project for Mexico's economy, we estimated monthly data for GDP and some other macroeconomic variables, given their quarterly series (Klein et al., 2007). Along with retaining the quarterly totals, our procedure emulates the quarterly growth pattern in the estimated high-frequency data. To explain, let us consider two successive quarterly values x and y – the former gives the initial condition and the latter is the quarterly total that is to be subdivided into three monthly values. The goal is to find an average monthly growth index g for the second quarter so that

$$g\frac{x}{3} + g^2\frac{x}{3} + g^3\frac{x}{3} = y.^5 \tag{11.4}$$

Substituting the quarterly growth index $h = y/x$ in formula (11.4) yields $g + g^2 + g^3 = 3h$. Although an exact solution cannot be found, we determine which solution of the form $g = h^k$ minimizes the error when $h \approx 1$:

$$h^k + h^{2k} + h^{3k} = 3h, \text{ or}$$

$$h^{k-1} + h^{2k-1} + h^{3k-1} = 3. \tag{11.5}$$

We know that h is close to 1, say, $h = 1 + \delta$, with $|\delta| < 1$. The binomial series expansion of $1 + \delta$ is $(1 + \delta)^n = 1 + n\delta + \delta^2(\ldots)$.

Applying this series expansion to each term on the left side of formula (11.5), in order to find the value of k for the best approximation, transforms (11.5) into

$$1 + (k - 1)\delta + \delta^2(\ldots) + 1 + (2k - 1)\delta + \delta^2(\ldots)$$

$$+ 1 + (3k - 1)\delta + \delta^2(\ldots) = 3,$$

$$\text{i.e. } (6k - 3)\delta + \delta^2(\ldots) = 0.$$

Hence $k = 1/2$ gives the best approximation.

The need to formulate specific algorithms to disaggregate time series and switch between different frequencies has diminished with the advancement in computing and econometric software. Thus EViews software provides a number of interpolation methods for estimating high-frequency series from an underlying low-frequency series. It supports the following interpolation methods for disaggregation of low-frequency data: constant, when the sum or average of the high-frequency observations matches the low-frequency observation; linear, when the low-frequency observation is assigned to the last high-frequency observation, with all the intermediate observations connected by a straight line; quadratic, which fits a local quadratic polynomial for each observation of the low-frequency series, with a following use of this polynomial to fill in all observations of the high-frequency series; cubic spline, which assigns each value in the low-frequency series to the last high-frequency observation associated with the low-frequency period and then places all intermediate points on a natural cubic spline, similar to the one given in Section 2.1, connecting the points (EViews 5 User's Guide, pp. 108–11).

3. THE USE OF ECONOMETRIC MODELS AT MIXED FREQUENCIES

3.1 Specification and Joint Solutions

The specification of the high-frequency econometric model is

$$y_t = Ay_t + A_1Ly_t + \ldots + A_pL^py_t + Bx_t + e_t, \tag{11.6}$$

where y_t is an n-element column vector of endogenous variables; x_t is a k-element column vector of exogenous variables; $A, A_1, \ldots, A_p$ are $(n \times n)$ matrices of coefficients multiplying endogenous variables, i.e. elements of vector y_t, measured at time $t, t-1, \ldots, t-p$; B is an $(n \times k)$ matrix of coefficients multiplying exogenous variables, i.e. elements of vector x_t; and e_t is an n-element column vector of error terms.

The specification of the low-frequency model is

$$y_s = Ay_s + A_1Ly_s + \ldots + A_qL^qy_s + Bx_s + e_s, \tag{11.7}$$

where y_s is an m-element column vector of endogenous variables; x_s is an r-element column vector of exogenous variables; $A, A_1, \ldots, A_q$ are $(m \times m)$ matrices of coefficients multiplying endogenous variables, i.e. elements of vector y_s measured at time $s, s-1, \ldots, s-q$; B is an $(m \times r)$ matrix of coefficients multiplying exogenous variables, i.e. elements of vector x_s; and e_s is an m-element column vector of error terms.

Lag operator L is used for manipulating lagged variables: $Ly_t = y_{t-1}$. A polynomial in the lag operator L is built with the account of different lengths of lags, namely, p for the high-frequency model and q for the low-frequency model. The last terms of the polynomial are, respectively, $L^py_t = y_{t-p}$ and $L^qy_s = y_{s-q}$.

A general solution of models (11.6) and (11.7) exists if their respective polynomials in the lag operators $(I - A - \ldots - A_pL^p)$ and $(I - A - \ldots - A_qL^q)$ are non-singular and invertible. Since in applications all the lagged values are computed at the start of a successive iteration, the 'tail' of lagged variables can therefore be found by a straightforward computation:

$$y_t^0 \equiv A_1y_{t-1} + \ldots + A_py_{t-p} \text{ and } y_s^0 \equiv A_1y_{s-1} + \ldots + A_qy_{s-q}, \tag{11.8}$$

where y_t^0 and y_s^0 are vectors of the summation results for the high-frequency and low-frequency model, respectively.

Vectors y_t^0 and y_s^0 defined in identities (11.8) play the role of an adjustment component for constant terms in the iterative process. These vectors can be combined with b_1, the first column in matrix B; thus b_1 becomes a variable column that must be recomputed at the beginning of a recurrent iteration:

$$b_{1t} = b_1 + y_t^0, b_{1s} = b_1 + y_s^0.$$

Matrix B changes to $B_t = (b_{1t}, b_2, \ldots, b_k)$ for the low-frequency model and $B_s = (b_{1s}, b_2, \ldots, b_r)$ for the high-frequency model. The solutions for the adjusted systems (11.6) and (11.7) are

$$\hat{y}_t = A\hat{y}_t + B_t x_t, \text{ or } \hat{y}_t = (I - A)^{-1} B_t x_t$$

for the high-frequency model, and

$$\hat{y}_s = A\hat{y}_s + B_s x_s, \text{ or } \hat{y}_s = (I - A)^{-1} B_s x_s \tag{11.9}$$

for the low-frequency model.

When the two models are used jointly for a medium-term period, the high-frequency model generates a forecast for 12 months forward that can be aggregated into an annual solution. The latter will likely be different from the first-year solution from the low-frequency model. It is presumed that the annual solution in the high-frequency model absorbs more detailed and richer information than its counterpart from the low-frequency model. Therefore, if the first-year low-frequency solution is moved close to or replaced by a high-frequency forecast, the low-frequency forecast will be updated and adjusted sequentially in tune with the high-frequency forecast.

In order to bring the solutions of the two models as close as possible to each other, we minimize the discrepancies between the solutions with the use of specially designed loss functions, which are also called penalty functions in the literature. In an alternative approach, we obtain an 'exact' joint solution by importing the values of key variables from the high-frequency into the low-frequency system. These two options, the use of a loss function and an exact joint solution, are considered in turn.

A loss function is a measure of discrepancies between a selected subset of m_1 solutions $(y^l_{1s_0}, \ldots, y^l_{m_1s_0})$ from the low-frequency model and $(y^h_{1s_0}, \ldots, y^h_{m_1s_0})$ from the high-frequency model, at $s = s_0$. We use two forms of loss functions, linear and quadratic, but there are also variations: they may have equal or unequal weights, and measured in levels or growth rates. A loss function is to be minimized subject to constraints formed from the equations of system (11.7) for the low-frequency model.

We base loss functions on a small subset of key variables that play an important role in determining other economic variables, either directly or indirectly. The adjustment of these key variables in tune with the high-frequency data will consequently help adjust and update other variables as well. Considering that the GDP and the price index are used to measure economic growth and macroeconomic stability, the two major goals for economic policy, we have specified loss functions in applications for Ukraine and Mexico in terms of these variables.

The formation of a loss function is easy to explain when it is based only on the GDP variable. The goal is to minimize the difference $|Y - Y_{HF}|$

between the GDP solutions Y from the low-frequency model and Y_{HF} from the high-frequency models. In what sense do we specify such a minimization, i.e. what GDP, low-frequency or high-frequency, is forced to move in the direction of the other one? Clearly, we manipulate the GDP from the low-frequency model in this process and want it to come as close as possible to the GDP from the high-frequency model. Hence we find Y_{HF} first, with the latter becoming a constant, not a variable. Generally, the minimization of the difference between a variable and a constant is equivalent to the minimization of the variable itself. But, in the case of an absolute difference, the solution will depend on whether $(Y - Y_{HF})$ is positive or negative. If Y is greater than $Y_{HF,}$ the problem turns into:

$$\text{Minimize } Y \tag{11.10}$$

subject to low-frequency equations specified as equals-or-greater-than inequalities, plus an additional constraint $Y \geq Y_{HF}$.

The objective function (11.10), in combination with the added constraint, ensures that Y will move in the direction of Y_{HF} from above.[6] If, on the other hand, Y approaches Y_{HF} from below, the objective is to maximize Y, with the direction of the added constraint reversed, that is:

$$\text{Maximize } Y \tag{11.11}$$

subject to low-frequency equations specified as equals-or-less-than inequalities, and $Y \leq Y_{HF}$.

When several variables are included in a loss function, choosing which problem to formulate, minimization or maximization, becomes more complicated. Suppose we use the GDP Y and price index P for that purpose. If they are both either above or below their counterparts from the high-frequency model, the cases are similar to problems (11.10) or (11.11). However, when Y and P are on different sides of Y_{HF} and P_{HF}, it is not clear whether minimization or maximization is appropriate. Instead, minimization of a quadratic function can be performed since the direction of subtraction does not play a role in this case:

$$\text{Minimize } [w_1(Y - Y_{HF})^2 + w_2(P - P_{HF})^2], \tag{11.12}$$

(with weights $w_1 + w_2 = 1$) subject to low-frequency equations specified as equals-or-greater-than inequalities. As in the linear case, Y and P are treated as variables in formula (11.12) and Y_{HF} and P_{HF} must be found first.

In applications, a goal might be to bring the growth rates of key low-frequency variables, not their levels, as close as possible to the solution from the high-frequency model. If Y and P are measured discretely, their growth can be expressed in index form as $g = Y_t/Y_{t-1}$ and $h = P_t/P_{t-1}$, respectively. The problem can be formulated in growth rates as:

$$\text{Minimize } [w_1(g - g_{HF})^2 + w_2(h - h_{HF})^2] \tag{11.13}$$

subject to low-frequency equations specified as equals-or-greater-than inequalities, plus $g \geq Y_t/Y_{t-1}$ and $h \geq P_t/P_{t-1}$.[7]

In another approach to bringing high-frequency and low-frequency forecasts as close as possible to each other, we import the values of key variables from the high-frequency into the low-frequency system. Suppose that a one-year forecast for monthly values of GDP is generated in the high-frequency model. The yearly GDP obtained by their summation can be viewed as a counterpart of the first-year GDP from the low-frequency model. In the importation procedure, the GDP value from the low-frequency model is suppressed and replaced by the estimate from the high-frequency model. The procedure turns the GDP variable in the low-frequency model into exogenous, and it is excluded from the set of endogenous variables. The total number of endogenous variables for the first year is reduced from m to $(m-1)$, but for the remaining years in the period it remains m. It is desirable to recalculate the low-frequency model every year of a moving medium period.

To formalize the procedure, assume that the GDP is the first element of vectors y_t^h for monthly observations in the high-frequency model and y_s^l for annual observations in the low-frequency model. The annual value of the GDP from the high-frequency model is $y_{11}^l = \sum_{t=1}^{12} y_{1t}^h$. The procedure partitions the first-year solution for vector y_s^l: $y_1^l = (y_{11}^l, y_1^{l1})$, where y_1^{l1} is an $(m - 1)$-element vector of the remaining first-year components: $y_1^{l1} = (y_{21}^l, \ldots, y_{m1}^l)$. For the first year of a medium-term period, solution (11.9) of the low-frequency model is therefore modified as

$$\hat{y}_1^{l1} = A^1\hat{y}_1^{l1} + B_1^1 x_1^{l1},$$

where an $(m - 1)$-element vector $\hat{y}_1^{l1}$ replaces an m-element vector $\hat{y}_s^l$; a $(k + 1)$-element vector x_1^{l1} replaces a k-element vector x_s^l, after adding an exogenous element y_{11}^l; an $(m - 1 \times m - 1)$ matrix A^1 replaces an $(m \times m)$ matrix A; and an $(m - 1 \times k + 1)$ matrix B_1^1 replaces an $(m \times k)$ matrix B_s, after shifting the first element from endogenous vector y_s^l to exogenous vector x_s^l.

3.2 Applications

We applied the described methodology to the Ukrainian and Mexican economies (Klein and Kushnirsky, 2005; Klein et al., 2007). The purpose of the Ukrainian project, which was undertaken first, was to test the methodology. Two simplified models were built for Ukraine's economy. The high-frequency model consisted of several equations to reflect trends of key variables that could affect other macroeconomic variables in a systematic way. The low-frequency model was more detailed and included the following variables: GDP *Y*, capital stock *K*, commissioned capital stock *DK*, total investment *I*, average annual number of workers *L*, and average annual loan interest rate *RKN*. The time series from 1985 to 2003 were used in estimation, with all monetary variables in 1996 constant prices.

Table 11.1 gives four forecasts for Ukraine for 2004–08. The first forecast is based on an independent solution of the low-frequency model for a five-year period, 2004–08. Three other forecasts were modified to agree with the solution of the high-frequency model, as explained in Section 3.1. In the first modification, a loss function was employed to minimize the difference between the 2004 solutions for the GDP, computed in the high-frequency forecast and unknown in the low-frequency forecast. In the second modification, the 2004 GDP was imported from the high-frequency model, with the low-frequency model adjusted to make the GDP variable exogenous for that year. The last modification was also based on the importation of the first-year GDP from the high-frequency model, but, in addition, the solution of the low-frequency model for the rest of the period was modified to incorporate a targeted growth rate.[8]

The solutions in Table 11.1 differ not only in magnitudes, but also in pattern of growth. Statistical data that were used in estimation were affected by dramatic transformations in Ukraine's economic history since independence and, in turn, caused the three first solutions in Table 11.1 to incorporate a rather depressed pattern of growth. The fourth solution that reflects an average pattern of growth since 2000 seems to be the most reliable projection for the five-year period.

The Mexican project was more elaborate than the Ukrainian project. The time series from 1980 to 2005 were used for Mexico's low-frequency model with annual observations, and from 1994 to 2005 for the high-frequency model with monthly observations. The high-frequency model contains 19 endogenous and 22 exogenous variables, and the low-frequency model 18 endogenous and 15 exogenous variables. The high-frequency forecast for Mexico was built for 2006, and the low-frequency forecast for 2006–10.

To bring the low-frequency forecast as close as possible to the high-frequency forecast, we use a loss function to minimize the discrepancies

Table 11.1 Comparison of four forecasts from the low-frequency model for Ukraine

Year	*Y*	*K*	*DK*	*I*	*L*	*RKN*
I. Independent solution of the low-frequency model						
2004	90 238.43	543 501.2	5 845.722	20 530.31	21.47951	22.7636
2005	90 443.75	547 753.1	5 935.423	20 657.07	21.43481	20.5173
2006	90 713.73	552 105.3	6 040.934	20 806.22	21.41528	18.2710
2007	91 050.38	556 575.8	6 162.797	20 978.44	21.42092	16.0247
2008	91 455.50	561 183.1	6 325.431	21 174.37	21.45173	13.7784
II. Solution with 2004 GDP from the loss function						
2004	87 023.00	542 386.1	4 862.391	19 140.60	21.47951	22.7636
2005	90 349.32	546 458.2	5 772.451	20 426.80	21.43481	20.5173
2006	90 611.41	550 694.7	5 933.778	20 654.82	21.41528	18.2710
2007	90 944.85	555 114.5	6 112.553	20 907.49	21.42092	16.0247
2008	91 351.48	559 737.2	6 309.214	21 185.43	21.45173	13.7784
III. Solution with 2004 GDP from the high-frequency model						
2004	120 185.10	551 818.5	13 180.440	30 896.51	21.47951	22.7636
2005	91 056.38	556 202.5	6 085.400	20 869.14	21.43481	20.5173
2006	91 332.98	560 687.9	6 192.553	21 020.57	21.41528	18.2710
2007	91 676.59	565 293.1	6 316.115	21 195.21	21.42092	16.0247
2008	92 089.05	570 036.4	6 456.543	21 393.67	21.45173	13.7784
IV. Solution with targeted growth rates (2004 GDP from the high-frequency model)						
2004	120 185.10	551 818.5	13180.44	30 896.51	21.47951	22.7636
2005	126 194.30	565 984.1	14711.38	33 060.19	21.90910	19.3942
2006	132 504.00	581 904.6	16315.91	35 327.87	22.34729	16.0247
2007	139 129.20	599 659.6	17997.71	37 704.76	22.79423	11.6553
2008	146 085.70	619 322.8	19760.64	40 196.32	23.25012	9.2858

Note: *Y* = GDP; *K* = stock of fixed capital; *DK* = commissioned capital stock; *I* = investment in fixed capital; *L* = labor employment; *RKN* = average loan interest rate.

between the 2006 solutions from the two Mexican models for: (a) the GDP *Y*, (b) a combination of the GDP *Y* and price index *P*, and (c) the growth rates of *Y* and *P*. For the combination of *Y* and *P*, as well as their growth rates, linear and quadratic minimization problems are solved. In addition, when both *Y* and *P* are included in a loss function, we assign either equal weights to them or give a priority to *Y* (and its growth rate) over *P*, with the selection of weights of 0.6 and 0.4, respectively. The unequal treatment of the two variables is based on an assumption that the GDP affects the level of all other macroeconomic variables in a systematic way and, therefore, bringing it closer to the high-frequency solution will push other variables to move in the same direction, too. This is not necessarily the case for the price index.

Another approach to bringing the short-term and medium-term forecasts for Mexico's economy close to each other is based on the importation of the GDP and the price index from the high-frequency model into the low-frequency solution. Similarly to the case of a loss function, the procedure modifies the first-year solution for Mexico's low-frequency model. Given a set of methods offered by EViews for a down conversion, from monthly to yearly observations, we obtain the annual value of the GDP by the summation of monthly values, while for the price index we average the monthly values.

Table 11.2 gives selected key variables from the Mexican low-frequency forecast for the 2006–10 period obtained by the application of the described methods: GDP Y, price index P, employment L, and exports XD. For each variable, there are five columns: an independent low-frequency solution, three solutions obtained by the use of loss functions (linear, non-linear, and in growth rates), and a solution with the 2006 Y and P values imported from the high-frequency model. The last row gives an average annual growth rate for each solution; it is measured as an average percentage over the five-year period with respect to the 2005 actual value posted in the first row of the independent solution. For example, Table 11.2 shows that the average growth rate for Y is a stable 2.7 percent across all the solutions. The greatest variation in the growth rate occurs for P, from 1.2 percent to almost 4 percent; different solutions thus respond differently to the fact that the price index has been volatile for Mexico.

The comparison of forecasts in Table 11.2 is illustrated in Figures 11.1 and 11.2 for Mexico's GDP Y and price index P, respectively. Three trajectories are given for each variable: an independent low-frequency forecast for 2006–10 ('Independent low-frequency forecast'), a low-frequency forecast for 2006–10 with the 2006 solution obtained from the use of a loss function in growth rates ('2006 forecast from growth loss function'), and a low-frequency forecast for 2006–10 with the 2006 solution imported from the high-frequency model ('2006 forecast from high-frequency model'). The first segment for the last forecast, that connects 2006 and 2007 points, is in a different form from the rest of the curve, to stress that the 2006 value is obtained from the high-frequency model.

Figure 11.1 shows that the trajectories for all three solutions for the GDP follow a relatively close pattern. This is not the case for the price index in Figure 11.2. As one can see from Figure 11.2, the solution based on the use of a loss function in growth rates for 2006 is distinctly different from the two other solutions for P. At the same time, for both Y and P in

Table 11.2 *Comparison of forecasts: independent, based on loss functions and on importation of variables from the high-frequency model*

Year	*Y*					*P*				
	Independent	Linear loss	Non-linear loss	Growth rates loss	GDP_{HF} and P_{HF}	Independent	Linear loss	Non-linear loss	Growth rates loss	GDP_{HF} and P_{HF}
2005	1 756 206	–	–	–	–	476.610	–	–	–	–
2006	1 829 874	1 818 180	1 846 850	1 818 290	1 846 854	508.118	394.597	523.999	395.153	523.999
2007	1 885 727	1 878 101	1 896 866	1 878 172	1 896 869	524.747	389.238	541.619	389.895	541.619
2008	1 939 067	1 933 888	1 946 616	1 933 936	1 946 618	542.243	436.350	555.170	436.862	555.169
2009	1 951 537	1 948 480	1 955 756	1 948 509	1 955 757	550.958	468.309	560.666	468.708	560.666
2010	2 006 118	2 003 774	2 009 544	2 003 795	2 009 545	570.917	506.233	578.549	506.544	578.549
% growth	2.70	2.67	2.73	2.67	2.73	3.68	1.21	3.95	1.23	3.95
Year	***L***					***XD***				
	Independent	Linear loss	Non-linear loss	Growth rates loss	GDP_{HF} and P_{HF}	Independent	Linear loss	Non-linear loss	Growth rates loss	GDP_{HF} and P_{HF}
2005	42.082	–	–	–	–	168 386	–	–	–	–
2006	43.120	42.931	43.394	42.932	43.394	154 336	160 775	153 435	154 336	153 435
2007	44.314	44.190	44.494	44.191	44.494	158 298	165 985	157 341	165 947	157 341
2008	45.438	45.355	45.560	45.355	45.560	180 979	186 985	180 246	192 902	180 246
2009	45.801	45.751	45.869	45.752	45.869	191 082	195 770	190 531	195 747	190 531
2010	46.569	46.531	46.625	46.532	46.625	199 237	202 906	198 804	203 714	198 804
% growth	1.60	2.03	2.07	2.03	2.07	3.42	3.80	3.38	3.88	3.38

Note: Y = GDP; P = output price index; L = labor emploment; XD = exports.

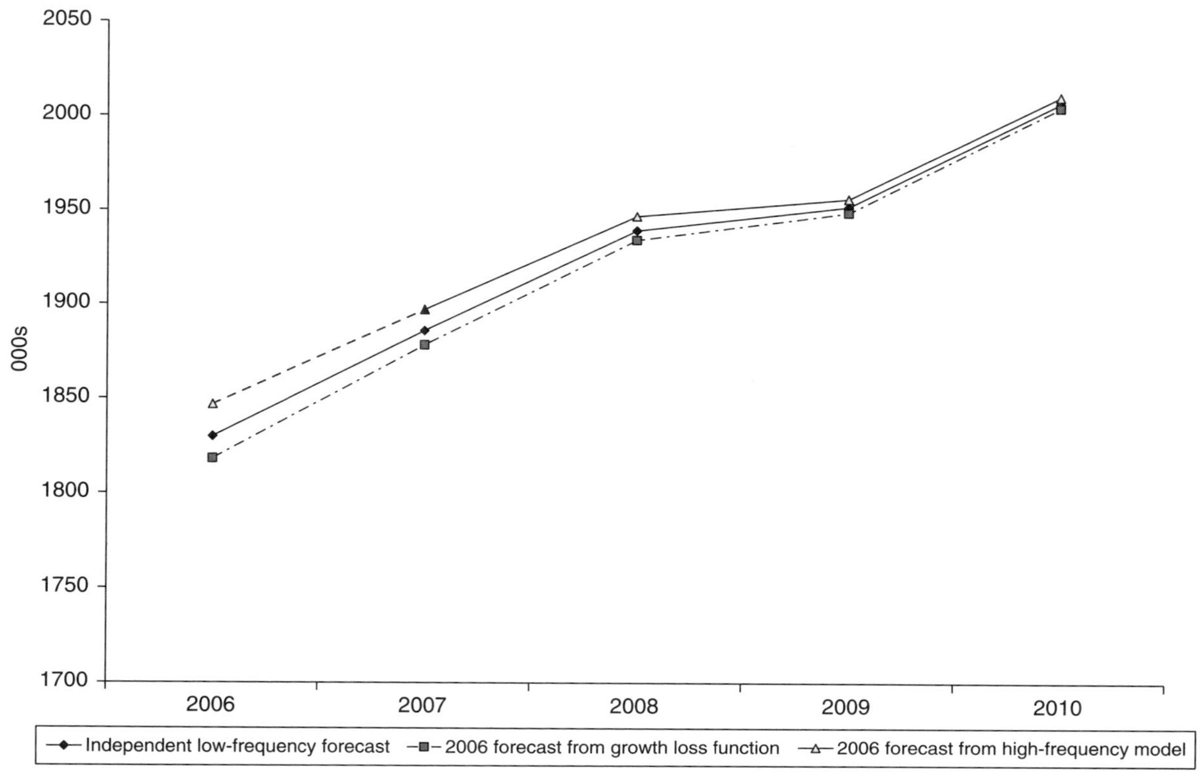

Figure 11.1 Comparison of Mexico's GDP forecasts

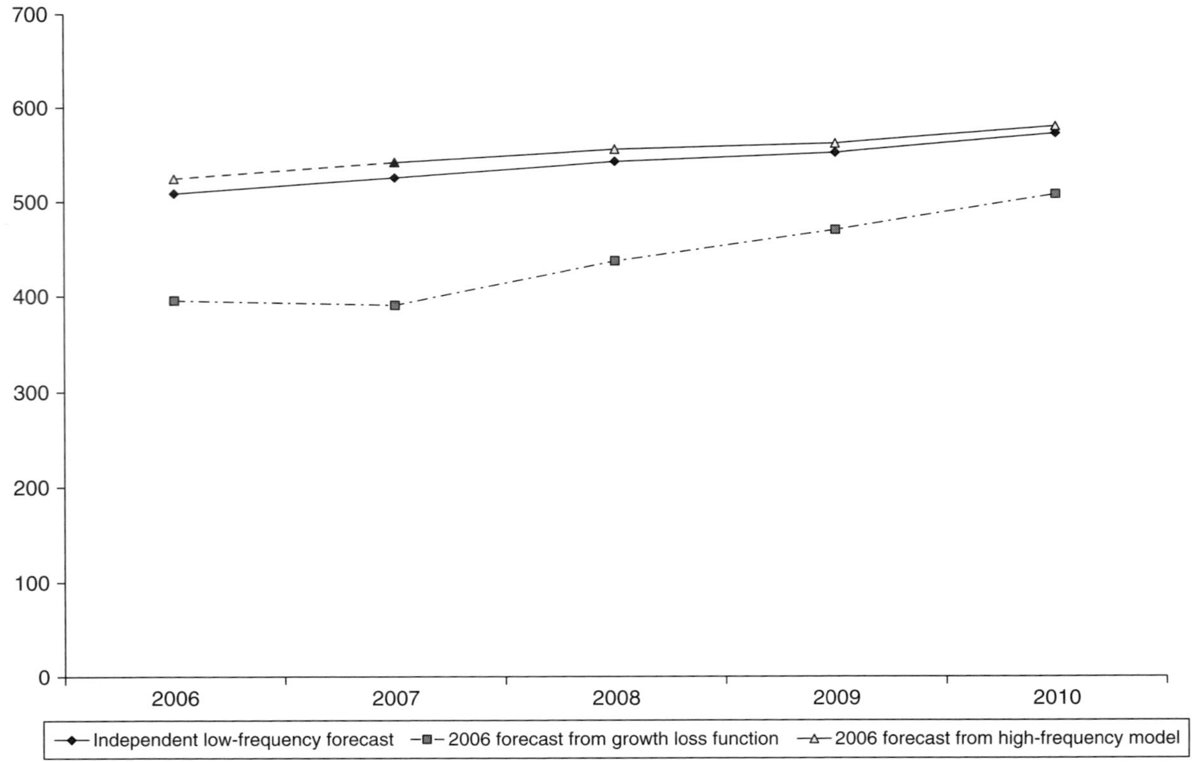

Figure 11.2 Comparison of Mexico's price index forecasts

Figures 11.1 and 11.2, as well as for other variables from Table 11.2, the distances between the three trajectories gradually decline toward the end of the five-year period. Such a tendency towards 'convergence' is especially visible for an independent forecast and a forecast with the 2006 solution imported from the high-frequency model. This implies that the transfer of new initial conditions forces the low-frequency forecast to divert from its independent trajectory, but primarily for the first year. The further away from the first year, the lesser the influence of new initial conditions and the greater the role of inertia built into the low-frequency model.

These findings signify the fruitfulness of using the combination of high-frequency and low-frequency models for updating medium- and long-term forecasts at least once a year, with the account of new information provided by a high-frequency forecast for the 'moving' new first year. In this capacity, the high-frequency model turns out to be handy for tuning up forecasts to ever-evolving economic trends, eliminating the need for conventional add factors.

Do we always want different approaches to the estimation of the same variables to yield similar results? On the one hand, the fact that different solutions are close to one another is a sign of consistency. On the other hand, the purpose of using the high-frequency model is to introduce corrections to the long- and medium-term patterns of growth exhibited by the variables of the low-frequency model. If, in this process, newly available high-frequency data signal significant changes in prevailing economic trends, which have not been captured by low-frequency estimates, the modification of a medium-term forecast in order to move it away from an otherwise 'undisturbed' independent forecast proves to be effective.

4. *EX-POST* FORECAST AT MIXED FREQUENCIES: ECONOMIC GROWTH DURING FOX'S ADMINISTRATION IN MEXICO

During Vicente Fox's presidential campaign, he aimed to achieve an average annual growth of 7 percent for the Mexican economy. Fox's six-year term in office was December 2000 to November 2006. The second row of Table 11.3 gives Mexico's actual annual GDP growth rates for that period.[9] The GDP is defined as in Table 11.2, i.e., as the value added in all aggregate economic sectors. As can be seen, the promised 7 percent rate never materialized. The average rate of 2.28 percent for that six-year period was the lowest in recent Mexican history, especially if compared to an average 5.1 percent achieved by the Zedillo Administration. The Fox government blamed the slowdown in the US economy for low growth, a

Table 11.3 Mexican GDP growth rates for 2000–06, %

Forecast	2001	2002	2003	2004	2005	2006	Period average
Actual growth rates	−0.16	0.83	1.35	4.18	2.80	4.77	2.28
Forecast from 2001	0.68	0	1.35	4.18	2.96	5.16	2.37/2.28
Forecast from 2002	NA	1.96	1.54	1.76	3.02	2.35	2.12/2.77
Forecast from 2003	NA	NA	1.38	2.73	3.22	2.55	2.46/3.27

view which to an extent is supported by analysts (see, e.g., Loria, 2007). However, while the events of 11 September 2001 in the USA generated an adverse shock for Mexico, too, the USA did not have a recession in 2001 (with a growth rate of 0.8 percent) as Mexico did, and in 2002–03 US growth was more than twice that of Mexican.

An unanticipated recession of 2001 hurt growth in the following years as well, but Mexican analysts point to a continuous stream of miscalculations on the part of the government. For example, in 2002 it projected a 3 percent GDP growth for 2003 (*Economic News & Analysis on Mexico*, May 2003); from Table 11.3, the actual rate was 1.35 percent. As late as November 2004, the Fox Administration was insisting that its target growth of 3.5 percent was attainable for 2005. Within several months the administration agreed to reduce that forecast to 3 percent, in line with other projections, which, as Table 11.3 shows, was close to actual 2.8 percent (SourceMex, 2005-11-02).

Why were negative short-term economic developments not used by Mexican officials for significant downward corrections in longer-term projections? Excluding political considerations, a reason could be that the inertia built into statistical time series played a role and the series were not properly adjusted for the new reality.

In order to see how models at mixed frequency could help in such situations, we use the created Mexican high-frequency and low-frequency macroeconometric models to generate several *ex-post* forecasts for the period of Fox presidency. Rows 3 through 5 in Table 11.3 give these forecasts. The first forecast was generated for the entire 2001–06 period, with equations in the high-frequency model estimated with observations from 1994 to 2000, and in the low-frequency model from 1980 to 2000. The next forecast was generated for 2002–06, with equations in both models estimated with additional data for 2001. And the last forecast, for 2003–06, was generated based on equations estimated with the account of 2002 data.

In all three forecasts we use the method of importation to the low-frequency model of key economic variables from the high-frequency model. For example, in the first forecast the high-frequency model is solved for 2001, which is followed by a two-stage solution of the low-frequency model, for 2001 and then for 2002–06. In the first stage, the equations for the GDP and the price index are excluded from the low-frequency model for 2001 and the values of these variables are imported from the solution of the high-frequency model, with an appropriate conversion from monthly to annual frequencies. In the second stage, the 2002–06 low-frequency solution is obtained based on the 2001 solution; this ensures that the five-year forecast is linked to its 2001 'mixed' solution. Forecasts for 2002–06 and 2003–06 in rows 4 and 5 are generated in the same fashion.

The last column in Table 11.3 gives average growth rates achieved in the period of Fox's presidency and those following from our forecasts. In the forecast rows two such rates are given: the forecast in the numerator and the actual for the relevant period in the denominator. The numbers show that the best approximation to actual growth rates is achieved in the first forecast and the worst in the last one. It is hard to explain the pattern, if any, based on this experiment. A contributing factor could be that adjustments are made only in the low-frequency model, but no adjustments are made in the high-frequency model. It is thus reasonable to expect that corrections in high-frequency relationships introduced based on actual economic fluctuations could further improve the combined forecasts.

5. CONCLUSION

We consider the use of statistical data and econometric models at mixed frequencies for estimation and forecasting. We first discuss how unknown values of economic variables are estimated by means of either interpolation or statistical methods when aggregation or, more challenging, disaggregation of time series is required. A traditional approach is based on the use of interpolation polynomials including the Lagrange polynomial and linear, quadratic and cubic splines, which are most popular in computational software. We also review selected statistical methods of obtaining time series of higher frequency when most often only aggregate data, annual or quarterly, are given.

Following the discussion of the role that statistical data at mixed frequencies play in estimation, we then suggest the application of models at mixed frequencies for medium- and long-term forecasting. The methodology of combining high-frequency and low-frequency econometric models for forecasting was developed by Klein and Kushnirsky (2005). Two applied projects were accomplished in order to test the methodology, first for the

Ukrainian economy and then for the Mexican economy. High-frequency and low-frequency models built for Ukraine were intentionally simplified, whereas the Mexican project was more elaborate and detailed.

Constructing and employing models at mixed frequencies make it possible to modify the solution at the beginning of a medium- or long-term forecast based on the use of either a loss function or the importation of variables from the high-frequency to the low-frequency model. A loss function enables one to minimize the distance between a selected set of variables in the two models and, as a result, force them to move as closely as possible to each other. The importation of key variables from the high-frequency model to the low-frequency model helps improve the accuracy for these variables, with a consequent adjustment of other variables in the forecast.

The outlined methodology is based on the premise that high-frequency forecasts are on average more accurate at the beginning of a medium- or long-term period than a low-frequency forecast. A reason is that aggregate low-frequency data do not fully interpret fluctuations over short-term intervals and cannot identify specific economic forces that are not materialized in historical data used for equation estimation. The modification of the low-frequency forecast with the account of new high-frequency data as suggested by our methodology is a compelling alternative to the use of add factors in econometric forecasting. In applications, the add factors are an *ad hoc* way to compensate for a poor match between historical data and new trends exhibited at the start of the forecast period. The use of add factors is subjective but often inescapable when it is clear that forecast values produced cannot pass a reality check. Since there is no information letting the researcher adjust the forecast to reality, the initial conditions are 'corrected' to counter the discrepancy.

A conventional approach to the use of models at mixed frequencies differs from our methodology in that a high-frequency model would be employed there to forecast for the first year of a medium-term period, and a low-frequency model for the rest of the period. That is, the short-term forecast on the basis of the high-frequency model would absorb recent trends, while the low-frequency model is expected to provide some hypothetical snapshot of the future development, rather a specific forecast. The low-frequency model can, of course, be updated as a new set of annual observations becomes available; but extending the sample enhances not only the properties of consistency and efficiency, but the built-in inertia as well. To ensure a smooth transition from the historical to forecast period in this type of situation, the researcher should have found a way to give a greater emphasis to recent rather than to past trends. However, attempts at adjusting accordingly the weights of observations in equation estimation are as arbitrary as the use of add factors. Our approach to modify the first-year solution of the low-frequency model, to comply with the high-frequency projections, is a viable answer to this seeming quandary. It was demonstrated in applications that the methodology retains the desired properties of large samples and, at the same time, provides computational procedures to make the generated low-frequency forecasts respond to newly emerging economic trends.

Ex-post forecasts help assess predictive ability of econometric models because they enable the researcher to compare the forecast with actual historic data. We generate *ex-post* forecasts for Mexico for the presidency of Vicente Fox (2001–06). We use a combination of high-frequency and low-frequency econometric models for three periods: 2001–06, 2002–06 and 2003–06. The adjustment of solutions of the low-frequency model based on high-frequency solutions turns the entire two-step forecast into a dynamic process that demonstrates how some miscalculations in actual planning of economic growth could have been avoided.

NOTES

1. Research leading to this chapter was supported by Temple University Summer Research and Grant-in-Aid programs.
2. The add factors are used for an arbitrary adjustment in econometric equations to compensate for a poor match between historical data used for equation estimation and new economic trends at the start of the forecast period.
3. Such an approach was pioneered at Wharton Econometrics, where two models of the USA, quarterly and annual, were used so that the solution of the annual model was forced to agree with the values obtained in the quarterly model (see, e.g., Klein and Barger, 1954; Preston, 1972).
4. The term 'spline' refers to thin flexible rods used by draftsmen to make smooth curves. The graph of a cubic spline approximates the shape that arises when such a rod is forced to pass through the given $n + 1$ data points.
5. Since there is no information on a monthly distribution of the value for the first quarter, the computation here is based on an average monthly value for the first quarter, i.e. $x/3$.
6. The information on whether Y is above or below Y_{HF} may become available from the comparison of independent high-frequency and low-frequency forecasts obtained prior to setting a loss function.
7. The subtraction of growth indices in both parentheses (11.13) is equivalent to the subtraction of growth rates.
8. In the process of importation of variables from the high-frequency model, their values have to be transformed from monthly to annual, which involves using frequency conversion. In EViews, frequency conversion is performed by creating a database, storing a high-frequency variable in this database, and, at the last step, fetching the variable from the database into the low-frequency model.
9. The source of the data is the *World Development Indicators 2007* of the World Bank. The data coincide with Mexican official statistics that we used in building our high-frequency and low-frequency macroeconometric models.

REFERENCES

Boot, G.C.G., W. Feibes and J.H.C. Lisman (1967), 'Further methods of derivation of quarterly figures from annual data', *Applied Statistics*, **16**(1), 65–75.

Chow, Gregory and An-loh Lin (1971), 'Best linear unbiased interpolation, distribution and extrapolation of time series by related series', *The Review of Economics and Statistics*, **53**, 372–5.

Denton, Frank T. (1971), 'Adjustment of monthly or quarterly series to annual totals: an approach based on quadratic minimization', *Journal of the American Statistical Association*, **66**(333), 99–102.

Di Fonzo, Tommaso (1990), 'The estimation of *M* disaggregate time series when contemporaneous and temporal aggregates are known', *The Review of Economics and Statistics*, **72**(1), 178–82.

Gerald, Curtis and Patrick Wheatley (2003), *Applied Numerical Analysis*, Reading, MA: Addison-Wesley.

Klein, L.R. and H. Barger (1954), 'A quarterly model of the United States economy', *Journal of the American Statistical Association*, **49**, 413–37.

Klein, L.R. and F.I. Kushnirsky (2005), 'Econometric modeling at mixed frequencies', *Journal of Economic and Social Measurement*, **30**, 251–77.

Klein, Lawrence R., Fyodor I. Kushnirsky and A. Delgado Mercado (2008), 'Econometric forecasting at mixed frequencies: application to Mexico's economy. Part I. Mexican high frequency and low frequency econometric models' and 'Part II. Combined use of high frequency and low frequency models', *Journal of Economic and Social Measurement*, **33**, 179–217 and 271–308.

Loria, Eduardo (2007), 'Causes of the slow rate of economic growth in Mexico', Conference on Finance and Economic Growth in Mexico, San Diego, June.

Preston, R.S. (1972), *The Wharton Annual and Industry Forecasting Model*, Economics Research Unit, University of Pennsylvania.

Rossi, Nicola (1982), 'A note on the estimation of disaggregate time series when the aggregate is known', *The Review of Economics and Statistics*, **64**, 695–6.

12. Using sentiment surveys to predict GDP growth and stock returns[1]

Giselle Guzmán

1. INTRODUCTION

The *American Heritage Dictionary* defines 'sentiment' as 'a thought, view, or attitude, especially one based mainly on emotion instead of reason.' By the same token, it defines something that is 'not endowed with reason' to be 'irrational.' Hence, 'sentiment' is largely regarded as 'emotional' and 'irrational.' Classical asset pricing theory makes no provision for such an irrational component in determining asset prices, particularly in long-run equilibrium. Yet it remains a favorite statistic for financial media and popular press, and is the source of endless commentary by market pundits and economists alike. Indeed, the financial press often credits or blames 'sentiment' for a rising or falling stock market. If markets do, in fact, react to reports of changes in sentiment, then this indicates that the reality of asset pricing contradicts the theory of asset pricing. This suggests an oversight on the part of the academic literature in failing to give sentiment the importance it may warrant in the theory of asset pricing.

Academics have only recently begun to examine what role, if any, sentiment may have in the theory of asset pricing. However, consensus is lacking regarding its most basic characteristics. The literature remains divided not only about whether or not sentiment matters for asset prices, but also about what sentiment actually is, and how best to measure and incorporate it in a theoretical framework. I focus here on the empirical aspects of sentiment, its measurement and its predictive power for the real economy as well as for financial markets.

Sentiment has no explicit role in traditional asset pricing models. The omission of sentiment from classical finance is rather curious, considering the key role played by emotion in the theories of Bentham (1781), one of the most influential early utilitarian philosophers. Bentham's concept of utility meant 'that property in any object, whereby it tends to produce benefit, advantage, pleasure, good, or happiness . . . or . . . to prevent the happening of mischief, pain, evil, or unhappiness to the party whose interest is considered. . .' As Lowenstein (2000) notes, neoclassical economists later rendered the utility construct devoid of its emotional content in a process that 'culminated in the development of ordinal utility and the theory of revealed preference, which construed utility as an index of preference rather than of happiness'. Classical finance has evolved around the mathematical concepts of mean-variance optimization, rational maximization of preferences, equilibrium analysis and no-arbitrage arguments, but it has largely neglected a key ingredient of financial markets: human emotion.

The pioneering work of Katona (1951, 1957, 1975) seeks to address the confluence of emotions and economics. His psychological approach to consumption prescribes that both *capacity* and *willingness* to buy are primary determinants of the consumption function. From this treatment one can infer that sentiment, i.e. something generally regarded as irrational, should be considered a *bona fide* component of expectations formation. Katona's theories build upon the notion of 'animal spirits' put forth by Keynes (1936). Notable contributions to the theory of emotions in economics are later made by Elster (1998), Lowenstein (2000), Thaler (2000) and Romer (2000). Romer succinctly echoes Katona's theories by stating that 'economists can usefully segregate decision mechanisms into two broad categories: those based on thoughts and those based on feelings', and suggests that the profession should 'treat thoughts and feelings more symmetrically'.

In this chapter, I aim to establish a definitive role for sentiment in macroeconomic forecasting and asset pricing by answering the following question: do the attitudinal data obtained from sentiment surveys contain any predictive power for economic growth and asset prices beyond the predictive information contained in macroeconomic and financial data? To answer this question, I examine 16 popular sentiment surveys of businesses and households, and test their ability to predict GDP growth as well as aggregate excess stock returns. I construct a composite sentiment factor using all of the sentiment survey indexes and then create separate factors for the sentiments of businesses and of households, for a total of three composite measures – All (APC), Business (BPC) and Household (HPC). I use the technique of principal components analysis to extract the common elements from sentiment surveys and create the composite factors. This signal-extraction technique allows a large collection of dynamic factors to be distilled into a few key measures that illustrate the joint effects of many popular surveys.

Section 2 presents a review of the related literature. Data and methodology are discussed in Section 3. The relation between sentiment indexes and macroeconomic factors is the focus of Section 4, as is the use of sentiment surveys in conjunction with the current quarter model (CQM) of Klein and Sojo (1989), a high-frequency model used to forecast GDP growth (see Chapter 1 in this volume for more details). Section 5 investigates the predictive power of sentiment for excess returns of aggregate stock indexes, controlling for macroeconomic factors and lagged stock returns, and Section 6 concludes.

2. LITERATURE REVIEW

2.1 Sentiment Measures

There are various purported measures of investor sentiment in the literature, but most of them are indirect, and no consensus is reached regarding the appropriate measure. Perhaps the most controversial of these hypothesized sentiment proxies is the closed-end fund discount (CEFD), i.e. the difference between the price of the fund and its net asset value (alternatively measured as the fund premium divided by its net asset value). The closed-end fund discount is first noted by Wiesenberger (1946). The concept is later refined by Zweig (1973), Malkiel (1977), Lee et al. (1991), and further investigated by Swaminathan (1996), with all of these authors claiming that the discount on closed-end funds is a measure of investor sentiment that has predictive power for stock returns. Lee et al. (1991) contend that closed-end funds are held mainly by individual investors and the discount shows a relation to the performance of small stocks, which are also disproportionately held by individual investors; hence, the discount reflects the sentiments of individual investors. However, other researchers, including Chen et al. (1993) and Elton et al. (1998), dispute the validity of the CEFD as a measure of investor sentiment and its ability to predict returns.

Other researchers construct sentiment measures from a variety of indicators, extracting purported sentiment factors from a collection of noisy proxies. Brown and Cliff (2004) use the Kalman filter technique and principal components analysis to create a sentiment factor from a collection of indicators, including the number of advancing issues to declining issues on the NYSE (New York Stock Exchange), the Arms index, the percentage change in margin borrowing, the percentage change in short interest, the odd-lot ratio, the ratio of CBOE (Chicago Board Options Exchange) equity puts to calls, the number of IPOs (initial public offerings), and net purchases of mutual funds. They report that the sentiment proxies have little ability to predict short-run stock returns, but display a strong contemporaneous relationship with returns. Baker and Wurgler (2006) use principal components analysis to construct a sentiment factor from the

CEFD, NYSE share turnover, the number of IPOs, the average first-day returns on IPOs, the share of equity issues in total equity and debt issues, and the dividend premium. The authors note an inverse relationship between their purported sentiment measure and subsequent returns.

Evidence on the ability of the commonly cited indirect sentiment measures to forecast stock returns is mixed. The conventional wisdom seems to be that if these measures have any power to predict returns, they can do so only for small-capitalization stocks. The problem with using market-based statistics as proxies for investor sentiment is that these indirect measures might be reflections of sentiment, but they might also be the result of other market forces. For example, Chen et al. (1993) point out that the closed-end fund discount may not be a proxy for market-wide investor sentiment, but only an indication of investor confidence in the closed-end funds themselves. Manski (2004) emphasizes that 'observed choice behavior may be consistent with many alternative specifications of preferences and expectations'. Because market measures are indirect, their accuracy as measures of investor sentiment cannot be known with any degree of certainty, as they are merely by-products of market activity, and that activity need not necessarily be a result of sentiment. Therefore it is also possible that the indirect measures, i.e. sentiment proxies, and the direct measures, i.e., sentiment surveys, may not measure the same thing.

2.2 Survey Data

The most obvious way to measure investor sentiment is by directly polling market participants and soliciting their opinions. Surveys ask respondents to report probabilistic expectations of significant personal financial or general economic events. Financial market participants can be broadly categorized as either households or businesses. Households participate in markets as both investors and consumers. Consumers influence stock prices not only by purchasing goods and services from publicly traded companies, thereby affecting sales and reported earnings, but also because consumer spending represents approximately two-thirds of GDP in the US. With the increased popularity of discount brokerages and online investing over the past couple of decades, many consumers are now also individual investors involved in direct trading, in addition to participating in the stock market via mutual funds and 401Ks. Households, consisting of consumers and investors, have gained increased exposure to, and influence in, the stock market in recent years.

Businesses are also important market participants. They are the listed companies themselves, or the suppliers, customers, or strategic partners of the listed companies, and their economic health determines general economic growth as well as the discount rates used in asset valuation. Thus, today's stock market brings together households and businesses as never before, highlighting the need to identify a direct and sensible way to measure the perceptions, sentiments and expectations of these market participants and determine whether or not they contain any predictive power for economic quantities of interest.

Over the years, survey data have had their share of detractors who sought to discredit their use in economic forecasting. Opponents argue that people do not always do as they say, and many economists dismiss the use of subjective data out of hand. Nevertheless, there are some legitimate concerns about the quality of the data elicited from surveys. Campbell (2004) points out that the most serious concern is whether respondents answer survey questions accurately. Most surveys cannot be used to track expectations of particular individuals through time, since they are series of cross-sections and not complete panels. Additionally, surveys are always subject to sampling error and other measurement issues. Additional concerns pertain to the manner in which questions are posed and responses elicited. Dominitz and Manski (2003) point out that certain phrases in survey questions such as 'better off', may be subject to interpretation. Survey data are imprecise because they represent an attempt to construct a *quantitative* measure of human attitudes that are inherently *qualitative*.

But it is clear that observed-choice data alone are insufficient for empirical analysis of decisions made when the information set is imperfect, as in the sense of Grossman and Stiglitz (1980), or incomplete. Manski (2004) contends that the assumption of rational expectations is implausible in decision-making with partial information. He advocates measuring expectations with survey data using subjective probabilities rather than the standard practice of revealed preference analysis, i.e. inferring decision processes from data on observed choices. The goal is to use self-reported data on expectations to relax or validate the assumptions regarding expectations that underlie economic models.

It appears that survey data may indeed be on the verge of a renaissance, with many researchers now taking an interest in sentiment surveys, and exploring their ability to explain how investors form expectations and their usefulness in forecasting the economy and asset returns.

2.3 The Predictive Power of Survey Data – The Evidence So Far

2.3.1 Consumer sentiment – macroeconomic literature

Most of the early work on expectations derived from surveys examines the University of Michigan's Surveys of Consumers and its ability to predict consumer spending. Klein and Lansing (1955) find that survey questions on buying intentions, feelings of financial well-being and price expectations are predictive of consumer expenditures on durable goods.[2] Mueller (1963) reports that lagged values of the University of Michigan surveys have predictive power for household expenditures on durable and non-durable goods.

Some researchers contend that surveys lose their predictive power once other financial and macroeconomic variables enter the specification. Hymans et al. (1970) find that the University of Michigan Index of Consumer Sentiment (ICS) can forecast automotive spending, but that lagged values of income, consumer prices and changes in stock prices can forecast the ICS. Mishkin (1978) finds that the University of Michigan ICS significantly predicts consumer expenditures on durable goods, but this relationship does not hold once financial variables are taken into account. Leeper (1992) uses a vector autoregression (VAR) framework to examine the relationship between consumer sentiment, industrial production and unemployment, and also finds that the relationship significantly weakens once stock prices and treasury bill rates are included in the analysis.

Garner (1991) asserts that consumer confidence indexes aid in forecasting aggregate consumption only during major economic or political events. Similarly, Throop (1992), using a five-variable vector error correction model (VECM), finds that in times of turbulence such as the Gulf War and the 1987 stock market crash, consumer sentiment can move independently of economic fundamentals, thus providing unique insights into future consumer expenditures. However, Throop notes that during normal periods, forecast results are slightly worse when sentiment is included in the specification than when it is omitted. The notion that sentiment is a particularly valuable forecasting tool during times of turmoil concurs with Katona's (1975) suggestion that the University of Michigan Surveys of Consumers reflects psychological factors that become pronounced during extraordinary periods of social, political, or economic upheaval.

Matsusaka and Sbordone (1995) find that fluctuations in consumer sentiment account for between 13 percent and 26 percent of the variance of GNP innovations, even after controlling for a collection of economic indicators, demonstrating that expectations play a non-trivial role in forecasting output. Bram and Ludvigson (1998) run a horserace of the University of Michigan ICS versus the Conference Board's Consumer Confidence Index (CCI) and compare their relative abilities to forecast five categories of household expenditures: total, motor vehicles, all goods excluding motor vehicles, services, and durable goods excluding motor vehicles. The authors report that sentiment can help predict consumption, even after including control variables, and also suggest that consumer attitudes may provoke economic fluctuations.[3] Howrey (2001) finds that the University of Michigan ICS is a statistically significant predictor of real GDP growth and provides an informative signal about the probability of recession. Klein and Özmucur (2002, 2004) demonstrate that models incorporating sentiment surveys of consumers, producers, or managers forecasting economic quantities such as personal consumption expenditures, personal income and industrial production, perform significantly better than models that do not include the surveys.

2.3.2 Surveys and the stock market – asset pricing literature

Despite their potential methodological shortcomings, surveys uniquely provide a direct measure of investor expectations. Yet most of the literature concerning the predictive power of surveys has focused on macroeconomic forecasting and limited use has been made of examining the predictive power of sentiment surveys in forecasting stock market returns. De Bondt (1993) considers the American Association of Individual Investors (AAII) survey and finds that the sentiment of small investors displays a bias towards extrapolation of past market trends. Otoo (1999) examines the relation between stock returns and the University of Michigan ICS and Conference Board CCI surveys, and reports that returns share a strong contemporaneous relation with the surveys, but lagged changes in sentiment have no explanatory power for stock returns. Fisher and Statman (2000) investigate the Merrill Lynch survey of sell-side strategists, the AAII survey of individual investors, and the Investors Intelligence (II) survey of investment newsletter writers, and conclude that the sentiments of these three groups of market participants are not identical.[4] Lee et al. (2002) employ a GARCH (generalized autoregressive conditional heteroskedasticity) model to examine the relation between the II survey and stock returns, and report that sentiment is a significant factor in explaining both excess returns and conditional volatility of returns.

Guzmán (2003) finds that the Union Bank of Switzerland/Gallup Index of Investor Optimism surveys (UBS) have significantly more predictive power than either the Michigan ICS or the Conference Board CCI surveys. Brown and Cliff (2005) study the relationship between the II survey and market-implied pricing errors from an independent valuation model, and find that the relationship is positive. Additionally, they report that sentiment is negatively related to future returns over multi-year horizons. Charoenrook (2005) examines the University of Michigan ICS and finds a negative relation with future excess returns at horizons of one month and one year. In addition, the author reports that the predictive power of consumer sentiment appears to be unrelated to economic cycles or time-varying expected returns. Lemmon and Portniaguina (2006) investigate the relationship between returns and the University of Michigan ICS and Conference Board CCI, and determine that the surveys forecast returns of small stocks and stocks with low institutional ownership. Finally, Verma and Verma (2007) use the II survey as a proxy for the sentiments of institutional investors and the AAII survey as a proxy for the sentiments of individual investors, and conclude that the former are more rational than the latter.

To my knowledge, this chapter is the first to examine a large collection of sentiment surveys of distinct respondent universes, extract their common signal, and test its ability to predict GDP growth and excess stock returns.

3. DATA AND METHODOLOGY

I study a total of 16 sentiment surveys. They are:

1. Institute for Supply Management Purchasing Managers' Index (ISM)
2. National Association of Purchasing Management – Chicago Business Barometer Index (NPM)
3. The Philadelphia Federal Reserve Business Outlook Survey (FED)
4. National Association of Home Builders–Wells Fargo Builders Index – headline (HMI)
5. National Association of Home Builders–Wells Fargo Builders Index – next six months (HM6)
6. National Association of Home Builders–Wells Fargo Builders Index – present conditions (HMP)
7. National Association of Home Builders–Wells Fargo Builders Index – traffic (HMT)
8. University of Michigan Index of Consumer Sentiment – headline preliminary (MIP)
9. University of Michigan Index of Consumer Sentiment – current conditions preliminary (MCP)
10. University of Michigan Index of Consumer Sentiment – expectations preliminary (MXP)
11. Conference Board Consumer Confidence Index – headline (CBH)
12. Conference Board Consumer Confidence Index – present situation (CBP)
13. Conference Board Consumer Confidence Index – expectations (CBX)
14. Union Bank of Switzerland/Gallup Index of Investor Optimism – headline (UBS)

15. Union Bank of Switzerland/Gallup Index of Investor Optimism – personal financial (UBP)
16. Union Bank of Switzerland/Gallup Index of Investor Optimism – economic (UBE)

Broadly speaking, the first seven of these can be classified as surveys of businesses and the remainder can be classified as surveys of households. A brief description of each survey follows.

The Institute for Supply Management (ISM) publishes the Manufacturing ISM Report On Business (ROB) each month. The ROB is based on data compiled from purchasing and supply executives nationwide. The Purchasing Managers' Index (PMI) is a composite index featured in the ROB based on the seasonally adjusted diffusion indexes for the following five indicators, with varying judgmental weights applied: new orders 30 percent, production 25 percent, employment 20 percent, supplier deliveries 15 percent, inventories 10 percent. A PMI reading above 50 percent indicates that the manufacturing economy is generally expanding; below 50 percent indicates that it is generally contracting.[5]

The National Association of Purchasing Management – Chicago compiles a monthly survey and a composite diffusion index of business conditions in the Chicago region. The Chicago Business Barometer™ survey registers manufacturing and non-manufacturing activity. Investors care about this indicator because the Chicago region mirrors the nation in its distribution of manufacturing activity. The NAPM–Chicago survey often moves together with the ISM index, but is reported one day in advance.[6]

The Philadelphia Federal Reserve Business Outlook Survey has been produced monthly since 1968. This survey is a check-box variety sent to about 250 large manufacturing firms located in the Third Federal Reserve District.[7] Participants indicate the direction of change in overall business activity and in the various measures of activity at their plants: employment, working hours, new and unfilled orders, shipments, inventories, delivery times, prices paid, and prices received.[8]

The National Association of Home Builders (NAHB) and Wells Fargo and Company produce the National Association of Home Builders–Wells Fargo Builders Index, a monthly survey of home builder sentiment, to gauge the demand side of the single-family housing market in the USA. The headline Housing Market Index (HMI) is a weighted average of responses to survey questions asking respondents to rate three aspects of their local market conditions: current sales of single-family detached new homes, expected sales of single-family detached new homes over the next six months, and traffic of prospective buyers in new homes.[9]

The University of Michigan Surveys of Consumers are conducted by the Survey Research Center at the University of Michigan and were developed in 1946 with the direction of George Katona. Each monthly survey contains approximately 50 core questions covering three broad areas of consumer sentiment: personal finances, business conditions and buying conditions. Five of these core questions form the Index of Consumer Sentiment (ICS). The survey is based on approximately 500 telephone interviews of adult men and women living in households in the coterminous USA. The sample is designed to maximize the study of changes by incorporating a rotating panel sample design in an ongoing monthly survey program. This design provides for the regular assessment of changes in attitudes and behavior, both at the aggregate and at the individual level. Three indexes from the University of Michigan Surveys of Consumers are considered in this study: University of Michigan Index of Consumer Sentiment – Headline Preliminary (MIP), University of Michigan Index of Consumer Sentiment – Current Conditions Preliminary (MCP), University of Michigan Index of Consumer Sentiment – Expectations Preliminary (MXP).[10,11]

The Conference Board Consumer Confidence Survey is conducted monthly by TNS.[12] The Consumer Confidence Index is based on responses to five questions included in the survey. The questionnaires are mailed to a nationwide representative sample of 5000 households, of which roughly 3500 typically respond. Each month, a different panel of 5000 households is surveyed. The survey asks respondents to give their: (1) appraisals of current business conditions, (2) expectations regarding business conditions six months hence, (3) appraisals of the current employment conditions, (4) expectations regarding employment conditions six months hence, and (5) expectations regarding their total family income six months hence. The indexes are then averaged together as follows: the Consumer Confidence Index is the average of all five indexes; the Present Situation Index is the average of indexes for questions 1 and 3; and the Expectations Index is the average of indexes for questions 2, 4 and 5.[13]

Union Bank of Switzerland and the Gallup Organization formed a partnership in October of 1996 to create a new index that would systematically track investor perceptions of the economy on a monthly basis. For the Union Bank of Switzerland/Gallup Index of Investor Optimism, an investor is defined as a male or female head of household with investments totaling $10000 or more.[14] 'Average investors' are those having between $10000 and $100000 of investable assets and represent about two-thirds of all investor households, while households having investments of $100000 or more are classified as 'substantial investors' and account for one-third of all investor households. Gallup interviews a random sample of approximately 1000 US investor households during the first two weeks of every month, and the results are reported at the end of the month. The survey methodology is the same as that used for the Gallup poll.[15] Seven questions are used to construct the Indexes of Investor Optimism. The questions are designed to measure two dimensions of optimism: three questions measure the personal financial dimension and four questions measure the general economic dimension.

This study examines the *changes* in survey-derived expectations and their relation to GDP growth and excess stock returns. Therefore most of the survey data are transformed using the difference of logs. The exceptions are the Philadelphia Federal Reserve Business Outlook Survey, which is transformed using the first difference, and the Union Bank of Switzerland/Gallup Index of Investor Optimism – Personal Financial and Economic Index, which are transformed using the first relative difference.[16] Note that the Union Bank of Switzerland/Gallup survey was conducted sporadically from October 1996 through January 1999, and has been conducted monthly since February 1999.[17] For the purposes of this study, data from October 1996 through January 1999 are interpolated to create a monthly series of comparable length to the other series.[18,19]

Table 12.1 provides summary statistics for the transformed series of sentiment survey changes, quarterly observations from February 1997 to May 2007.[20] The time-series properties are also presented. Autocorrelations for each series are provided at one, three and twelve lags, and none displays significant autocorrelation. Augmented Dickey–Fuller tests reject at better than the 1 percent level the hypothesis that any of the series has a unit root. Some of the data are highly correlated, hence it is intuitively appealing to extract the common elements from this group of surveys and test the predictive power of the shared components.

Two main data techniques are employed in this chapter – the Almon or polynomial distributed lag (PDL) technique and principal components analysis (PCA). They are described briefly in this section.

A polynomial distributed lag is employed for the sentiment factor on the right-hand side of several regression equations. This is because the data are significant at more than one lag, but using more than one individual lag may induce multicollinearity and produce biased *t*-statistics on the individual regression coefficients. The PDL allows the use of more than one lag (with some constraints on coefficients) and alleviates the multicollinearity concern. Additionally, the use of a PDL is consistent with Katona's (1975) notion that expectations follow a slow social learning process. Hence the sentiment variable is assumed to follow a simple distributed lag of finite length n:

$$y_t = \sum_{i=0}^{n} w_i X_{t-i} + \varepsilon_t \qquad \text{for } t = 1, 2, \ldots, T. \tag{12.1}$$

Table 12.1 Sentiment changes and the first principal component of All, Business, and Household sentiment

Quarterly average data – 41 observations	Mean	Median	Std. Dev.	AC1	AC3	AC12
ISM – ISM Purchasing Managers Index	−0.066	−0.539	2.134	0.071	−0.202	−0.196
NPM – NAPM Chicago Business Barometer	0.047	0.000	3.161	−0.268	0.102	0.073
FED – Philadelphia Fed Business Outlook Survey	−0.098	0.016	1.192	0.038	−0.003	0.062
MIP – Michigan Preliminary ICS – Headline	−0.088	0.209	2.207	−0.328	0.114	0.027
MCP – Michigan Preliminary ICS – Current Conditions	−0.027	−0.029	1.808	−0.297	0.137	−0.176
MXP – Michigan Preliminary ICS – Expectations	−0.136	0.115	3.065	−0.409	0.091	0.009
CBH – Conference Board CCI – Headline	−0.044	0.097	3.662	−0.288	−0.237	0.042
CBX – Conference Board CCI – Expectations	−0.104	0.398	4.879	−0.444	−0.268	0.147
CBP – Conference Board CCI – Present Situation	0.016	0.146	3.552	0.267	0.057	−0.066
UBS – UBS/Gallup Investor Optimism – Headline	−0.390	−0.223	21.180	−0.487	−0.058	−0.020
UBP – UBS/Gallup Investor Optimism – Personal Financial	5.794	0.139	43.312	−0.236	−0.040	−0.050
UBE – UBS/Gallup Investor Optimism – Economic	4.098	0.508	24.297	−0.037	−0.054	−0.035
HMI – NAHB/WF Builders Index – Headline	−0.345	0.000	3.129	0.193	0.097	−0.205
HM6 – NAHB/WF Builders Index – Next 6 Months	−0.213	0.000	3.339	−0.103	0.118	−0.092
HMP – NAHB/WF Builders Index – Present Conditions	−0.388	0.000	3.175	0.230	0.052	−0.190
HMT – NAHB/WF Builders Index – Traffic	−0.330	0.647	3.708	0.070	0.149	−0.250
APC1 – All Sentiment Principal Component 1	0.000	−0.290	2.634	−0.256	−0.047	−0.105
APC2 – All Sentiment Principal Component 2	0.000	0.342	1.746	0.118	0.075	−0.034
APC3 – All Sentiment Principal Component 3	0.000	0.193	1.386	−0.119	−0.009	0.007
BPC1 – Business Sentiment Principal Component 1	0.000	−0.491	1.948	0.149	0.099	−0.204
BPC2 – Business Sentiment Principal Component 2	0.000	−0.063	1.280	−0.161	0.017	−0.039
BPC3 – Business Sentiment Principal Component 3	0.000	−0.074	1.017	0.078	−0.089	0.030
HPC1 – Household Sentiment Principal Component 1	0.000	−0.070	2.429	−0.342	−0.057	−0.002
HPC2 – Household Sentiment Principal Component 2	0.000	0.203	1.218	0.117	0.009	0.043
HPC3 – Household Sentiment Principal Component 3	0.000	−0.020	0.946	−0.329	−0.009	−0.214

Macroeconomic variables lagged according to data reporting lags	Mean	Median	Std. Dev.	AC1	AC3	AC12
NEW_ORDERS(*t*–2)	0.014	−0.064	1.648	−0.352	0.267	−0.124
UNFILLED_ORDERS(*t*–2)	0.136	0.058	1.212	0.233	0.285	−0.045
HOUSING_STARTS(*t*–1)	−0.029	−0.403	6.009	−0.424	−0.063	−0.146
CONSTRUCTION(*t*–2)	0.271	0.365	1.077	0.200	0.208	−0.097
BUILDING_PERMITS(*t*–1)	0.041	−0.193	3.514	−0.274	0.009	0.063
HOURLY_EARNINGS(*t*–1)	0.065	0.069	0.271	0.190	−0.094	−0.091
AVG_WEEKLY_HOURS(*t*–1)	−0.017	0.000	0.251	−0.457	0.083	−0.005
CPI(*t*–1)	0.212	0.186	0.254	0.246	−0.083	−0.142
PPI(*t*–1)	0.187	0.222	0.577	0.108	0.187	−0.182
RETAIL_SALES(*t*–1)	0.205	0.208	1.075	−0.370	−0.061	−0.067
TRADE-WEIGHTED_EXCHANGE_RATE(*t*–1)	−0.192	−0.131	1.178	0.306	0.002	−0.088
MONEY_SUPPLY(*t*–1)	0.300	0.308	0.399	0.300	0.142	0.000
CONSUMER_CREDIT(*t*–2)	0.326	0.282	0.394	0.276	0.074	0.074
INVENTORY_SALES_RATIO(*t*–2)	−0.024	0.000	0.816	−0.329	0.117	−0.151
NET_GOV_RECEIPTS(*t*–1)	−0.360	−1.214	3.249	−0.264	0.356	0.820
UNEMPLOYMENT_RATE(*t*–1)	−0.006	0.000	0.126	−0.101	0.184	0.015
TIPS-IMPLIED_INFLATION(*t*–1)	−0.006	0.003	0.222	0.291	−0.110	−0.016
FED_FUNDS_RATE(*t*–1)	0.000	0.003	0.182	0.666	0.500	0.019
PRIME_RATE(*t*–1)	0.000	0.000	0.177	0.708	0.531	0.036
CORPORATE_BOND_RATE(*t*–1)	−0.015	−0.040	0.166	0.178	−0.104	−0.146

Table 12.1 (continued)

Macroeconomic variables lagged according to data reporting lags	Mean	Median	Std. Dev.	AC1	AC3	AC12
TBILL_3M(*t*–1)	−0.002	0.012	0.199	0.453	0.426	0.110
EXPORT_IMPORT_RATIO(*t*–2)	0.016	−0.001	0.195	0.008	0.000	−0.005
TBOND_YIELD_1YEAR(*t*–1)	−0.005	0.000	0.201	0.445	0.305	−0.042
TBOND_YIELD_10YEAR(*t*–1)	−0.014	−0.043	0.216	0.161	0.008	−0.169
TBOND_YIELD_20YEAR(*t*–1)	−0.015	−0.050	0.185	0.125	−0.012	−0.214
30-YR_FIXED_MORTGAGE(*t*–1)	−0.013	−0.020	0.127	0.533	0.021	−0.269
DISPOSABLE_PERSONAL_INCOME(*t*–1)	0.258	0.284	0.725	−0.185	−0.154	0.026
INDUSTRIAL_PRODUCTION(*t*–1)	0.211	0.243	0.541	0.078	0.186	0.088
NON–FARM_EMPLOYMENT(*t*–1)	0.103	0.119	0.131	0.649	0.617	0.309
MANUFACTURING_AND_TRADE_SALES(*t*–1)	0.226	0.278	0.739	−0.358	0.128	−0.074

This is based on the assumption that the lag weights lie on a polynomial of degree $p < n$:

$$w_i = \sum_{j=0}^{P} \lambda_j i^j \qquad \text{for } i = 0, 1, \ldots, n. \tag{12.2}$$

The specification used throughout the chapter is $p = 2$ (quadratic polynomial) and $n =$ three lags.[21] End-point restrictions are imposed, with both the near end and the far end constrained to zero. Experiments with alternate PDL specifications did not improve the model. The sum of the PDL coefficients is reported.

Principal components analysis is a technique used to reduce multidimensional data sets to lower dimensions for analysis (see Chapter 9 for an excellent exposition). The use of PCA allows for a large set of correlated variables to be employed together, without the problem of multicollinearity, as the extracted factors are pairwise orthogonal. Sensitivity to units of measurement is avoided by standardizing the variables to have mean zero and unit variance, before calculating the principal components. Principal components of the indicators are formed by extracting the characteristic roots of the correlation matrix of the variables. The result is a linear combination of the indicators that allows for a common signal to be distilled from the data, measuring the collective impact of several indicators at once while conserving degrees of freedom. I use PCA to extract a composite sentiment factor $S_{i,t}$ from a large set of survey indexes $X_{i,t-n}$. The survey data are set at the appropriate n-period data reporting lag, to reflect how they enter the information set at time t, i.e., the $t-n$ values of the sentiment surveys are known. Let the ith principal component of the sentiment surveys be denoted

$$S_{i,t} = \sum_{i=1}^{m} \gamma_i X_{i,t-n} \qquad \text{for } i = 1, 2, \ldots, m. \tag{12.3}$$

Principal components are calculated using the 16 surveys: ISM, NPM, FED, HMI, HM6, HMP, HMT, MIP, MCP, MXP, CBH, CBP, CBX, UBS, UBP and UBE. The goal is to capture the common component among the different sentiment indexes, and test whether their joint effect has any predictive power for GDP growth and stock returns.

From these 16 surveys, three composite sentiment factors are constructed: (1) an aggregate sentiment factor constructed from all surveys of the various respondent groups, APC, using all 16 surveys ($m = 16$); (2) a Business sentiment factor, BPC, formed from the seven surveys of businesses ($m = 7$); and (3) a Household sentiment factor, HPC, constructed from the nine surveys of households, comprising consumers and investors ($m = 9$). The principal components are formed using the quarterly average values of changes in the surveys.

Table 12.2 shows the eigenvectors and the variance proportions captured by the first three principal components of each group: All, Business, and Household. The first principal component of All surveys, APC1, explains 42.3 percent of the variance, while the first three principal components, APC1, APC2 and APC3, together capture 72.6 percent of the total variance of the system. The first principal component of Business surveys, BPC1, explains 52.9 percent of the variance, while the first three principal components, BPC1, BPC2 and BPC3, reflect 90.2 percent of the total variance of the Business group. The first principal component of Household surveys, HPC1, explains 64 percent of the variance, while the first three principal components, HPC1, HPC2 and HPC3, collectively represent 89.8 percent of the total variance of the Household group.

A macroeconomic factor $M_{i,t}$ is also constructed using principal components analysis. The goal is to determine if sentiment surveys merely reflect macroeconomic information, as some researchers have postulated, or if the surveys contain unique information. A broad collection is formed of 30 macroeconomic variables that are generally regarded as indicative of the economic cycle, such as new orders, housing starts, inflation, unemployment and industrial production, etc. The set of 30 macroeconomic indicators, hypothesized to have *a priori* importance for economic growth and asset prices, is loosely based on Matsusaka and Sbordone (1995), Klein and Özmucur (2002), and Stock and Watson (2002). I construct the composite macroeconomic factor $M_{i,t}$ using principal components at time t with each indicator $I_{i,t-n}$ lagged appropriately to reflect its own n-period data reporting lag. For example, CONSUMER_CREDIT enters the information set with a two-period reporting lag, while INDUSTRIAL_PRODUCTION is reported with a one-period lag. Thus the principal components are calculated with each variable lagged to reflect how it enters the agent's information set at time t. Let the ith principal component of the macroeconomic indicators be denoted

$$M_{i,t} = \sum_{i=1}^{30} \gamma_i I_{i,t-n} \qquad \text{for } i = 1, 2, \ldots 30 \qquad (12.4)$$

Table 12.1 presents descriptive statistics for the macroeconomic indicators, as well as their associated data reporting lags. Most of the indicators were transformed using the difference of logs, with the exception of ratios and yield data, which were transformed using first differences. Whenever possible, the pre-update series is used rather than the revised historical series, as the goal is to replicate as closely as possible the real-time information set that is available to market participants. The augmented Dickey–Fuller (ADF) tests reject at the 1 percent level the hypothesis that any series has a unit root, with the exception of the three-month US treasury bill (TBILL_3M)

Table 12.2 Principal components and eigenvectors – sentiment

Sentiment - first three principal components
Sample: 1997Q1–2007Q2; quarterly average data include 41 observations

All sentiment (APC)				Business sentiment (BPC)				Household sentiment (HPC)			
	Comp 1	Comp 2	Comp 3		Comp 1	Comp 2	Comp 3		Comp 1	Comp 2	Comp 3
Eigenvalue	6.770	2.975	1.874	Eigenvalue	3.702	1.600	1.009	Eigenvalue	5.757	1.448	0.873
Variance prop.	0.423	0.186	0.117	Variance prop.	0.529	0.229	0.144	Variance prop.	0.640	0.161	0.097
Cumulative prop.	0.423	0.609	0.726	Cumulative prop.	0.529	0.757	0.902	Cumulative prop.	0.640	0.801	0.898
Eigenvectors:				Eigenvectors:				Eigenvectors:			
Variable	Vector 1	Vector 2	Vector 3	Variable	Vector 1	Vector 2	Vector 3	Variable	Vector 1	Vector 2	Vector 3
ISM	−0.169	−0.061	−0.215	ISM	−0.156	0.635	−0.296				
NPM	−0.117	−0.127	−0.249	NPM	−0.068	0.713	−0.045				
FED	−0.010	−0.077	0.550	FED	0.060	−0.211	−0.942				
MIP	−0.326	−0.125	0.236					MIP	−0.370	0.241	0.330
MCP	−0.224	0.047	0.376					MCP	−0.240	0.369	0.538
MXP	−0.315	−0.189	0.137					MXP	−0.366	0.145	0.188
CBH	−0.333	−0.181	0.119					CBH	−0.382	0.166	−0.329
CBX	−0.329	−0.193	0.065					CBX	−0.382	0.027	−0.041
CBP	−0.184	−0.095	0.242					CBP	−0.205	0.438	−0.671
UBS	−0.330	−0.170	−0.144					UBS	−0.379	−0.201	−0.052
UBP	−0.286	−0.129	−0.343					UBP	−0.295	−0.533	−0.036
UBE	−0.253	−0.130	−0.364					UBE	−0.327	−0.491	−0.031
HMI	−0.222	0.467	−0.017	HMI	−0.514	−0.079	−0.005				
HM6	−0.225	0.413	0.107	HM6	−0.466	−0.183	−0.123				
HMP	−0.187	0.481	−0.035	HMP	−0.498	−0.060	0.016				
HMT	−0.242	0.398	−0.109	HMT	−0.488	−0.010	0.092				

and total non-farm employment (NON-FARM_EMPLOYMENT), for which the unit root hypothesis is rejected at the 5 percent level, and federal government net receipts as a percentage of GDP (NET_GOV_RECEIPTS), for which the hypothesis cannot be rejected. The data are transformed and standardized prior to computing the principal components. Once again, quarterly average values are utilized.

Only the first principal component is employed in the analysis, and it captures 17.3 percent of the total variance of the system of macroeconomic indicators. The eigenvector of the first principal component of macroeconomic indicators is given by

$$
\begin{aligned}
M1 = {} & 0.057\, NEW\_ORDERS(t-2) \\
& + 0.046\, UNFILLED\_ORDERS(t-2) \\
& - 0.099\, HOUSING\_STARTS(t-1) \\
& + 0.093\, CONSTRUCTION(t-2) \\
& - 0.079\, BUILDING\_PERMITS(t-1) \\
& - 0.132\, HOURLY\_EARNINGS(t-1) \\
& + 0.050\, AVG\_WEEKLY\_HOURS(t-1) \\
& + 0.155\, CPI(t-1) \\
& + 0.147\, PPI(t-1) \\
& - 0.047\, RETAIL\_SALES(t-1) \\
& - 0.025\, TRADE\text{-}WEIGHTED\_EXCHANGE\_RATE(t-1) \\
& - 0.230\, MONEY\_SUPPLY(t-1) \\
& - 0.143\, CONSUMER\_CREDIT(t-2) \\
& + 0.008\, INVENTORY\_SALES\_RATIO(t-2) \\
& - 0.052\, NET\_GOV\_RECEIPTS(t-1) \\
& - 0.156\, UNEMPLOYMENT\_RATE(t-1) \\
& + 0.175\, TIPS\text{-}IMPLIED\_INFLATION(t-1) \\
& + 0.284\, FED\_FUNDS\_RATE(t-1) \\
& + 0.280\, PRIME\_RATE(t-1) \\
& + 0.269\, CORPORATE\_BOND\_RATE(t-1) \\
& + 0.328\, TBILL\_3M(t-1)
\end{aligned}
$$

$$+ 0.060\, EXPORT\_IMPORT\_RATIO(t - 2)$$
$$+ 0.371\, TBOND\_YIELD\_1YEAR(t - 1)$$
$$+ 0.282\, TBOND\_YIELD\_10YEAR(t - 1)$$
$$+ 0.253\, TBOND\_YIELD\_20YEAR(t - 1)$$
$$+ 0.281\, 30\text{-}YR\_FIXED\_MORTGAGE(t - 1)$$
$$+ 0.025\, DISPOSABLE\_PERSONAL\_INCOME(t - 1)$$
$$+ 0.161\, INDUSTRIAL\_PRODUCTION(t - 1)$$
$$+ 0.200\, NON\text{-}FARM\_EMPLOYMENT(t - 1)$$
$$- 0.009\, MANUFACTURING\_AND\_TRADE\_SALES(t - 1)$$

The eigenvector of the first principal component reveals that the factor is essentially a proxy for the slope of the yield curve. The coefficient loadings of the eigenvector elements are also the correlation coefficients between the principal component and the underlying variables.

Due to serial correlation in the residuals, Newey–West (1987) heteroskedasticity and autocorrelation-consistent (HAC) standard errors are employed throughout the analysis.

4. SENTIMENT AND GDP GROWTH

I begin by testing the ability of the sentiment factors to explain future GDP growth. The baseline regression measures the relation between GDP growth at time *t*, lagged GDP growth, and the lagged composite macroeconomic factor. A fixed lag of one period and the PDL are each tested. The baseline model is

$$GDP_t = c + \beta_1 GDP_{lag} + \beta_2 M1_{lag} + \varepsilon_t. \tag{12.5}$$

The baseline results for the fixed lag are presented in Panel A of Table 12.3 and the results for the PDL are presented in Panel B. The one-period lag specification results in an adjusted R^2 of 0.079, while the PDL specification gives an adjusted R^2 of 0.277. The quarterly average macroeconomic factor, i.e. the first principal component of the macroeconomic indicators, is denoted MPC1 in Table 12.3, and it is significant at the 10 percent level for the one-period lag specification.

Next, the model is augmented to test whether any of the three composite

Table 12.3 Regressing GDP growth on lagged GDP growth, lagged macroeconomic factor, and lagged sentiment factor

Panel A	Baseline model – lag 1				Panel B	Baseline model – PDL			
Variable	Coeff.	t-stat.	Adj. R^2		Variable	Coeff.	t-stat.	Adj. R^2	
GDP(t–1)	−0.007	(−0.036)	0.079		GDP(pdl)	0.219	(4.654***)	0.277	
MPC1(*t*–1)	0.378	(1.785*)			MPC1(pdl)	−0.002	(−0.059)		
Panel C	**Sentiment-augmented model – lag 1**				**Panel D**	**Sentiment-augmented model – PDL**			
Variable	Coeff.	t-stat.	Adj. R^2	Increment	Variable	Coeff.	t-stat.	Adj. R^2	Increment
All sentiment					**All sentiment**				
GDP(*t*–1)	−0.007	(−0.037)	0.137	0.058	GDP(pdl)	0.181	(2.775***)	0.270	−0.007
MPC1(*t*–1)	0.265	(−1.199)			MPC1(pdl)	0.009	(−0.199)		
APC1(*t*–1)	−0.232	(−2.432**)			APC1(pdl)	−0.066	(−1.065)		
Business					**Business**				
GDP(*t*–1)	−0.018	(−0.093)	0.070	−0.009	GDP(pdl)	0.155	(2.785***)	0.296	0.020
MPC1(*t*–1)	0.362	(1.712*)			MPC1(pdl)	0.055	(−1.207)		
BPC1(*t*–1)	−0.133	(−1.199)			BPC1(pdl)	−0.105	(−2.818***)		
Household					**Household**				
GDP(*t*–1)	0.004	(−0.019)	0.141	0.062	GDP(pdl)	0.215	(3.517***)	0.256	−0.021
MPC1(*t*–1)	0.256	(−1.135)			MPC1(pdl)	−0.003	(−0.084)		
HPC1(*t*–1)	−0.259	(−2.888***)			HPC1(pdl)	−0.012	(−0.168)		

Note: Dependent variable is GDP growth. Estimation method is ordinary least squares. For one-period lag, sample period is 1997Q2–2007Q2, with 41 observations. For polynomial distributed lag, sample period is 1997Q4–2007Q1, with 38 observations. Newey–West HAC standard errors and covariance matrix with lag truncation = 3 are employed throughout. *T*-statistics given in parentheses with significance level indicated by * significant at 10%, ** 5%, *** 1%. Increment is the difference between adjusted R^2 of sentiment-augmented regression and adjusted R^2 of baseline specification of GDP growth regressed on lagged GDP growth and lagged macroeconomic factor only.

sentiment factors (All, Business, or Household) has predictive power for future GDP growth over the baseline equation. The inclusion of a composite macroeconomic factor in a model that tests the ability of sentiment to forecast an economic variable such as GDP growth efficiently addresses the concerns of researchers such as Mishkin (1978), Leeper (1992), Carroll et al. (1994), and Bram and Ludvigson (1998), who hypothesized that sentiment may be made redundant by macroeconomic and financial information. If sentiment is merely a reflection of macroeconomic and financial information, then the sentiment-augmented regression should not have any incremental predictive power over the baseline equation. The sentiment-augmented model is estimated as

$$GDP_t = c + \beta_1 GDP_{lag} + \beta_2 M1_{lag} + \beta_3 S1_{j,lag} + \varepsilon_t \qquad \text{for } j = 1, 2, 3 \tag{12.6}$$

In the interest of parsimony, only the first principal component is utilized. Panel C of Table 12.3 reveals that APC1, the composite factor for All sentiment, is significant at the 5 percent level for one lag. The sign of the coefficient is negative. However, Table 12.2 indicates that the eigenvector for APC1 is negative since all of the elements have negative coefficients. Thus APC1 is positively predictive of future GDP growth at one lag, even after controlling for the persistence of GDP and a lagged composite macroeconomic factor. When sentiment is high, future GDP growth is high. The addition of APC1 to the model increases the adjusted R^2 by 5.8 percent. This result is driven mainly by the sentiment of Households rather than Businesses, since the specification with HPC1 is incrementally predictive, but the specification with BPC1 is not. The Household sentiment factor, HPC1, is statistically significant at the 1 percent level, and increases the adjusted R^2 by 6.2 percent for the one-period fixed lag. Note again that the eigenvector of HPC1 is negative; hence the factor is positively predictive of future GDP growth. The reverse is true for the PDL specification, displayed in Panel D: BPC1 is statistically significant at the 1 percent level and adds 2 percent to the adjusted R^2, while HPC1 and APC1 are not statistically significant.

Next, I examine the predictive power of the composite sentiment factors when used in conjunction with the current quarter model (CQM) of Klein and Sojo (1989), for forecasting GDP growth in the USA. The baseline relationship is estimated as

$$GDP_t = c + \beta_1 CQM_t + \varepsilon_t \tag{12.7}$$

Table 12.4 Regressing GDP growth on quarterly average CQM forecasts and sentiment factor

Panel A. Baseline model

Variable	Coeff.	t-stat.	Adj. R^2
C	0.434	(0.523)	0.107
CQM	1.045	(3.520***)	

Panel B Sentiment-augmented model

All sentiment					Business sentiment					Household sentiment				
Variable	Coeff.	t-stat.	Adj. R^2	Incre-ment	Variable	Coeff.	t-stat.	Adj. R^2	Incre-ment	Variable	Coeff.	t-stat.	Adj. R^2	Incre-ment
C	0.247	(0.299)	0.123	0.016	C	0.257	(0.304)	0.119	0.012	C	0.294	(0.357)	0.110	0.003
CQM	1.111	(3.721***)			CQM	1.107	(3.673***)			CQM	1.092	(3.652***)		
APC1	−0.147	(−1.793*)			BPC1	−0.188	(−1.569)			HPC1	−0.129	(−1.165)		
C	1.151	(1.334)	0.164	0.058	C	0.530	(0.617)	0.103	−0.004	C	1.208	(1.422)	0.166	0.059
CQM	0.749	(2.397**)			CQM	1.002	(3.356***)			CQM	0.726	(2.284**)		
APC1(t−1)	−0.232	(−2.812***)			BPC1(t−1)	−0.147	(−1.614)			HPC1(t−1)	−0.257	(−3.168***)		
C	1.088	(1.403)	0.214	0.107	C	0.355	(0.404)	0.103	−0.004	C	1.267	(1.801)	0.221	0.114
CQM	0.769	(2.798***)			CQM	1.067	(3.492***)			CQM	0.692	(2.482**)		
APC1	−0.210	(−2.449**)			BPC1	−0.169	(−1.426)			HPC1	−0.237	(−2.119**)		
APC1(t−1)	−0.282	(−3.364***)			BPC1(t−1)	−0.107	(−1.128)			HPC1(t−1)	−0.345	(−3.845***)		
C	0.919	(1.421)	0.188	0.081	C	0.285	(0.345)	0.164	0.057	C	0.937	(1.482)	0.137	0.031
CQM	0.801	(3.019***)			CQM	1.057	(3.589***)			CQM	0.786	(2.763***)		
APC1(pdl)	−0.159	(−2.599**)			BPC1(pdl)	−0.126	(−3.829***)			HPC1(pdl)	−0.143	(−1.959**)		

Note: Dependent variable is GDP growth. Estimation method is ordinary least squares. For one-period lag, sample period is 1997Q2–2007Q2, with 41 observations. For polynomial distributed lag, sample period is 1997Q4–2007Q1, with 38 observations. Newey–West HAC standard errors and covariance matrix with lag truncation = 3 are employed throughout. t-statistics given in parentheses with significance level indicated by * significant at 10%, ** 5%, *** 1%. Increment is the difference between adjusted R^2 of sentiment-augmented regression and adjusted R^2 of baseline specification of GDP growth regressed on quarterly average CQM forecasts only.

Panel A of Table 12.4 presents the results of the baseline model of GDP growth regressed on the average of the CQM high-frequency forecasts made throughout the quarter. The relevant null hypothesis for the baseline regression is $\beta_1 = 1$. If the CQM is a good forecasting model, it should almost perfectly explain GDP growth. Indeed, the coefficient on the CQM model forecasts is statistically significant at better than the 1 percent level, with $\beta_1 = 1.045$. The adjusted R^2 is 0.107.

The equation is then augmented with the composite sentiment factors to determine whether sentiment can improve the performance of the CQM model. In this specification, only the first principal component of the sentiment surveys is utilized. The macroeconomic factor is not included since this information would already be reflected in the CQM forecast. The sentiment-augmented model is estimated as

$$GDP_t = c + \beta_1 CQM_t + \beta_2 S1_{j,lag} + \varepsilon_t \qquad \text{for } j = 1, 2, 3 \qquad (12.8)$$

A fixed lag of zero (contemporaneous relation), one period, and the PDL are each tested. Panel B of Table 12.4 reveals that the composite factor for All sentiment, APC1, is significant in all specifications, adding as much as 10.7 percent to the adjusted R^2. Once again, the coefficients for APC1 are negative, but the negative eigenvector indicates a positive relationship. The result appears to be driven in the short run by the sentiments of Households, as HPC1 is significant contemporaneously, at one lag, and with the PDL specification, increasing the adjusted R^2 by as much as 11.4 percent. The sentiment of Businesses appears to have more effect at longer lags since only the PDL of BPC1 is significant, adding 5.7 percent to the adjusted R^2. Both now-casting and forecasting of GDP growth are aided by the addition of sentiment data to the CQM model, since both the contemporaneous and lagged sentiment factors are statistically significant. The results suggest that macroeconomic forecasters should not hesitate to incorporate sentiment measures in their efforts to predict future GDP growth.

5. SENTIMENT AND STOCK RETURNS

Do the sentiment factors have any predictive power for aggregate excess stock returns? In order to investigate this question, a baseline model is presented that controls for the composite macroeconomic factor and momentum, i.e. lagged stock returns. If sentiment is nothing more than a reflection of recent stock returns and macroeconomic information, then the sentiment-augmented model should not have any incremental predictive power over the baseline model. The baseline equation is estimated as

$$(R_{i,t} - Rf_t) = c + \beta_1(R_{i,t-1} - Rf_{t-1}) + \beta_2 M1_{t-1} + \varepsilon_t \qquad (12.9)$$

The results of the baseline model are presented in Panel A of Table 12.5. Cumulative three-month (one quarter), six-month (two quarters) and nine-month (three quarters) excess returns (i.e. the gross return minus the risk-free rate, Rf_t) are examined for the S&P500 index (SPQ), the Russell 1000 Growth index (R1GQ), the Russell 1000 Value index (R1VQ), the Russell 2000 Growth index (R2GQ), and the Russell 2000 Value index (R2VQ), for a total of 15 test portfolios (five stock indexes and three time horizons, Q1, Q2 and Q3). The Russell 1000 indexes contain large-capitalization stocks, whereas the Russell 2000 indexes contain small-capitalization stocks.

Next, the baseline model is augmented with the composite sentiment factors to determine whether or not sentiment has any incremental predictive power. In this specification, the *first three* principal components of the sentiment surveys are utilized, relying on the arguments of Stone (1947). The augmented model controls for lagged excess returns of the relevant portfolio and the lagged composite macroeconomic factor. The inclusion of a composite macroeconomic factor in a model that tests the ability of sentiment to forecast stock returns efficiently addresses the concerns of researchers such as Brown and Cliff (2005), Lemmon and Portniaguina (2006) and Verma and Verma (2007), who hypothesized that sentiment may be made redundant by macroeconomic and financial information. If the lagged sentiment factors have any incremental ability to predict stock returns, then the *increment* to the adjusted R^2 should be positive. The sentiment-augmented model is estimated as

$$(R_{i,t} - Rf_t) = c + \beta_1(R_{i,t-1} - Rf_{t-1}) + \beta_2 M1_{t-1} + \beta_3 S1_{j,PDL} + \beta_4 S2_{j,PDL} + \beta_5 S3_{j,PDL} + \varepsilon_t \quad \text{for } j = 1, 2, 3 \qquad (12.10)$$

The results are presented in Panels B, C, and D of Table 12.5 for the sentiment of the All, Business and Household groups, respectively. A fixed lag of one period and the polynomial distributed lag are both tested, and both specifications have predictive power, but the results for the polynomial distributed lag are more robust. The robustness of the PDL specification indicates that the sentiment factor possesses non-linearity. Due to space limitations, only the results of the PDL are reported.

Panel B of Table 12.5 reveals that the sentiment factors of All respondent

Table 12.5 Regressing excess returns on lagged returns, lagged macroeconomic factor, and lagged sentiment factors (first three principal components)

Panel A Baseline		Panel B All (PDL)					Panel C Business (PDL)					Panel D Household (PDL)				
INDEX	Adj. R^2	APC1 (pdl)	APC2 (pdl)	APC3 (pdl)	Adj. R^2	Incre-ment	BPC1 (pdl)	BPC2 (pdl)	BPC3 (pdl)	Adj. R^2	Incre-ment	HPC1 (pdl)	HPC2 (pdl)	HPC3 (pdl)	Adj. R^2	Incre-ment
SPQ1	−0.039	−0.418	−0.233	−0.531	−0.066	−0.028	−0.124	0.251	0.480	−0.118	−0.080	−0.521	−0.903	−0.965	−0.032	0.006
		(−1.216)	(−0.896)	(−1.024)			(−0.385)	(0.311)	(0.656)			(−1.221)	(−1.618)	(−0.729)		
SPQ2	−0.049	−0.307	−0.126	−0.647	−0.117	−0.068	−0.183	−0.066	1.109	−0.111	−0.062	−0.401	−1.283	−1.824	−0.063	−0.014
		(−0.615)	(−0.281)	(−0.651)			(−0.382)	(−0.043)	(0.819)			(−0.658)	(−1.601)	(−0.802)		
SPQ3	−0.021	−0.167	0.427	−0.990	−0.055	−0.034	−0.610	−0.532	2.269	0.027	0.048	−0.225	−1.597	−1.618	−0.057	−0.035
		(−0.317)	(0.455)	(−0.709)			(−0.716)	(−0.284)	(1.364)			(−0.374)	(−1.355)	(−0.574)		
R1GQ1	−0.043	−0.450	−0.069	−0.612	−0.098	−0.055	−0.289	0.508	0.606	−0.117	−0.074	−0.488	−0.675	−0.549	−0.108	−0.065
		(−1.087)	(−0.191)	(−0.976)			(−0.711)	(0.444)	(0.644)			(−1.028)	(−1.238)	(−0.346)		
R1GQ2	−0.032	−0.425	0.255	−0.729	−0.094	−0.062	−0.566	0.211	1.092	−0.095	−0.063	−0.388	−1.016	−1.342	−0.105	−0.073
		(−0.717)	(0.351)	(−0.599)			(−0.767)	(0.101)	(0.641)			(−0.624)	(−1.067)	(−0.511)		
R1GQ3	−0.009	−0.347	1.161	−1.011	−0.023	−0.014	−1.308	−0.269	2.267	0.005	0.014	−0.227	−0.939	−0.338	−0.104	−0.096
		(−0.522)	(0.759)	(−0.594)			(−0.946)	(−0.111)	(1.085)			(−0.369)	(−0.616)	(−0.102)		
R1VQ1	−0.010	−0.404	−0.444	−0.458	0.004	0.014	0.064	0.080	0.368	−0.076	−0.067	−0.580	−1.080	−1.353	0.086	0.096
		(−1.372)	(−2.831***)	(−0.954)			(0.255)	(0.131)	(0.558)			(−1.563)	(−1.869*)	(−1.266)		
R1VQ2	−0.053	−0.196	−0.570	−0.709	−0.066	−0.013	0.228	−0.119	1.195	−0.054	−0.001	−0.411	−1.648	−2.410	0.048	0.101
		(−0.427)	(−2.384**)	(−0.796)			(0.729)	(−0.101)	(1.051)			(−0.664)	(−2.127**)	(−1.231)		
R1VQ3	−0.014	0.034	−0.314	−1.152	−0.008	0.006	0.081	−0.569	2.345	0.131	0.145	−0.183	−2.378	−2.918	0.130	0.143
		(0.065)	(−0.779)	(−0.929)			(0.185)	(−0.392)	(1.691*)			(−0.286)	(−2.369**)	(−1.226)		
R2GQ1	0.017	−0.618	−0.466	−1.894	0.090	0.073	−0.189	1.311	0.810	−0.011	−0.028	−0.710	−2.392	−0.847	0.103	0.086
		(−1.465)	(−1.498)	(−2.861***)			(−0.448)	(1.059)	(0.677)			(−1.502)	(−3.491***)	(−0.488)		
R2GQ2	−0.035	−0.265	−0.316	−2.569	0.001	0.036	−0.222	1.350	2.270	−0.067	−0.032	−0.293	−3.163	−1.679	0.001	0.036
		(−0.403)	(−0.588)	(−2.107**)			(−0.359)	(0.637)	(1.145)			(−0.399)	(−2.518**)	(−0.538)		
R2GQ3	0.007	0.233	0.698	−3.620	0.129	0.122	−0.886	1.034	4.575	0.094	0.087	0.343	−3.846	−0.526	0.082	0.075
		(0.311)	(0.594)	(−2.306**)			(−0.863)	(0.464)	(1.977*)			(0.434)	(−2.105**)	(−0.129)		

Table 12.5 (continued)

Panel A Baseline		Panel B All (PDL)					Panel C Business (PDL)					Panel D Household (PDL)				
INDEX	Adj. R^2	APC1 (pdl)	APC2 (pdl)	APC3 (pdl)	Adj. R^2	Increment	BPC1 (pdl)	BPC2 (pdl)	BPC3 (pdl)	Adj. R^2	Increment	HPC1 (pdl)	HPC2 (pdl)	HPC3 (pdl)	Adj. R^2	Increment
R2VQ1	−0.010	−0.478	−0.770	−1.035	0.087	0.097	0.242	0.513	0.093	−0.065	−0.055	−0.718	−1.955	−1.472	0.170	0.180
		(−1.619)	(−2.281**)	(−1.905*)			(0.711)	(0.642)	(0.116)			(−2.372**)	(−3.203***)	(−1.373)		
R2VQ2	−0.045	0.029	−1.029	−1.809	0.134	0.179	0.619	0.631	1.285	−0.005	0.040	−0.218	−3.169	−2.807	0.207	0.251
		(0.066)	(−2.111**)	(−1.968*)			(1.103)	(0.487)	(1.037)			(−0.387)	(−3.469***)	(−1.645)		
R2VQ3	−0.027	0.580	−0.877	−2.681	0.206	0.233	0.700	0.297	2.721	0.087	0.114	0.351	−4.590	−3.653	0.338	0.365
		(0.886)	(−1.669*)	(−2.081**)			(1.003)	(0.187)	(1.615)			(0.605)	(−3.573***)	(−1.766*)		

Notes: Dependent variable is excess return on portfolio *i* at time *t*. Estimation method is ordinary least squares. For polynomial distributed lag, sample period is 1997Q4–2007Q1, with 38 observations. Newey–West HAC standard errors and covariance matrix with lag truncation = 3 are employed throughout. *t*-statistics given in parentheses with significance level indicated by * significant at 10%, ** 5%, *** 1%. Increment is the difference between adjusted R^2 of sentiment-augmented regression and adjusted R^2 of baseline specification of excess returns regressed on lagged returns and lagged macroeconomic factor only.

SPQ1 is the one-quarter-ahead return on the S&P500 index. SPQ2 is the cumulative two-quarter-ahead return on the S&P500 index. SPQ3 is the cumulative three-quarter-ahead return on the S&P500 index. R1GQ1 is the one-quarter-ahead return on the Russell 1000 Growth index. R1GQ2 is the cumulative two-quarter-ahead return on the Russell 1000 Growth index. R1GQ3 is the cumulative three-quarter-ahead return on the Russell 1000 Growth index. R1VQ1 is the one-quarter-ahead return on the Russell 1000 Value index. R1VQ2 is the cumulative two-quarter-ahead return on the Russell 1000 Value index. R1VQ3 is the cumulative three-quarter-ahead return on the Russell 1000 Value index. R2GQ1 is the one-quarter-ahead return on the Russell 2000 Growth index. R2GQ2 is the cumulative two-quarter-ahead return on the Russell 2000 Growth index. R2GQ3 is the cumulative three-quarter-ahead return on the Russell 2000 Growth index. R2VQ1 is the one-quarter-ahead return on the Russell 2000 Value index. R2VQ2 is the cumulative two-quarter-ahead return on the Russell 2000 Value index. R2VQ3 is the cumulative three-quarter-ahead return on the Russell 2000 Value index.

groups have some modest predictive power, mostly, but not exclusively, for small-capitalization stocks. Large-capitalization value stocks have some limited predictability. The sentiment factors of All survey respondents show significant predictive power for small-capitalization stocks. The increments to the adjusted R^2 for the Russell 2000 Growth and Value indexes range from 3.6 percent for the cumulative two-quarter return on the Russell 2000 Growth index to 23.3 percent for the cumulative three-quarter return on the Russell 2000 Value index.

Panel C of Table 12.5 presents the results for the sentiment factors of the Business group. The Business sentiment factors show predictive power for all five of the major stock market averages. The sentiment-augmented equation for the cumulative three-quarter return on the S&P500 index is improved by 4.8 percent relative to the baseline equation. The increments to the adjusted R^2 for the Russell indexes range from an improvement of 1.4 percent for the cumulative three-quarter return of large-capitalization growth stocks to 14.5 percent for the cumulative three-quarter return of large-capitalization value stocks. Note that the significant coefficients in Panel C are positive. Table 12.2 reveals that the eigenvector of the third principal component of Business sentiment is mostly negative, and loads heavily on FED, the Philadelphia Federal Reserve Business Outlook Survey, which has a negative coefficient. This suggests that Business sentiment inversely anticipates the excess return on large-capitalization value and small-capitalization growth stocks. One possible interpretation is that business managers have a keen sense of the pulse of the economy. If managers detect improved business conditions, they may become more optimistic about future economic growth and respond to survey questions accordingly. As their optimism rises, their level of risk aversion declines, and thus they demand lower returns on their investments, creating a negative relation between changes in Business sentiment and future aggregate excess stock returns.

The results for the sentiment of Households are presented in Panel D of Table 12.5. The Household sentiment factors display significant predictive power for all portfolios except the large-capitalization growth stocks. The improvements to the adjusted R^2 range from 0.6 percent for the one-quarter return on the S&P500 to as much as 36.5 percent for the cumulative three-quarter return on small-capitalization value stocks. Note that the significant coefficients in Panel D are negative, and occur mostly for HPC2. Table 12.2 reveals that HPC2, the second principal component of Household sentiment, has mostly positive elements on the eigenvector, with the positive elements loading most heavily on the University of Michigan Index of Consumer Sentiment – Current Conditions Preliminary (MCP) and the Conference Board Consumer Confidence Index – Present

Situations (CBP). The combination of the positive loadings on the principal component with the negative coefficient in the regression suggests a negative relation between changes in these surveys and subsequent excess returns. However, note that HPC2 also loads *negatively* (and heavily) on all three of the Union Bank of Switzerland/Gallup Indexes of Investor Optimism – Headline, Personal Financial and Economic (UBS, UBP and UBE). The combination of the negative loadings on the principal component with the negative coefficient in the regression suggests a positive relation between changes in the Union Bank of Switzerland/Gallup surveys and subsequent excess returns.

One interpretation could be that this dichotomy is consistent with systematic overreaction by naïve investors such as that postulated by De Bondt and Thaler (1989), with an associated subsequent return reversal. This explanation is plausible given that the respondent groups of the University of Michigan and Conference Board surveys are households of ordinary consumers, who may not be particularly adept at interpreting economic data or anticipating stock market trends. Conversely, the respondents to the Union Bank of Switzerland/Gallup surveys are *investor* households, with a minimum of $10 000 in investable assets. The minimum asset requirement of the Union Bank of Switzerland/Gallup surveys may act as a filtering mechanism, creating a strategic universe of respondents who are sophisticated in financial matters, pay attention to economic trends, and correctly anticipate the direction of the stock market.

6. CONCLUSION

The economic magnitude of the predictability demonstrated in this chapter is significant. Consider the GDP growth regressions in Table 12.3. Panel C shows that the one-period lag specification for the All sentiment factor, APC1, has a coefficient of –0.232. From Table 12.1, note that the standard deviation of APC1 is 2.634. Multiplication of the coefficient with the standard deviation indicates that a one-standard deviation rise (decline) in APC1 predicts a decline (rise) of −0.611 percent in the following quarter's GDP growth. Similarly, from Panel D, a one-standard deviation rise (decline) in the Business sentiment factor, BPC1, predicts a decline (rise) of −0.205 percent in GDP growth over the following quarter.

Next, consider the excess stock returns regressions presented in Table 12.5. Panel B shows the results for the All sentiment factor, APC2. In the regression for R1VQ1, the one-quarter excess return on the Russell 1000 Value index, APC2 has a coefficient of −0.444. The standard deviation of APC2, given in Table 12.1, is 1.746. Multiplication of the regression coefficient with the standard deviation indicates that a one-standard deviation rise (decline) in APC2 predicts a decline (rise) of −0.775 percent in the following quarter's excess return on a broad portfolio of large-capitalization value stocks from its unconditional mean. In the regression for R2GQ3, the cumulative three-quarter excess return on the Russell 2000 Growth index, APC3 has a coefficient of −3.620. Table 12.1 shows that the standard deviation of APC3 is 1.386. This implies that a one-standard deviation rise (decline) in APC3 predicts a decline (rise) of −5.017 percent in the following nine months' excess return on a broad portfolio of small-capitalization growth stocks from its unconditional mean. Conversely, in the same regression for R2GQ3, Panel C shows that the Business sentiment factor, BPC3, has a regression coefficient of 4.575. Multiplication of the coefficient for BPC3 with its standard deviation of 1.017 obtained from Table 12.1 indicates that a one-standard deviation rise (decline) in BPC3 predicts a rise (decline) of 4.653 percent in the following three quarters' excess return on a broad portfolio of small-capitalization growth stocks from its unconditional mean.

Turning to the Household sentiment factors in Panel D, one can observe that in the regression for the cumulative three-quarter excess return on the Russell 1000 Value index, HPC2 has a coefficient of −2.378. The standard deviation of HPC2, given in Table 12.1, is 1.218. Multiplication of the regression coefficient with the standard deviation indicates that a one-standard deviation rise (decline) in HPC2 predicts a decline (rise) of −2.896 percent in the following nine months' excess return on a broad portfolio of large-capitalization value stocks from its unconditional mean. In the regression for the cumulative three-quarter excess return on the Russell 2000 Value index, HPC2 has a coefficient of −4.590. Multiplying by the standard deviation of HPC2 implies that a one-standard deviation rise (decline) in HPC2 predicts a decline (rise) of −5.591 percent in the following three quarters' excess return on a broad portfolio of small-capitalization value stocks from its unconditional mean.

The results presented herein shed new light on the question of whether or not sentiment surveys are relevant to forecasting economic growth and stock returns, and whether they contain information that is orthogonal to macroeconomic and financial data. One important benefit of survey data is that they are readily available on a high-frequency basis. Thus researchers have at their disposal an important and relatively underexploited tool for forecasting economic quantities and asset prices, as well as measuring expectations of different population groups. I have shown that sentiment surveys have significant predictive power for both GDP growth and excess stock returns, and that the result is robust to the inclusion of information pertaining to the macroeconomic environment and momentum.

Additionally, while the sentiment surveys share some common predictive signals, the sentiments of different respondent universes can be distinguished, and have non-identical predictive power. Furthermore, the findings reject the conventional wisdom that sentiment affects only small-capitalization stocks. The results suggest that it would behoove researchers to incorporate sentiment surveys in their forecasting models of economic growth and stock returns.

NOTES

1. All equations have been estimated with EViews by Quantitative Micro Software, LLC.
2. Klein and Lansing (1955) studied a 're-interview' sample of the 1953 Survey of Consumer Finances conducted by the Survey Research Center of the University of Michigan, a precursor to the University of Michigan's Index of Consumer Sentiment.
3. Bram and Ludvigson (1998) estimate the relation between the difference of logs in consumption and the ICS and CCI sentiment indexes, and include a vector of control variables that contains the lagged dependent variable, lagged growth in real labor income, lagged log first difference in the real S&P500 index, and lagged first difference of the three-month treasury bill rate.
4. These three surveys were omitted from this study because they are of questionable value. The Merrill Lynch survey of sell-side strategists is likely to have a pronounced optimistic bias towards overweighting stocks in its recommended asset allocation. The AAII survey suffers from self-selection bias (members can take the survey as often as they wish on the AAII website), while the II survey depends on a subjective classification of newsletter writers, which can be influenced by the personal opinions or cognitive biases of the newsletter readers who determine the classification.
5. Source: Institute for Supply Management website: http://www.ism.ws/ISMReport/content.cfm?ItemNumber=10706&navItemNumber=12957.
6. Source: National Association of Purchasing Management – Chicago website: http://napm-chicago.net/home/content/view/22/43/.
7. The Third Federal Reserve District comprises Delaware, New Jersey, and Pennsylvania.
8. Source: The Philadelphia Federal Reserve website: http://www.philadelphiafed.org/econ/bos/.
9. Source: National Association of Home Builders.
10. Source: Surveys of Consumers, Survey Research Center at the University of Michigan.
11. The final values for the Michigan ICS, Current and Expectations indexes are omitted in order to avoid information overlap, as the final indexes are sometimes released in the first few days of the subsequent month.
12. A caveat is in order regarding the Conference Board data. They are revised data and the Conference Board states that it does not maintain the preliminary data. The preliminary number is released at the end of the month for any given survey month. However, this number is overwritten with the final number at the end of the subsequent month. Thus the data may suffer from look-ahead bias. The Conference Board claims that the difference between the preliminary and final number is not statistically significant, so they were included in the analysis.
13. Source: the Conference Board.
14. According to UBS/Gallup, in 1996, about one in three households qualified as investors based upon this definition. By 2003, the proportion had increased to about 40%.
15. Source: UBS/Gallup.
16. This is because these series contained negative values; hence it was not possible to use difference of logs.

17. As of January 2008, UBS and Gallup dissolved their partnership to conduct the surveys.
18. Regression results were virtually identical using the interpolated series beginning in October 1996 and the non-interpolated monthly series beginning in February 1999.
19. The sample period under study begins in February 1997 due to the availability of TIPS data, which are used to calculate the implied inflation expectation that is included among the indicators employed in constructing the macroeconomic factor.
20. Quarterly observations are calculated as quarterly averages.
21. The specification includes contemporaneous and three lags, with near and far end-point restrictions imposed.

REFERENCES

Baker, M. and J. Wurgler (2006), 'Investor sentiment and the cross-section of stock returns', *The Journal of Finance*, **LXI** (4), 1645–79.

Bentham, J. (1781), *An Introduction to the Principles of Morals and Legislation*, Oxford: At the Clarendon Press: London, New York and Toronto: Henry Frowde.

Bram, J. and S. Ludvigson (1998), 'Does consumer confidence forecast household expenditure? A sentiment index horse race', *FRBNY Economic Policy Review*, June, 59–77.

Brown, G.W. and M.T. Cliff (2004), 'Investor sentiment and the near-term stock market', *Journal of Empirical Finance*, **11**, 1–27.

Brown, G.W. and M.T. Cliff (2005), 'Investor sentiment and asset valuation', *Journal of Business*, **78** (2), 405–39.

Campbell, J. (2004), 'Comment: perspectives on behavioral finance: does "irrationality" disappear with wealth? Evidence from expectations and actions' in *NBER Macroeconomics Annual 2003*, M. Gertler and K. Rogoff (eds), Cambridge, MA: MIT Press, pp. 194–99.

Carroll, C.D., J.C. Fuhrer and D.W. Wilcox (1994), 'Does consumer sentiment forecast household spending? If so, why?', *The American Economic Review*, **84** (5), 1397–408.

Charoenrook, A. (2005), 'Does sentiment matter?', unpublished manuscript. The Owen Graduate School of Management, Vanderbilt University, http://www2.owen.vanderbilt.edu/fmra/papers%20data/2005%20papers/does%20sentiment%20matter_aidd.pdf.

Chen, N., R. Kan and M. Miller (1993), 'Are the discounts on closed-end funds a sentiment index?', *Journal of Finance*, **48**, 795–800.

De Bondt, W.F.M. (1993), 'Betting on trends: intuitive forecasts of financial risk and return', *International Journal of Forecasting*, **9**, 355–71.

De Bondt, W.F.M. and R. Thaler (1989), 'Anomalies: a mean-reverting walk down Wall Street', *Journal of Economic Perspectives*, **3** (1), 189–202.

Dominitz, J. and C. Manski (2003), 'How should we measure consumer confidence (sentiment)? Evidence from the Michigan Survey of Consumers', Working Paper 9926, National Bureau of Economic Research.

Elster, J. (1998), 'Emotions and economic theory', *Journal of Economic Literature*, **36**, 47–74.

Elton, E.J., M.J. Gruber and J.A. Busse (1998), 'Do investors care about sentiment?', *Journal of Business*, **71**, 477–500.

Fisher, K. and M. Statman (2000), 'Investor sentiment and stock returns', *Financial*

Analysts Journal, March/April, Association for Investment Management and Research, 16–23.
Garner, C.A. (1991). 'Forecasting consumer spending: should economists pay attention to consumer confidence surveys?', *Federal Reserve Bank of Kansas City Economic Review* (May/June), 57–71.
Grossman, S. and J. Stiglitz (1980), 'On the impossibility of informationally efficient markets', *The American Economic Review*, **70** (3), 393–408.
Guzmán, G.C. (2003), 'GDP growth signals, investor psychology, and hedging pressure: a multivariate approach to forecasting returns on the S&P500 index', unpublished manuscript, The Wharton School, University of Pennsylvania, April.
Howrey, E.P. (2001), 'The predictive power of the index of consumer sentiment', *Brookings Papers on Economic Activity*, **2001** (1), 175–207.
Hymans, S.H., G. Ackley and F.T. Juster (1970), 'Consumer durable spending: explanation and prediction', *Brookings Papers on Economic Activity*, **2**, 173–206.
Katona, G. (1951), *Psychological Analysis of Economic Behavior*, New York: McGraw-Hill.
Katona, G. (1957), 'Federal Reserve Board committee reports on consumer expectations and savings statistics', *Review of Economics and Statistics*, **39**, 40–46.
Katona, G. (1975), *Psychological Economics*, New York: Elsevier.
Keynes, J.M. (1936), *The General Theory of Employment, Interest, and Money*, London: Macmillan for the Royal Economic Society.
Klein, L.R. and J.B. Lansing (1955), 'Decisions to purchase consumer durable goods', *Journal of Marketing*, **20**, 109–32.
Klein, L.R. and S. Özmucur (2002), 'The predictive power of survey results in macroeconomic analysis', in Wladyslaw Welfe (ed.), *Macromodels 2001*, Chair of Econometric Models and Forecasts, University of Lodz, Lodz, pp. 181–97.
Klein, L.R. and S. Özmucur (2004), 'Some possibilities for indicator analysis in economic forecasting', in Pami Dua (ed.), *Business Cycles and Economic Growth: An Analysis Using Leading Indicators*, Oxford: Oxford University Press, pp. 243–57.
Klein, L.R. and E. Sojo (1989), 'Combinations of high and low frequency data in macroeconometric models', in L.R. Klein and J. Marquez (eds), *Economics in Theory and Practice: An Eclectic Approach*, Dordrecht: Kluwer, pp. 3–16.
Lee, C.M.C., A. Shleifer and R.H. Thaler (1991), 'Investor sentiment and the closed-end fund puzzle', *The Journal of Finance*, **46** (1), 75–109.
Lee, W., C. Jiang and D.C. Indro (2002), 'Stock market volatility, excess returns and the role of investor sentiment', *Journal of Banking and Finance*, **26**, 2277–99.
Leeper, E.M. (1992), 'Consumer attitudes: king for a day', *Federal Reserve Bank of Atlanta Economic Review*, **77**(4), 1–15.
Lemmon, M. and E. Portniaguina (2006), 'Consumer confidence and asset prices: some empirical evidence', *The Review of Financial Studies*, **19** (4), 1499–529.
Lowenstein, G. (2000), 'Emotions in economic theory and economic behavior', *The American Economic Review*, **90** (2), 426–32.
Malkiel, B.G. (1977), 'The valuation of closed-end investment company shares', *Journal of Finance*, **32**, 847–59.
Manski, C. (2004), 'Measuring expectations', *Econometrica*, **72**, 1329–76.
Matsusaka, J.G. and A.M. Sbordone (1995), 'Consumer confidence and economic fluctuations', *Economic Inquiry*, **33**, 296–318.

Mishkin, F.S. (1978), 'Consumer sentiment and spending on durable goods', *Brookings Papers on Economic Activity*, **1**, 217–32.
Mueller, E. (1963), 'Ten years of consumer attitude surveys: their forecasting record', *Journal of the American Statistical Association*, **58** (304), 899–917.
Newey, W. and K. West (1987), 'A simple, positive definite, heteroscedastic and autocorrelation consistent covariance matrix', *Econometrica*, **55**, 703–8.
Otoo, M.W. (1999), 'Consumer sentiment and the stock market', Board of Governors of the Federal Reserve System.
Romer, P.M. (2000), 'Thinking and feeling', *The American Economic Review*, **90** (2), 439–43.
Stock, J.H. and M.W. Watson (2002), 'Macroeconomic forecasting using diffusion indexes', *Journal of Business & Economic Statistics*, **20** (2), 147–62.
Stone, R. (1947), 'On the interdependence of blocks of transactions', *Supplement to the Journal of the Royal Statistical Society*, **9** (1), 1–45.
Swaminathan, B. (1996), 'Time-varying expected small firm returns and closed-end fund discounts', *Review of Financial Studies*, **9**, 845–87.
Thaler, R.H. (2000), 'From homo economicus to homo sapiens', *Journal of Economic Perspectives*, **14** (1), 133–41.
Throop, A.W. (1992), 'Consumer sentiment: its causes and effects', *Federal Reserve Bank of San Francisco Economic Review*, **1**, 35–59.
Verma, R. and P. Verma (2007), 'Are survey forecasts of individual and institutional investor sentiments rational?', *International Review of Financial Analysis* (2007), doi:10.1016/j.irfa.2007.04.001.
Wiesenberger, A. (1946), *Investment Companies Services*, New York: Warren, Gorham, and Lamont.
Zweig, M.E. (1973), 'An investor expectations stock price predictive model using closed-end fund premiums', *Journal of Finance*, **28**, 67–78.

Appendix: preliminary analysis of Brazil

Andrei Rudoi

The attractive acronym, BRIC, referring to a group of promising expansionary economies, is being widely used in international discussions. For this volume we present full chapters on Russia, India and China, but an entire chapter is not devoted to the Brazilian case. Brazil, however, has been studied by the main techniques presented in this volume by Dr Andrei Rudoi, and he has provided a brief analysis of Brazilian GDP and inflation.

To assure the reader that we have full capabilities for dealing with estimates for Brazil, similar to those for the other diverse country studies, Dr Andrei Rudoi prepared, using principal components analysis, materials for forecasting GDP and CPI values to demonstrate that the BRIC countries can all be analyzed by our methods.

Dr Rudoi has used 30 indicator values and computed a forecast equation for the GDP of Brazil. This is a quarterly treatment, covering 1993Q1 to 2005Q4.

The case of inflation is measured by monthly movements of the CPI from June 1995 through May 2006. For treatment of seasonal variation he has introduced two 'dummy' variables for GDP movements and four 'dummy' variables for CPI. As many as 60 indicator values are used. The Brazilian equations and out-of-sample extrapolations to test forecasting capabilities are given below.

$$\begin{aligned} GDP = {} & \underset{(13.02)}{89.00} + \underset{(4.06)}{2.00D_2} + \underset{(2.27)}{1.10\,D_3} + \underset{(4.92)}{0.28\,GDP(-3)} + \underset{(13.75)}{2.14PC_1} \\ & - \underset{(4.41)}{1.32PC_2} - \underset{(6.01)}{2.01PC_3} + \underset{(1.07)}{0.18PC_4} + \underset{(3.78)}{1.31PC_8} + \underset{(2.12)}{0.92PC_{10}} \\ & + \underset{(2.66)}{0.77PC_2(-2)} - \underset{(2.42)}{0.81PC_3(-3)} + \underset{(5.27)}{0.80AR(1)} - \underset{(3.57)}{0.64AR(2)} \end{aligned}$$

$$+ \underset{(2.43)}{0.41\text{AR}(3)} - \underset{(2.80)}{0.39\text{AR}(4)} + \underset{(33.97)}{0.94\text{MA}(5)}$$

$$R^{-2} = 0.99 \qquad \text{DW} = 2.05$$

D_2 and D_3 are seasonal dummy variables for the second and third quarters.

In the case of CPI forecasting, it was necessary to introduce a dummy variable, for a crisis that occurred from October through December 2002, as well as seasonal dummy variables for February, July and August.

$$\text{CPI} = \underset{(2.90)}{2.15} + \underset{(8.21)}{1.73\text{D}_C} - \underset{(1.96)}{0.40\text{D}_2} + \underset{(2.86)}{0.57\text{D}_7} - \underset{(1.65)}{0.34\text{D}_8}$$

$$+ \underset{(69.2)}{1.73\text{CPI}(-1)} - \underset{(28.8)}{0.74\text{CPI}(-2)} - \underset{(3.37)}{0.30\text{PC}_1} + \underset{(2.80)}{0.03\text{PC}_2}$$

$$- \underset{(1.71)}{0.16\text{AR}(1)} + \underset{(2.17)}{0.20\,\text{AR}(2)} - \underset{(2.64)}{0.24\,\text{AR}(3)}$$

$$+ \underset{(1.99)}{0.06\text{PC}_4(-1)} + \underset{(2.20)}{0.21\text{PC}_1(-2)} - \underset{(36.49)}{0.60\text{MA}(2)} + \underset{(33.71)}{0.55\text{MA}(10)}$$

$$R^{-2} = 0.99 \qquad \text{DW} = 2.02$$

D_C is the dummy variable for crisis.

The indicators used for extraction of principal components (CPI and GDP) are listed below. Figures A.1–A.4 and Tables A.1–A.3 give the information in detail.

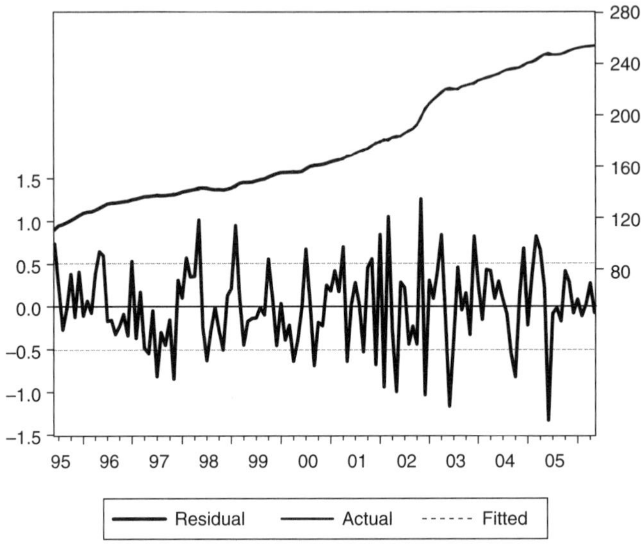

Figure A.1 *CPI regression residual plot (December 1994 = 100)*

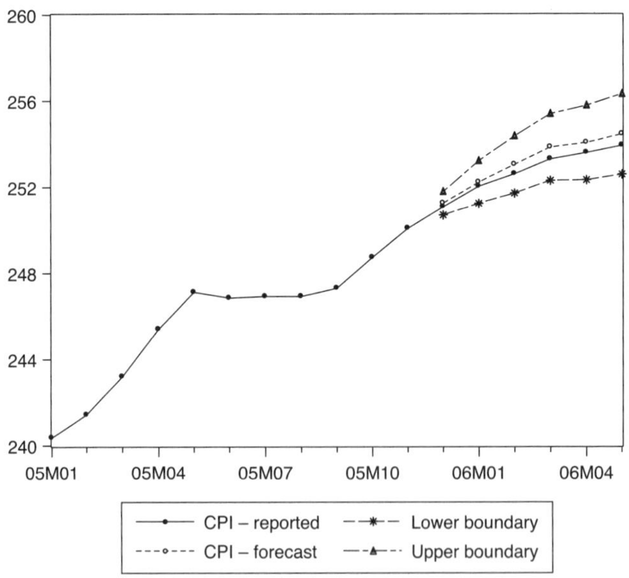

Figure A.2 *CPI – forecast accuracy testing: +/– one standard error confidence interval (historical sample reduced by six months) (December 1994 = 100)*

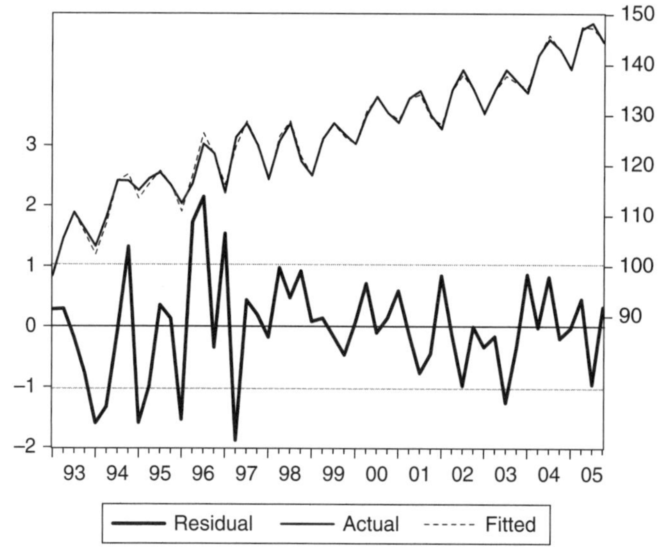

Figure A.3 *GDP regression residual plot*

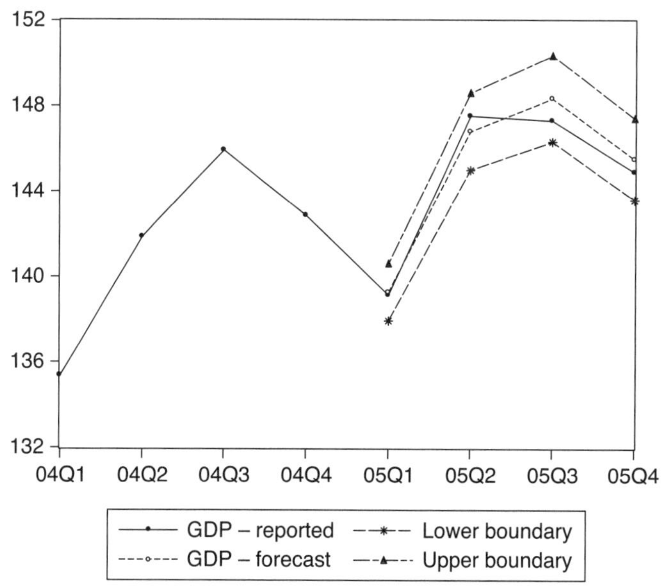

Figure A.4 *GDP – forecast accuracy testing: +/– one standard error confidence interval (the historical sample was reduced by four quarters) (average quarterly GDP in 1990 = 100)*

Table A.1 CPI month-on-month % change

	Reported	Forecast
Dec. 04	0.86	
Jan. 05	0.57	
Feb. 05	0.44	
Mar. 05	0.73	
Apr. 05	0.91	
May 05	0.70	
Jun. 05	−0.11	
Jul. 05	0.03	
Aug. 05	0.00	
Sep. 05	0.15	
Oct. 05	0.58	
Nov. 05	0.54	
Dec. 05	0.40	0.47
Jan. 06	0.38	0.39
Feb. 06	0.23	0.32
Mar. 06	0.27	0.32
Apr. 06	0.12	0.08
May 06	0.13	0.15

Table A.2 Partial derivatives and correlations

	Partial derivative of CPI with respect to	Correlation between CPI and
Money supply – currency outside banks	0.052	0.978
Money supply – demand deposits	0.052	0.974
Money supply – savings deposits	0.050	0.954
Money supply – private securities held by the public	0.053	0.936
Money supply – items representing the difference between M3 and M2	0.051	0.973
Money supply – federal, state and municipal securities held by the public	0.049	0.897
Exchange rate – US$ (purchase) – period average	0.042	0.813
Credit operations in the financial system – to federal public sector	**−0.011**	**−0.335**
Credit operations in the financial system – to state and municipal public sector	**−0.032**	**−0.514**
Credit operations in the financial system – to industrial private sector	0.053	0.975

Table A.2 (continued)

	Partial derivative of CPI with respect to	Correlation between CPI and
Credit operations in the financial system – to housing sector	**−0.046**	**−0.748**
Credit operations in the financial system – to rural private sector	0.052	0.946
Credit operations in the financial system – to commerce private sector	0.052	0.911
Credit operations in the financial system – to individuals	0.053	0.950
Credit operations in the financial system – to other services private sector	0.054	0.975
Long-term interest rate	**−0.025**	**−0.610**
Minimum wage	0.053	0.985
Formal employment – mining	0.034	0.510
Formal employment – non-metallic minerals	0.033	0.493
Formal employment – metallurgy	0.040	0.610
Formal employment – mechanics	0.042	0.684
Formal employment – electrical and communications equipment	**−0.028**	**−0.650**
Formal employment – transport equipment	0.023	0.243
Formal employment – furniture	0.049	0.913
Formal employment – publishing and printing	0.011	0.041
Formal employment – tobacco, leather and related products	0.042	0.670
Formal employment – chemicals and pharmaceutical products	0.042	0.686
Formal employment – textiles, clothing and leather goods	0.036	0.543
Formal employment – footwear	0.050	0.923
Formal employment – food and beverages	0.016	0.199
Formal employment – public utilities	**−0.034**	**−0.726**
Formal employment – building material	**−0.041**	**−0.852**
Formal employment – commerce	0.052	0.910
Formal employment – services	0.051	0.875
Formal employment – public administration	0.044	0.776
Formal employment – crops and livestock, horticulture, hunting and fishing	0.015	0.150
Import prices (US$/kg) – machines and apparatus for domestic use	**−0.036**	**−0.614**

Table A.2 (continued)

	Partial derivative of CPI with respect to	Correlation between CPI and
Import prices (US$/kg) – furniture and other household equipment	0.022	0.378
Import prices (US$/kg) – household appliances	**−0.015**	**−0.334**
Import prices (US$/kg) – passenger vehicles	**−0.007**	**−0.239**
Import prices (US$/kg) – beverages and tobacco	0.026	0.476
Import prices (US$/kg) – food	**−0.035**	**−0.576**
Import prices (US$/kg) – pharmaceutical products	**−0.008**	**−0.026**
Import prices (US$/kg) – textiles and clothing	0.008	**−0.182**
Import prices (US$/kg) – intermediate products – building materials	0.020	0.451
Import prices (US$/kg) – intermediate products – food	**−0.021**	**−0.362**
Import prices (US$/kg) – intermediate products – mineral products	0.019	0.434
Import prices (US$/kg) – intermediate products – chemicals and pharmaceuticals	**−0.014**	**−0.162**
Import prices (US$/kg) – fuels	0.043	0.803
Export prices (US$/kg) – coffee, not roasted	**−0.028**	**−0.555**
Export prices (US$/kg) – meat	**−0.039**	**−0.777**
Export prices (US$/kg) – iron ore and concentrates	0.034	0.561
Export prices (US$/kg) – cane sugar, raw	**−0.020**	**−0.490**
Export prices (US$/kg) – aluminum, unwrought	0.017	0.284
Export prices (US$/kg) – ferroalloys	0.039	0.544
Export prices (US$/kg) – passenger vehicles	**−0.017**	**−0.404**
Export prices (US$/kg) – instant coffee	**−0.029**	**−0.638**
Export prices (US$/kg) – fuel oils	**−0.001**	0.155
Government revenues	0.050	0.950
Government expenditures	0.051	0.942

Notes:
Total number of indicators: 60.
Number of indicators with negative partial derivatives: 20, of which 19 indicators are also negatively correlated with CPI.
The remaining indicator has a low correlation with GDP (0.155).

Table A.3 Partial derivatives: GDP with respect to:

Employment – commerce	−0.161
Employment – public administration	−0.295
Employment – services	−0.341
New vehicle sales/registrations	0.591
Real capital goods production	0.128
Real consumer durables production	0.284
Real consumer semidurables and nondurables production	0.984
Real intermediate goods production	0.936
Real mining production	0.819
Real manufacturing production	0.847
Ratio of consumer price index to construction price index	−1.498
Ratio of consumer price index to wholesale price index	−1.080
Ratio of government expenditures to government revenues	0.006
Real effective exchange rate	0.943
Imports – capital goods, US$	0.874
Imports – consumer durable goods, US$	0.450
Imports – fuels and lubricants, US$	−0.362
Imports – intermediate products and raw materials, US$	0.734
Imports – consumer nondurable goods, US$	0.693
Exports – coffee, US$	0.638
Exports – meat and poultry, US$	−0.034
Exports – soybeans and soybean products, US$	0.396
Exports – aluminum and aluminum products, US$	0.270
Exports – iron and iron products, US$	−0.471
Exports – sugar, US$	0.858
Exports – automobiles and automobile parts, US$	0.096
Exports – airplanes, US$	0.699
Exports – other primary products, US$	−0.013
Exports – other semimanufactured products, US$	0.693
Exports – other manufactured products, US$	0.151

CONSUMER PRICE INDEX

Indicators Used for the Extraction of Principal Components

- Money supply – currency outside banks
- Money supply – demand deposits
- Money supply – savings deposits
- Money supply – private securities held by the public
- Money supply – items representing the difference between M3 and M2

- Money supply – federal, state and municipal securities held by the public
- Exchange rate – US$ (purchase) – period average
- Credit operations in the financial system – to federal public sector
- Credit operations in the financial system – to state and municipal public sector
- Credit operations in the financial system – to industrial private sector
- Credit operations in the financial system – to housing sector
- Credit operations in the financial system – to rural private sector
- Credit operations in the financial system – to commerce private sector
- Credit operations in the financial system – to individuals
- Credit operations in the financial system – to other services private sector
- Long-term interest rate
- Minimum wage
- Formal employment – mining
- Formal employment – non-metallic minerals
- Formal employment – metallurgy
- Formal employment – mechanics
- Formal employment – electrical and communications equipment
- Formal employment – transport equipment
- Formal employment – furniture
- Formal employment – publishing and printing
- Formal employment – tobacco, leather and related products
- Formal employment – chemicals and pharmaceutical products
- Formal employment – textiles, clothing and leather goods
- Formal employment – footwear
- Formal employment – food and beverages
- Formal employment – public utilities
- Formal employment – building material
- Formal employment – commerce
- Formal employment – services
- Formal employment – public administration
- Formal employment – crops and livestock, horticulture, hunting and fishing
- Import prices (US$/kg) – machines and apparatus for domestic use
- Import prices (US$/kg) – furniture and other household equipment
- Import prices (US$/kg) – household appliances
- Import prices (US$/kg) – passenger vehicles
- Import prices (US$/kg) – beverages and tobacco

- Import prices (US$/kg) – food
- Import prices (US$/kg) – pharmaceutical products
- Import prices (US$/kg) – textiles and clothing
- Import prices (US$/kg) – intermediate products – building materials
- Import prices (US$/kg) – intermediate products – food
- Import prices (US$/kg) – intermediate products – mineral products
- Import prices (US$/kg) – intermediate products – chemicals and pharmaceuticals
- Import prices (US$/kg) – fuels
- Export prices (US$/kg) – coffee, not roasted
- Export prices (US$/kg) – meat
- Export prices (US$/kg) – iron ore and concentrates
- Export prices (US$/kg) – cane sugar, raw
- Export prices (US$/kg) – aluminum, unwrought
- Export prices (US$/kg) – ferro-alloys
- Export prices (US$/kg) – passenger vehicles
- Export prices (US$/kg) – instant coffee
- Export prices (US$/kg) – fuel oils
- Government revenues
- Government expenditures

GROSS DOMESTIC PRODUCT

Indicators Used for the Extraction of Principal Components

- Employment – commerce
- Employment – public administration
- Employment – services
- New vehicle sales/registrations
- Real capital goods production
- Real consumer durables production
- Real consumer semi-durables and non-durables production
- Real intermediate goods production
- Real mining production
- Real manufacturing production
- Ratio of consumer price index to construction price index
- Ratio of consumer price index to wholesale price index
- Ratio of government expenditures to government revenues
- Real effective exchange rate
- Imports – capital goods, US$
- Imports – consumer durable goods, US$

- Imports – fuels and lubricants, US$
- Imports – intermediate products and raw materials, US$
- Imports – consumer nondurable goods, US$
- Exports – coffee, US$, not roasted
- Exports – meat and poultry, US$
- Exports – soybeans and soybean products, US$
- Exports – aluminum and aluminum products, US$
- Exports – iron and iron products, US$
- Exports – sugar, US$
- Exports – automobiles and automobile parts, US$
- Exports – airplanes, US$
- Exports – other primary products, US$
- Exports – other semimanufactured products, US$
- Exports – other manufactured products, US$

Index